DEMON POSSESSION

DEMON POSSESSION

A Medical, Historical, Anthropological
and Theological Symposium

Papers presented at
the University of Notre Dame
January 8-11, 1975
under the auspices of the
Christian Medical Association

Edited by
John Warwick Montgomery

BETHANY HOUSE PUBLISHERS
MINNEAPOLIS, MINNESOTA 55438
A Division of Bethany Fellowship, Inc.

Copyright © 1976
Bethany Fellowship, Inc.
All rights reserved

Published by Bethany Fellowship, Inc.
6820 Auto Club Road, Minneapolis, Minnesota 55438

Printed in the United States of America

Library of Congress Cataloging in Publication Data:

Main entry under title:

Demon possession.

    Bibliography: p.
    Includes indexes.
    1. Demonology—Congresses. I. Montgomery, John
Warwick. II. Christian Medical Society.
BF 1501.D45   235'.4   75-19313
ISBN 0-87123-102-6 pbk.

For
MARCUS R. BRAUN
Kansas City, Missouri

John Warwick Montgomery is Dean and Professor of Jurisprudence at the Simon Greenleaf School of Law, Orange, California, and Director of its annual summer program at the International Institute of Human Rights, Strasbourg, France.

He holds eight earned degrees besides the LL.B.: the A.B. with distinction in Philosophy (Cornell University; Phi Beta Kappa), B.L.S. and M.A. (University of California at Berkeley), B.D. and S.T.M. (Wittenberg University, Springfield, Ohio), M.Phil. in Law (University of Essex, England), Ph.D. (University of Chicago), and the Doctorat d'Université from Strasbourg, France.

He is author of over one hundred scholarly journal articles and more than thirty-five books in English, French, Spanish, and German. He is internationally regarded both as a theologian (his debates with the late Bishop James Pike, death-of-God advocate Thomas Altizer, and situation-ethicist Joseph Fletcher are historic) and as a lawyer (barrister-at-law of the Middle Temple and Lincoln's Inn, England; member of the California, Virginia, and District of Columbia Bars and the Bar of the Supreme Court of the United States). He is one of only six persons to have received the Diploma of the International Institute of Human Rights *cum laude*, and was the Institute's Director of Studies from 1979 to 1981. From 1980 to 1983 he served on the Human Rights Committee of the California Bar Association.

He is honored by inclusion in *Who's Who in America, Who's Who in American Law, The Directory of American Scholars, Contemporary Authors, Who's Who in France, Who's Who in Europe, International Scholars Directory* (editor-in-chief), and *Who's Who in the World.*

Preface

On January 8-11, 1975, on the campus of the University of Notre Dame, the Christian Medical Society held an historic conference—a worthy successor to its Symposium on the Control of Human Reproduction (Portsmouth, New Hampshire, 1968) out of which came the significant volume, *Birth Control and the Christian* (Tyndale House, 1969). The latest CMS conference, like its predecessor, dealt with a subject of the most central importance for all those who heal and all those concerned with healing in our contemporary society: "A Theological, Psychological, Medical Symposium on the Phenomena Labeled As 'Demonic.' "

Symposium participation was by invitation only, and a stellar group of twenty-five specialists in the field spent intensive days working through one of the most difficult and challenging problem areas where theology, psychology, psychiatry, medicine, law, anthropology, sociology, literature, missions, and pastoral care converge. Though the discussions were privileged, owing to the sensitive nature of the subject matter, the general Christian public can now benefit from the fruits of this vital symposium, the present volume offering a large percentage of the conference essays to a wider audience.

Readers will be aware immediately of two striking characteristics of the papers comprising this book: their common commitment and their breadth of treatment. All symposium invitees were committed, as is the Christian Medical Society which graciously and perceptively brought them together, to the historic, biblical, evangelical faith; for them the Bible is without apology God's Word, and when He speaks man is to listen and not talk back. At the same time, participants represented the most impressive spread of academic and practical vocations—from psychiatry to literature to missionary anthropology—and thoroughly believed that all these areas of knowledge, being reflections of God's hand in a fallen world, could and should illumine scriptural truth. The value of the present book lies precisely at this point: a wealth of data and interpretation of the demonic which cannot be found under a single cover anywhere else—and yet all of it infused with a unified, overarching conviction of biblical reality.

"Reality" is perhaps the best single word to sum up both the symposium and this book; here readers will find minimal naïveté and minimal rationalization. A respectable number of the participants had had personal experience with the paranormal, the occult, and demonic, and were thus well beyond superficial attempts to "explain away" these phenomena. Those whose contact with this realm had been limited to documented accounts of others found their own beliefs intensified and broadened by personal narratives (only a few of them appear in the essays) such as that of English psychiatrist R. K. McAll, who lives in a former residence of Sir Arthur Conan Doyle, and whose children and others of his acquaintance had verifiable contact with the shade of that paradoxical rationalist and spiritualist, and who participated in the exorcistic laying of his ghost.

One was—and is—reminded of solicitor Cathcart in the classic but almost forgotten novel, *The Necromancers*, by Robert Hugh Benson (1871-1914), perhaps the greatest literary condemnation of the demonic nature of spiritualism ever written. Only "old Cathcart" of the novel's many religious, non-religious, and anti-religious characters really believes that the devil can and does obsess and possess through the cult of spiritualism: only he, converted from spiritualism to Christianity, knows the true name of the Watcher on the Threshold who lurks at the other side of consciousness to prevent the one in trance from reentering this world after his unholy wanderings in the realm of the spirits. A fellow lawyer, Morton, finds Cathcart utterly inexplicable:

> It seemed to him quite amazing that a sensible man like Cathcart could take such rubbish seriously. In every other department of life the solicitor was an eminently shrewd and sane man, with, moreover, a youthful kind of brisk humour that is perhaps the surest symptom of sanity that it is possible to have. He had seen him in court for

years past under every sort of circumstance, and if it
had been required of him to select a character with which
superstition and morbid humbug could have had nothing
in common, he would have laid his hand upon the senior
partner of Cathcart and Cathcart. Yet here was this sane
man, taking this fantastic nonsense as if there were
really something in it. . . . To hear him speak of materiali-
sation as a process as normal (though unusual) as the production of radium, and of planchette as of wireless tele-
graphy—as established, indubitable facts, though out of
the range of common experience—this had amazed this
very practical man. Cathcart had hinted too of other
things—things which he would not amplify—of a still more
disconcertingly impossible nature—matters which Morton
had scarcely thought had been credible even to the darkest medievalists; and all this with that same sharp, sane
humour that lent an air of reality to all that he said.

. . . .

    In the underground the two talked no more; but Mr.
Morton, affecting to read his paper, glanced up once or
twice at the old shrewd face opposite that stared so steadily
out of the window into the roaring darkness. And once
more he reflected how astonishing it was that anyone in
these days—anyone, at least, possessing commonsense—
and commonsense was written all over that old bearded
face—could believe such fantastic rubbish. . . . Here was
the twentieth century; here was an electric railway, padded
seats, and the *Pall Mall*! Was further comment required?

It is hoped that readers of the essays by the "Cathcarts"
who have contributed to this book *will* make the required
further comment: the "air of reality" in all that's said here
has a most disarming explanation, namely, that it derives
from the genuine reality of Holy Scripture and attested experience.

JOHN WARWICK MONTGOMERY

30 March 1975:
Easter Day: the Festival of
the Resurrection of Our Lord

Table of Contents

Introduction

LYNN R. BUZZARD

> The man who denies the phenomena of spiritism today
> is not entitled to be called a skeptic; he is simply ignorant.

These words of Dr. Thomason Hudson are illustrative of the extent of occult phenomena in our time. Concurrent with perhaps the most extensive naturalism, rationalism, and materialism in human history is the meteoric rise of interest in the occult, in the mysterious, and the psychic.

It is hardly necessary to document today's interest in the occult; from playing with ouija boards to communication with the dead to the dissemination of information on witchcraft and demonism, the occult has captured the interest and imagination of persons of every age and social class, and penetrated into virtually every field of human endeavor. Our age seems to be, as Dr. Louis Schlan, Chicago psychiatrist observed, "ripe for the occult."

The interest in the devil has likewise assumed proportions which would only a few years ago have seemed impossible in the "civilized" world. Modern civilization was supposed to have relegated the devil to primitive and unenlightened peoples. *The Exorcist* is but one example of such fascination. It is now possible in novel and film to study how one might be possessed of the devil, have a child of the devil, or worship the devil. Anton LaVey's Satanist Church is only the most radical and most publicized of a vast interest in the devil, his power and personality leading to the establishment of cultic devil worship which has assumed astonishing proportions in western nations.

Our age seems to have a deep fascination with evil, the bizarre, and the inexplicable. It thrives on horror and repulsion. What makes one faint or vomit or experience nightmares has a kind of magnetic charm. Mary Knoblauch summed up this fascination in commenting on *The Exorcist*: "Perhaps the most frightening thing about the EXORCIST is that thirst for and fascination with evil that lies buried in us all, surfacing with savage swiftness at the right incarnation." The moment of that incarnation seems to be upon us. What was buried has arisen and dances unashamedly in the streets.

Why all of this fascination with evil, the devil and the demonic? Why has the occult captured the imagination of author and dramatist? Why have so many youths been enamored by its charm? And why this, precisely when our society and culture had supposedly learned that such notions had long since been banished in the face of our enlightenment? As painful as the rise of such phenomena may be to the Christian observer, as repulsive as the occult and devil worship may be, it seems clear that they are but one expression of the failure of naturalism and materialism to fill the deepest needs of man. Is it not in part a quest for the mystery of life, for something beyond a mere bio-chemical view of man—an expression of longing in the very soul of man for something to worship? Here we confront man's declaration that the mere random action of molecules and atoms, the mere flow of electrical impulses in the brain, cannot and must not explain life and the universe. Man's psyche rebels against those who would reduce him and his universe to mere trivia and bury the supernatural. Director William Friedkin significantly commented on the film version of *The Exorcist*: "It's going to bring people back to the mystery of faith. That was my point in making it."

Such phenomena alone would call for serious study and exploration by biblical, theological, pastoral, and psychiatric disciplines. But the evil which confronts us in *The Exorcist* or in occult practice seems only to be a sample, and not even a very large one, of the evil which encompasses humanity. The Rev. John Nicola, technical consultant in the filming of *The Exorcist*, went beyond the film when he commented on our "gnawing inability to explain in purely human terms the origin of a complex web of evil which constantly seeks to engulf humanity." The introductory paragraph in the Roman ritual of exorcism makes the same point:

> Man, above all the Christian, must reckon with the

realm of the prince of darkness and his legions, not presuming that Satan has no existence outside the product of fable, superstition, or figment—an error endemic in materialists of any age—not minimizing his power over the human person or in human affairs, without on the other hand seeing him lurk in every nook and crevice, like some of the ancient desert fathers, or for that matter like certain exotic cults of the present day. There is a world of demons, as revealed religion teaches, and even if revelation were not so absolute, we could conjecture that the devil is a real person and that his sway is tremendous—a legitimate inference from the magnitude of evil to which our times, no less than past history, bear witness.

The task which faces the church is surely more intensive and extensive than simply facing the more bizarre forms of the occult. A whole theology of evil is at stake. The despair, the alienation, the nihilism and neurosis of man himself is directly involved in the struggle against evil. Theodore Roszak, though writing from a very different world view, nevertheless caught something of this larger evil which faces us (*Where the Wasteland Ends*):

> Why do nihilism and neurosis brood over what we please to call the "developed" societies, taking as great a toll of human happiness as gross physical privation in the third world?
>
> Is it not clear enough that these are the many twisted faces of despair? We conquer nature, we augment our power and wealth, we multiply the means of distracting our attention this way and that . . . but the despair burrows in deeper and grows fatter; it feeds on our secret sense of having failed the potentialities of human being. A despairing humanity is not merely an unhappy humanity; it is an ugly humanity, ugly in its own eyes—dwarfed, diminished, stunted, and self-loathing. These are the buried sources of world war and despotic collectivism, of scapegoat hatred and exploitation. Ugly hates beautiful, hates gentle, hates loving, hates life. There is a politics of despair. . . . Out of despair, they grow burdened with moral embarrassment for themselves, until they must at last despise and crucify the good which they are helpless to achieve. And that is the final measure of damnation: to hate the good precisely because we know it is good and know that its beauty calls our whole being into question.
>
> Once we fall that far, we may soon enough begin to yearn for the peace of annihilation.

In the face of such, neither the church nor the world will any longer tolerate a veil of silence regarding evil,

Satan, and the demonic. It is essential that the church speak with authority and power regarding these issues, offering clear words of guidance and truth, of freedom and grace. Serious and profound questions must be asked and answered. What can one make of occult phenomena which only the most blind can deny? What of widespread Christian assumptions regarding the extensive demon possession of Christian and non-Christian alike? What is the biblical understanding of demons and their activity? How are we to receive the often strange and discomforting reports from the mission field regarding demon activity? What insights can the disciplines of anthropology and psychiatry give to our understanding of the nature of man and evil? What is a proper pastoral stance for the church in our day? What is the biblical and pastoral word for those obsessed with or possessed by evil powers? These and many like questions are crucial for those who minister, whether as pastor, doctor, counselor, or even neighbor. It is time to expose patent fallacies, declare eternal verities—and be honest about our ambiguities and confusion. We must raise the nagging questions, and delineate the acceptable alternatives. Nothing less will do than to grapple with these profundities, using all the insight and wisdom which in God's grace we have, while remaining open to the broadening of our own perspectives.

Dangers

As optimistic as we might be that the shared insights of our differing disciplines and our common commitment to God in Christ will provide clear directions and perspectives, we must recognize that the enterprise is not without its dangers.

"Simple About Evil"

To begin with, let us recall Paul's advice to the church at Rome (Rom. 16:19): "I would have you wise unto that which is good and simple concerning that which is evil." While Paul urges upon the church a sophistication, a wisdom regarding that which is good, he suggests that the Christian maintain a simpleness about evil. That fascination with evil of which we spoke earlier may ensnare even the Christian student of evil. What begins as interest may become fascination, and the fascination may lead to seduction. It is possible to be a little too clever, a little too sophisticated about evil. One must never forget that the issue is one of "principalities and powers," which cannot be approached casually with a naïve disregard of their ensnaring capacities. C. S. Lewis doubtless had this in mind when he warned that there are two errors regarding the devil: one was not to believe in him at all, and the other was to pay too much attention to him. The word of Scripture surely is not a call to be a simpleton, and no excuse for foolish thinking. But it is a warning which can be disregarded only at great risk.

Mystery of the Demonic

A second danger is the illusion that in our efforts we shall grasp in finality the nature and sum of evil, successfully analyze and delineate it, and be done. On the contrary, just as the Christian has to recognize that he cannot fully define, describe or delineate the scope of God in His grace, so he must expect only partial answers relative to the kingdom of evil. We see through a glass darkly. We are, as it were, a landlocked people. Our perception of such realities is severely handicapped. So when we have enhanced our knowledge, listened to the voice of the Spirit in Holy Scripture, benefited from the insights of one another, and examined our own souls, we will have attained (perhaps fortunately) but slight awareness of the geography and boundaries of the kingdom of evil. To think otherwise would be a gross act of pride which indeed goeth before a fall.

Foster Misunderstanding

A further danger in attempting to deal with the nature of the demonic is that such an effort in and of itself may result in confusion and misunderstanding by both church and society. In the first place, to focus on the devil himself may be misunderstood as encouraging the phenomenon sadly present in some Christian circles where the devil gets more attention than God himself: the devil is lifted up as exciting, clever, perhaps even omniscient and omnipresent, while God comes off as a boring, predictable, unexciting, unimaginative deity. If this symposium were to result in giving the devil more publicity, we should have failed. The devil is not the agenda of the Christian. The direction and focus of the Christian and his church is toward God, not toward Satan and his counter-kingdom.

We would have further encouraged confusion if we fostered the identification of all evil in the world with demonic possession. "The devil made me do it" is not an acceptable theological stance, but rather a demonic form of escapism to avoid confrontation with personal sin within. How easy it would be if one could thus exorcise guilt and responsibility and the need for personal repentance and conversion! But the Scriptures themselves warn against casting out demons without something to replace them; other evils rush in and the result is worse. Identification of all evil with demonic possession may also disastrously draw attention away from the wider realm in which evil operates in the world—ideas, institutions, structures—principalities and powers. To encourage the focusing of the church's attention upon one narrow and dramatic aspect of the problem would be to leave the major area of evil and demonic activity untouched. The proclamation of the church and of this conference must be to name evil in all its expressions and particularly those in which its operations are so cleverly disguised.

A further confusion which an emphasis upon the demonic may produce is the notion that evil is openly and always abhorrent. Would that that were so! *Time* magazine, in reviewing *The Exorcist*, observed that the devil represented therein was an "easy devil." The evil with which the world and the Christian are so regularly confronted does not come with such clear credentials; its arrival can be soft and gentle, and its appearance that of an angel of light. The demonic evil infesting the world is far more subtle and infinitely more seductive than any *Exorcist* style demon ever dreamed of. A sound theology of evil must recognize that possession is not among the cleverest works of the devil.

Centered in Christ

Let it be clearly stated that this symposium will have profoundly failed if its result should be to direct people's attention away from Christ. The primary declarations which we have to make are not about the devil, but about Christ. The truths we have to delineate about evil are, paradoxically, not truths about demons, but truths about God, for He alone offers the assurance of victory over the evil powers. The foundation of this symposium, if not its direct content, must therefore be the Gospel, the Cross, and the Atonement. The hope of this conference is not that somehow we might grasp some truth about the demonic, but rather that we should see more profoundly the truth of the Good News. The aim of this symposium is not that we might design tools of exorcism, but that we might more clearly and decisively express the words, "Greater is he that is in you than he that is in the world," and "Thou wilt keep him in perfect peace whose mind is stayed on thee." The declaration of this conference must not be a fearful admission of the overwhelming power of the demonic, but the declaration which Paul made to the Colossian church (Col. 2:15): "He disarmed the principalities and powers and made a public example of them, triumphing over them in him." Underlying all that is here declared, debated and espoused must be that declaration of and confidence in the victory already won in Christ, who is not only our Lord but Lord of all.

DEMON POSSESSION

PART ONE

Demonology in the Bible

1

The Demythologization of the Demonic in the Old Testament

DENNIS F. KINLAW

The Difficulty of the Subject

Our subject in these sessions is difficult by its very nature. Objectivity is needed but the subjective character of the search complicates our problem. We are seeking to know about a world we cannot see. It is known only through the inner self. Yet the line between our spirits and that world of other spirits is elusive. Our imaginations can play tricks on us and make us confuse identities rather easily.

Our problem is further complicated by our obvious affinity for evil. Man as we know him, fallen man, is much more easily intrigued by evil than by good. The imagination is typically susceptible. Dorothy Sayers understood this when she suggested that the playwright who introduces into her cast of characters the devil has an almost insuperable problem. How to keep the evil one from becoming the hero! Malcolm Muggeridge had his finger on the same thing when he suggested that fiction was a better medium for evil than good in that evil is always better in imagination than reality, while the good tastes better in fact than in imagination. This is confirmed by the ease with which such subjects as Faust, Frankenstein, or Rosemary's Baby can be dramatized in print, in film, or on the tube. It will be awhile before the best-seller lists or the television ratings help sell the story of a Fenelon, a Wesley, or a Brainerd.

We have particular need for divine guidance and protection from illusion. That is why we turn to the Scripture.

Only through it can we with certainty protect ourselves from delusion self-generated or otherwise.

The Importance of Scripture
and Especially the Old Testament

The importance of the Scriptures can hardly be over-emphasized. And by the Scriptures we mean all of the written Word. We live in a day that tends to take the New Testament for the Word of God. And some at times seem to prefer only certain portions of it. The witness of the whole Bible must be sought here.

The Old Testament must be taken seriously. It is as certainly Scripture as the New. How can one ignore the book which Jesus and the earliest Christian Church loved and accepted as the Word of God? To do so, as history so bountifully documents, almost inevitably leads to error. We must remember that Genesis is revelation as much as St. John and that in many things is essential to any true interpretation of John. If all we had were the Pentateuch, we would certainly be impoverished but our religion would still be as unique among the religions of the world as Jesus is among mankind's many "saviors."

The Old Testament is especially relevant here in that its people lived in a world remarkably like our own in its preoccupation with the sensual, the occult, and the demonic. Israel knew well three cultures—Assyro-Babylonian, the Egyptian, and the Canaanite. In each the demonic was a prevalent factor. As with so many cultures of history, the affairs of life were felt to be under the control of spirits. Petty annoyances like a toothache or a fall, more serious evils such as disease and plague, and even one's emotions of love, hate, or jealousy were felt to be the result of the activity of spirits. There even seem to have been special fiends with special concern for special parts of the body. No matter what was wrong there was always someone to blame. It was a simple view of life in that there was an identifiable cause for every evil happening.

It had its negative side though, for life tended to become enveloped in fear. Even the gods had their problems. Death, disease, and other misfortunes could befall them too. Little wonder that popular religion was largely concerned with how to control the baleful world of demons who threatened both gods and men. Magic, witchcraft, sorcery, divination and all of the occult arts inevitably flourished.

It was like much of Africa where there is a knowledge of one creator God who is good. His part though in daily religion is negligible. It is the spirits of the ancestors and the demons that get the attention. They are the ones that bring danger and threaten one's daily existence. Why worry about the benign one? Thus popular religion becomes a matter of sacrifices, incantations and spells to appease and manipulate the world of spirits. That kind of religion was very familiar to Israel.

Israel's neighbors believed that these spirits could do things not only to you but in you. The evidence is that spirit-possession was familiar in Babylon, Egypt, and Canaan. This manifested itself in all manner of aberrant behavior from frenzy or catalepsy to apparent clairvoyance. From the earliest times in the ancient Near East there were priests whose business it was through magical incantations and occult rites to expel the evil spirits. The extant exorcistic literature is substantial.

The Old Testament Data

What a surprising contrast when one turns to the Old Testament! It reflects a completely different world. Only one clear case in thirty-nine books is recorded where an evil spirit comes upon a man, Saul, and then that evil spirit is from Yahweh. The relief that is brought to him comes not by magical incantation or spell but by the singing of the psalmist, David. And as for instruction in or ceremonies for the exorcising of the demonic there is absolute silence.

There is acknowledgment of the world of the dead and the possibility of communion with it by the living. But the story of the witch of Endor gives its own witness to the uniqueness of Israel. Her practice is forbidden and when it is exercised it gives no help. Life is determined by moral realities, not magical. The witch can bring up Samuel but can do nothing to help a lost Saul. He is in Yahweh's hands and Yahweh cannot be manipulated. Hearkening to Yahweh is what determines the issues of life, not witchcraft or idolatry.

Josephus tells us that Solomon was wise in incantations by which illnesses were relieved, and gave forms for exorcism by which demons could be driven out, never to return (*Antiquities*, VIII. ii.5). The apocryphal Tobit tells us of Tobias, his son, who was led by the angel Raphael to marry a virgin who had been widowed seven times. On each of the previous occasions when her new husband entered the marriage chamber, he was immediately slain by Asmodeus, a demon. Tobias, instructed by the angel Raphael, burned the heart and liver of a special fish. This expelled the demon who fled to Egypt where Raphael pursued and bound him. Tobias was then able to take in safety and with righteous joy Sarah for his wife.

Josephus and Tobit bear witness to the pervasiveness of the belief in demon possession and the possibility of exorcism. It is significant though that the thirty-nine traditionally received canonical books are remarkably silent on such a subject.

It is not that the Old Testament does not know about such spirits. It does. We see it particularly in the reference to the *shedim* and the *šecirim* and perhaps to *lilîth*.

Lilith is known from the Babylonian literature as a female night demon. The *shedim* were demons (perhaps "the black ones") to whom Israel's neighbors offered sacrifice, even their own sons and daughters (Deut. 32:17; Ps. 106:37). The *šecirim* were demon-satyrs ("the hairy ones") who frequented the fields and the deserts. There are only two references to the *shedim*, Deut. 32:17 and Ps. 106:37. In the first, in Moses' song, we are told of how Israel after deliverance from Egypt provoked Yahweh in the wilderness to jealousy by sacrificing to the *shedim*. In Psalm 106 we are told how Israel refused to destroy the nations as Yahweh commanded, intermingled with their neighbors, accommodated themselves to their ways, and sacrificed their sons and daughters to the *shedim*. These two references exhaust the Old Testament teaching on the *shedim*.

There are only four references to the *šecirim*. In Lev. 17:7 Israel was forbidden to make sacrifices to these field demons. "And they shall no more offer their sacrifices unto devils, after whom they have gone a whoring." Undoubtedly the insistence upon sacrificing at the central sanctuary under the watchful eye of a priest was one means of protecting the Hebrew from yielding to the temptation to take his neighbors' routine precautions against mishap. The passage in Chronicles (2 Chron. 11:15) records how Rehoboam, when he followed his own self-willed way, appointed priests to sacrifice to the goat and calf idols and thus brought judgment from Yahweh on His people. The pressure from its environs to turn to the demonic and the occult is clear in the

Old Testament in that departure from faith in Yahweh and obedience to His laws *always* brought a flood of such.

There are two other references to the *śᵉᶜirim* in the Old Testament, in Isa. 13:21 and 34:14. In both passages a land is described that has come under judgment from Yahweh. In the desolation that results the wild animals are able to establish their dominion in the ruins. In each case the *śᵉᶜirim* are listed among the wild creatures. But the question now is, does *śaʿir* mean "satyr-demon" or simply "wild goat"? The evidence for simply "goat" is strong.

This brings us to a most remarkable tendency in Israel. In striking contrast to her neighbors who were geniuses at creating a mythology, we find a perpetual tendency or power in Israel to demythologize life. Take for instance the word *lîlîth*, well known as the Assyrian female night demon and succuba who had intercourse with men in their dreams. Later Jewish literature makes her the first wife of Adam who flew away and became a demon, stole and destroyed new-born infants, and brought disease. In her one appearance in the Old Testament she is in a list of real animals and birds, with the jackals and wildcats, the pelicans, and the owls. The LXX renders the *hapax legomenon* by a word which means something like a tail-less monkey!

Resheph was a Canaanite god of plague and pestilence. He is documented from Mari, Ugarit, Zenjirle, Karatepe, Crete, Egypt and Carthage in literature from 1800 to 350 B.C. He was almost omnipresent in the Near East. The word occurs a number of times in the Old Testament but never with a mythological or demonical overtone. It is simply the Hebrew word for "flame" or "fire-bolt."

The same could be said for many other words which Israel used. Before Yahweh became their God these words were loaded with mythological and supernatural significance. The impact of Yahweh was to strip them of all but their natural meaning. The Old Testament acknowledges the spirit world but seems bent upon minimizing, demythologizing, or marginalizing it. Wherever it does occur, it *always* has its origin in Yahweh and its role and domain determined by His sovereignty. No autonomous domain, independent of Yahweh, or outside His immediate control, exists to threaten man.

The treatment of Satan in the Old Testament is comparable. He is the tempter who can mislead an Eve or a David and thus contribute to their coming under Yahweh's judgment (Gen. 3:1ff. and 1 Chron. 21:1ff.). He is the adversary who can accuse a Joshua, the high priest (Zech. 3:1ff.), or complicate life for a Job. But we are told also that he was made by Yahweh (Gen. 3:1), is one of His servants under His control (Job 1 and 2), and can do nothing without His explicit permission (Job 1 and 2). His person and role develop so slowly in the Old Testament that it takes centuries for the noun "satan" or "adversary" (Num. 22:22) to become a personal name (Zech. 3). This primary evil one in the Old Testament carries about him none of the aura of numinous fear and terror which marked the novel and the film, *The Exorcist.*

In the Old Testament Yahweh alone was to be feared. He had neither rival nor competitor. He alone is man's ultimate concern and only ultimate help. No concessions were to be made to the popular pressure to turn to the crutches of magic, idolatry, or the occult to deal with daily fears or anxieties. Whether in the temple, in the home, or in the field with their multiple problems, Yahweh alone was to be their dread or their security. His fear was the beginning of wisdom. He alone was God and there was no savior beside Him. Perfect peace was found by keeping one's mind stayed on Him. No easy religion, but the Old Testament demand, and a striking contrast to all that was around.

Why This Treatment?

The faith that is found in the Old Testament was unique. It gives the lie to any notion of continuity that Israel's faith emerged as an evolutionary variant in the ancient Near Eastern world of religion. It was a disjunction. It was unique not only in its new elements but in the way it treated the elements held in common with its neighbors such as the demonic.

In this sense the Gospels in the New Testament are more like the literature of Israel's neighbors, for, there we find the demonic appearing openly and rather extensively. The difference between the atmosphere of Malachi and Matthew is striking. What happened? Can all of this be explained as the influence of Persian dualism or Jesus' concession to popular superstition? It must be noted that when one gets to Rom. 1:1 the atmosphere changes again. The demonic is in the background and has little definition. The expressions "principalities," "powers," "rulers of the darkness of this world," and "spiritual wickedness in high places" satisfy few of our questions and excite, not satisfy, our imaginations. Again, in this literature written to humble believers in pagan cities of the first century where the demonic was commonplace, there is no word of explanation about possession or how to handle it. All rituals for exorcism developed later. They were not in Paul's instructions to his brothers.

Why this playing down and ignoring of a familiar problem whether in Abraham's day or in Paul's? Why the demonic under wraps? A few suggestions may be appropriate.

1. The Old Testament obviously takes very seriously the doctrine of *creatio ex nihilo*! In the beginning there was Yahweh plus nothing. The monotheism here is radical. There is one *ultimate* because there is one *primus* and that is Yahweh. There is no world either good or evil that exists alongside Him as equal or rival. He reigns and reigns alone. Evil must be transferred from the metaphysical, as in other regions of the world, to the moral realm.

2. It makes man's responsibility for his own evil unavoidable at every point. Nowhere is it necessary to posit the demonic to account for human evil. Man's own freedom is enough. No cosmic evil principle exists that makes sin necessary. Satan may entice man to sin, but he is finite like the mortal creature he tempts and is subject to the same righteous judgment of Yahweh. The serpent could only encourage Eve to misuse her freedom as he had misused his.

3. This approach takes seriously man's present affinity for evil and his tendency to dramatize it. It recognizes the old principle that whatever gets your attention gets you. Therefore the center of the stage is reserved exclusively and solely for Yahweh. It is to be noted that hell, Satan and the demonic are most fully treated in the Gospels and the Apocalypse of John. Could it be that God is content to let us see that negative world only in the presence of the incarnate Christ? The veil is never parted to show us Moses and Satan, Elijah and Satan, or Paul and Satan. Satan and the demonic appear with clarity and definition only when Jesus is present. And at this point fallen imaginations find their susceptibility to be enchanted by the demonic broken and an ability to see things as they are. To God be the glory for this revelation and the freedom which it brings.

2

Response

GORDON R. LEWIS

Two little six-year-olds struggled with the problem of demythologizing the demonic when they were heard arguing about the existence of the devil. One little boy said, "Oh, there isn't any devil." The other little boy who was very upset by this said, "What do you mean there isn't any devil? It talks about him all the way through the Bible." The first little boy said in a very knowing way, "Oh, that's a lot of nonsense, you know. Just like Santa Claus, the devil turns out to be your daddy."

Some demythologizers would go as far as that little boy with the demonology that pervaded the nations surrounding Israel and the demonology in the Bible. Rudolph Bultmann is the father of demythologization, if not an Old Testament scholar. He assumed that reality was exhausted in a closed continuum of cause and effect which leaves no room for divine or demonic activity.[1] No interruption or perforation of the causal continuum by supernatural powers is thought possible. History is an unbroken whole, complete in itself. This also rules out activities of God in Christ for the salvation of the world. "For modern man the mythological conception of the world, the conceptions of eschatology, of redeemer and of redemption are over and done with." [2] Bultmann thinks it impossible to use electric lights and modern medical and surgical discoveries and at the same time believe in the biblical world of spirits and miracles.[3]

The cozy, completely predictable world Bultmann assumed has been found more complex than he imagined. Few recent writers imagine that they live in a neat, surprise-free world. At any time a person may come face to face with the unexpected. As Peter Berger, the sociologist-theologian, says, many think that human life gains the greatest part of its richness from any experience of stepping outside the take-for-granted reality of everyday life, any openness to the mystery that surrounds us on all sides.[4]

The danger now is that people may be returning to the extreme preoccupation with the demonic that characterized Israel's neighbors. Dennis Kinlaw has very helpfully shown that the Old Testament avoided obsession with demons and taught that they were not intermediaries between man and God but subordinates of Satan who was in turn a creature under the control of God. This view takes the force out of the mythology around Israel without going to the unbiblical and unrealistic extreme of Bultmann.

Bultmann assumed that nature is a closed continuum; Israel's neighbors assumed an open and meaningless world at the caprice of demons. The Christian, A. Berkeley Mickelsen suggests, affirms that God has established nature's laws, but is not the prisoner of His own laws. "Hence orthodoxy, insisting on *a controlled continuum*, is actually asserting the freedom of God. That God is free to act becomes clear in the miracles of Jesus." [5] Within the divine control, Kinlaw shows, is the power of Satan and demons.

Deliverance from the tension and fear of Israel's superstitious neighbors, Kinlaw wisely asserts, is rooted in a proper understanding that metaphysically the *ultimate* is God, not nature, not the demonic and not the spirits of dead people. Writing on the idea of power in the Old Testament, Walter Grundmann agrees. A personal God replaces the forces of nature, and so the predominant feature is not force or power, but the will of God. Religion replaces magic. The important things are obedience, prayer and sacrifice, not magical incantations, instruments and ceremonies.[6]

That Old Testament writers distinguished demons from consulting with the spirits of the dead is supported by Werner Foerster in his article on demons. He concludes: "When we survey the whole development from the reserved attitude of the Old Testament to that more or less complete triumph of the popular view by way of the outlook of the pseudepigrapha, we may conclude that the decisive feature in Jewish demonology is that the demons are evil spirits and that the link with the souls of the dead is broken." [7]

On the following considerations, I question Kinlaw's

statement that the witch of Endor brought up the soul of Samuel (p. 4): (1) Saul recognized Samuel; he did not have to take the witch's word for it. (2) Samuel spoke like Samuel, not through the witch's mouth. (3) The medium was startled and her usual procedure was cut short. (4) The message Samuel gave was biblical in content and not contrary to the pleasure of God. (5) To say that a medium can talk with the spirits of the dead is inconsistent with the rest of Scripture.

Insightfully Kinlaw suggests that Old Testament statements attributing evil to the Lord teach the absoluteness of monotheism, which is a reflex of the doctrine of creation out of nothing. Although he says Aristotelian distinctions are not drawn by the Old Testament, and verbally he is correct, he explains Yahweh is responsible for all that exists (Aristotle's final cause) and that moral evil is the result of the activity of creatures that came from His hand (Aristotle's efficient or blameworthy cause). To say that Yahweh is responsible though Yahweh himself never produced evil is to say that He is the final cause but not the blameworthy cause, is it not? While there are differences between Old Testament thought and that of the Greek philosophers, their frames of reference are not totally other. Some biblical scholars in their enthusiasm to magnify the differences seem unwilling to admit similarities which are to be expected since both Hebrews and Greeks were humans created in the image of God, lived in the same world and struggled with many of the same problems.

I agree with Kinlaw that no appeal to the demonic can displace the responsibility of evil-doers. But I wonder if apart from a demonic factor we can account for the enmity between the seed of the woman and Satan. Apart from demonic opposition to the coming Christ, would Cain have killed Abel? Would pharaoh have killed the male babies in Egypt? Would Haman have sought to annihilate the Jews? Would Herod have slaughtered the male infants at the time of the Messiah's birth?

J. I. Packer underscores one of Kinlaw's helpful points in the following terms: "Our demonology cannot be any more true or adequate than our doctrine of God is. We can see the truth about the devil only in the light of truth about God. Demonology concerns one aspect—the basic aspect—of the mystery of evil; evil has to be understood as a lack, a perversion of good; and we know what good is only when we know what God is. Only through appreciating God's goodness can we form any idea of the devil's badness." [9]

The inferiority of the satanic role is made more graphically by Chambers who imagines a conversation between himself and Satan. Toynbee pointed out that when the devil tempts a creature, God himself is thereby given the opportunity to recreate the world.[10] Chambers asks the devil if there may not be an end to his dialectics. The devil says: "I have brought man to the point of intellectual pride where self-extermination lies within his power. There is not only the bomb, . . . there are the much less discussed delights of bacteriological annihilation. And it is only a question of time until whole populations can be driven insane in time of war by sound which their ears cannot hear but their nerves cannot bear."

"Just what do you get out of it?" asked the pessimist.

"My friend," said Satan, "you do not understand the Devil's secret. But since shamelessness is part of my pathos, there is no reason why I should not tell you. The devil is sterile. I possess the will to create (hence my pride), but I am incapable of creating (hence my envy). And with an envy raised to such power as mortal minds can feel, I hate the Creator and His creation. My greatest masterpiece is never more than a perversion—an ingenious disordering of another's grand design, a perversion of order into chaos, of life into death. Why? . . . Perhaps, it is simply, as every craftsman knows, that nothing enduring, great or small, can ever be created without love. But I am as incapable of love as I am of goodness. I am as insensitive to either as a dead hand is to a needle thrust through it." [11]

Notes

1. Rudolf K. Bultmann, *Jesus Christ and Mythology* (New York, N.Y.: Charles Scribner's Sons, 1958), p. 65.

2. *Ibid.*, p. 17.

3. H. W. Bartsch, ed., *Kerygma and Myth* (New York, N.Y.: Harper, 1961), p. 5.

4. Peter L. Berger, *A Rumor of Angels* (Garden City, N.Y.: Doubleday, 1969), p. 94.

5. A. Mickelsen, *Interpreting the Bible* (Grand Rapids, Mich.: Eerdmans, 1963), pp. 8-9.

6. Gerhard Kittel, ed., *Theological Dictionary of the New Testament,* trans. G. Bromiley, II (Grand Rapids, Mich.: Eerdmans, 1964), 290-94.

7. *Ibid.*, p. 15.

8. Rousas John Rushdoony, "Demons, Demonology," *Encyclopedia of Christianity*, ed. Philip E. Hughes, IV (Marshallton, Del.: National Foundation for Christian Education, 1972), 352.

9. "The Devil," *Eternity*, April, 1964, p. 8.

10. Arnold J. Toynbee, *A Study of History*, Vol. I (New York: Oxford University Press, 1934), p. 284; in the one-volume abridgement by D. C. Somerville, p. 63.

11. Wittaker Chambers, "The Devil," *Life Magazine*, 24 (February 2, 1948), pp. 84-85.

3

Jesus and the Unclean Spirits

J. RAMSEY MICHAELS

Nothing is more certain about the ministry of Jesus than the fact that He performed exorcisms. Wherever we take soundings in the synoptic tradition—Mark, the so-called "Q" source, Matthew, and Luke—we find narratives and controversies centering on Jesus' ability to cure those who were demon possessed. Only the Gospel of John lacks this kind of material, and even here the controversies are at least echoed in the charge that Jesus himself is demon possessed (7:20; 8:48, 52; 10:20).

The Exorcisms

The primary source of descriptions of actual exorcisms is the Gospel of Mark. The Markan evidence consists of four incidents (1:23-28; 5:1-20; 7:24-30; 9:14-29) and a number of summary statements which include the driving out of demons among Jesus' characteristic acts (1:32-34, 39; 3:7-12). A brief consideration of each passage in turn, with a comparative glance at parallel passages in the other Gospels, will enable us to construct a picture of Jesus' warfare with the demonic world as Mark conceives it.

1. *The Demoniac in the Synagogue* (Mark 1:23-28; cf. Luke 4:33-37). After the call of the first disciples (1:16-20), Jesus entered the synagogue at Capernaum and began to teach (1:21). His teaching caused wonder among the people, "for he was teaching them as one having authority, and not as the scribes" (1:22). This impressive statement, which in Matthew becomes the conclusion and response to the Sermon on the Mount (cf. Matt. 7:28-29), is reinforced in

Mark by an account of an exorcism in the Capernaum synagogue (1:23-28). After the demoniac has been healed, the
people ask each other in amazement, "What is this? A
new teaching with authority! He commands even the unclean spirits, and they obey him" (1:27). The function of the
exorcism for Mark, therefore, is to drive home a point about
the authority of Jesus' teaching, a point which Matthew
makes in a very different way and without reference to
the expulsion of demons.

As for the story itself, it is told with classic brevity
and simplicity, involving several basic, indispensable elements: the situation (a demon-possessed man in the synagogue, v. 23), the demon's challenge to Jesus (v. 24), the
rebuke and exorcism (v. 25), the departure of the unclean
spirit (v. 26), and the response of the onlookers (vv. 27f.).
The demoniac is described as "a man in an unclean spirit"
(ἄνθρωπος ἐν πνεύματι ἀκαθάρτῳ). This expression occurs only
in Mark (here and in 5:2). Both times it is changed by
the other evangelists. The parallel in Luke 4:33 speaks of
"a man having an unclean demon," while the parallel passages to Mark 5:2 read "a certain man . . . having demons"
(Luke 8:27) or "two demoniacs" (Matt. 8:28).

The phrase "a man in an unclean spirit" is reminiscent
of Paul's strange reference to himself in 2 Corinthians
12:2 as "a man in Christ" (ἄνθρωπος ἐν Χριστῷ). In the latter
case the reference is not simply to the continuing "in Christ"
relationship of which he speaks frequently in his epistles,
but to an exceptional ecstatic experience of being totally
possessed by Christ so as to receive special messages and
visions.

In somewhat parallel fashion the demoniac in Mark 1:23
ff. is "inspired." He "knows" something about Jesus and
speaks what he knows "in the spirit," except that the spirit
by which he speaks is "unclean." He is in a sense the precise
opposite counterpart to the inspired Christian prophet. His
opposition to Jesus, even while voicing a kind of confession,
is seen in the contrast between ἀκάθαρτος ("unclean spirit,"
v. 23) and ἅγιος ("Holy One of God," v. 24)[1] as well as in
the formula "What have we to do with you?" (lit., "What
to us and to you?") in verse 23. Thus his recognition of
Jesus as "the Holy One of God" is in no sense equivalent
to the confession, "Jesus is Lord," which according to Paul
can be uttered only at the impulse of the Holy Spirit (1
Cor. 12:3). If the two were equivalent, the Markan narrative

would be in contradiction to the Pauline principle. Even as it is, the silencing of the demons (1:34; cf. v. 25) may have something to do with the fact that for them to acknowledge Jesus as God's unique messenger is considered inappropriate by Jesus and/or the gospel writer. Instead of suppressing the fact that this was what took place, Mark has faithfully recorded the tradition while being careful to append to it Jesus' command not to speak (cf. also 3:12).[2]

It is noteworthy in this account that the unclean spirit, not Jesus, initiates the confrontation. Strictly speaking it is the afflicted man who utters the words recorded in Mark 1:24, but in reality they are not the words of "a man" but of "a man in an unclean spirit." Twice in verse 24 the use of the plural "us" makes it clear that the real speaker is indeed the demon. It is important, however, not to read the situation of Mark 5:1-20 back into this incident. The plural does not indicate that the man is possessed by more than one demon (as in 5:9), only that the demon speaks as one of a class of beings who have a similar attitude toward Jesus, sharing common fears of destruction at His hands. The demon addresses Jesus with a singular verb ("*I* know who you are . . .") and in turn is addressed with singular pronoun and imperatives (v. 25). At the word of Jesus the demon is put to silence and, with one last shudder and cry, departs from his victim. The reader learns nothing of his fate or the fate of the man. The conclusion of the story focuses rather on the amazement of the witnesses and the subsequent spread of Jesus' fame throughout the surrounding region in Galilee (vv. 27-28).

2. *The Gerasene Demoniac* (Mark 5:1-20; cf. Matt. 8:28-34; Luke 8:26-39). The longest and most remarkable exorcism in the New Testament takes place in the region of Gerasa just after the stilling of the storm (Mark 4:35-41). The same basic elements are present as in the account of the demoniac in the synagogue: the situation is sketched, this time in considerable detail (5:1-5); the demon challenges Jesus in much the same way as before (5:6-7); Jesus commands the unclean spirit to depart from the man (5:8-12) and he finally does so (5:13), but only after an interchange which is unparalleled in any other Gospel incident; finally the reactions of those affected by the miracle are described (5:14-20).

Mark preserves this order of narration even while offering a clue that the actual sequence of events was different.

Verses 8-10 appear to be an explanatory insertion, moderating the abruptness of verse 7 by giving some additional circumstances which led up to the outburst, "What have I to do with you, Jesus, son of the Most High God? I ask you to swear to God that you will not torment me!" [3] Thus verses 8-10 are a kind of flashback: "For he had said to him, 'Come out of the man, you unclean spirit.' And he had asked him 'What is your name?' and he said to him 'My name is Legion, for we are many.' And so he kept pleading with him that he should not send him out of that region."

If this implied original order of events is correct, then in this case the initiative lay with Jesus, at least as soon as the demoniac fell at His feet. Whether the apparent insertion represents merely the awkwardness of Mark's style or whether Mark is editing and supplementing (from additional information he possesses) an earlier written account consisting of 5:1-7, 11f. is uncertain. If the latter is the case, it appears that Matthew has followed the shorter account, for his Gospel lacks any parallel to verses 8-10. That Mark is capable of working backwards from an incident or saying to describe parenthetically the events which led up to it is made clear on a more extensive scale in 6:17-29, where a series of statements introduced by γάρ (vv. 17, 18, 20) is used to explain Herod's references to John the Baptist in 6:14, 16. Here in chapter five the effect of the "insertion" (if such it is) is to explain why the demons are plural in verses 12-13. The demoniac speaks in the singular in verse 7 (contrast 1:24), and there is no preparation of a shift to the plural apart from verse 9.

Matthew, by contrast, uses plurals already in 8:29 (his parallel to Mark 5:7), so that the plurals in 8:30ff. (the parallel to Mark 8:11ff.) come as no surprise. Thus no parallel to Mark 5:8-10 is necessary.

Luke, on the other hand, follows Mark in using an explanatory statement introduced by γάρ (Luke 8:29, parallel to Mark 5:8) but weaves into this statement additional material about the man's personal history (parallel to Mark 5:4f.). But Luke's parallels to Mark 5:9-10 (i.e., Luke 8:30-31) do not belong to this "flashback," but apparently pick up the order of the account interrupted at 8:28. Thus Matthew and Luke, each in his own way, have edited Mark in the interests of a smoother narrative.

A further function of Mark 5:8-10 is to indicate just how the spirits feared that Jesus would "torment" them.

The μ̄ με βασανίσῃς of verse 7 is explained by the ἵνα μὴ αὐτὰ - ἀποστείλῃ ἔξω τῆς Χώρας in verse 10. They feared that Jesus would send them out of the region of the Gerasenes, which appears to be their home for the time being and in that sense a "haunted" place. The reason for the sending of the demons into a herd of swine (vv. 11-13) is much-debated.[4] At the very least, the account has the effect of stressing the multiplicity of the demons. In the present form of the narrative the "legion" of verse 9 is dramatically reinforced by the picture of two thousand swine drowning in the lake. There were demons enough in this one man to galvanize two thousand pigs and send them to their deaths! Beyond this, little can be said. The fact that unclean spirits are sent into unclean animals is hardly accidental. They have asked to be allowed to go to a place that is natural for them, and there is no need to draw the conclusion that Jesus has somehow tricked them or sent them to their final destruction.

The reader of Mark's Gospel can hardly overlook the fact, however, that the effect of Jesus' ministry is precisely to break down the distinction between the clean and the unclean. By His word Jesus makes all foods clean (Mark 7:19), thus displaying in a different way His lordship over what Paul calls the "elements of the world." [5]

We are not intended to speculate about the immediate fate of the unclean spirits in 5:11-13. What matters is that their power over the demoniac has been broken, and their days are shown to be numbered. They take possession of swine because the swine are unclean, and they seem to thrive in the region of the Gerasenes and the Decapolis because this region is inhabited by gentiles (also considered unclean by pious Jews). But these are precisely the traditional distinctions which, according to Mark, Jesus has come to abolish. His exorcism of demons becomes for Mark a paradigm of His "exorcism" of traditions about clean and unclean, particularly when these distinctions are applied to people as well as animals and food (cf. Mark 7:1-23).

The reaction to the miracle is negative on the part of the Gerasenes (5:14-17) and positive on the part of the man (5:18-20). He wants to leave the region with Jesus, but is told to return to his home and family and "tell them what the Lord has done for you [ὅσα ὁ κύριός σοι πεποίηκεν] and how he has had mercy on you" (v. 19). He does so, proclaiming in the Decapolis "what Jesus had done for him [ὅσα ἐποίησεν αὐτῷ ὁ Ἰησοῦς] and all were amazed" (v. 20). The implicit identification of "Jesus" with "the Lord" (made even sharper in Luke 8:39) [6] is a striking note on which to end the narrative.

3. *The Syro-Phoenician Woman* (Mark 7:24-30; cf. Matt. 15:21-28). The next exorcism narrative in Mark, appropriately enough, has to do with the daughter of a (gentile) Syro-Phoenician woman (7:24-30). To the request that Jesus drive the demon out of her daughter, Jesus replies, "Let the children first be fed. It is not good to take the bread of the children and throw it to the dogs" (7:27). But when the woman shows persistence and ingenuity, Jesus performs the exorcism at a distance, and the child is made well. The placing of this incident between the feeding of the 5,000, on Jewish territory, and the feeding of the 4,000, in a predominantly Gentile region, strengthens the point made by the exchange between Jesus and the woman.[7]

4. *The Boy with a Deaf-Mute Spirit* (Mark 9:14-29; cf. Matt. 17:14-21; Luke 9:37-43a). As Jesus, with Peter, James, and John, returns to His disciples from the Mount of Transfiguration, He finds a crowd gathered around a man who has brought for healing his son, possessed by a "mute spirit" (πνεῦμα ἄλαλον, 9:17). As in the other cases, the situation is described (9:18, 21-22) including the symptoms and the inability of the disciples to drive out the spirit (9:18). The latter feature is distinctive to this particular story. The point is not only that Jesus has the power to expel demons, but also that others as well have this power, at least theoretically. Therefore when they fail to do so, Jesus sees it as symptomatic of a "faithless generation" (9:19). The keys to the exercise of this power are faith and prayer. When the boy's father says to Jesus, "If you can do anything, take pity on us and help us," Jesus replies, "What do you mean, 'If you can'? Everything is possible for him who believes" (9:23). After the exorcism, Jesus' disciples ask Him privately why they were unable to drive out the demon. Jesus' answer is that "this kind can come out only by prayer" (9:29). [8] Mark's purpose in this narrative is to emphasize not only what Jesus did in one instance but also what every disciple can do through faith and prayer. The point is one which comes out more clearly in 11:22-24, in connection with the cursing of the fig tree.

Several conclusions emerge from this brief survey of the Markan exorcism stories. In each instance, Mark has reasons of his own for telling the story. Each has a function in the author's overall plan for his Gospel, a function which goes beyond merely an interest in demon possession and exorcism for their own sake.

In 1:23-28 the function is to reinforce the impression of Jesus' authority given in 1:22. This emphasis reappears in 4:35-41, just prior to the second exorcism, when Jesus addresses the storm in much the same language with which He addressed the unclean spirit in chapter one:

1:25	4:39
And Jesus sternly command-ed him, [ἐπετίμησεν αὐτῷ] say-ing 'Be quiet [φιμώθητι] and come out of him.'	And he got up and sternly commanded the wind [ἐπετίμη- σεν τῷ ἀνέμῳ] and said to the lake 'Be still. Keep quiet' [πεφίμωσο].

The response to Jesus' authority is also much the same in each case:

1:27	4:41
'What is this? A new teach-ing, with authority. He even gives orders to the unclean spirits and they obey him' [ὑπακούουσιν αὐτῷ].	'Who then is this, that even the wind and the lake obey him' [ὑπακούει αὐτῷ]?

The story of the Gerasene demoniac which follows immediately in Mark reinforces this impression with its concluding identification of Jesus as "Lord" (5:19-20), but in so doing provides also the most extensive example of an exorcism told for its own sake. This narrative more than any of the others helps to satisfy the reader's curiosity about the specific nature of demon possession. The plurality of the spirits, their conversation with Jesus, extending beyond simply acknowledging Him as Son of God, their need to remain in the Gerasene region, their entrance into the two thousand swine, the radically changed character and appearance of the man—all such details are vivid and unforgettable, reflecting without a doubt the testimony of eyewitnesses. They serve us well, therefore, in describing the phenomena which confronted Jesus in His ministry.

The story of the Syro-Phoenician woman, on the other hand (7:24-30), shows no interest in the daughter for her own sake nor in the exorcism as such. The concern is rather with the mother as a representative Gentile seeking help from Jesus the Jew. The only distinctive feature of the exorcism itself is that, like the healing of the gentile centurion's servant (Matt. 8:5-13; Luke 7:1-10; cf. John 4:46-54), it takes place from a distance. Functionally, this exorcism in Mark (and Matthew) is no different from the healing story as found in Matthew, Luke, and John.

In the case of the boy with a deaf-mute spirit (9:14-29), the exorcism is similarly subordinate to the teaching on faith and prayer, yet it is described in considerable detail. The one new significant point which emerges here is that the victory over demons belongs not to Jesus alone but to every disciple of His who prays in faith. This is entirely in line with the general Markan insistence that Christians after the resurrection may (and will) succeed where the original disciples failed.[9] The emphasis on prayer may also suggest that what Mark commended to his readers was not "exorcism" in a limited technical sense, but individual and corporate prayer on behalf of those who were possessed in Mark's own day.[10]

5. *The Summaries* (Mark 1:32-34; cf. Matt. 8:16-17; Luke 4:40-41. Mark 1:39; cf. Matt. 4:23; Luke 4:44. Mark 3:7-12; cf. Matt. 4:24-25; 12:15-16; Luke 6:17-19). In addition to specific incidents told with some detail, there are three passages in Mark which provide general summaries of Jesus' ministry of exorcism. Mark 1:32-34 summarizes the healings and the exorcisms side by side: "they brought to him all the sick and the demon-possessed . . . and he healed many who were sick with various diseases and drove out many demons, and he did not permit the demons to speak, for they knew him." Sickness and demon possession are here closely associated, yet kept distinct. The same is true in Mark 3:10-12: "for he had healed many, so that those with diseases were falling down before him [ἐπιπίπτειν αὐτῷ] to touch him, and the unclean spirits, when they saw him, fell down before him [προσέπιπτον αὐτῷ] and cried out, saying 'You are the Son of God.' And he commanded them sternly not to make him known." Again healing and exorcism are described together and in somewhat similar terms, but without blurring the distinctions between them. The special character of demon possession and thus of exorcism is carefully kept in view.

It is somewhat different in Matthew, where "demon possessed" are listed among "all who were sick with various diseases and suffering severe pain," along with "epileptics" and "paralytics" (Matt. 4:24). All these groups together are "healed" (4:25; Mark never in so many words speaks of demoniacs as being "healed"). The summary in Matt. 8:16-17 begins with exorcisms ("they brought to him many who were possessed by demons, and he drove out the spirits with a word") and then extends the range by speaking of healings in general ("and he healed all those who were sick"). The latter is evidently taken to include the former, for Matthew appends a quotation from Isaiah to cover both: " 'He bore our sicknesses and carried our diseases' " (8:17). In much the same way the Matthean parallel to Mark 1:39 replaces Mark's reference to "driving out the demons" with "healing every disease and every infirmity among the people" (4:23). And in Matt. 10:1, "authority over unclean spirits" results in "healing every disease." Thus the tendency of Matthew is to put demon possession within the general category of illness, and exorcism within the general category of healing.

The Lukan parallel to Mark's first summary statement is content to leave exorcism and healing side by side much as Mark has done (Luke 4:40-41), but Luke 6:18 (parallel to Mark 3:9-10) moves in a direction not unlike that which Matthew has taken. Luke speaks of a large crowd of people "who had come to hear him and to be healed of their diseases; and those who were troubled by unclean spirits were healed" (ἐθεραπεύοντο). Here as in Matthew, "healing" refers almost interchangeably to disease and to demon possession. Elsewhere, in a passage uniquely his own, Luke speaks of a woman who had a "spirit . . . of infirmity" (πνεῦμα . . . ἀσθενείας) for eighteen years (Luke 13:10). Jesus tells her, "Woman, you are set free from your infirmity" (13:12). Later He defends His action by saying, "Then should not this woman, a daughter of Abraham, whom Satan has kept bound for eighteen long years, be set free on the Sabbath day from what bound her?" (13:16). Is this a healing or an exorcism? The lines between the two, not perfectly drawn even in Mark, have become more and more difficult to define. Peter in the book of Acts sums up Jesus' ministry in a way that similarly groups healing and exorcism under the same rubric. Peter describes how Jesus "went around doing good and healing all who were under the power of the devil, because God was with him" (Acts 10:38).

The evidence of these summaries, particularly as we move from Mark to Matthew and Luke, shows how the phenomenon of demon possession underwent interpretation, or at least classification, even within the synoptic tradition itself, so as to become simply one category of "disease," while exorcism, correspondingly, came to be classed as one kind of "healing." This is perhaps why the lists of spiritual gifts in 1 Cor. 12 include "healing" and "miraculous powers" but not "exorcism" as such (12:9f., 28f.).[11] The tendency to extend or extrapolate the definition of the demonic to include phenomena other than actual possession, or conversely to subsume possession under the broader heading of illness, is thus present already in the New Testament itself.

The implications of this for the present-day minister or psychiatrist must be carefully weighed. On the one hand, it is possible to conclude that *all* sickness is demonic and must be exorcised, with or without accompanying medical attention. On the other hand, some might assume that all cases of demon possession belong under the category of physical or mental illness and should therefore be treated exclusively according to acceptable medical or psychiatric methods, with no particular involvement of the church.

Another question is a hermeneutical one. Should this extrapolation which goes on within the New Testament even be accepted as valid? Should not Mark, as the earliest and most "primitive" gospel witness, be taken as normative, and the tendencies present in Matthew and Luke simply disregarded as distortions? These are important and difficult questions, and somewhat beyond the scope of this paper, which proposes simply to deal with the New Testament evidence. Tentatively I believe that two classes of phenomena should be recognized: first, a specific, limited experience of "possession," described almost clinically by Mark in chapters 5 and 9, and second, a wider sphere of disease and mental illness in which, admittedly, many of the same symptoms will appear. In the case of the second, Christians have no hesitancy in making use of *both* prayer and medical treatment. Therefore perhaps in the rare cases which can today be assigned with some probability to the first category, exorcism and psychiatric help should not be regarded as mutually exclusive options. It is of such cases that Jesus said, "This kind can come out only by prayer." Prayer in fact seems to be the indispensable common factor in the treatment of afflictions in both the narrower and the broader categories.

The Controversy

The synoptic stories of the expulsion of unclean spirits

are of interest not only for their own sake but also because of the controversy to which they lead. The so-called Beelzebub controversy, attested by both Mark and Q, centers around the charge that Jesus himself is demon possessed. This charge, together with Jesus' response to it, marks a watershed in His ministry, for it is here that rejection of Him begins to take root and grow.

1. *Mark.* The account in Mark (3:22-30) is both preceded and followed by references to the family of Jesus (3:21, 31-35). In 3:21 His relatives go out to bring Him home because it was rumored (ἔλεγον) that He was out of His mind. When they arrive in verses 31ff., He turns to "those around him" (the disciples, presumably), saying, "Here are my mother and my brothers." One of the functions of what comes in between is to explain further the charge that Jesus is insane. The ἔλεγον of 3:22 helps explain the ἔλεγον of verse 21. Those making the charge are specifically identified as "the scribes who came down from Jerusalem." The charge itself is spelled out as being possessed by Beelzebub (Βεεζεβοὺλ ἔχει, v. 22), and rephrased in retrospect as being possessed by an unclean spirit (πνεῦμα ἀκάθαρτον ἔχει, v. 30). Thus a kind of equivalency is established between possession by demons and possession by Satan. "Beelzebub" is identified as an "unclean spirit" (v. 30) or as "the ruler of the demons" (v. 22), and yet when Jesus answers the charge, He does so with reference to "Satan" (vv. 23, 26).

Jesus' reply to the charge against Him has two parts: the first, *ad hominem;* the second, entirely serious and direct. First He brands the suggestion that He drives out demons by the power of Beelzebub, the ruler of the demons, as self-contradictory and absurd. This He does by the use of "parables" or analogies (3:23), leading to a *reductio ad absurdum.* First He poses a rhetorical question: "How can Satan drive out Satan?" (v. 23). Then using the twin analogies of a kingdom (v. 24) and a household (v. 25), each introduced by καὶ ἐάν and phrased in much the same way, He makes the point that no institution divided against itself can survive. Finally He brings the illustrations to bear on the question with which He started: "So if [καὶ εἰ] Satan has really risen against himself and is divided, he cannot stand but has come to an end." The charge is thus dissolved in a paradox; if Satan is indeed driving out Satan in the ministry of Jesus, then he is divided and his power is at an end. He cannot even stand, much less bring the unclean spirits into subjection.

The serious part of Jesus' answer does not begin until 3:27, where the words ἀλλ' οὐ δύναται mark a heightening of significance: "Yes and what's more . . ." or "But what is more important, no one can enter the house of the strong man and carry off his goods unless he first bind the strong man, and then he shall rob his household." This final "parable" represents Jesus' real answer to the charge that He is in league with Satan. His exorcisms prove that the "strong man" (i.e., Beelzebub or Satan) is indeed already bound, so that those whom he has taken captive can now be set free. The expulsion of the unclean spirits means that Satan himself is defeated in principle.[12]

Although Jesus' answer has been well reasoned and not without flashes of wit and humor (cf. vv. 23-26), its undercurrent of anger emerges in verses 28-30. The sayings about the "blasphemy against the *Holy* Spirit" in Mark are directly connected with the preceding accusation against Jesus that "he has an *unclean* spirit" (3:30). The implication is that the Holy Spirit has been blasphemed by being referred to as unclean. The scribes from Jerusalem are themselves in danger of committing the "unforgivable sin," which thus receives a very precise historical context. The significance of the passage for today is as a serious warning to exercise great care and caution in labelling as "demonic" any phenomenon (e.g., tongues, healing, or even exorcism itself) which may in actuality be a work of the Spirit of God.

2. *Matthew and Luke.* The Beelzebub controversy in both Matthew and Luke is introduced not by a rumor that Jesus is insane but by a specific instance of exorcism. The narrative in Matthew follows a summary in which many people follow Jesus and (characteristically for Matthew) Jesus "healed them all" (12:15) and "commanded them" (ἐπετίμησεν, just as He commanded the demons in Mark) "that they should not make him known" (12:16). After a typically Matthean Scripture quotation (vv. 17-21), the narrative resumes with the healing (ἐθεράπευσεν) of a "blind and mute demoniac" (12:22). The crowd's reaction is to ask if Jesus can be the Son of David, but the Pharisees bring the charge that He performs His exorcisms by Beelzebub, ruler of the demons (12:24). Strictly speaking, the charge is not (as in Mark) that Jesus is possessed by Beelzebub, but simply that He is in league with him for the purpose of performing exorcisms.

Clearly, Matthew is following Mark, but just as clearly, he is drawing on another source as well. In Matthew (12:25) and in Luke (11:17), the charge is not made publicly, but Jesus "knows their thoughts." The "parables" of the kingdom and of the household are adapted from Mark with only minor revisions (Matt. 12:15-26; Luke 11:17-18). Moreover, both the *ad hominem* part and the serious part of Jesus' answer to the charge are expanded in Matthew and Luke. This expansion (Matt. 12:27-28, Luke 11:19-20) is usually considered to be "Q" material. Jesus first speaks *ad hominem*, extending the irony of His references to a kingdom or a household.

If exorcisms mean that one is in league with Beelzebub, then what about exorcisms performed by Pharisees themselves? This is the only reference in the Gospels to exorcisms performed by Pharisees or Rabbis, and not done in Jesus' name, but there is ample evidence of such activity outside the New Testament.[13] "They shall therefore be your judges," Jesus adds. Coming to the serious part of His answer (v. 28), Jesus prefaces the reference to the strong man with yet another "if" clause paralleling the one about Satan in verse 26 and especially the one about the Pharisees themselves in verse 27: "If I by the Spirit of God ['finger of God' in Luke] drive out demons, then the kingdom of God has come upon you" (Matt. 12:28; cf. Luke 11:20). This reinforces the point already made in Mark: Jesus' exorcisms are a sign that the Kingdom of God is already at work; this is what the binding of the strong man really means.

The strong note of anger which characterized the Markan account is also strengthened in Matthew and Luke. Both conclude the Beelzebub story with a severe word of warning —first to the immediate hearers, but then to any who refuse to recognize the Spirit of God at work in Jesus and His followers: "He who is not with me is against me, and he who does not gather with me scatters" (Matt. 12:30; Luke 11:23). This represents a remarkable variation on a saying found in a different context, but one having to do with exorcism, in Mark and Luke: "For he who is not against me is for me" (Mark 9:40; Luke 9:50). It is possible that the same, or two originally interchangeable, sayings of Jesus have been adapted for use in two contrasting situations. In the "Q" material relating to the Beelzebub tradition, it is a question of blasphemy: those who fail to recognize God's Spirit at work in Jesus automatically put themselves in opposition to Him.

In Mark 9:38-40 and Luke 9:49-50 the situation is entirely different. Here someone who definitely does recognize the Spirit at work in Jesus has for that very reason used the name of Jesus to the same end—to free people from the dominion of unclean spirits. The use of Jesus' name for this purpose makes it unlikely that such a person doubts the power of the name or intends to blaspheme either Jesus or the spirit of God working through Him. The narrative of the seven sons of Sceva in the book of Acts, however, indicates the perils of using the name of Jesus lightly or as a magic formula (Acts 19:13-16). The seldom-discussed passage in Mark and Luke about the "strange exorcist," should, however, serve as a guideline for evaluating contemporary exorcists who are in some sense "Christian" but whose orthodoxy is open to question.

To return to the Beelzebub incident and its ramifications, the note of anger and warning preserved in Matt. 12:30 and Luke 11:23 is continued by each evangelist in his own way. Matthew, like Mark, continues with the pericope about the blasphemy of the Holy Spirit (12:31-32) but lacks Mark's specific reference back to the charge that Jesus "has an unclean spirit." The reason is presumably that this precise charge has not been recorded in Matthew. But Matthew does go on to record some very strong words of Jesus in 12:33-37 directed to the "brood of vipers" (v. 34) about good and bad trees and fruit, and about the necessity of accounting for "every idle word" at the day of judgment (v. 36). In the following section about the sign of Jonah (12:38-42), Jesus denounces the "evil and adulterous generation" (12:39; cf. vv. 41f.) which looks for signs. Finally, Matthew records a remarkable "Q" passage about an unclean spirit who is driven out of a man and returns, after wandering through desert places. Finding his previous home swept clean, he fetches seven other spirits worse than himself, so that "the last state of that man is worse than the first" (12:43-45). This frightening possibility is reminiscent of the "Legion" in Mark 5, but Matthew makes it unmistakable what his application is: "So it will be with this evil generation" (12:45).

The idea that a whole generation can be demon possessed puts the whole discussion out of the sphere of the medical and into that of the sociological and political. One is reminded of the "principalities and powers" in Paul or of the "three unclean spirits, like frogs" in Rev. 16:13, who deceive the nations and lead them to the battle of Armageddon, but such areas are outside the scope of the present study.

Luke brings out the anger of Jesus, and His condemnation of those who accused and tempted Him, more simply. In Luke the original charge was made not by scribes from Jerusalem, as in Mark, and not by Pharisees, as in Matthew, but by "some" in the crowd (11:15; the reference to "your sons" in v. 19, however, probably indicates that Pharisees are in view). Luke picks up on the charge that Jesus is in league with Beelzebub by attaching the "Q" passage about the "return of the unclean spirit" directly to his account of the Beelzebub controversy. His point is unmistakable: the accusers are themselves in danger of the worst kind of demon possession (far worse than that connected with a particular set of physical and psychological symptoms). They are in danger of spiritual blindness which misses the work of God going on in Jesus (cf. 11:33-36, 37-53). The challenge to Jesus for a sign from heaven (11:16) is picked up in 11:29-32: "This generation is an evil generation. It looks for a sign. . . ." But before it all, Luke recorded a positive word of assurance: the Father will give the Holy Spirit (some mss. read "a good spirit") to those who ask Him (11:13). This is God's only alternative to the unclean spirits (11:24-26) which threaten all (even entire generations) who reject the work of God.

3. *John.* Even though the Beelzebub controversy as such does not appear in the fourth Gospel, the charge that Jesus is demon possessed is echoed in several Johannine passages. When Jesus accuses "the Jews" of trying to kill Him, they reply, "You have a demon! Who is trying to kill you?" (7:20). In this context, "You have a demon!" is virtually equivalent to "You're crazy!" In John 10:20, some of the Jews say of Jesus, "He has a demon and is insane." The second accusation serves to explain the first. The tendency in the synoptics to interpret demon possession in terms of other things (e.g., sickness, insanity, or spiritual blindness) is clearly present here as well. When others ask, "How could a demon open the eyes of the blind?", we cannot help but be reminded of the Beelzebub controversy and especially Mark 3:23 ("How can Satan drive out Satan?"). In John 8:48f. ("you are a Samaritan and have a demon"), the charge of demon possession has become a part of an almost stereotyped kind of name-calling, and again seems to have lost any specific reference to "posses-

sion" as a psychological phenomenon.

The Beelzebub passage raises the question of how far the work of Satan and the work of demons can be regarded as interchangeable. A number of considerations (some of them outside of the passage itself) suggest that they can, and yet the point should perhaps not be allowed to stand without qualification. As we have seen to "have Beelzebub" (3:22) and to "have an unclean spirit" (3:30) can be equivalent because Beelzebub is himself called "the ruler of the demons" (v. 22). Moreover, the fact that Jesus replies to the charge about Beelzebub by asking "How can Satan drive out Satan?" (3:23) seems to complete the equation. John, in fact, presents the defeat of Satan as a great and decisive act of exorcism: "Now is the judgment of this world; now is the ruler of this world driven out" (ἐκβληθήσεται, John 12: 31).

It is obvious that Satan and the demons are both personifications of evil, that both exercise dominion over human beings, that both are capable on occasion of recognizing Jesus as the Son of God (for Satan, cf. the temptation accounts in Matthew and Luke), and that both are destined for destruction (cf., e.g., Matt. 8:29; 25:41). But the similarities have limits. As we have seen, the unclean spirits are terrified at the very sight of Jesus (e.g., Mark 1:24; 5:7, 10; cf. James 2:19), while Satan approaches Him boldly to hurl challenges against Him (Matt. 4:1-11; Luke 4:1-13). The demons carry out their work by means of "possession" in a very specific sense, or by means of physical handicaps or illness. Satan works rather through human sin: through Judas the traitor (Luke 22:3; John 13:2) or through the well-meaning Peter (Mark 8:33; cf. Luke 22:31). Satan is uniformly described in Scripture as a supernatural or superhuman figure, while the demons are perhaps more accurately regarded as subnatural or subhuman. There is nothing in their conversations with Jesus to indicate that they are necessarily superior to man in power or intelligence.[14] Jesus addresses them as He might address an animal or as He does in fact address the storm in Mark 4:39. If it is true that on occasion they are able to gain the mastery over human beings, it must be admitted that the same is true of animals when humans make the mistake of walking unprotected through jungles. This ability to master or even to kill is not the mark of any inherent superiority, only of ill will taking advantage of man's temporary vulnerability.

Notes

1. For the same contrast, cf. 1 Cor. 7:14.

2. It is unlikely that φιμώθητι in 1:25 can be classed as a real injunction to secrecy of the kind referred to in v. 34. The parallel with Jesus' quieting of the storm in 4:39 (πεφίμωσο) suggests that it is merely Jesus' way of commanding the demon to cease his outcry and relinquish his victim. There is no clear evidence that it belongs to Mark's much-discussed "secrecy phenomena."

3. The use in 5:7 of ὁρκίζειν, from which the English word "exorcism" is derived, is striking. Here it is used (with τὸν θεόν) by the demoniac in addressing Jesus, while in Acts 19:13 it is used (with τὸν Ἰησοῦν) by some Jewish "exorcists" in addressing those who were possessed. Such flexibility suggests that it has not yet acquired the fixed technical meaning of "exorcize." (If it had, the demon would here be "exorcizing" Jesus!)

4. For a list of various theories, cf. H. Ridderbos, *The Coming of the Kingdom* (Philadelphia, Pa.: Presbyterian and Reformed, 1962), pp. 113ff.

5. Cf. Gal. 4:3, 9; Col. 2:20.

6. In Luke, when the man is commanded to "tell what *God* has done for you," he proclaims in the city "what *Jesus* had done for him."

7. Cf. B. van Iersel, "Die wunderbare Speisung und das Abendmahl in der synoptischen Tradition," *Novum Testamentum* (1964), pp. 188f.

8. The words "and fasting" are not found in the earliest and best Greek manuscripts. See B. M. Metzger, *A Textual Commentary on the Greek New Testament* (London and New York: United Bible Societies, 1971), p. 101.

9. See, e.g., D. J. Hawkin, "The Incomprehension of the Disciples in the Marcan Redaction," *Journal of Biblical Literature* XCI (1972), 491-500. This is more plausible than the better known argument of T. J. Weeden (*Mark-Traditions in Conflict* [Philadelphia: Fortress, 1971]) that Mark is carrying on an actual polemic against the original disciples.

10. Cf. the procedure used in healing according to James (5:13ff.).

11. The "ability to distinguish between spirits" (12:10) appears to be a different matter, more closely related to prophecy than to healing or exorcism.

12. See, e.g., G. E. Ladd, *The Presence of the Future* (Grand Rapids, Mich.: Eerdmans, 1974), pp. 149-70.

13. The most complete collection of material is found in H. L. Strack and P. Billerbeck, *Kommentar zum Neuen Testament aus Talmud und Midrasch*, IV, Pt. 1 (Munich: C. H. Beck, 1956), Excursus 21, "Zur altjüdische Dämonologie," 501-535.

14. The fact that they are cohorts of Satan implies nothing about their intelligence, anymore than the fact that men belonging to God makes them equal to God. The demons' insight into who Jesus was seems attributable not to superhuman intelligence but, as we have seen, to a kind of quasi-prophetic revelation. Especially in Mark 5 the unclean spirits seem irrational and bent on destruction, whether of their victim (vv. 3-5) or of themselves (vv. 11-13).

4

Response

JOHN P. NEWPORT

In general, the commentator is in agreement with the material in the paper. It is a straightforward descriptive paper.

For the sake of discussion, a number of emphases in the paper can be questioned and some omissions noted.

1. One statement to be questioned is that Mark's purpose in reciting stories about demon possession and exorcism is to make a teaching or doctrinal point (pp. 1, 6, 7). For example, the paper states that Mark 1:23-28 is given to drive home a point about the authority of the teaching of Jesus (p. 1). Mark 7:24-30 is given to show the mother in the story as a representative gentile seeking help from Jesus the Jew (p. 7). Mark 9:14-19 indicates that exorcism is subordinate in the story to the teaching on faith and prayer (p. 7).

Should not a strictly descriptive or phenomological approach to Mark's Gospel reflect the fact that Mark's primary emphasis is on Jesus' almost total concern with the defeat of the demonic powers? If anything, the significance of the demonic grows in depth and breadth as Mark unrolls the ministry of Jesus.[1]

There is a tendency in the paper, as described above, to stress the ultimate priority of the significance of the words or teachings of Jesus as against the deeds as seen in His exorcisms. Is it not more accurate to say that Mark's primary emphasis is on the deeds of Jesus which represents the power of God unleashed in the world rather than on His words? Priority of deeds, of course, is contrary to the basic assumption of many form critics. The typical form critic would emphasize that the words of Jesus came first and

His miracles and deeds were a later accretion. The form
critics see the deeds or miracles as an attempt to glorify
or exaggerate the power of Jesus with an incrustation of
legendary mighty works. Thus Martin Dibelius contends
that "this Tale-making often, but not always, means a de-
generation of the tradition, removing it ever further from
the historical reality." [2]

There is a tendency, even among evangelicals, to be
influenced by the negative side of Form Criticism. Form
Criticism can sometimes degenerate from a scientific study
into a filter designed to screen out that which modern man
finds distasteful.[3] We have a difficult time, for example,
in applying or reinterpreting the demonic today. Therefore,
we tend to down play the centrality of the demonic in Mark's
Gospel. We are influenced by those who say that this radical
emphasis on the demonic was really an accretion added
by the church. But to be honest to the text we must accept
the pervasive and all-touching role of the demonic in Mark
and the other Synoptic writers.[4]

2. Some scholars would question the statements of the
paper that Matthew and Luke tend to put demon possession
under the category of illness and exorcism within the general
category of healing.

Are not demon possession and exorcism the larger categories under which illness and healing should be subordi-
nated?

Kallas and Langton contend that Mark teaches that one
of the ways in which Satan rules his captured realm is
through diseases. Thus when Jesus heals disease He is pushing back the kingdom of Satan. In the field of ordinary
physical maladies Jesus sees the hand of the Evil One.
The lady who was crippled (Luke 13:11, 16) was under the
bondage of Satan. Even ordinary fever is an evidence of
demonic activity or oppression.[5]

A further contention of Kallas refers to the tendency
among scholars to adapt the message of Jesus to a generation that no longer believes that sickness is a scourge of
Satan. But this cannot change the fact that the Synoptic
Gospels make it clear that the command to announce the
Kingdom of God (which meant the defeat of Satan) was
seldom given apart from the command to cure diseases
and to rout demons (which, also, meant the defeat of Satan).
(Cf. Matt. 9:35; 10:7, 8; 8:16-17; Luke 9:2, 6; 10:1, 9; 4:17-
19.)[6]

3. Would it not have been helpful if the paper had discussed the background of the concept of the demonic in the Old Testament and intertestamental periods?

Some scholars see a background of the demonic in the Old Testament picture of God as surrounded by a heavenly host of spirits who serve Him and do His bidding (Ps. 82:1; 89:6; Dan. 7:10).

Deut. 32:8, where the RSV has "sons of God," is seen as a reflection of the idea that God superintended the nations through subordinate spiritual beings (cf. also Dan. 10:13, 20, 21). In Job 1-2 Satan is portrayed as one of these "sons of God" who appears before God to accuse Job and to receive permission to put him to the test.[7] The paper does not attempt to deal with the relation of the Synoptics and the demonic views of the apocryphal and pseudepigraphic literature, the Dead Sea Scrolls, and the earlier strata of the Talmud.

Such a background study raises the difficult questions of progressive revelation and the problem of sources in relation to revelation and inspiration. The paper omits all such questions.

It also would have been helpful if the paper had shown similarities and differences between the intertestamental sources and the New Testament.

4. As a descriptive study, the paper has relatively little discussion of the relevance of New Testament materials for the contemporary age. It does not attempt to cope with the idea that Jesus merely adapted himself to the concepts of His age or the suggestion that Jesus was a child of His day and mistaken in His belief about demons. These criticisms need to be answered because the Synoptic Gospels portray demon exorcism as an activity at the heart of His messianic mission.[8]

5. Does not the paper make too much of a distinction between Satan and demons? The paper emphasizes that demons are subnatural or subhuman, while Satan is supernatural or superhuman. There is nothing, the paper maintains, to indicate that demons are necessarily superior to man in power or intelligence.

Is it not more accurate to see Satan and demons as an integral part of a tight-knit lethal organization? One important distinction between New Testament demonology and animism is that animism portrays evil spirits as disorganized and chaotic while the New Testament sees Satan and demons as closely aligned and highly organized. Futhermore, the demon in Mark 1:24 is described as having an insight into the mission and significance of Jesus which the disciples had not attained.[9]

Notes

1. James Kallas, *Jesus and the Power of Satan* (1968), pp. 202f.
2. Martin Diebelius, *From Tradition to Gospel* (1935), p. 99.
3. Kallas, p. 98.
4. *Ibid.*, pp. 80, 82, 210.
5. James Kallas, *The Significance of the Synoptic Miracles* (1961), pp. 63, 65; and E. Langton, *Essentials of Demonology* (1949), p. 151.
6. Kallas, *Significance*, p. 80.
7. E. Jacob, *Theology and the Old Testament* (1958), pp. 70-72; and Kallas, *Significance*, chap. 4.
8. George E. Ladd, *A Theology of the New Testament* (1947), pp. 52ff.
9. *Ibid.*, pp. 50f.

PART TWO

Demonology in History & Law

5

The Occult Revival in Historical Perspective

RICHARD LOVELACE

The aim of this paper is to set forth a historical overview of the various components within the occult movement, and to examine the light which this history sheds on the remarkable upsurge of interest in the occult in recent years. The earlier section of the paper is based on the assumption that there is an underlying dynamic unifying all the differing forms of the occult, as well as many common external insignia, and I think the data we examine will support this conclusion. It is hazardous business for a historian to attempt to interpret the spiritual significance of events, especially those which are as close to us as the occult revival, but at the end of this essay I will take some hesitant steps in that direction.

A Historical Analysis of the Occult Spectrum

It is difficult to fix on a definition of the occult which will properly encompass all of its forms and not spill over boundaries into such adjacent territories as comparative religion, cults, and flying saucer research. The etymology of the word is little help today, since the occult in all its manifestations is no longer "hidden," but rather the object of an intensive publicity campaign. After some observation of the kinds of birds which have been flocking together in response to this propaganda, I have concluded that the subject can be divided into two major subtypes: what might be called soft-core occult disciplines—astrology, parapsychology, spiritualism, prophecy, and Eastern and neognostic cults; and the hard-core occult, which includes white and black witchcraft and Satanism. Some items at the beginning of this spectrum may appear relatively innocuous, but each succeeding form of the occult seems to incorporate all the forms which precede it on the list, so that we find exponents of witchcraft like Sybil Leek and Hans Holzer writing as trained technicians in the areas of astrology and ESP. It appears that there is a kind of vortex effect in operation, so that persons who are initially attracted to some of the more respectable forms on the periphery of the occult are automatically swept in toward the center, guided inward by gradually stronger admixtures of hard-core teaching.

Historical analysis of the various occult disciplines confirms the hypothesis that they are part of a more or less unified system with a gravitational center in the region of serious witchcraft. At first glance this does not always seem to be true. In the case of astrology, for instance, there might even appear to be a biblical warrant for some types of judicial and physical astrology—applications dealing with the interpretation of world events and meteorology, as distinguished from natal and horary astrology, which involve the casting of personal horoscopes and the making of decisions. Genesis 1 states that the heavenly bodies were created "for signs," [1] and apparently the astrological investigations of the Magi were the cause of their coming to the Christ-child.[2] Perhaps because of these fragmentary scriptural references some important theologians have taken a soft approach to astrology. Thomas Aquinas felt that the stars had some influence over human passions, and even a reformer like Philip Melanchthon did not renounce the discipline.

But the normative attitude within the church has been to regard metaphysical astrology as a pernicious superstition. Augustine gave it up when he learned that a landowner and a slave had been born at the same instant. Another early father allowed that the Magi had been drawn to Christ through the stars, but added that this was the last event in history in which the stars could serve as a signpost, and that henceforth our attention should be fixed on the Christ.

Examination of the ultimate historical origins of astrology confirms this judgment. The discipline is of great antiquity, and found among all the ancient civilizations: the Chaldeans, the Babylonians, the Egyptians, the Druids, the Chinese and East Indians, and the Aztecs and Incas in the new world. In the Babylonian form, which may be the prototype for all the others, astrology was connected with the worship of deific powers associated with the heavenly bodies, and also with the cult of the Baalim. The biblical record bears this out. In Isa. 47:12, 13, in an oracle against Babylon, astrology is connected with sorcery and condemned as a superstitious vanity.[3] The account of Manasseh's apostasy in 2 Chron. 33:3-4, 6 suggests the occult context within which astrology was most frequently found:

> ...he rebuilt the high places which Hezekiah his father had broken down; he also erected altars for the Baals and made Asherim, and worshipped all the host of heaven and served them.... He built altars for all the host of heaven in the two courts of the house of the Lord. And he made his sons pass through the fire in the valley of Ben-hinnom; and he practiced witchcraft, used divination, practiced sorcery, and dealt with mediums and spiritists.[4]

Throughout the Christian Era the practice of astrology has continued for the most part to be associated with the occult religious underworld suggested by this passage. Despite the qualified indulgence of a few church leaders, the medieval church, and later the majority of protestants, condemned the discipline. This did not stop some very intelligent and influential, and even religious, figures from using the stars for guidance; among them Christopher Columbus, Sir Isaac Newton, and Benjamin Franklin. The foundations for modern astrology were laid in the *Tetrabiblos* of Ptolemy. But when Copernicus overthrew the Ptolemaic system he did not utterly reject the validity of astrological calculations.

The place of astrology within the occult revival in our own time can be exemplified by the story of its growth in America since the late nineteenth century. The germinal force behind its expansion was the career of Evangeline Adams, who began to practice publicly in the 1890's and made such important converts as Edward VII, Caruso, Mary Pickford, and J. P. Morgan. In 1930 Miss Adams went on radio, and in 1932 the first periodicals devoted specifically to astrology appeared. Carroll Righter, a convert of Miss Adams, continued to spread the popularity of the discipline among leaders in the entertainment world, among them Marlene Dietrich, Susan Hayward, Robert Cummings, Tyrone Power, Van Johnson, Peter Lawford, and Ronald Reagan (who now professes indifference). The ability of media leaders such as these to influence culture is an important factor in the expansion of astrology during the 1940's and 1950's.

In the period following World War II the practice seems to have exploded both in America and Europe. An account of the astrological boom in France, in 1964, described it as a $650,000,000-a-year business with 500,000 astrologers involved, and traces its popularity to the decline of organized religion combined with a widespread public need for new sources of reassurance.

In 1969, the opening number of the musical *Hair* called the attention of the American public to the place of astrology within the counterculture. *Time* magazine's cover story on astrology during the same year estimated that there were 10,000 full-time and 175,000 part-time astrologers practicing in America, and noted that the average age of their clients had fallen from 45 to 25. The connection between the youth culture and the American astrology boom is underlined by the fact that Dell paperbacks dealing with the subject jumped from sales of one million in 1962 to eight million in 1965, during a period when the rock- and drug-culture were undergoing their initial expansion.[5]

Many professional astrologers today would probably deny that the discipline has anything at all in common with the occult. Zoltan Mason, for example, comments that confidence in astrology is usually positively correlated with strong faith in God, and Carroll Righter defines the Age of Aquarius as the era of Christ the Water-Bearer, a time of new spiritual beginnings, amity, brotherhood, wide learning, the shedding of inhibitions, new aspirations, joy, science, and the life of Christ.[6] This outlook on the present and future is remarkably similar to the postmillennial Christian optimism of Jonathan Edwards, expressed in the latter sections of his *History of Redemption*. Righter's division of the ages in history is also reminiscent of the periodization of Joachim di Fiore. The Age of Aries the Ram (2000 B.C. until the birth of Christ) is the Age of the Father. The Age of Pisces the Fish (from Christ until the present century) is the Age of the Son, a time of death, sorrow, the cross, skepticism, and disillusionment. The Aquarian age, whose beginning is variously located by the astrologers in 1904, 1933, or elsewhere in the twentieth century, seems to correspond to Joachim's predicted Age of the Holy Spirit.

On the other hand, astrologer Barbara Birdfeather, whose connection with the occult world is explicit, defines the ages from a very different perspective. Ms. Birdfeather, who is also a rock music disc jockey, says that in the cycle of the 12 great ages, each of 2100 years duration, we are now moving away from the Piscean Era, the age of Christ the Fisher of Men, into an Aquarian age in which energy will be used "purely, intellectually, and electrically." The present Christian church she views as "the dregs of the Piscean Age." [7] And New England astrologer Constella doubts that her discipline reinforces a belief in the God of Scripture: "We're afraid to say no, no, no to the bearded man upstairs," she says, "until we have a substitute." [8] It seems clear that in the life of the average follower, astrology replaces the roles occupied by the Word and the Spirit in the Christian life: it gives him a kind of mirror in which he can behold his own identity and find himself, and it lights up his daily pathway with a substitute for the lamp of Providence.

Parapsychology is another instance within the soft-core occult realm which seems on the surface to be compatible with Christianity. The researches of Dr. J. B. Rhine and others at Duke University have at least partially established an image of scientific respectability and religious neutrality for parapsychological occurrences. There are evangelical authorities who hold that some types of *psi* phenomena, such as clairvoyance (paranormal vision of contemporary events) and telepathy are "normal" and can be found among Christians. My own research tends to confirm this. Charles Haddon Spurgeon, the great evangelical preacher of the late nineteenth century, interrupted his sermons on several occasions with comments about specific sins and situations among his congregation that must have required some kind of preternatural knowledge.[9] Many of us know of instances in which Christians have become supernormally aware in moments when death or danger has threatened loved ones. The "word of knowledge," one of the nine gifts of the Holy Spirit commonly accepted by Pentecostals, is usually defined in terms of this kind of extrasensory awareness focused on a particular person or event. On the other hand, the fringes of the charismatic movement today are littered with cases in which apparently false charismata have had a blasting effect on the spiritual lives of those who were seeking parapsychological gifts without sufficient care and discrimination.

Some helpful distinctions emerge in a survey of the history of parapsychology. Kurt Koch has provided us with a useful typology of the occult in a little book called *The*

Devil's Alphabet which helps to display some of the forms of parapsychological gifts, although it reveals a much more pessimistic outlook on the supposed neutrality of *psi* phenomena.[10] It is immediately apparent, however, that Koch takes a less hopeful view of the neutrality of some *psi* factors. Under the first of three general headings, Extra-Sensory Perception, Koch lists three subcategories: Spiritism (including apparitions, telekinesis in the form of tumbler-moving, table-lifting, trance-speaking, and automatic writing); Hyperesthesia (including the sooth dream, telepathy, clairvoyance, clairaudience, and clairsentience); and Mantic (cartomancy or card-laying, palmistry, astrology, and rod-and-pendulum divination). Koch's second main category, Extra-Sensory Influence, includes a similar mixture of respectable and improper phenomena: magic, blood-pacts, fetichism, and incubi and succubi; and his third category, Extra-Sensory Apparitions (including ghosts and materializations), is wholly beyond the usual scope of science. Walter Martin, who is more tolerant than Koch in admitting clairvoyance and telepathy as neutral phenomena, nevertheless condemns precognition, telekinesis, and medium trances as necessarily demonic in origin.

It is doubtful that any scientific parapsychologist would be happy with Koch's handling of his field, but it does under-line the fact that most *psi* phenomena are found in occult history, as well as the current practice of shamans and witch doctors. In the era of preternatural knowledge, the ubiquity of seers, soothsayers, and oracles in ancient and primitive cultures is too well known to need comment. Parapsychology as a discipline, however, is a much more recent phenomenon in history, which emerges first in the late eighteenth century with the discoveries of Anton Mesmer, and begins to flower in the late nineteenth century with the foundation of the British Society for Psychical Research in 1882 and its American counterpart in 1888. Both of these institutions, which gained the respect and participation of men of the caliber of William James and Henri Bergson, were originally concerned with matters which reveal a mix-ture of occult and scientific interest: *psi* factors involving the mutual influence of human minds, hypnotism, extra-sensory perception, apparitions of the living and dead, and the "laws of spiritualism." The research at Duke University, begun in 1927 by William McDougall and augmented by the addition of the Rhines in 1930, further refined the dis-cipline by an increased use of controlled and repeatable experiments, variation of parameters, and the application of statistics.

Two other factors have contributed to an upsurge of interest in parapsychology in the past several decades: the employment of sensitives such as Peter Hurkos and Gerard Croiset in criminal detection, and the recent development of parapsychological research in Russia.

The Russian experiments were inaugurated as part of the Cold War, in response to a news report that American naval personnel had experimented with telepathic communication to the crew of the atomic submarine Nautilus during a voyage in 1960. The Russian research, as described in a paperback which became a runaway best-seller in America in 1970, began with ordinary parapsychological investigations into telepathy, telekinesis, and psychometric detection, but ended up dealing with a number of areas not normally respectable within the ideological framework of atheistic humanism: astrology, dowsing, the photography of auras and the theory of astral bodies, and healings administered by witches and warlocks.[11] All of these were explained, however, in terms of the ordinary official materialism. There is an eery reminiscence here of C. S. Lewis' *That Hideous Strength*, in which a scientific organization proceeding on the basis of pure naturalism discovers ultimately that its experimental achievements have been literally enabled and governed directly by the devil.

Spiritualism—or, as evangelicals usually refer to it, Spiritism—is a movement which has been with us openly for so long during this century that it has an aura of domesticity, and is usually treated as a cult rather than as part of the occult. The line between cults and occult is often indistinct, however, and we have already observed a link between mediumship and other forms of occult activity in the Societies for Psychical Research, and in the biblical passage about Manasseh previously quoted. And in fact this occult connection goes back to prehistory. In primitive societies there is apparently continuum between animistic polytheism and the Cult of the Dead. In ancient China, the worship of ancestors was practiced partly in order to avoid obsession or possession of the living by the spirits of the dead, which could take the form of a somnambulistic or hypnotic trance. The person so possessed was commonly gifted with clairvoyancy, the raising of apparitions, psychometry, and other parapsychological abilities, as well as an ability to perform miraculous healings.[12] The possessing personality commonly demanded to be worshipped in return for its services, and the response to this was usually the development of a local cultus, but occasionally primitive forms of exorcism were attempted.

John Livingston Nevius, a missionary in China in the late nineteenth century who is still perhaps the most balanced Christian writer on the subject of demon possession, encountered many instances of such shamanistic possession in his ministry. He treated them as demonic, and found that they could be broken up fairly rapidly by simple prayers of exorcism, or even in some cases simply by the persistent reading of Scripture in the vicinity of the possessed person, creating an unpleasant environment for the possessing spirit.[13] Among Indo-European cultures, there is a similar intermixture of phenomena attributed to the dead with cultus and behavior associated with nonhuman spirits. The Orphic and Eleusinian mysteries in Greece involved mediumship and the production of apparitions through what today would be called the extrusion of ectoplasm, and the Delphic oracle was thought to be possessed by a chthonic deity. The *elohim* of Babylon and Assyria— "gods," which the Old Testament refers to derisively as *elilim*, "feeble ones" or "vanities"—were associated with spirits of the dead, as were the *baalim* mentioned in the book of Judges, which were thought to be the spirits of departed heroes.[14]

During most of the Christian Era, communication with the spirits of the dead has been branded as necromancy in Western Christendom, and so has necessarily continued its course within the occult underground. Just as in the case of astrology and parapsychology, it begins to surface again in respectable regions in the nineteenth century.

J. K. van Baalen traces three major waves of increase in the movement, one following the wide publicity given to the spirit-rapping phenomena associated with the Fox sisters in 1848, and the other two following each of the world wars, probably because of the widespread grief among bereaved parents of servicemen. Local organizations were begun in the United States between 1850-72. The National Spiritualist Association of the United States of America was founded in 1893, and by 1923 there were 682 Spiritualist churches in America with a membership of 126,000.[15] In 1852, American mediums announced that the spirits of the dead were predicting the spread of the movement to England, and after this invasion occurred on schedule there was a similar development in the organizational expression of the movement in the British Isles and in the rest of Europe. We have already pointed to the founding of the Society for Psychical Research in 1882. It is interesting that another major surge of interest in Spiritualism was occurring in England in 1904-5, just at the time when a major religious revival was taking place in Wales and at Keswick.

In America, the spread of the movement during the past four decades has been closely connected with the career of medium Arthur Ford, who has recently become extremely well known because of his connection with Bishop James Pike. Pike, who before his own death was seeking to communicate with the spirit of his son, a suicide, found in the former a confirmation of survival after death which he had been unable to obtain from the church's doctrine. Arthur Ford also finds no inconsistency between Christianity and his profession, and claims as forerunners of Spiritualism St. Francis, St. Teresa, George Fox, Alexander Campbell, and John Wesley, as well as Moses and Jesus.[16] Sherwood Eddy's *You Will Survive After Death* is a much more plausible reconciliation of Spiritualism with a Christianity which sounds almost evangelical, but it is interesting that his most theologically literate contact in the spirit world, an identity calling itself Father Tobe, has an adoptionist Christology along with many other aberrations.[17]

As Victor Ernest points out, the spirit clientele of different mediums ranges from those who sound like departed fundamentalists to those who are blatantly obscene, heretical, or blasphemous.[18] Again the vortex effect is at work to sweep the convert in toward the darker center. The public currently shows little discernment in detecting the anti-Christian roots of the movement, however. In my own area, Elwood Babbitt, the "medium of Massachusetts," commonly consorts with some rather dubious company among the spirits, but a photograph of ectoplasm taken at a recent seance in which the spirit of Bertrand Russell was invoked was presented in the *Boston Globe* as a "photograph of God" by an awestruck reporter whose agnosticism had been shattered.

Prophets—both forth-tellers for the gods, and foretellers of the future—are rooted as deeply in prehistory as Spiritism. In many instances it is hard to distinguish the two. The Bible focusses particular attention on the phenomena of false or counterfeit prophecy, which can be detected either by its incorporation of heresy or by the failure of predictions about future events.[19] Both Testaments state that there is a demonic energy behind false prophecy, and not simply human deception.[20] Paul's exorcism of a demon controlling the Philippian seeress is a dramatic instance of this. The attitude of the church toward prophecy during the Christian Era has been delicately ambivalent. The medieval church adopted a cautious if respectful attitude toward the predictions of St. Catherine of Siena and others who affirmed the papal system, and condemned those like Joachim di Fiore who did not. The ambiguous predictions of the French Astrologer Michel de Nostredame (Nostradamus) were condemned by the Catholic congregation of The Index in 1781 after attracting wide public interest.

In our century, two American figures have become increasingly associated with the image of prophecy in the public mind. The first, Edgar Cayce, did not particularly engage in predictive prophecy, but began as a healer and later moved into the sphere of religious teaching. His biographer, Thomas Sugrue, intentionally connects Cayce with Christian sources, stressing his early training in a Church of Christ Sunday School and even mentioning a meeting with D. L. Moody. Sugrue notes the fact that Cayce's grandfather was a dowser, and could make brooms dance and plants grow, but presents Cayce as an awkward but idealistic youth with a wholly altruistic desire to serve mankind but no gifts to do so.

The subsequent story sounds a little like an occult episode of *The Waltons.* Cayce is visited by a shining spirit who endows him with the potential for extraordinary gifts, such as memorizing the contents of spelling books simply by sleeping near them, and, later, diagnosing and prescribing medicines for sick people, also while asleep, and sometimes even at a distance. The medicines advised by Cayce's "unconscious," which is what his alternate personality calls itself, are often merely folk remedies, but in most instances they effect almost miraculous cures. Cayce continues to exercise his healing gift, although frequently troubled by his inability to judge whether it is from God or from Satan, until a gentleman who has had some contact with the occult proposes that they ask Cayce's "unconscious" some religious questions. This new vein of inquiry opens up an apparently inexhaustible supply of information. Cayce's unconscious informs them that true Christianity, in the form of early Gnosticism, has been lost to the world for centuries, and the present Christian Church is a body of imposters.[21] Jesus, according to Cayce's "unconscious," was in reality an occult master, who taught the necessity of being born again—that is, reincarnation—and died on the Cross to atone for negative karma.[22]

The religious teachings of Cayce's "unconscious" are still being subjected to theological mining and smelting several decades after his death in 1945, and a center for healing and religious studies at Virginia Beach, administered by his son Hugh Lynn Cayce, has continued to attract pilgrims and disseminate literature. At this point in America Edgar Cayce has almost reached the status of an industry.

The other major American prophetic figure, Jeane Dixon, specializes in predictive prophecy. Mrs. Dixon is a devout Roman Catholic, attends mass daily, and reputedly repeats the 23rd Psalm every morning while facing east. According to biographer Ruth Montgomery, each morning in her devotions Jeane Dixon asks God the question, "What do I need to know today to help humanity?" The resulting revelations of the future, however, can come to her via the full paraphernalia of serious occultists, including visions, dreams, inner voices, numerology, ESP, telepathy, Tarot cards, and personal "vibrations" assessed by the touch of a finger. She first became aware of her gifts in a contact with an old Gypsy woman who read her palm when she was a child, assured her that she was destined to become a great seeress, and gave her a crystal ball which is still one of her most treasured possessions. Her prophecies, which have concerned events of such magnitude that she has been the counsellor of many persons in high government office, have had enough accuracy to appear to be preternatural, and enough inaccuracy not to appear divine.[23] In a little book by her own hand, *Reincarnation and Prayers to Live By*, she professes Trinitarian belief, but also states the opinion that all religions lead to the true God, and offers as one of her prayers a devotional to an Indian goddess.

Examining Edgar Cayce and Jeane Dixon, one is left with a sense of bafflement and pity for human beings who are straining to be altruistic, but are quite apparently being used for purposes and by forces which are beyond their comprehension. It is interesting in the instance of Cayce to note the similarity of his uncanny healing ability using worthless medicines to Nevius' Chinese energumens, and to shamans and witch doctors in many other cultures. It is apparent by this time that a common feature of most forms of occult behavior is the influence, and sometimes the total control, of alternate personalities over the minds of those involved. One of the questions which must be addressed in this conference is the matter of the possible psychological and theological explanations for this recurring phenomenon. It is interesting that Edgar Cayce was preceded by a number of other somnambulistic healers in the nineteenth century, among whom was the first hypnotic subject treated by Anton Mesmer, whose gift came to him in the hypnotic process. The medical implications of this are also profound and complex. A final theological question which needs exploration is the status of prophetic gifts within the charismatic movement, and such major predictions as David Wilkerson's vision, which seems to parallel the darker projections of current futurologists. The issue which emerges is this: Are occult prophecy and other para-psychological phenomena mimics or counterfeits of legitimate Christian gifts, or is any attempt to seek for paranormal gifting in danger of producing false gifts?

The gnosticism of Edgar Cayce's "unconscious" leads us naturally to the last category of the occult which I have designated as soft-core, that of certain religious counterfeits for Christianity which are either strongly gnostic in form or else derivative from Eastern religion. Both of these sub-types have in common antipathy to the physical creation and its Maker, the idea of salvation by the reception of hidden knowledge, and the concept that the godhead is found at the root of one's own inner being.

A classical example of occult gnosticism is the Ancient Mystical Order of the Rose Cross, an uncanny survival which recapitulates most of the features of the early gnostic systems. A more recent instance is the Process Church of the Final Judgment, which was inaugurated in London in the 1960's by a High Church Anglican architect with a rather Gothic name, Robert de Grimston Moor. De Grimston (as he now prefers to be called) married a spiritualist medium, and shortly afterward began an intensive religious search involving dream interpretation and the study of the Bible and other scriptures. In the mid-1960's De Grimston and the community which had gradually collected around him were directed by spirits to migrate to the Yucatan peninsula, near a Mayan ruin named Xtul, where they received a series of religious revelations from discarnate entities. In 1970 and the subsequent years the spirits directed them in a number of mission tours in Europe, Cambridge in Massachusetts,

Chicago, and New Orleans. The doctrine of "the Process" might be described as monotheistic pantheism refracted polytheistically through four deific symbols: Jehovah, Lucifer, Satan, and Christ. Each of these terms stands for "powers" which summon up resonant affinities in every human being, in varying mixtures: Jehovah, the quality of stern legal righteousness; Lucifer, the quality of artistic sensibility; Satan, the quality of unbridled libido; and Christ, the quality of reconciling love. The first three of these "powers" are opposed to one another in a "game" of antagonism, but the Christ-power (which is equivalent to the oversoul or underlying deity in each of us) has come to reconcile the three to one another. The way which Jesus brings involves the casting aside of all tendencies to feel guilt for sin or to blame others for it.

There are nevertheless three laws of ethical behavior which we should strive for: the Golden Rule, karma (the accumulation of merit or demerit by our actions), and love for our enemies, including Satan. Baptism is "in the name of the Unity of the Lord Christ and Satan." Local assemblies or communes of the Process vigorously and single-mindedly engaged both in evangelism and social action, as anyone knows who has been in their vicinity. The group now numbers some 40,000 members in Cambridge, including students and college professors, and several hundred thousand adherents elsewhere. A breakaway group which has renounced as impractical the command to love Satan now exists.[24] It should be noted that the Process cannot be considered as explicitly Satanist, despite its quaternity and the Dracula-capes affected by its adherents. It is much too subjective for this; its deities are almost symbols for human passions, somewhat in the manner Euripides utilizes the Greek pantheon in his dramas. There is, as a matter of fact, something deeply Hellenic about this blend of gnosticism and spiritism.

Eastern forms of the occult with a similar morphology begin to make their appearance in the West, once again, in the nineteenth century. Some of the writings of Emerson and the work of Mary Baker Eddy are American examples of Hindu influence. Around the turn of the century Madame Blavatsky and Annie Besant introduced an amalgam of Tibetan Buddhism and pantheistic gnosticism called Theosophy, with much closer connections to the occult and paranormal realms. Beginning with Jack Kerouac and other writers of the Beat Generation era in the early 1950's, and notably as a result of the work of interpreters like D. T. Suzuki and the ex-Anglican Alan Watts, a great upsurge of interest in Eastern religion (particularly Zen Buddhism) accompanied the growth of the counterculture in America, possibly because the East afforded an avenue for profound religious exploration which did not restrain sexual life-styles.

In the late 1960's a wave of variations on Hinduism swept through the counterculture leadership, as some turned from chemical mind-expanders to search for natural and per-manent highs. The Beatles experimented with the Transcen-dental Meditation of the Maharishi Mahesh Yogi, and later with the Hare Krishna movement of A. C. Bhaktivedanta. (It is interesting that ex-Beatle George Harrison continues to advertise Hare Krishna, just as two other very fine mu-sicians, James Seals and Dash Crofts, are aggressive evangelists for Bahaism, a Mohammedan offshoot.)

In the 1970's two other examples of Eastern evangelism swept through the United States, Guru Maharaj Ji and the Divine Light Mission of the Word Unification Church, the creation of Sun Myung Moon of Korea. Maharaj Ji, still in his teens, is simply the best promoted of a number of young Indians who have recently proclaimed themselves to be avatars of the deity with a command to spread forms of Hinduism in both the East and the West. Mr. Moon is rather unusual in that his teaching is not primarily Eastern in influence, but is a heretical offshoot of Korean Christianity blended with spiritualism. Mr. Moon intimates that his ministry is the fulfillment of the biblical prophecy of the Second Coming of Christ, and predicts an "outpouring of spirits" to accompany the last days.[25] It is interesting that Christians on secular college campuses who have ex-perienced an increasing openness to evangelicalism among students had simultaneously noticed an influx of promoters of Eastern religion.

Some of the new Eastern variants have features which are significant in the context of this conference: vegetarian diets, systems of exercise such as the different forms of yoga, and techniques of meditation involving the repetition of mantras (words or phrases embodying supernatural power, according to Hinduism). It is well known that the exponents of Transcendental Meditation are attempting to introduce this practice into schools and other public pro-grams under the guise of a religiously neutral form of psy-chological therapy. I know of one Trappist monastery in the South in which all the monks recently enrolled in a program of Transcendental Meditation under the direction of an Eastern guru. The one exception was a Catholic Pentecostal brother, but he was involved in a course of Silva Mind Control, an even more overtly occult discipline with many attendant paranormal phenomena.

This bring us to the forms of the occult which I have designated as hard-core, witchcraft and Satanism. There are two main theories of the historical origins of witchcraft: that of Margaret Murray, who in 1921 proposed the thesis that witchcraft in Western Europe was only a survival of the pre-Christian pagan worship of the male Horned God and female goddess akin to Ashtaroth and Diana; and the strongly opposing thesis of Montague Summers, a Roman Catholic scholar, who insists that the witches were self-conscious worshippers of the devil, who signed blood pacts with him and had all the characteristic features which their Christian inquisitors attributed to them. Summers took the occult powers of the witches quite seriously, and vigorously attacked Miss Murray's contention that they were innocuous followers of a nature cult.[26] We shall see that both Miss Murray and Summers are supported by evidence within the modern witchcraft movements.

Summers contends that the forerunners of witches were abhorrent even to respectable pagans. He notes that in 721 B.C. the ruling Roman triumvirate banished all astrologers and charmers, and that later Maecenas called on Augustus to exile sorcerers and magicians as despisers of the gods, which set a precedent for similar action by Tiberius, Claudius, and Vespasian.[27] Charles Williams comments that the motivation for the pagan attack on witchcraft was primarily the desire to eliminate all possible centers of political disaffection, as in the parallel instance of the persecution of Christians.[28] Williams notes that the early church adopted an ambivalent attitude toward witchcraft, on the one hand attacking it as a powerless superstition, and on the other, trying to eradicate it as if it were a plague.[29] He might have added that as the Middle Ages developed, popular Catholicism incorporated many elements which are suspiciously similar in form, including the practice of candle-burning before saints and the elevation of the Virgin Mary to a position practically equivalent to that of the female deity in the typical bitheistic pairing noted by Miss Murray.

As the medieval period developed, uneasiness about the powers of darkness among Christians and occult interest among the populace seem to have increased. Summers associates a concurrent expansion of witchcraft with the appearance of heretical gnostic sects like the Bogomils, Paulicians, and Albigenses around the turn of the millennium, and feels that there is a connection between gnosticism and witchcraft.[30] In an able and fascinating article in *Church History*, Donald Nugent observes that the first great flowering of witchcraft during the Christian Era occurred during the Renaissance.[31] In 1258, Pope Alexander IV directed a bull to the Franciscan Inquisitors initiating the attack in 1484, and in 1490 the Jesuits Heinrich Kramer and James Sprenger produced their classic Christian manual on witchcraft, the *Malleus Maleficarum*. Apparently the numerical high point of the witchcraft explosion occurred just before and during the Protestant Reformation. By 1700, somewhere between thirty thousand and several millions of witches had been tried and executed. The Reformation, however, launched a biblical attack on magical elements in contemporary Christian practice, and on the occult world outside the church, which began to restrain the world of superstition.[32] The eighteenth-century Enlightenment further reduced the incidence of sorcery, to such an extent that even the existence of professing witches became an article of doubt. Nevertheless there continued to be an underground stream of witchcraft and Satanism during the eighteenth and nineteenth centuries. Peter Gay, who contends that the Enlightenment itself was a neo-Pagan revival, notes that in the left wing of the movement, among libertines such as the Marquis de Sade, sexual magic and a semi-serious demonolatry were practiced in places like the Hellfire Caves of France and England.[33]

In the late nineteenth century the stream begins to surface quietly, first in the rather respectable and domesticated magic of A. E. Waite's Order of the Golden Dawn and then in the virulent Satanism of Aleister Crowley. J. K. Huysmans' novel *La-Bàs* indicates the existence of similar movements in France. C. S. Lewis comments that he was aware of, and attracted to, several circles of magical interest in London during the 1920's and 30's.[34] According to Margaret Murray's thesis, the work of Gerald Gardner, an anthropologist and practicing warlock, disseminated a form of witchcraft in the 1930's and 40's in England. After the repeal of the Witch Act in Britain in 1951, English witchcraft began to proliferate openly, and in the 1960's Sybil Leek and other articulate exponents rose into prominent view in the media, conducting a skillful public relations campaign to advance the image of Wicca, the "old knowledge," as they preferred to call their religion.

The inertial momentum of the post-Enlightenment disbelief in witchcraft was still sufficiently strong, however, that scholars of the caliber of E. E. Evans-Pritchard, Pennethorne Hughes, and H. R. Trevor-Roper continued concurrently to assert the nonexistence of witchcraft. In the late 1960's the media were presenting so much evidence of a witchcraft revival that this kind of scholarly ignorance became increasingly difficult.

In 1967 a group of hippies surrounded the Pentagon and conducted an exorcism. In 1968, on Halloween, WITCH—the Women's International Terrorist Conspiracy from Hell—held a demonstration. In England, reports of grave robberies began to appear, and Anglican and Catholic clergy found themselves reviving the practice of exorcism in desecrated churches. There were ritual murders in New Jersey and California, and the supreme horror of the Manson murder case. There were rumors that the Rolling Stones dedicated their performances to Satan. Alice Cooper changed his name to that of one of the witches executed at Salem at the direction of a ouija board. And rock acts appeared which seemed to have more in mind than publicity in their occult references, such as Arthur Brown and Black Sabbath. In 1971 *Newsweek* estimated that there were some 80,000 white witches in America.[35] *Time's* cover story in 1972 noted that one airline was offering a "psychic tour of Britain" for $629, and estimated that somewhere between three and seven million Germans were involved seriously in the occult.[36] Writing in *His Magazine* in 1970, Robert Evans of the Greater Europe Mission stated that there were more warlocks in Germany than Protestant pastors, and more in France than the number of doctors. He noted also the existence of a school for witches in Ulting, England. This kind of institution seems to exist also in a number of American cities.[37]

Just as in the case of the counterculture and the Jesus movement, the media are quieter now about witchcraft. But in each of these instances the silence may be simply existing because the phenomenon in question has become a normal and accepted part of the current landscape, not because it has receded or vanished. The serious witchcraft movement in America today is as organized and vigorous in its growth as evangelical Christianity. It has its own publishing houses—more than half a dozen of them—producing books with titles like *The Caldron Cookbook, The Stock Market and Witchcraft, Sexual Power through Witchcraft,* and even children's books which beautify the witch's image. There is even a journal called the *Occult Trade Review,* which is not surprising since the movement generates a multi-million-dollar industry. Witchcraft has its own travelling evangelists, chief among them Sybil Leek, Hans Holzer, and Martin Ebon. There are also resident spokespersons who act as pastors and bishops in different locales. In my own area, a young woman named Laurie Cabot who runs a witchcraft shop and has styled herself "The Witch of Salem" gives lectures to local PTA's, and is establishing an occult institute to train disciples on the North Shore. Hans Holzer has written an instructive *vade mecum* which tours the major cities in America and lists the varieties of witchcraft available in their covens, which include Sicillian, Welsh, Druidic, Haitian, and many others.

Some covens practice black or malefic witchcraft, attempting to raise the "cone of power" to destroy their enemies—and there are wars among the witches, according to Holzer. The established exponents of witchcraft are publicly critical of black witchcraft; it gives the craft a bad name. Some covens practice sexual magic in the Gardnerian tradition, initiating new members in the "Great Rite," an act of ceremonial intercourse. Some, like California's Feraferia, seem as elfin and innocuous as a Tolkien story. The most significant common feature of all these covens is the worship of a duad of gods, one male and one female. It appears that Margaret Murray's theory is borne out of the surviving remnants of the witch cults, unless these have been consciously modelled after her thesis. Modern witchcraft is a revival of the pagan pattern represented by the worship of Baal and Ashtaroth.[38]

This does not mean that Montague Summers' thesis is not equally supported by some data. Aleister Crowley, the son of Plymouth Brethren parents, concluded after a reading of the book of Revelation that he was the Great Beast predicted in it, and devoted the rest of his life to acts of sexual magic attempting to beget the Antichrist, under the direction of a discarnate entity named Aiwaz. He is apparently the figure on whom Roman Castavet, in *Rosemary's Baby,* is based. There is little doubt that Crowley was an intentional Satanist.[39]

Anton LaVey's Church of Satan in California, on the

other hand, seems to be a collection of basically agnostic swingers using Nietzschean philosophy as an excuse for hedonism. But Mike Warnke, an evangelical converted from the ranks of Satanism in Berkeley, tells of a different kind of Satanism in which the involvement with demon worship is conscious and deliberate. If what he tells us is correct, there are ascending circles of evil within the witchcraft movement in which the higher levels are intentionally given over to the worship of ultimate evil. The relative frequency of verifiable murders involving the ritual sacrifice of infants and adults, a practice quite beyond the scope of most witchcraft covens, seems to confirm this. It is difficult to know how seriously to take Warnke's report, which revives the old story of the Illuminati, the secret order dedicated to the promotion of atheism and anarchism, which is discredited today except among adherents of the John Birch Society. The picture he presents, however, is that of a kind of occult Mafia, with its headquarters somewhere near the site of the witchcraft trials in Salem Village.[40]

The Nature and Causes of the Occult Revival

There is a famous aphorism of C. S. Lewis to the effect that the devil is equally pleased when he is feared and when he is ignored.[41] The biblical reason behind this is that when he is up against Christians who are fully aware of their resources and their authority, there are only two things he can do to avoid giving ground: he can bluff and he can hide. The devil is a little bit like the hognose snake, a harmless but evil-looking reptile which responds to the threat of danger by two ruses. First, it impersonates a pit-viper, coiling, striking, and hissing viciously. If this fails to intimidate the attacker, the snake turns belly-up, opens its mouth and lolls its tongue out, and plays dead. If it is picked up and placed right side up, it simply turns over again and resumes the death ruse again, because it seems to realize that if it cannot bluff, it has to mimic death.

The devil has been playing dead in Western Christendom for the past several centuries—roughly since 1692, the date of the Salem witchcraft scandal. In the pre-Reformation period, his strategy was rather to bluff—to terrify Christians, as well as tempting and oppressing them and taking advantage of every deficiency in the Catholic understanding of redemption. The pre-Christian Era, and even the medieval period within the church's history, were ages of superstition about the powers of darkness. One of the possible etymologies of the word "superstition" interprets the root combination of *super* and *stare* to mean "overcommitment" or "overbelief." In contrast to the relatively terse and chaste treatment of angelic and demonic powers in the Bible, the pagan world developed a luxuriant overgrowth of belief in superhuman agencies, and Christianity itself came to be infected with the same attitude.

The Reformation made an effort to return to a biblical balance in confronting the powers of darkness, although the Puritan casuistry that was developed to handle witchcraft still retains traces of overbelief. One of the most dangerous of these was the fear that sorcerers could actually cause harm to Christians supernaturally, despite the principle stated in Num. 23:23 that "there is no omen against Jacob, nor is there any divination against Israel."

Christian apologists in the late seventeenth century were also making use of witchcraft and other evidences of demonic reality to prove the existence of God. When the misuse of spectral evidence (hallucinatory or demonic apparitions of accused witches) at Salem resulted in disastrous injustice, skeptics were able to turn the tide against superstition by making any belief in demonic agency seem not to be respectable. The rug was neatly pulled from under a good deal of Christian apologetics, and the devil went underground as the Western world moved into a new era of what might be called "*substition.*" There are perfectly natural causal explanations for the whole sequence, but there are also things about it that make us suspect a little direct devilish intervention. Certainly the devil had a lot more freedom to carry out his characteristic strategems of deceiving, accusing, tempting and otherwise manipulating Christians and non-Christians in the clean, well-lighted room which was the post-Enlightenment universe, in which all created beings intermediate between God and man had supposedly suffered intellectual fumigation.

We have seen that virtually all forms of occult practice have been enjoying a renaissance since the late nineteenth century, at first in a relatively covert and quiet way, and then openly and dramatically within the last decade or so. The structure and timing of this revival must be understood by analogy with the growth of the evangelical movement during the twentieth century, I believe. The present apparent upswing in evangelical renewal is not an outpouring of the Spirit in discontinuity with the past, but rather the result of decades of reformational ploughing and evangelistic sowing which have finally led to a time of extensive reaping. In a similar way, the occult revival is the end result of something which has been steadily building throughout the twentieth century, but has gone unnoticed until recently.

Why has this steady buildup occurred? Authorities on the occult have ventured a number of answers. One of the most ingenious is that of Os Guinness. Guinness suggests that the doctrinal decay of Protestantism in the twentieth century has permitted us to be reinfested by the same forms of superstition which the Reformation drove back. The Western world today is consequently like a clearing in the jungle in which the central fire has burned low at night, and now the camp is surrounded with a ring of encircling eyes belonging to the jungle creatures which have moved in close.

Guinness and Francis Schaeffer also suggest that the pervasive anti-rationalism in many sectors of the twentieth-century intellectual climate has helped breed this kind of movement.[42] Donald Nugent strikes some similar notes. He notes that the occult revival during the Renaissance and the present occult expansion have many factors in common. There is in both a degree of primitivism and psychic atavism, with an underlying substratum of despair. Both are eras where power is sought by the disenfranchised, especially women—Nugent comments that in the Renaissance one finds only one warlock for every 10,000 witches—and both have seen a growth of sexual license and pornographic literature. Each has been influenced by a new measure of contact with Eastern culture, and each has seen an increase in the use of psychedelic drugs.[43] If we postulate that late medieval Christianity is decadent, so that it both provokes and is powerless to restrain a rebellious neopagan movement with an occult fringe, we have an etiology which closely resembles that suggested by Guinness.

It might be argued with equal force, however, that the occult revival is one instance among many of the gradual re-emergence of paganism from the underground existence forced upon it by the theocratic restraints of the Middle Ages. Western Christendom accepted Locke's principle of a free market of ideas at least theoretically, but it took several centuries for a post-theocratic outlook to penetrate its institutions. A double bind of legal restrictions and societal taboos has kept many deviant forms of behavior under cover, and hence has limited their growth, until quite recently. As we have seen, the laws against witchcraft have remained in force if not in use until the middle of this century. The surfacing of the occult underground could well be compared to the emergence of the homosexual minority which has come "out of the closet" in the last decade. The lesson would seem to be that if Christians adopt a hands-off policy with respect to the corporeal restraint of paganism, sooner or later they are going to see the return of at least a little paganism, and perhaps a great deal of it. And the occult is simply one of the common forms of paganism. From this perspective, what we are observing today may be merely a return to normal, and not an unnatural, result of decline.

Another explanation for the occult revival is suggested by Theodore Roszak's analysis of the counterculture. According to Roszak's first book, the hippie movement was a religious counter-revolution among young people disgusted by the failure of scientific technocracy.[44] In his second book, *Where the Wasteland Ends*, Roszak celebrated the potential for a religious renaissance based on a return to old-fashioned paganism.[45] Judging from what we have seen, there is no more authentic form of paganism than the occult movement. For the first time in centuries, the biblical condemnation of the worship of Baal and Ashtaroth is beginning to have direct reference to contemporary culture. If we are nearing the end of history, the Scriptures may turn out to speak more bluntly than we might have imagined to the habits of the greatest mass of humanity in history.

Among Christians, the conviction that these are the last days has seized upon the occult revival as further confirmation. Those who expect the culture to get more and more corrupt with the approach of the end can easily interpret the growth of the occult as the visible manifestation of the eruptions of demonic powers from the pit described in Rev. 9:1-11 and 16:13-16. This is certainly one possible theological approach to the data, and it does not necessarily rule out any combination of the more immanent causative factors already mentioned.

As a church historian, I am automatically rather cautious about the assumption that these are literally the last days. There is no depressed era in Christian history which has not felt itself to be on the verge of Christ's return. And as a historian of revival, I have observed that depressed eras have a way of turning into Christian resurgences that regain the lost ground and move beyond it to embrace a larger area with purer expressions of the Gospel. There is one possible scenario for the future in which misdirected technology, the god that failed, combines with religious decay to destroy humanity. There is another one which postulates that a revived and reformed Christianity regains a degree of dominion over the conscience of the Western world, and technology is harnessed to solve at least partially the ecological, population, and hunger problems of the underdeveloped countries, while these are simultaneously experiencing powerful Christian development.

The second scenario would be that which the greatest theologian of revival, Jonathan Edwards, would project. Edwards conceived of the Christian movement as a kind of army of spiritual liberation moving out to free the world from an occupying force of demons which had already been defeated in principle at the Cross. Any army experiences assaults, defeats, withdrawals, and counterattacks resulting in the gaining of more ground and the occupation of new territory. The ebb and flow of spiritual power within the church and the similar fluctuation of depravity in the world are not meaningless nodes on a sine-curve; they are the way the fortunes of battle are perceived in Christian consciousness. According to Edward's postmillennial optimism, Christianity is destined to sweep outwards in a series of such pulsations until the whole earth is full of the knowledge and the glory of God, as the waters cover the sea.

History may be considered as a series of stages in which one territory is substantially conquered for Christ, then a contraction occurs as the war is opened within a wider radius, and then a renewed Christian assault sweeps outward to widen the diameter of the reign of Christ. Phenomenologically, a "revival" of the opposing forces, the powers of darkness, seems to occur in three situations: first, when the Christian forces are spiritually at a low ebb themselves; second, when they are relatively strong, but a new and wider mission front has opened up; or third, when a renewed Christian offensive is simply being met by a counterattack from the other side. Thus a revival of paganism, or atheistic humanism for that matter, is not necessarily a sign of Christian weakness. It may simply be a signal that our troops are on the move, and that a wider field is opening.

I am personally inclined to believe that from the standpoint of transcendent causes there is an element of all three of the possibilities mentioned above involved in the occult revival, along with a mixture of the immanent causes

already mentioned. During the first half of the twentieth
century, the Christian church was considerably weakened
and divided, and during this period many forms of devilish
ideology gained considerable ground in the West. The occult
was one. Atheistic humanist materialism was a considerably
more dangerous antichrist, and some of the most effective
activities of Satan were probably within the Christian church
itself. Since the middle of the century the evangelical sector
of the church has begun to be revived and reformed, and
at the moment there are many evidences that other areas
of professing Christendom are being touched, although it
is still a question whether the bulk of the institutional church
is enjoying the awakening which is occurring around its
edges among the young people. In the meantime, technological revolutions in the areas of transportation and communication have turned the world into a village, as Marshall
McLuhan says.

Under these conditions *all* ideologies have an unusual
missionary opportunity. The drugs, the sitar music and the
occult mysticism of the East flow into the Western world.
If the water pressure is strong enough, the Christianity of
the West must inevitably flow into the East in return. To
use another metaphor: Christianity is like a fire, which
periodically develops a vigorous blaze, but is each time
covered with increasing quantities of green wood which it
must dry out before it can ignite. At the present moment
in history, virtually all of the available wood on the planet
is about to go on fire. The outcome of this may be terminal
apostasy and great tribulation, or it may be revival of the
church and response to the Kingdom. But unless we have
some revelation of the imminence of the end which is surer
than all those in the past, our posture had better be an
aggressive acting out of the words of Jesus: "Occupy until
I come." [46]

Notes

1. Gen. 1:14.
2. Matt. 2:2.
3. Cf. also Jer. 10:2-3.
4. 2 Chron. 33:3-4, 6.
5. "Astrology: Fad and Phenomenon," *Time*, March 21, 1969, pp. 47-48.
6. "Digging the Stars," *Newsweek*, January 13, 1969, pp. 78-79.

7. From an interview with Ms. Birdfeather conducted by Nat Freedland and presented on side 1 of a double-record album, *The Occult Explosion* (United Artist Records, 1973).

8. "Astrology: Fad and Phenomenon," *loc. cit.*

9. Ernest W. Bacon, *Spurgeon: Heir of the Puritans* (Grand Rapids, Mich.: Eerdmans, 1968). pp. 154-56.

10. Kurt Koch, *The Devil's Alphabet* (Grand Rapids, Mich.: Kregel, 1971).

11. Sheila Ostrander and Lynn Schroeder, *Psychic Discoveries Behind the Iron Curtain* (New York: Bantam, 1971).

12. Lewis Bayles Paton, *Spiritism and the Cult of the Dead in Antiquity* (London, New York: Macmillan, 1921), pp. 29-35.

13. John Livingston Nevius, *Demon Possession and Allied Themes* (Old Tappan, N.J.: Revell, 1894), pp. 75-76, 129-31.

14. Paton, *op. cit.*, pp. 258-59.

15. J. K. van Baalen, *The Chaos of Cults* (Grand Rapids, Mich.: Eerdmans, 1938), pp. 22-24.

16. Arthur Ford, *Unknown but Known* (New York: Harper and Row, 1968).

17. Sherwood Eddy, *You Will Survive after Death* (New York: Rinehart, 1950), pp. 9-13, 148-65.

18. Victor Ernest, *I Talked with Spirits* (Wheaton, Ill.: Tyndale House, 1970).

19. Deut. 13:1-3; 18:20, 22.

20. 1 Kings 22:19-23; 1 John 4:1-3.

21. Thomas Sugrue, *There Is a River* (New York: Dell, 1967 [first published in 1945]).

22. Anne Read, *Edgar Cayce on Jesus and His Church* (Paperback Library, 1970), pp. 70ff.

23. Ruth Montgomery, *A Gift of Prophecy* (New York: Bantam, 1969).

24. James A. Gittings, "The Process Church of the Final Judgment," *A.D.*, November, 1973, pp. 36-42.

25. Young Oon Kim, *Divine Principle and Its Application* (Assoc. for the Unification of World Christianity, 1969).

26. Montague Summers, *The History of Witchcraft* (New Hyde Park, N.Y.: University Books, 1956), pp. 31-45; cf. Margaret Murray, *The Witch Cult of Western Europe* (London: Oxford University Press, 1962 [first published in 1921]), and *The God of the Witches* (London: Oxford University Press, 1970).

27. Summers, *op. cit.*, pp. 11-12.

28. Charles Williams, *Witchcraft* (New York: Meridian Books, 1959 [originally published in 1941]), pp. 18-21.

29. *Ibid.*, pp. 72-75.

30. Summers, *op. cit.*, pp. 20-29.

31. Donald Nugent, "The Renaissance and/of Witchcraft," *Church History*, XL (March, 1971), 69-78.

32. Cf. Keith Thomas, *Religion and the Decline of Magic* (New York: Scribners, 1971).

33. Peter Gay, *The Enlightenment* (New York: Knopf, 1967 [first published in 1966]).

34. C. S. Lewis, *Surprised by Joy* (London: Geoffrey Bles, 1955), pp. 165-68.

35. "Evil, Anyone?", *Newsweek*, August 16, 1971, pp. 56-57.

36. "The Occult: a Substitute Faith," *Time*, June 19, 1972, pp. 62-68.

37. Robert Evans, "The Lure of the Black Arts," *His* (Inter-Varsity Christian Fellowship), April, 1970, pp. 9-12.

38. Hans Holzer, *The Witchcraft Report* (New York: Ace, 1973).

39. Aleister Crowley, *Moonchild* (New York: Avon, 1971).

40. Mike Warnke, *The Satan- Seller* (Plainfield, N.J.: Logos, 1972).

41. C. S. Lewis, *The Screwtape Letters* (London: Macmillan, 1943); and *Screwtape Proposes a Toast* (London: Bles, 1961), p. 19.

42. Os Guinness, *The Dust of Death* (Chicago: InterVarsity Press, 1973), pp. 276 ff.

43. Nugent, *loc. cit.*

44. Theodore Roszak, *The Making of a Counter-Culture* (New York: Doubleday, 1969).

45. Theodore Roszak, *Where the Wasteland Ends* (New York: Doubleday, 1973).

46. Luke 19:13.

6

Not Suffering Witches to Live:

A Brief Reappraisal of Witch Trial Theory and Practice

JOHN WARWICK MONTGOMERY

When confronted with the matchless claims of Christ—His life of perfect holiness, His atoning death to give fallen man the gift of heaven—unbelief finds itself hard put to sustain its negative posture. One of the counter-arguments most consistently employed by unbelievers since the dawn of modern secularism has centered on the witchcraft trials of the fifteenth through the seventeenth centuries: these horrors, it is argued, belie the claims of Christianity, for they were the direct and consistent product of its theology and religious practice; only with the rise of Enlightenment rationalism and the modern spirit did such abominations cease.

Though the literature of the witch trials is enormous, as witnessed alone by the Andrew Dickson White collection at Cornell University or by Henry Charles Lea's three-volume *Materials Toward a History of Witchcraft*, the subject needs perpetual reappraisal in the light of its function as a standard weapon in the armory of unbelief. Critics of Christianity by way of the witchcraft trials need to be reminded of the beam in their own secular eye; as Robert H. Jackson boldly stated in his closing address in the Nuremberg War Crimes Trial: "The terror of Torquemada pales before the Nazi inquisition." And Christian believers need to understand the true nature of the problem reflected in the witch prosecutions, so that when they repent they will repent intelligently, pouring no unnecessary oil on the smouldering fires of unbelief.

The Issue Sharpened

Critics of the witch trials almost invariably concentrate their salvos on the phenomenon of the demonic *per se*. They argue aprioristically that "no sensible person can accept the real existence of witches, much less demons," and consider it therefore self-evident that the whole concept of the witch trial was sheer madness.

It is not our task here to deal with the question of the ontological reality of the demonic, of demon possession, or of witchcraft—particularly since we have done so *in extenso* elsewhere.[1] To the convinced rationalist we would merely say: whatever you do, if you wish to deny the existence of personal, supernatural evil, do *not* examine the empirical data; for no facts in history are better established (except perhaps those relating to the incarnation of God in Christ)!

But wholly apart from the ontological question, the critics who pose such objections display a woeful lack of historical perspective. George Lyman Kittredge concluded his impeccable scholarly study of *Witchcraft in Old and New England* with these theses:

> To believe in witchcraft in the seventeenth century was no more discreditable to man's head or heart than it was to believe in spontaneous generation or to be ignorant of the germ theory of disease.
> The position of the seventeenth-century believers in witchcraft was logically and theologically stronger than that of the few persons who rejected the current belief.
> The impulse to put a witch to death comes from the instinct of self-preservation. It is no more cruel or otherwise blameworthy, in itself, than the impulse to put a murderer to death.[2]

These sentiments are entirely confirmed by the best of recent specialized studies. Thus, after examining the records of some seven hundred witch trials in the duchy of Lorraine, Etienne Delcambre concluded that the judges were anything but "monsters of hypocrisy and dishonesty": "Their language can reflect the highest spirituality—inspired, it would seem, by passages from *The Imitation of Christ*. . . . Their hearts were not hardened, nor was their love for their neighbor feigned."[3] In the same vein, Edmund Heward's careful biography of Sir Matthew Hale, Lord Chief Justice in the reign of Charles II, rehabilitates his activity in the Bury St. Edmunds witchcraft case of 1664 from Lord Campbell's incredible charge that he "murdered" old women. Argues Heward:

In his charges to the jury Hale stated that he had no doubt that there were such creatures as witches as the scriptures affirmed it. To a man such as Hale who believed in the supernatural and the revelations contained in the scriptures this would be irrefutable evidence.

All other nations had laws against witches. This would be regarded as weighty evidence by Hale as he set great store by the accumulated wisdom of mankind.

There had been an Act of Parliament on this subject only sixty years before, drawn up by the advice of eminent lawyers including Sir Edward Coke. How could a judge with Hale's education and background be expected to deny his religion, his experiences and a recent Act of Parliament? [4]

Except for isolated instances of judicial perversity (which are hardly limited to this single aspect of legal history—or of life in general!), those who participated in the witch trials ought not to be regarded as untouchables; they do not deserve to be faulted for holding beliefs inherent to the worldview of their day—and beliefs which (I would submit) have a disquieting veracity transcending the epochs of the trials. Proper criticism of the witch trials lies at a different point: the legal operation itself, as viewed in terms of *substantive* law (ought witchcraft to have had a legal remedy?) and *adjective* law (trial procedure and the laws of evidence). Here, if anywhere, legitimate criticism of the trials exists; and here, therefore, theological and juridical lessons are to be learned. Let us first examine the question of procedure in the witch trials.

Torture and "Exceptional" Procedure in Continental Law

It is a commonplace that torture was used to extract confessions of witchcraft and that rules of evidence were "relaxed" in the witch trials. The accompanying judgment is also widespread that the responsibility for such an appalling state of affairs lay squarely with Christianity, as represented by the medieval church and its Reformation offshoots. But, as in the case of most "obvious" truths, the truth lies elsewhere.

One must first of all distinguish between two different systems of law operating in the geographical areas associated with the witch trials: the "civil" law tradition of the European continent (operating in France, Spain, the Holy Roman Empire of the German nation, etc.), and the "common" law that became an identifiable legal system in England after the Norman conquest and was transmitted to America by the English colonists. The continental civil law did finally come to approve of torture in a certain range of cases, including witchcraft; but this was due not to the church, but to the revival of absolutistic Roman law. In the Anglo-American common law tradition, torture was never condoned, except in rare instances where the common law was modified by statute.

On the continent judicial torture is virtually unheard of from the fall of Rome to the revival of Roman law. Where it occurred, it was roundly condemned by Christianity. At the time of the fall of the western Roman empire (5th century), Augustine had castigated the use of torture to extort confessions.[5] Influential popes of the early Middle Ages, such as Gregory the Great (6th century) and Nicholas I (9th century), reiterated his position and applied it to specific cases. The Saxon annals for the year 928 record that "good King Wenceslas," duke of Bohemia, destroyed gibbets and instruments of torture that some judges had employed. The twelfth century Decretum of Gratian unqualifiedly repudiates torture as a means of extorting confessions.[6] Concludes Lea: "This position was consistently maintained until the revival of the Roman law familiarized the minds of men with the procedures of the imperial jurisprudence."[7]

A. Esmein of the Paris Law Faculty is equally explicit in his great *History of Continental Criminal Procedure*:

> Torture is an institution of Roman origin. . . . It is, therefore, not surprising that the diffusion of torture coincides, in modern history, with the revival of the half-forgotten Roman law by the criminalists of the Bologna school. The transformation of the procedure by the substitution of torture for ordeals really begins to manifest itself from the end of the 1100s. . . . At the end of the 1300s torture had become a general custom.[8]

By the thirteenth century powerful efforts were being made by continental European monarchs to destroy the local autonomy which was the hallmark of feudalism and to create centralized "modern" states; in these efforts, Roman law— the law of an absolutistic empire in which the emperor had come to function as a demi-god—was an irresistible tool.

During the same time period, the medieval Roman church was endeavoring to increase its power through the parallel centralization of its administrative controls; Roman law here became the model for church law. Torture and inquisitional procedure thus entered the church itself. "The canon law had permitted it by virtue of the predominating influence of the Roman law" (Esmein, p. 91). On the European continent, therefore, the tragic irony came to pass that the church, which had endured the persecution of half-mad emperors during Rome's twilight, finally approved and practiced the same methods toward its deviants.

This gross inconsistency, however, was not lost on many influential Christian thinkers during the height of the witch mania. The endeavors of Protestants Johann Weyer or Wier [9] and Reginald Scot [10] to substitute reason for torture are well known. Innumerable other efforts by concerned Christians have been buried in a general outcry against the trials; for example, few recall the painstaking and model investigations by seventeenth century Spanish inquisitor Alonso de Salazar y Frías, conducted with full regard for the civil rights of the accused,[11] or the eloquent arguments of French jurist Augustin Nocolas who asserted in his work, "Whether Torture Is a Sure Means of Verifying Secret Crimes" (1682): "I shall never accept as legitimate ground for conviction what has been admitted under torture, for it is an invention of the devil and has never been condoned by Scripture." [12]

Biblical Influence on Anglo-American Law

In England, the development of legal institutions followed a different pattern from that of the continent; in particular, Roman codifications had a much less pervasive influence. "Much of the common law of England was founded upon Mosaic law. The primitive Saxon Codes re-enacted certain precepts taken from the Holy Scriptures, and King Alfred in his Doom Book adopted the Ten Commandments and other selections from the Pentateuch, together with the Golden Rule in the negative form, as the foundation of the early laws of England." [13] The Common law of England thus did not allow secret tribunals and interrogation by torture. By the seventeenth century, observes Esmein (pp. 322-23):

Everywhere upon the continent, in France and elsewhere, the inquisitorial procedure, secret and written, was now established, a product of the Roman and the Canon law, with their defects more or less accentuated according to the country. One European nation, however, had resisted and escaped the contagion, and was destined later to serve, to a large extent, as a model for the legislation of the French Revolution. This was England.

Predictably, the loss of civil rights and the use of torture appear in England at times when the crown endeavors by any and all means to extend its royal power: the infamous Star Chamber of the Tudor and Stuart monarchs. But such a phenomenon was never seen as "normal" within the framework of English law, and the Star Chamber was abolished as contrary to the Magna Carta by the Long Parliament in 1641.[14] The most severe of the witchcraft statutes, that of 1541, was the product of one of the most absolutistic of English kings, Henry VIII, whose own spiritual life—it need hardly be added—was not above reproach.[15]

Far from being the center of the witch trial craze, as is often alleged, England and her Puritan colonies, influenced as they were by a biblically orientated legal system, maintained a remarkably balanced approach to the witchcraft issue. Kittredge has irrefutably rehabilitated both King James I (author of the influential *Daemonologie*) and the New England Puritans from the scurrilous attacks made against them by modern critics. As for King James, whose name is permanently associated with the Authorized Version of the Bible, his knowledge of Scripture was too profound to allow him the psychological luxury of witch hunting; after a detailed refutation of the charges leveled against him by Trevelyan and others, Kittredge writes (p. 328):

> Our scrutiny of King James' record is finished. No summing up is necessary. The defendant is acquitted by the facts. One final remark, however, may be made, in lieu of a peroration. Diligent search has so far brought to light less than forty executions for witchcraft throughout England in the reign of James I, or an average of about *two a year*. Contrast with this statement the fact that in ten years of the same reign (6-15 James I), at least thirty-two persons were pressed to death in the single County of Middlesex for refusing to plead in cases of felony (not witchcraft), or an average of over *three a year*, and that, in the same county for the same period, at least seven hundred persons were hanged for felonies other than witchcraft, or an average of *seventy a year*. These figures call for no commentary. We may double or treble the number of witch-hangings, if we will, in order to allow for incompleteness in the published records, and it still remains true that the reign of James I was not, in this regard, a dark and bloody period.

A similarly careful study of Puritan witch trials leads Kittredge to the following theses:

> The total number of persons executed for witchcraft in New England from the first settlement to the end of the century is inconsiderable. . . .
>
> The public repentance and recantation of judge [Samuel Sewall] and jury in Massachusetts have no parallel in the history of witchcraft. . . .
>
> The record of New England in the matter of witchcraft is highly creditable, when considered as a whole and from the comparative point of view.
>
> It is easy to be wise after the fact,—especially when the fact is two hundred years old.[16]

The Desanctification Process

To be sure, in spite of Christian precept and its jurisprudential application in a not inconsiderable number of witch trials, many instances of flagrant judicial inhumanity did occur. In the continental civil law, this came about through the application of the Roman theory of the *crimen exceptum*—crime so heinous (e.g., treason) as to allow the court to dispense with the protections to which the accused was ordinarily entitled. Noting that "in 1468, witchcraft was expressly designated as a *crimen exceptum*,"[17] Lee writes:

> In atrocious or "excepted" crimes, not only was the punishment severer, but the wholesome rules as to the character of the witnesses and of the evidence admitted were relaxed, showing that it was not simple justice but punishment that was sought. All doubts were resolved by resort to torture, both of the accused and of witnesses. It is true that careful and minute prescriptions were current as to what justified torture, but in discussing them the conclusion is reached that in the end everything is left to the discretion of the judge. It is the same with the severity, duration and repetition of torture. It is described as almost equivalent to death and worse than the amputation of both hands, but there was practically no limit to its severity except that if it killed the accused the judge was subject to investigation. Theoretically it was admitted that a confession extorted by illegal torture did not condemn the accused, but in practice this was illusory, for to admit it condemned the judge, and there was no one to pronounce it illegal. There was one redeeming feature—the accused was entitled to a copy of the evidence and to competent time to answer it; but this could be set aside by the will of

the legislator. He could also have an advocate, unless he had an evil reputation or was caught *in flagranti*, but the advocate was not to induce him to suppress the truth. As to confrontation, when the accused under torture denounced others, she was in their presence to be lightly tortured again and repeat the denunciation—the reason given for which was that it was better sometimes that the guilty should escape than that the innocent should be afflicted with dire torments. Such was in brief the system of jurisprudence which developed the witch madness.[18]

The use of such methods was bad enough when carried out by secular authority; even more reprehensible was their employment by the church itself in the late medieval period. Torture—categorically condemned by the early church and its theologians, as we have seen—came finally to be permitted by Canon law as a result of the revival of Roman law. Thus the infamous activities of the exceptional tribunals of the Holy Inquisition.

Even common law countries were not entirely exempt from such deviations where witchcraft was concerned. Both England and New England accepted so-called "spectral evidence" in witch trial prosecutions. Observes Christina Hole: "Evidence that would have been unacceptable in any other case was freely admitted in witch trials. Michael Dalton in *The Country Justice,* published in 1618, says that magistrates must not always expect direct evidence against witches, 'seeing that all their works are the works of darkness, and no witnesses present with them to accuse them.' "[19] Significantly, specter testimony was done away with in New England as early as 1693—largely as a result of the arguments of Robert Pike, who effectively queried, "Is the devil a competent witness?"[20] More ominous was the theoretical possibility of torture in New England trials: the "Body of Liberties," the first code of the Massachusetts colonists, provided for the use of torture in eliciting evidence and as a means of punishment.[21]

How could such a sad state of affairs have come about? How could Christian believers—whose religious beliefs had been classed as treasonable and therefore a *crimen exceptum* in the days of the Roman empire—have themselves jettisoned the legal safeguards of the accused in the witch trials? Two reasons can be identified, and there are important present-day lessons to be learned from each.

First, witchcraft was considered such a heinous crime and so difficult to detect and punish that "special" procedures were justified to stamp it out. The distinguished French jurist Jean Bodin, in his *De la démonomanie des sorciers*, reasoned that since witchcraft was so monstrous, "whatever punishment we can order against witches by roasting and cooking them over a slow fire is not really very much," and "one accused of sorcery must never be fully acquitted unless the calumny of his accuser is clearer than the sun, inasmuch as the proof of such crimes is so obscure and difficult that not one witch in a million would ever be accused or punished if regular legal procedure were observed." [22] This extraordinary admission makes patent that the evils of the witch trials were due in large part to the fatal moral error that the end can justify the means employed to attain it.

In our day we readily and properly identify this fallacy with the Marxist-Leninist philosophy and with situation ethics;[23] but are we equally aware of its operations in today's anti-Communist witch hunting? Rolf Hochhuth's *The Deputy*—whether we agree or not with its theme that Pius XII was willing to tolerate even the racist horrors of the Third Reich rather than give up Germany as a "bulwark against Communism"—is a sober reminder of how easy it is even for Christian believers to sacrifice human rights in over-zealous crusades to rid the world of genuine evils.

Allowing the end to justify the means is but the surface of the iceberg, however; there was an even more basic moral failing involved when Christians allowed legal illegality in the witch trials. They forgot that God was still in His heaven and that His promise of a last judgment expressly applies to crimes unprovable in human tribunals: "There is nothing covered that shall not be revealed, neither hid that shall not be known" (Luke 12:2-3, and parallels). Faced with the near impossibility of making their case against witchcraft in the courts of this world, they perverted human justice instead of leaving the judgment to the Great Assize. They refused to let God be God. They *played* God and—inevitable product of such a game—dehumanized themselves.

The Question of Legal Remedy

Our examination of the adjective law of the witch trials (procedure and evidence) has thus brought us directly to a central question of substantive law: Should witchcraft have been subject to human legal sanctions at all?

Here the modern critic of Christianity gleefully cites Ex. 22:18 and related Old Testament verses: "Thou shalt not suffer a witch to live." But such passages, though they certainly have been used to rationalize witchcraft persecution, do not necessarily justify it at all. There are many verses in the Bible that pronounce in no uncertain terms a death penalty upon evil, but which do not at all imply that human courts should deliver or carry out that sentence. "The wages of sin is death," declares the Apostle in Rom. 3:23, but the implication is hardly that human tribunals should sentence all sinners to the gallows! And even if one concedes that the Israelites were expected to punish witchcraft with the death penalty, this in no way commits the children of the new covenant to such activity—unless at the same time one would bring the New Testament church under the bondage of Old Testament ceremonial law, dietary rulings, and slaughters of Amalekites, all of which served a special purpose in preparation for the coming of Messiah but which are abrogated after His incarnation (Acts 10; Gal. 2; Col. 2:16-17).

The proper function of human law is to regulate conduct so as to prevent injustice among men; it is not to regulate ideas or to coerce opinions. But, as Rossell Hope Robbins emphasizes in the introduction to his standard *Encyclopedia of Witchcraft and Demonology:* "Witchcraft was not primarily concerned with acts; it was concerned with opinions and ideas." No objection could be raised to prosecuting a witch for murder when adequate evidence was able to be marshalled to show that she had in fact killed someone, but the difficulty lay in showing a connection between her demonic *beliefs* and actual harm to others. Montesquieu, in his *Spirit of the Laws* (bk. XII, chap. v), gives classic expression to the issue:

> It is an important maxim, that we ought to be very circumspect in the prosecution of witchcraft and heresy. The accusation of these two crimes may be vastly injurious to liberty, and productive of infinite oppression, if the legislator knows not how to set bounds to it. For as it does not directly point at a person's actions, but at his character, it grows dangerous in proportion to the ignorance of the people; and then a man is sure to be always in danger, because the most exceptionable conduct, the purest morals, and the constant practice of every duty in life, are not a sufficient security against the suspicion of his being guilty of the like crimes.

Some witchcraft ordinances made the salutary distinction between belief and practice; for example, "the Carolina of 1532 (based on the Bamberg Halsgerichtsordnung of 1507) punishes with death only injurious sorcery." [24] Sad to say, however, examples can be multiplied in the opposite direction. The learned Melchior Goldast, in his *Rechtliches Bedencken*,[25] cites the Schauenburg Policey-Ordnung of 1615 and other territorial Ordnungen to the effect that whoever makes a pact with the devil shall be burned alive even though he works no evil to anyone; "therefore those, whether Catholic or Protestant, are wholly wrong who teach that witches and sorcerers who give themselves to the devil and renounce God, but do no harm to man or beast, are not to be executed, but, like heretics, are to be received to repentance and absolution, with public church-discipline." [26] Thus the witch trial courts frequently obliterated the distinction between sin and crime and set themselves to the work of a miniature last judgment—but without benefit of divine omniscience.

It is vital, however, not to attribute this grave jurisdictional mistake solely to spiritual insensitivity or even perversity. Until very recent times, western man has not thought in terms of church-state separation in any serious way, and the assumption that state and church were fundamentally doing the same work lies at the root of much of the excesses of the witch trials. From Constantine's recognition of Christianity as the official religion of the empire in the early fourth century to the minority pleas of the Reformation Anabaptists for the separation of Church and State in sixteenth century—pleas that took another two centuries and more to be acted upon—the almost universal rule was "cujus regio, eius religio." The operation of this principle was especially powerful in the centuries when the witch trials were most frequent. To be sure, there was halting recognition theologically that something was wrong, as is evidenced by the insistence of the Holy Inquisition that those they found guilty must be turned over to the secular arm for actual punishment. But the great insight of Augustine in separating the City of God from the City of Man and Luther's fundamental distinction between Law and Gospel and the Two Kingdoms were not brought to bear on the issue of church-state relations or on the vital collateral question of the proper jurisdiction of human courts.

The blending of church and state is of course a spiritual problem in itself. Luther rightly emphasized that whenever Law and Gospel are confused—whenever a mélange of the Two Kingdoms occurs—human pride and works righteousness lie at the root. Man wants to carry out God's functions; he wants to build new towers of Babel to reach heaven. Not satisfied with the areas of civil and legal control given to him ("subdue the earth"—Gen. 1:28), man tries also to subdue hell. In the case of the witch trials, irony is piled upon irony, for in an effort to conquer the devil by whatever means, man falls directly into the clutches of the evil one. It was the primal sin of Lucifer to say, "I will be like the most High" (Isa. 14:12-15). Thus did the son of the morning become the prince of darkness; and thus were the Christians who played God in the witch trials historically tainted with the mark of the beast they endeavored to subdue in an unscriptural way.

Again, the witch trials hold out a warning for the contemporary church. We also—with no excuse available by way of established religion, since the separation of church and state is integral to our constitutional law—press for the expansion of legal remedies in moral and spiritual realms. Evangelicals have a long and sorry history of pushing for the legal enforcement of morals (local option campaigns, Sunday closing laws, and the like). Where, as in the case of literary censorship, the causal connection between wrong belief and direct injury is as hard to establish as it was in the witchcraft trials, are we not doing the Faith a great disservice to press for legal sanctions? Ought we not to keep before us the fundamental distinction between God's tribunal and man's, between His kingdom and ours, between eternal gospel and temporal law? Our task is not to correct every moral failing by human legislation; we are rather to legislate where provable harm to the body politic will arise in the absence of law. Thus we must prosecute stealing, but not profanity; perjury and misrepresentation of the terms of a contract, but not lying in general; child abuse, but not the teaching of atheism; murder, but not belief in witchcraft. God is still in His heaven, and the evils we are powerless to correct in accord with His Word He will most assuredly remedy on the last day.

Some Witch Trial Lessons Summarized

History is a good schoolteacher. Here, in summary, are

lessons which contemporary Christians can and should learn from the witch trials.

(1) Properly distinguish state from church, human courts from the last judgment, Law from Gospel.

(2) In correcting evils, never yield to the situationist principle of the end justifying the means.

(3) Be most careful not to assimilate the evil methods of your adversaries in combatting them. As a result of taking the gold of the Egyptians, the Israelites had the wherewithal to make a golden calf; medieval Christians, having conquered ancient Rome, uncritically absorbed her law, thereby acquiring a positive view of judicial torture and "extraordinary" procedures inimical to civil rights and scriptural humanitarianism.

(4) Never underestimate your spiritual opposition. Even after all appropriate qualifications have been made, the devil achieved more through the witch trials than he could possibly have gained by demonic activity apart from them.

Notes

1. *Principalities and Powers: The World of the Occult* (Minneapolis: Bethany Fellowship, Inc. 1973). This book is now available in a paperback edition.

2. Harvard University Press, 1929.

3. Groningen, 1953, pp. 408-415.

4. Vol. I, chap. xvii.

5. *City of God*, bk. XIX, chap. vi.

6. "Quod vero confessio cruciatibus extorquenda non est," Caus. XV, qu. 6, can. 1.

7. *Superstition and Force: Essays on the Wager of Law—the Wager of Battle—the Ordeal—Torture*, 2d ed. (New York: Greenwood Press reprint, 1968), p. 370.

8. Trans. Simpson (Rothman Reprints, 1968), p. 9.

9. *De praestigiis daemonum* (1563).

10. *The Discoverie of Witchcraft* (1584).

11. See Julio Caro Baroja, *The World of the Witches*, trans. Glendinning (Chicago: University of Chicago Press, 1964), chap. xiv.

12. See also Roland Villeneuve, *Les proces de sorcellerie* (Verviers, Belgium: Marabout, 1974), chap. ix.

13. H. B. Clark, ed., *Biblical Law* (2d ed., 1944), para. 70; cf. Montgomery, *Jurisprudence: A Book of Readings* (Washington, D.C.: Lerner Law Books, 1974).

14. See William Holdsworth, *The History of English Law*, 3d ed., I, 508-516.

16. P. 373; cf. John M. Taylor, *The Witchcraft Delusion in Colonial Connecticut* (1908), pp. 27-28.

17. Henry Charles Lea, *Materials Toward a History of Witchcraft,* I, 244.

18. *Ibid.*, II, 901-902.

19. *Witchcraft in England* (New York: Scribner, 1947), p. 62; cf. her *Mirror of Witchcraft* (London: Chatto & Windus, 1957), pp. 181ff.

20. *Dictionary of American Biography,* VII, 598, *in loco*; cf. C. W. Upham, *Salem Witchcraft* (1867), Vol. II.

21. See Max Farrand's edition of the *Body of Liberties* (1929), p. 50, and cf. Max Radin, *Handbook of Anglo-American Legal History* (1936), para. 50.

22. Paris, 1580, bk. IV, chap. v.

23. See my debate with Joseph Fletcher: *Situation Ethics: True or False* (Minneapolis: Bethany Fellowship, Inc., 1972).

24. Lea, *op cit.*, I, 244.

25. Bremen, 1661.

26. Lea, *op. cit.*, bk. II, 805.

PART THREE

Demonology in Literature

7

The Cosmocrats:

Diabolism in Modern Literature

D. G. KEHL

In his poem "The Second Coming," written in 1919, William Butler Yeats envisaged the broken center of modern civilization and the subsequent loosing of the apocalyptic beast upon mankind:

> Turning and turning in the widening gyre
> The falcon cannot hear the falconer;
> Things fall apart; the center cannot hold;
> Mere anarchy is loosed upon the world,
> The blood-dimmed tide is loosed, and everywhere
> The ceremony of innocence is drowned;
> The best lack all conviction, while the worst
> Are full of passionate intensity.
>
> Surely some revelation is at hand;
> Surely the Second Coming is at hand. . . .
> And what rough beast, its hour come round at last,
> Slouches toward Bethlehem to be born?

Diverging somewhat from the common interpretation of the poem, one might regard the "rough beast" as the apocalyptic, diabolic one, and the anarchic, "blood-dimmed tide" as demonic hosts loosed upon mankind, loosed from the moorings of traditional belief.* "When half-gods go,/The gods

---

* [The literary argument comprising the opening portion of this essay is summarized by the author on page 111: "Writers who make the most effective, responsible use of diabolism are those who make neither too much nor too little of the devil, giving him his place but not giving place to him."

[Most of the books listed in this article are documented in the bibliography at the end of the article, making it unnecessary to repeat some of the data in the notes or in the text itself—*editor.*]

arrive," Emerson wrote—or perhaps more accurately, when the true God is given only halfhearted allegiance or when He is totally rejected or declared "dead," the false gods of this world are there to fill the void.

At the first coming, when Christ walked upon this earth, the demonic powers openly opposed Him, making a concerted effort to thwart the redemptive plan. Now, as the second coming draws nearer, the Adversary, knowing his time is short, mobilizes his demonic forces in a climactic effort. Thus the second coming of Christ is vividly foreshadowed by the "second coming" of diabolism. Accordingly, Arthur Lyons entitled his book *The Second Coming: Satanism in America* and *Time* magazine (June 19, 1972) announced on its cover, "Satan Returns." Of course, Satan and his cosmocrats have not really "returned," for they have not been gone: Diabolus and his demons do not take vacations or even sabbaticals. As one writer puts it, "We are dealing with personalities who have been assigned to frustrate and to defeat the will of God for us as God's children. They serve Satan faithfully without interruption in their service. They don't punch in at eight and go home at four-thirty with a half-hour off for lunch and two coffee breaks a day, so that there are times when you are free from their activity because they are off the job." [1]

St. Paul told the Ephesians that Christian believers "are contending not against flesh and blood, but against the world rulers of this present darkness," against "the cosmocrats of the dark eon," as the Greek reads. If believers must contend *against* these spiritual hosts of wickedness in heavenly places, readers of modern literature must contend *with* these cosmocrats in *literary* places. In his *Studies in Classic American Literature* (p. 83), D. H. Lawrence wrote: "You *must* look through the surface of American art, and see the inner diabolism of the symbolic meaning. Otherwise it is all mere childishness." The reader of modern literature, American or otherwise, must heed Lawrence's advice. For, as St. Marc Girardin has said, "Formerly the imagination created saints for its legends, but today it makes devils for its novels."

According to the German mystic Jacob Böhme, when Satan was once asked why he left Paradise, he replied, "I wanted to be an author." Perhaps this anecdote does much to illuminate the authorship of some current diablerie. Although one may not be prepared to go so far as H. G. Wells did in stating that "Satan is a celestial raconteur,

[that] he alone makes stories," [2] one underestimates, to his critical detriment, the pervasive literary role of diabolism, just as one underestimates, to his spiritual peril, the pervasive moral influence of diabolism.

"Lucifer looms large in literature," Maximilian Rudwin wrote forty years ago. "The 'Morning Star,' hurled from heaven, shines brilliantly in the firmament of fiction. The discrowned archangel has waxed truly formidable in literary stature. Beelzebub bears on his shoulders the burden of belles-lettres. It is significant that Diabolus has been the principal motif of inspiration for the world's great masterpieces. . . . Sorry, indeed, would the plight of literature be without the Devil. Lacking the Devil, there would simply be no literature. With the Devil eliminated, there would be no plot, no complication, and consequently no story. Syllogistically stated, the idea may perhaps be expressed as follows: All real stories depend upon plots; all plots depend upon the intervention of the Devil; consequently all real stories depend upon the Devil." [3] Similarly, poet W. D. Snodgrass has said, ". . . In this racket [writing] if the devil isn't on your side you'd better give up. . . . The snake has all the best lines, metaphorically speaking. . . . The most important part of your work has to come out of the satanic side of yourself or at least that side which you consider satanic. That side you will have repressed and so may have gathered some power" (in a letter to the present author, November 3, 1974).

Perhaps Rudwin, Wells, and Snodgrass overstate the case, or state it without necessary qualification, for "the Fiend" is not, as Rudwin says, "the fountainhead of all fiction." Satan is the fountainhead of all lies, yes. But even though fiction is the little lie we make about the big lie we live, genuine literary art is the truth even if it never really happened, as Chief Bromden says in Ken Kesey's *One Flew Over the Cuckoo's Nest* (N.Y.: Signet, 1962, p. 13), as Helen Bober tells Frank Alpine in Bernard Malamud's *The Assistant* (N.Y.: Dell, 1957, p. 117), as Joyce Cary suggests in *Art and Reality* (Garden City, N.Y.: Doubleday, 1958).

Nor is the devil "a creative fellow," as Sterling North and C. B. Boutell have made him out to be. [4] He is canny and crafty but not *creative*. Satan never *created* anything (*bara*, "out of nothing"); he can only *imitate*. He cannot *consecrate*—only *desecrate*; he cannot *cultivate*—only *violate, invalidate, degenerate*. The fountainhead of the true poem (from the Greek *poiema*, "to make") is not the counterfeiter but the Divine Creater, the Master Poet, who has created us "in Christ Jesus unto good works," making us His "workmanship," His *poiema* (Eph. 2:10; cf. the same word in Rom. 2:20, translated "the things that are made"). Further, it should be remembered that it was *before* Satan appeared in the Garden that Adam exercised his God-given power of *naming*, the essence of the belletristic process.

To argue, as Rudwin does, that belles lettres could not exist without the devil is to indulge in a curious form of critical *felix culpa*. Rudwin's logic is specious, his syllogism both invalid and unsound:

> *Major premise*: "All real stories depend upon plots." (Such an assertion in its unqualified form is unsound.)
> *Minor premise:* "All plots depend upon the intervention of the Devil." (Again, the soundness depends upon clarification of terms, particularly "intervention of the Devil.")
> *Conclusion*—"Consequently, all real stories depend upon the Devil." Besides being unsound, this assertion is invalid because of the undistributed middle term.

> Validly constructed, the syllogism would read as follows:

> *Major premise:* Conflict is the basis of literary art.
> *Minor premise:* The influence of the devil is the basis of conflict.
> *Conclusion:* Therefore, the influence of the devil is the basis of literary art.

Perhaps Keith L. Roos validly expressed the place of Satan in literary art: "People have always shown a deep interest for (Satan's) literary incarnations, whether or not they believe in the devil's spiritual entity. Men of all languages have unanimously approved his fitness as a fictional character. Indeed, as a poetic personage, the devil has had few equals in history." [5]

It would seem that some belletrists and literary critics have fallen into what C. S. Lewis called the "two equal and opposite errors into which our race can fall about the devils. One is to disbelieve in their existence. The other is to believe, and to feel an excessive and unhealthy interest in them. They themselves are equally pleased by both errors. . . ." [6] The contrapuntal errors of making too much or making too little of the devil were illustrated in a recent UPI story about a man summoned before the judge to answer for a felony charge. His alibi "The devil made me do it" makes *too much* of the devil, rationalizing one's own guilt; the judge's response, "I'm sorry but the devil does not come under the jurisdiction of this court," makes *too little* of the devil. The literary critic who insists upon the Fiend as "the fountainhead" of all belles lettres makes too much of Satan. Conversely, the critic who ignores the devil's role in literature or who, like Emerson, holds a monistic view of evil as "merely privative," as cold is the privation of heat, "so much death and nonentity" ("Divinity School Address"), thus removing any possibility of real conflict, is making *too little* of the devil, reducing literature to a sip of cambric tea.

"There is danger . . . in taking the Devil too lightly," according to a *Time* magazine writer, "for in doing so man might take evil too lightly as well. Recent history has shown terrifyingly enough that the demonic lies barely beneath the surface, ready to catch men unawares with new and more horrible manifestations. But the Devil taken too seriously can become the ultimate scapegoat, the excuse for the world's evils and justification for men's failure to improve themselves." "Perhaps," the *Time* article continues, "the ideal solution would be to give the Devil his due, whether as a symbolic reminder of evil or a real force to be conquered—but to separate him, once and for all, from 'magic' " (June 19, 1972, p. 68). Those who read and believe the Scriptures know, of course, that the devil is neither merely a "symbolic reminder of evil" nor simply a "force." Writers who make the most effective, responsible use of diabolism are those who make neither too much nor too little of the devil, giving him his place but not giving place to him. Poet Howard Nemerov has said: "I should be very chary in talking about the Devil, lest I be thought to be invoking him. So too I rather more than half believe that much to discuss the mystery of iniquity is to contribute to its power" (in a letter to the present author, October 22, 1974).

Separating the devil from mere "magic" involves, first of all, recognizing that he exists as a real personality. "The Devil's cleverest wile," Baudelaire wrote in his *Short Prose Poems*, "is to convince us that he does not exist." Similarly, a character in Joris-Karl Huysmans' *La Bàs* (*Down There*): *A Study in Satanism* remarks, "Satan is forgotten by the great majority. . . ; the wiliest thing the Devil can do is to get people to deny his existence." Andre Gide, in the Journal of *The Counterfeiters* (Vintage, 1927, pp. 416, 435), wrote: "The more we deny him the more reality we give him. The Devil is affirmed in our negation.... Vincent gradually lets himself be permeated by the diabolic spirit.... He feels that the more he succeeds in disbelieving in the real existence of the Evil One, the more he becomes the pawn of Satan." Denis de Rougemont, in his book *The Devil's Share* (pp. 19-21), expresses the point as follows:

> *Satan dissembles himself behind his own image.* He chooses to don a grotesque appearance which has the sure effect of making him inoffensive in the eyes of educated people. For if the Devil is simply the red demon armed with a large trident, or the faun with a goatee and the long tail of popular legend, who would still go to the trouble of believing in him, or even of declaring that he does not believe in him? ... What appears to be incredible is not the Devil, not the Angels, but rather the candor and the credulity of the sceptics, and the unpardonable sophism of which they show themselves to be the victims: "The Devil *is* a gent with red horns and a long tail; *therefore* I don't believe in the Devil." And so the Devil has them precisely where he wants them.

Reinforcing this point, Screwtape, in C. S. Lewis' *The Screwtape Letters*, tells Wormwood:

> I wonder you should ask me whether it is essential to keep the patient in ignorance of your own existence.... Our policy, for the moment, is to conceal ourselves. Of course this has not always been so. We are really faced with a cruel dilemma. When the humans disbelieve in our existence we lose all the pleasing results of direct terrorism, and we make no magicians. On the other hand, when they believe in us, we cannot make them materialists and sceptics.... The fact that "devils" are predominantly *comic* figures in the modern imagination will help you. If any faint suspicion of your existence begins to arise in his mind, suggest to him a picture of something in red tights, and persuade him that since he cannot believe in that ... he therefore cannot believe in you.

An increasing number of modern writers, however, do seem to show evidence of belief in the reality of the demonic. John Updike, for example, in his introduction to *Soundings in Satanism* (ed. F. J. Sheed; N. Y.: Sheed and Ward, 1972, pp. vii-viii, x), writes: " ... In our Protestantism, ... we judge our Judge; and we magnanimously grant our Creator his existence by a 'leap' of our own wills, incidentally reducing his 'ancient foe' to the dimensions of a bad comic strip.... I would, timidly, in my capacity as feeble believer and worse scholar, open the question of the devil as a metaphysical possibility, if not necessity. . . . A century of progressivism bears the fruit of Hitler; our own super-technology breeds witches and warlocks from the loins of engineers.''

Responding to a question about Updike's remarks, novelist D. Keith Mano has said: "Updike is too cautious: that's why, while a fine stylist, he is not an important writer. . . . I'm a Flannery O'Connor man. The devil is both dramatic necessity for the writer and, for any Christian worth his salt, a spiritual necessity" (in a letter to the present author, November, 1974).

Such is the view of Flannery O'Connor, one of the highly regarded writers of twentieth century American literature. Noting that she saw "from the standpoint of Christian orthodoxy" [8] that "the meaning of life is centered in our Redemption by Christ," O'Connor said, "My subject in fiction is the action of grace in territory held largely by the devil" (p. 32). The devil, to O'Connor, is both a real personality and a dramatic necessity. "To insure our sense of mystery," she wrote, "we need a sense of evil which sees the devil as a real spirit who must be made to name himself, and not simply to name himself as vague evil, but to name himself with his specific personality for every occasion. Literature, like virtue, does not thrive in an atmosphere where the devil is not recognized as existing both in himself and as a dramatic necessity for the writer" (p. 117). Accordingly, there appears in her novel *The Violent Bear It Away*,[9] this dialogue between Young Tarwater and the stranger, a demonic figure, the latter speaking first: " 'The way I see it,' he said, 'you can do one of two things. One of them, not both. Nobody can do both of two things without straining themselves. You can do one thing or you can do the opposite.' 'Jesus or the devil,' the boy said. 'No no no,' the stranger said, 'there ain't no such thing as a devil. I can tell you that from my own self-experience. I know that for a fact. It ain't Jesus or the devil. It's Jesus or *you*.' " Here again is the devil's "cleverest wile": the attempt to convince us that he does not exist.

In another, ironic, sense, however, there is a modicum of truth in what the stranger says, for the spirit of self *is* the spirit of the devil (see the recurrence of the solipsistic "I will" in Isa. 14:13-14). If the devil can get a man to live for *himself*, he has won a victory. What need is there for subtle, chthonian devices? As Pogo expressed it, "We have met the enemy and he is *us*."

The demonic forces have a powerful ally, a fifth column within every man—the old man, the Adamic nature, the flesh, which, along with this worldly system and the devil, forms a powerful triad of evil, caricature of the Holy Trinity. Novelist and poet Charles Williams, in his preface to his study of witchcraft (*Witchcraft*, pp. 9, 10), noted the power of the human heart as a demonic ally: Witchcraft "is one exhibition among many—and more flagrant than some—of a prolonged desire of the heart; few studies of the past can present that heart more terribly . . . in its original and helpless corruption. . . . No one will derive any knowledge of initiation from this book; if he wishes to meet 'the tall, black man' or to find the proper method of using the Reversed Pentagram, he must rely on his own heart, which will, no doubt, be one way or other sufficient."

Graham Greene, another major twentieth century writer, posits the notion that belief in the reality of God logically entails belief in the reality of Satan. Bendrix, the unbelieving narrator of *The End of the Affair* (N.Y.: Viking, 1951, pp. 70-71), says: "I have never understood why people who can swallow the enormous improbability of a personal God boggle at a personal devil. I have known so intimately the way that demon works in my imagination." What Bendrix, who never for a moment doubts the reality of "the demon in the mind," cannot admit but by the end of the novel is coming to, is that the reverse is also true: the existence of a personal devil demands also the existence of a personal God. Poet W. D. Snodgrass has remarked, "I'm myself an atheist, so I guess it would be improper for me to believe in the devil if I don't believe in God" (in a letter to the present author, November 3, 1974). The irony of all ironies is that belief in the existence of the former can sometimes lead to belief in the existence of the latter. For example, Joris-Karl Huysmans, after his investigations into Satanism convinced him of the existence of a supernatural of evil, became convinced also of a supernatural of good. He summarized it as follows: "With his hooked paw, the Devil drew me toward God" (preface to *La Bàs*, pp. xxvi-xxvii).

God does indeed "make the wrath of men [and even devils] to praise him," as the Psalmist said (76:10). Paradoxically, "*all* things work together for good to them that love God, to them who are the called according to his purpose" (Rom. 8:28)—even the diabolical. In *Notes from the underground*, Dostoevsky wrote: "The dialectic of good is set in motion through suffering—and often through sin."

Thomas Mann expressed much the same idea in the twentieth century. And more recently critic Ihab Hassan has written: "... Grace, if it is to be found at all, lies deep in the soft core of violence. The saint and the criminal stand back to back on either side of the demonic." [10]

Similarly, the Satanism of Baudelaire was, in the opinion of T. S. Eliot, "an attempt to get into Christianity by the back door" and was thus "redeemed by meaning something else." [11] This "something else" is "the possibility of damnation" and therefore also of personal salvation. Elsewhere in his study of the demonic influence, Eliot remarked, "Most people are only a very little alive; and to awaken them to the spiritual is a very great responsibility: it is only when they are so awakened that they are capable of real Good, but that at the same time they become first capable of Evil." Such then is one of the great merits of literary art: "to awaken them to the spiritual"—to both spiritual evil and spiritual good, to the demonic and to the heavenly beatific, perhaps even to the latter through the former.

"Perhaps evil is the crucible of goodness.... Perhaps even Satan—Satan in spite of himself—somehow works out the will of God." This remark of Lankester Merrin's in William Peter Blatty's *The Exorcist* (p. 370)—borrowed from a sermon by John Henry Newman—is well illustrated in Flannery O'Connor's *The Violent Bear It Away*. Novelist John Hawkes has said that O'Connor is "on the devil's side without knowing it," just as Shelley said that Milton was. Hawkes has written: "... A good many readers would mistake Flannery O'Connor's belief in the Holy for its opposite.... In the most vigorously moral of writers the actual creation of fiction seems often to depend on immoral impulse." [12] But a closer examination of the novel reveals that rather than O'Connor being on "the devil's side without knowing it," she depicts the *devil* working on *God's* side without knowing it. Young Tarwater comes to regard Rayber as the Old Prophet's "bait," and, paradoxically, it is the rape of Tarwater by the diabolic stranger that leads to his purgation and his beatific vision.

The references to Baudelaire, to Dostoevsky, to Huysmans, point up the necessity—if one is to "look through the surface" of recent literature and "see the inner diabolism of the symbolic meaning"—to consider briefly the historical underpinnings of diabolism in literature. In a letter to me poet Howard Nemerov has sketched this literary development as follows:

Mark the progress of Satan from Easter week of thirteen hundred, when Dante saw him helpless in hell chomping on three major sinners, through near four centuries after which Milton saw him get up, take council, make trouble, through another century and a half till Blake (who put Milton straight) figured him as Energy, Bright Day, fiery Orc, and perhaps Los himself; and down to this pupil present, where you may take the evidence of Wallace Stevens as to his decease ("The death of Satan was a tragedy/For the imagination"—"Esthetique du Mal," VIII) or the evidence of, for example, Bernanos or de Rougemont that he still stalks abroad seeking whom he may devour. I've got a sort of pet notion that the first great change, from Dante to Milton, corresponded to a technological change as well as the Copernican cosmological one: from the wheel that moves by power applied to the rim, as with the potters' wheel, the mill wheel, the windmill, God's stillness moving the spheres from outside, by desire . . . to the wheel that is moved by power applied to the center as in all our marvelous machines (in a letter to me, October 22, 1974).

Nemerov's concept is a fascinating one indeed, its image harking back to Yeats' "widening gyre." If the modern wheel, moved by power applied to its center rather than its circumference, parallels, perhaps even influenced, the development of the diabolic in literary art, Yeats reminds us that "the center cannot hold": the wrong kind of power applied to the center breaks it, and "things fall apart."

More immediate antecedents to writers treating diabolism in the modern period are suggested by Archibald MacLeish: the diabolism is "all part of the current fashion for what is called 'evil'. . . . (The best brief current comment is the name of that motorcycle rider who fell in the river.). . . . George Sand and Flaubert discussed it in 1874 or 5 and it hasn't changed since" (letter to me, October 19, 1974). Flaubert's novel *The Temptation of St. Anthony* (based in part on Brueghel's painting) and George Sand's *The Devil's Pool* (based in part on Holbein's woodcuts) do in fact serve to illustrate yet another turn, another revolution, in the widening gyre. George Sand's remarks in her introduction to *The Devil's Pool* (p. 12), concerning the purpose of diabolism in literature, provide apt commentary on the more facile, sensational treatment of diabolism in such recent works as *Rosemary's Baby* and *The Exorcist*:

> We shall not refuse to artists the right to probe the wounds of society and lay them bare to our eyes; but is the function of art still to threaten and appall? In the litera-

ture of the mysteries of iniquity, which talent and imagination have brought into fashion, we prefer the sweet and gentle
characters, which can attempt and effect conversions, to the
melodramatic villains, who inspire terror; for terror never
cures selfishness, but increases it. . . . The novel of today
should take the place of the parable and the fable of early
times. . . . The artist has a larger and more poetic task than
that of suggesting certain prudential and conciliatory mea-
sures for the purpose of diminishing the fright caused by
his pictures.[13]

Perhaps the "modern" period of diabolism in literary
art "began" with Baudelaire—whom T. S. Eliot characterized as "essentially a Christian, born out of his due
time" [14]—and Joris-Karl Huysmans, whose work, according to Eliot, is typified by the "fee-fi-fo-fum decor of medi-
evalism" (Eliot, p. 66). Huysmans' *La Bàs* does in fact
hark back to the medieval, but it also looks ahead to the
modern. As Durtal, the protagonist-writer puts it: "I had
to occupy myself with Gilles de Rais and the diabolism
of the Middle Ages to get contemporary diabolism revealed
to me" (p. 258). Huysmans attempted in the novel to adopt
a new artistic technique, a dichotomous "spiritual naturalism" or "supernatural realism" inspired by Grunewald's
Crucifixion, a "masterpiece at the same time infinite and
of earth earthy." Who can look upon "this coarse, tear-
compelling Calvary" (p. 8) and doubt either the powerful
reality of the diabolic, particularly its evil within us all
in nailing there the innocent Son of God, or, on the other
hand, the powerful reality of divine love, which impelled
Him to this crux? Here then is diabolic grotesquerie at
its worst, its lowest, and here, too, is divine grace at its
best, its highest. Such seems to be what Huysmans attempted to convey in his study of Satanism, and perhaps he at
least partially succeeded.

La Bàs, utilizing the framing device of story-within-
story, deals with a novelist, Durtal, who is researching
and writing the story of the fifteenth century mystic-turned-
Satanist, Gilles de Rais. In the course of his investigations,
Durtal encounters virtually every form of diabolism, which,
he learns, is basically demon influence or possession:

> The external semblance of the Demon is a minor mat-
> ter. He has no need of exhibiting himself in human or
> bestial form to attest his presence. For him to prove him-
> self, it is enough that he choose a domicile, in souls which
> he ulcerates and incites to inexplicable crimes. Then, he

can hold his victims by that hope which he breathes into them, that instead of living in them as he does, and as they don't often know, he will obey evocations, appear to them, and deal out, duly, legally, the advantages he concedes in exchange for certain forfeits. Our very willingness to make a pact with him must be able often to produce his infusion into us (pp. 114-15).

From his friend Des Hermies, Durtal learns that "the most important thing about Satanism is the black mass"— "that and witchcraft and incubacy and succubacy. . . . Sacrilegious mass, spells, and succubacy. There you have the real quintessence of Satanism" (p. 71). Later he learns, at first hand, the truth of these statements. He is mysteriously seduced by Mme. Chantelouve, his Hyaoinabe girl, whom he learns is not only an active Satanist but a demon-possessed vixen with "three distinct beings in her" (p. 223), an indulger in incubacy, and herself an unearthly succubus. She takes him to a Black Mass, an indescribably blasphemous rite conducted by a defrocked priest who has had the figure of Christ tattooed on his heels the better to trample Him underfoot. "Durtal, terrified, saw through the fog the red horns of Docre, who, seated now, frothing with rage, was chewing up sacramental wafers, taking them out of his mouth, wiping himself with them, and distributing them to the women, who ground them underfoot, howling, or fell over each other struggling to get hold of them and violate them. The place was simply a madhouse, a monstrous pandemonium of prostitutes and maniacs. Now, while the choir boys gave themselves to the men, a little girl, who hitherto had not budged, suddenly bent over forward and howled, howled like a dog" (p. 272; cf. the same desecration of the holy in such works as Graham Greene's "The Hint of an Explanation"). Leaving the mass, Mme. Chantelouve conducts Durtal to a musty room above a shoddy bar, where she seduces him on a bed strewn with fragments of hosts.

Durtal is also introduced to a godly man of faith, Carhaix, the cathedral bell-ringer, who asks the novelist, " 'What do you hope for if you have no faith in the coming of Christ?' " Durtal replies, " 'I hope for nothing at all.' 'I pity you. Really, you believe in no future amelioration?' 'I believe, alas, that a dotard Heaven maunders over an exhausted earth.' The bell-ringer raised his hands and sadly shook his head" (p. 294). The novel ends with remarks about the future by Carhaix, Des Hermies, and Durtal, each conveying an element of truth. Carhaix says:

"On earth, all is dead and decomposed. But in heaven!
Ah, I admit that the Paraclete is keeping us waiting.
But the texts announcing his coming are inspired. The future is certain. There will be light," and with bowed head
he prayed fervently.

Des Hermies rose and paced the room. "All that is
very well," he groaned, "but this century laughs the glorified Christ to scorn. It contaminates the supernatural and
vomits on the beyond. Well, how can we hope that in the
future the offspring of the fetid tradesmen of today will be
decent? Brought up as they are, what will they do in Life?"

"They will do," replied Durtal, "as their fathers and
mothers do now. They will stuff their guts and crowd out
their souls through their alimentary canals" (pp. 316-17).

And so it is in the "enlightened" seventies of the twentieth century, eighty-five years after *La Bàs* was conceived.
For *we* are the offspring of whom they spoke. Like Carhaix,
true believers eagerly await the Second Coming of Christ,
but meanwhile the "second coming" of Satan and his cosmocrats wreaks upon the earth a far greater desecration than
even Durtal and his friend envisaged. If what Gévingey,
the astrologer in the novel, said was true in the late nineteenth century, it is more pervasively and perversely ap-
plicable today: " 'It's a two-sided age. . . . People believe
nothing, yet gobble everything' " (p. 312). And Durtal's comment about his own age applies even better to the present:
" 'What a queer age. . . . It is just at the moment when
positivism is at its zenith that mysticism rises and the follies
of the occult begin.' " To which Des Hermies replies:
" 'When materialism is rotten-ripe, magic takes root. This
phenomenon reappears every hundred years' " (p. 261).

Here again is the "widening gyre" of Yeats, the spiral,
the cycle, of demonic activity in the affairs of men. More
recent literature has added virtually nothing new to the
diabolism of *La Bàs* and earlier works; it has only sophisticated it, making it more profitably marketable, in some
cases, by sensationalizing it. It has, in short, illustrated
another turn of the wheel with its broken center. There
is, after all, little that *can* be added, for Satan has not
changed his basic strategies through the centuries. He only
accommodates, making adjustments to match the current
Zeitgeist, which, by the way, he has largely effected. "The
devil keeps advertising," says a character in *The Exorcist*
(p. 400); "the devil does lots of commercials." Similarly,
W. H. Auden wrote in *New Year Letter* (London: Faber
and Faber, 1941, p. 35):

> The Devil, as is not surprising,
> —His business is self-advertising—
> Is a first-rate psychologist,
> Who keeps a conscientious list,
> To help him in his ticklish deals,
> Of what each client thinks and feels,
> His school, religion, birth and breeding,
> Where he has dined and who he's reading.

Ever since he used a Madison Avenue soft-sell appeal to Eve in the Garden, Satan has been similarly advertising, producing what J. B. Priestley in another context has called "Admass—a consumer's race with donkeys chasing an electric carrot." [15] For centuries Satan and his cosmocrats have used the old donkey-carrot trick. Except for electrifying his carrot to adjust to the technological age, he has kept his techniques virtually unchanged. And why not? They have always been highly effective—and obviously still are. As Auden has put it: "Millions already have come to their harm, / Succumbing like doves to his adder's charm" ("Danse Macabre").

Such are the grotesque, bestial metaphors of Diabolus: the adder charming the dove, the dimpled spider with fly or moth, the wolf in sheep's clothing fleecing the lamb, the lion stalking what kid he may devour,

> A scapegoat aged into a steer; boar-snouted;
> His great limp ears stuck sidelong out in air;
> A dewlap bunched at his breast; a ram's-horn wound
> Beneath ear; a spur licked up and out
> From the hide of his forehead; bat-winged, but in bone;
> His eye a ring inside a ring inside a ring,
> That leers up, joyless, vile, in meek obscenity—
> This is the devil.[16]

Or the devil and his cosmocrats are, and make their dehumanized victims become, the grotesque mass of beetles, their wings folded but at the very instant of loosing, as depicted in Charles Williams' novel *All Hallows Eve* (N.Y.: Noonday, 1969; originally published in 1948). But perhaps most pernicious of all is their dissimulation as angels of light such guises as that of the kindly stranger, the "pale, lean, old-looking young man" with lavender shirt, panama hat, and cream-colored car in O'Connor's *The Violent Bear It Away.*

Whatever their guise or strategy, the demonic cosmocrats are powerful fallen angels, and their influence underlies diabolism and the occult. "All magic," the demonic

Theron Ware says in James Blish's novel *Black Easter*, "*all* magic, with no exceptions whatsoever—depends upon the control of demons. By demons I mean specifically fallen angels." [17] Demonic activity takes various forms, as indicated in Scripture and illustrated in modern literature. Perhaps in sequential order of severity and often of progression, demonic activity takes these forms: (1) demonic *impression*, often through *expression;* (2) demonic *repression*, both the putting down, the hindering of good, and the forcing of ideas or impulses into the subconscious; (3) demonic *obsession*, whereby the victim is greatly preoccupied with the unholy and/or unwholesome and, in some cases, with the Evil One himself; (4) demonic *depression*; (5) demonic *oppression*, just short of (6) demonic *possession*.

These forms or stages of demonic activity involve all the faculties of man, but each is directed toward particular faculties. For example, demonic impression is directed toward the mind: Paul warned Timothy that in the latter times some would "depart from the faith, giving heed to seducing spirits, and doctrines of demons" (1 Tim. 4:1); consequently, we are to bring into captivity every thought to the obedience of Christ (2 Cor. 10:5).

Demonic repression is also directed primarily at the mind: Paul said that "the god of this world has blinded the minds of them that believe not, lest the light of the glorious gospel of Christ . . . should shine unto them" (2 Cor. 4:4). It is the Wicked One who comes and snatches away the seed sown in the heart (Matt. 13:19). Or he subtly implants unwholesome, unholy impulses in the subconscious mind, where they remain unevaluated, uncriticized, and undiscerned until triggered to rise to the surface as powerful attitudinal predispositions. If the demonic cosmocrats cannot corrupt our minds (2 Cor. 11:3) or *defile* them (Titus 1:15) or *blind* them (2 Cor. 4:4) or *confuse* them (2 Thess. 2:2) or *unsettle* them (Luke 12:29) or *divert* them (James 1:4; 4:8) or *discourage* them (Heb. 12:3), they seek to *bypass* our conscious minds, subtly appealing instead to the irrational or sub-rational, a form of subliminal seduction.

Demonic obsession involves both mind and heart, a subtle attraction, perhaps beginning with either the intellect or emotions and leading to an unwholesome-unholy preoccupation. "Set your affection on things above, not on things on the earth," Paul admonishes (Col. 3:2). Demonic depression, and its accompanying distress, is directed primarily at the emotions. A major demonic tool is discouragement and depression; therefore, we are admonished to "consider him . . . lest we become weary and faint-hearted" (Heb. 12:3).

The next form, demonic oppression, is directed primarily toward the emotional and, in some cases, the physical. Demonic possession, of course, involves all the human faculties, all of which are manipulated.

The question of whether or not a believer can be possessed by a demon, a topic too broad to consider here, is controversial, with some cogent arguments mustered to support both sides. Perhaps most plausible is the view that because the Holy Spirit indwells the believer (Rom. 8:9; 1 Cor. 6:19), no unholy spirit can—"Greater is he that is in you than he that is in the world" (1 John 4:4). But some feel that one cannot presume to say so summarily that a believer long out of fellowship, unrepentant, having grieved and quenched the Spirit, having strayed so far that although he has the Spirit, the Spirit does not have him, brooks no access to an unholy spirit. Perhaps Whitman's vivid description of his sensuous "possession" through loss of counterpoise illustrates the point (*Song of Myself*):

> Immodestly sliding the fellow-senses away,
> They bribed to swap off with touch and go and graze at the
> edges of me. . . .
> The sentries desert every other part of me,
> They have left me helpless to a red marauder.

Unfortunately, many believers have become so preoccupied with demonic *possession* that they have almost failed to recognize the other forms of demonic activity, any one of which is often more than adequate to achieve the diabolic purpose. Some modern works of literature illustrate one or two forms of demonic activity and a few—for example Huysmans' *La Bàs*, O'Connor's *The Violent Bear It Away*, Blish's *Black Easter*, I. B. Singer's *Satan in Goray*[18]— illustrate all six forms.

Perhaps no work in modern literature better illustrates diabolic impression through expression, doctrines demon-taught, than does O'Connor's *The Violent Bear It Away*. The diabolic "stranger," besides attempting to convince Tarwater that the devil does not exist, derogates Old Tarwater as being "crazy," variously flatters and taunts the boy, implanting doubt about the veracity of the old man's word and about his own prophetic "calling." He presents a specious argument against resurrection and future judgment:

"... Don't you think any cross you set up in the year 1952 would be rotted out by the year the Day of Judgment comes in? Rotted to as much dust as his ashes if you reduced him to ashes? And lemme ast you this: What's God going to do with sailors drowned at sea that the fish have et and the fish that et them et by other fish and they et by yet others? And what about people that get burned up naturally in house fires? Burnt up one way or another or lost in machines until they're pulp? And all those sojers blasted to nothing? What about all those there's nothing left of to burn or bury?" (p. 324).

It is typical of the demonic impression that the stranger urges Tarwater to burn rather than bury the old man, who had insisted that his body be buried ten feet deep "to keep the dogs from digging it up." This passage is reminiscent of the first section of Eliot's *The Waste Land*, "The Burial of the Dead":

> The corpse you planted last year in your garden,
> Has it begun to sprout? Will it bloom this year? . . .
> Oh keep the Dog far hence, that's friend to man,
> Or with his nails he'll dig it up again.

The dogs are perhaps the same in both cases, as are the "corpses." Cleanth Brooks has said of Eliot's lines: "I am inclined to take the Dog [the capital letter is Eliot's] as Humanitarianism and the related philosophies which, in their concern for man, extirpate the supernatural—dig up the corpse of the buried god and thus prevent the rebirth of life." [19] The implication in both Eliot and O'Connor seems clear: to the extent that a philosophy, including Humanism, extirpates the supernatural, it is demonic or at least diabolically inspired.

Rayber, in O'Connor's novel, is a dehumanized, machine-like humanist and the devil's emissary. Similarly, Professor Weston, who becomes the grotesque Un-man in C. S. Lewis' *Perelandra*, [20] seeks to make a diabolic, damning impression upon the Green Lady, by arguing for a specious *felix culpa*. In other cases, the demonic impression, the initial access, the "in," is made through the senses, as in the case of the tannis root charm in Ira Levin's *Rosemary's Baby*, or through the emotions—for example, Guy's ambition for success, in the same novel, or Regan's curiosity about the ouija board in *The Exorcist*. Often the demonic cosmocrats capitalize upon legitimate, God-given needs and desires—knowledge, a measure of success, security, children and happiness as in Rosemary's case—with the purpose

of getting the victim to attempt to satisfy them in an illegiti-
mate, distorted way rather than in a God-ordained way.
Thus there is not only the temptation to do right for the
wrong reasons, as Eliot suggests in *Murder in the Cathedral*,
but also the temptation to do wrong for the right reasons—the
notion that it is right to do wrong in order to do right or
get the chance to do right.

It is this latter which seems to have motivated the Watergate wrongdoing. The relevance of Watergate to this discussion of diabolism is perhaps suggested in these remarks
written in 1891 by the Harvard scholar Barrett Wendell:

> ...Mental and moral degeneracy—credulity and fraud
> —seem almost invariably to entangle themselves with oc-
> cult phenomena that many cool-headed people are dis-
> posed to assert the whole thing a lie. To me...it does
> not seem so simple. I am much disposed to think that
> necromancers, witches, mediums—what not, —actually do
> perceive in the infinite realities about us things that are
> imperceptible to normal human beings; but that they
> perceive them only at a sacrifice of their higher faculties—
> mental and moral—not inaptly symbolized in the old tales
> of those who sell their souls. If this be true, witchcraft is
> a thing more subtly dangerous still.[21]

Diabolism is so subtly dangerous because it is so danger-
ously subtle. And it is such because, among other reasons,
once the initial impression is permitted, the expression heed-
ed, the argument accepted, the bill of goods "bought," the
incursion brooked, one becomes vulnerable to other forms
of demonic influence. If one does not wish to eat the devil's
apples, someone has said, he should stay out of the devil's
orchard. The second look becomes the leer, which becomes
the lust, which becomes the lascivious lunge into the dark.
Young Tarwater, in O'Connor's novel, listened to the demonic stranger's prattle until "he had lost his dislike for the
thought of the voice.... He began to feel that he was only
just now meeting himself..." (p. 324). Demonic mental
repression has begun, and physical repression occurs when
Rayber and the stranger seek to thwart Tarwater's full-
filling his vatic destiny.

Demonic obsession takes the form of excessive preoccupation with things, with unwholesome/unholy ideas, with
self, or with Satan himself. When his great uncle dies, young
Tarwater becomes obsessed with the diabolically urged idea
of independence, of freedom from the old man's influence.
Professor Weston, in Lewis' *Perelandra*, is obsessed with

the idea of "scientification," of spreading human corruption to other planets. Durtal, in *La Bàs*, becomes obsessed by the demonic Chantelouve, "burning for this unknown woman" (Huysmans, p. 99). Like the Galatians, who, according to Paul, were "bewitched" so as to be unable to obey the truth (Gal. 3:1), the townsfolk of Goray, in Singer's *Satan in Goray*, are bewitched, given the evil eye, charmed by the false messiah, Sabbatai Zevi, until they obsessively worship him. As Huysmans' *La Bàs* illustrates, monomania of the wrong kind can lead to demonomania, which can lead easily to demon possession. To be possessed with demon-inspired ideas can be the prelude, for unbelievers at least, to being possessed by the demon himself.

Demonic depression in its initial stage often takes the form of discouragement, faint-heartedness, and disillusionment through doubt. In O'Connor's novel, the demonic stranger attempts to convince Tarwater that God is oblivious to him: "You're left by yourself in this empty place with just as much light as that dwarf sun wants to let in. You don't mean a thing to a soul as far as I can see. . . . The truth is the Lord ain't studying about you. You ain't entered His Head" (pp. 324-25).

Consequent demonic distress takes a variety of forms, such as the sensuous unpleasantness accompanying the presence of demons in the opening of James Blish's *Black Easter*: "The room stank of demons. And it was not just the room. . . . No, the stench was something abroad in the world. . . . That exhalation from Hell-mouth was drifting up from the world below. . . , a pervasive, immensurable fog of rising evil. . . . The reek of evil had suddenly become much more pronounced" (pp. 15, 16, 17, 19). Similarly, in Singer's novel: "Rechele was well aware that the room was crowded with evil things. The brooms and mops stirred; long shadows swept along the walls like apparitions from another world" (p. 49). Later when Rechele was beset by mysterious ills, "some said she suffered from falling sickness, others that she was in the power of demons" (p. 53).

Distress caused by demons is often the prelude to more severe forms of demonic oppression, as in the case of Rabbi Benish in *Satan in Goray*: ". . . He could not fall asleep. A whistling and howling arose from the hearth, and now and then in the stagnant air a sigh as of a soul in torment. The rafter, piled high with ancient holy volumes no longer fit for us, shuddered, and dull thuds were heard from above, as though someone were moving heavy things about. . . .

Half awake and half asleep, his ears caught the sound of speech that seemed to be issuing from many mouths" (p. 75). When the Rabbi is physically injured, an example of demonic oppression, the townspeople whisper the same refrain: " 'It's because of *the others*, the demons. They're the ones to blame. . . .' Glucke, the trustee, swore that, unable to sleep all night, she had heard the noise of women chattering in the wind, and had concluded that the spirits were gathering together. Later, at the very moment when Rabbi Benish was injured, all the spirits had burst into laughter, mocking and clapping their hands—for they had avenged themselves on humans, had done them an injury" (p. 81).

Still later in the novel, when evil becomes rampant, widespread demonic oppression occurs. "On the night of Hoshana Rabba a dreadful thing happened: A woman who had gone to fetch water was thrown by demons into the well, where she was found dead the next morning, head down and feet up. The evil spirits also molested the old night watchman, tearing off half his beard" (p. 129). During prayers at the study house, "a completely unexpected fight broke out," and some "insisted that 'the others' had had a hand in the affair. . . . Even the women, as though devil-driven, attacked one another remorselessly, tearing bonnets, ripping shawls and jackets, savagely digging their nails into flesh, and filling the prayer house with their uproar" (p. 129). " . . . Not a day passed without incident or affliction" (p. 130). Perhaps there is no more graphically detailed, grotesque description of demonic oppression than that in Singer's novel:

> The destroyer demons had been reveling freely in the streets of Goray. Every night they beat on the window-panes. . . . When a candle was lit, the shadow of a bony hand with five outspread fingers could be distinguished on the wall opposite. . . . On Thursday imps overturned the dough troughs, spilling the dough for the white Sabbath bread; they threw handfuls of salt into the pots where dinner was being cooked, ripped the *mezuzot* from door posts. . . . Imps would hang on to the wheel-spokes of a wagon, dragging the wagon back and blinding the horse. Disguising themselves as he-goats, they danced to meet the women returning from the bathhouse. . . . Every night Satan visited Rechele to torment her. He was black and tall, fiery-eyed and with a long tail; his body was cold, his lips scaly, and he exhaled pitchfire. He ravished her so many times she was powerless to move. Then, rising,

he tormented her in numerous ways. Pulling the hairs
singly from her head, he wound them about her throat;
he pinched her in the hips and bit her breasts with his
jagged teeth. When she yawned he spat down her throat;
he poured water on her bedsheet and pretended she had
wet her bed. He made her show him her private parts and
drink slop. He seduced her into reciting the explicit name
of God and blaspheming Him; on Friday nights he forced
her to desecrate the Sabbath by tearing paper and touching
the Sabbath candlesticks. Sometimes Satan told Rechele
obscene tales, and Reb Gedaliya on the other side of the
wall would hear her loud, mad laughter resounding at
midnight. Once, Reb Gedaliya opened the door of the
Holy Ark to take out the Torah scroll, only to find the
scroll mantle slashed, and a piece of dung lying within. . . .
    Rechele suffered extraordinary tortures. At times the
evil one blew up one of her breasts. One foot swelled. Her
neck became stiff. Rechele extracted little stones, hairs,
rags, and worms from wet, pussy abscesses formed on
the flesh of her thigh and under her arms. Though she
had long since stopped eating, Rechele vomited frequently,
venting reptiles that slithered out tail first (pp. 144-46).

A similar kind of widespread demonic oppression is described in Blish's *Black Easter*. Mr. Baines, a director of
Consolidated Warfare Service, goes to Rome to commission
the diabolist Theron Ware to effect three diabolic acts: the
death of the governor of California; the death of scientist
Albert Stockhausen, who is on the verge of an unpatent-
able discovery which Baines' company already has made
and over which he wishes to maintain secret control; and
an insane experiment which he describes as follows: "I
would like to let all the demons out of Hell for one night,
turn them loose in the world with no orders and instructions—except of course that they go back by dawn or some
other sensible time—and see just what it is they would do
if they were left on their own hooks like that" (p. 108).
As if in a panel of Hieronymus Bosch, the diabolist
Ware summons infernal archangels of the Descending Hierarchy; then he, Baines and his contingent, and Father Domenico, sent to observe and, if possible, restrict the experiment, wait in the room to note what events might transpire.
At first, the news is disappointing to Baines—hardly different from reading any morning's newspaper: a major
train wreck in Colorado, a freighter floundering in a blizzard
in the North Sea, another hydrogen bomb detonated by the
Chinese, another raiding incident on the Israeli-Jordanian
border, a rape and massacre staged on a government hos-

pital in Rhodesia. But then on BBC comes such news, interspersed with singing commercials, as the Tate Gallery fire and the announcement that "there is no hope of saving the gallery's great collection of Blake paintings, which include most of his illustrations for the *Inferno* and *Purgatorio* of Dante" (p. 150).

Later it is learned that the supposed Chinese fusion test was actually a nuclear attack on Taiwan, that Western capitals are preparing for war after "the napalm murder of the U.S. president's widow in a jammed New York discotheque" (p. 154). Following a shock wave and widespread holocaust, Ware seeks to exorcise the demons which possess the world, but they refuse to return. Even Father Domenico is unsuccessful, for Armageddon has begun prematurely and without the appearance of the Antichrist.

The novel ends with the apocalyptic triumph of evil: "It would not be long now. In all their minds and hearts echoed those last three words. World without end. End without world. *God is dead*" (p. 165). Perhaps the most apt commentary on demonic oppression in both *Satan in Goray* and *Black Easter* is this remark in the preface to the former novel: "Once the core of faith is lost, Satan must triumph and the forces of evil overwhelm mankind." When things are wrong at the core, when the hub of the wheel is broken, things fall apart and the demonic tide is loosed upon mankind.

Sometimes demonic oppression, just short of possession of will and faculties, takes the form of temporary sensual "possession"—that is, supposed satanic intercourse and impregnation, incubacy, and succubacy. In *The Violent Bear It Away* young Tarwater, having accepted a ride from the diabolic stranger wearing the lavender shirt and panama hat, is drugged and raped. Similarly, Rosemary Woodhouse, in Ira Levin's *Rosemary's Baby*, is drugged and supposedly impregnated by Satan in a grotesque, surrealistic nightmare. In a comic novel, *The Devil's Own Dear Son*, published in 1949, James Branch Cabell tells the story of Diego de Arredondo Dodd, who discovers that his true father was Red Samael, the Seducer, youngest and most virile of the seventy-two Princes of Hell, a red-headed rogue who made his reputation centuries ago with Eve and Lilith. In Huysmans' *La Bàs*, Gévingey, an astrologer, tells Durtal (pp. 146, 148) that according to some theories:

> The incubi take the semen lost by men in dreams and make use of it. . . . Can a child be born of such a union?

The possibility of this kind of procreation has been up-
held by the Church doctors, who affirm, even, that children born of such commerce are heavier than others
and can drain three nurses without taking on flesh. . . .
If the woman is not the victim of a spell, if she voluntarily
consorts with the impure spirit, she is always awake when
the carnal act takes place. If, on the other hand, the woman
is the victim of sorcery, the sin is committed either while
she is asleep or while she is awake, but in the latter case
she is in a cataleptic state which prevents her from de-
fending herself.

Incubacy and succubacy, then, symbolize a form of
demonic oppression which may be a form of limited physical possession and which may lead to complete possession.
The relationship between sex and possession has been discussed most recently by William Sargant, in his book
*The Mind Possessed: A Physiology of Possession, Mysti-
cism and Faith Healing.* According to Mr. Sargant: "The
act of sex and orgasm . . . greatly increases suggestibility
and so facilitates the implantation of belief. . . . Repeated
induced orgasmic collapse has therefore been used to produce states of deep hysterical trance" (p. 88). (Cf. the
similar effect of drugs in relation to possession. Note the
suggested relationship in Levin's *Rosemary's Baby.*) The
tantric cults of the East have used sexual intercourse "to
strengthen religious group feelings and to bring about states
of possession by divine and demonic powers" (p. 89). Even
in Western cultures, where sexual methods have until
recently at least been driven underground by Christian
ethics, Satanist groups employ sex practices in which, according to Sargant, "the devotees believe themselves to be
possessed by the Devil and his minions" (p. 91).

That such sensualism is a form of limited or temporary
possession is suggested by William Faulkner's curious use
of the succubus-vampire image in describing the black
preacher as he delivers the Easter sermon in *The Sound
and the Fury* (New York: Random House, 1929, p. 367):
"With his body he seemed to feed the voice that, succubus
like, had fleshed its teeth in him." Brother Shagog, of course,
is "possessed," "inspirited," "entheosed" (cf. *enthusiasm*,
literally "a god within"), but with the *Holy Spirit* rather
than an *unholy spirit.* Just as Paul admonished believers,
"Be not drunk with wine, wherein is excess, but be filled
with the Spirit," so one might admonish by implication:
"As an unbeliever can be yielded to, possessed and con-

trolled by a demonic spirit, believers keep on being filled by the blessed Holy Spirit of God."

The phenomenon of spirit possession and of victory through Christ is depicted in graphic detail in the final chapter of James Baldwin's first novel *Go Tell It on the Mountain* (New York: Signet, 1954, pp. 167-68):

> ...Something moved in John's body which was not John. He was invaded, set at naught, possessed. This power had struck John, in the head or in the heart; and, in a moment, wholly, filling him with an anguish that he could never in his life have imagined, that he surely could not endure, that even now he could not believe, had opened him up; had cracked him open, as wood beneath the axe cracks down the middle, as rocks break up; had ripped him and filled him in a moment, so that John had not felt the wound, but only the agony, had not felt the fall, but only the fear; and lay here, now, helpless, screaming, at the very bottom of darkness.
>
> He wanted to rise—a malicious, ironic voice insisted that he rise—and, at once, to leave this temple and go out into the world.... In his turning the center of the whole earth shifted, making of space a sheer voice and a mockery of order, and balance, and time. Nothing remained: all was swallowed up in chaos.

Here again is the imagery of turning, with the center broken, shifting, causing things to "fall apart," disordered, chaotic.

And then, in "the darkness ... full of demons crouching, waiting to worry him with their teeth again" (p. 172), John

> saw the Lord for a moment only; and the darkness, for a moment only, was filled with a light he could not fear. Then, in a moment, he was set free; his tears sprang as from a fountain; his heart, like a fountain of waters, burst. Then he cried: "Oh, blessed Jesus! Oh, Lord Jesus! Take me through! ..." Yes, the night had passed, the powers of darkness had been beaten back. He moved among the saints..., one of their company now; weeping, he yet could find no words to speak of his great gladness; and he scarcely knew how he moved, for his hands were new, and his feet were new, and he moved in a new Heaven-bright air (p. 178).

But not all cases of demon possession in modern literature end with exorcism and the powers of darkness beaten back. According to the astrologer in *La Bàs*, victims of demon possession, including voluntary incubacy and succubacy, frequently die by suicide or some other form of violent death, or they end in madness (p. 148).

That Rayber, the Humanist schoolteacher in *The Violent Bear It Away*, is "possessed" by evil spirits becomes clear. His remark when Old Tarwater went to live with him applies ironically to himself and not to the Old Prophet: " 'Ha,' he said, 'my house is swept and garnished and here are the seven other devils, all rolled into one!' " (p. 344). Rayber's end is both madness and collapse—but only with a whimper, not a bang. He is last seen standing "woodenly," a dehumanized, mechanical contraption beyond feeling—resembling his nineteenth century predecessor, Roger Chillingworth, in Hawthorne's *The Scarlet Letter* (Columbus, Ohio: Ohio State University Press, 1962, p. 244), who turned into a very fiend and "positively withered up, shrivelled away . . . like an uprooted weed that lies wilting in the sun." But before their demise, both Rayber and Roger, despite their diabolic ends, unwittingly serve to effect the divine purpose, working on the Lord's side without knowing it. The words of the dying Arthur Dimmesdale apply equally as well to young Tarwater vis-à-vis the stranger and Rayber: "God is merciful! He hath proved his mercy most of all in my afflictions. . . . By sending yonder dark and terrible old man, to keep the torture always at red-heat! By bringing me hither to die this death of triumphant ignominy before these people! Had either of these agonies been wanting, I had been lost forever!" Like Dimmesdale, young Tarwater learns that "the mercy of the Lord burns."

Similarly, in Lewis' *Perelandra*, Professor Weston who, demon possessed, becomes the Un-man, serves to test the virtue of the Green Lady. "The weakest of all weak things," Mark Twain wrote in "The Man That Corrupted Hadleyburg" (*The Complete Short Stories of Mark Twain*, New York: Bantam, 1957, p. 383), "is a virtue which has not been tested in the fire." Weston became demon possessed when "he gave up his will and reason to the bent Eldil" (Lewis, p. 188): " 'I call that force into me completely. . . .' Then horrible things began happening. A spasm like that preceding a deadly vomit twisted Weston's face out of recognition. As it passed, for one second something like the old Weston reappeared—the old Weston, staring with eyes of horror and howling, 'Ransom, Ransom! For Christ's sake don't let them——' and instantly his whole body spun round as if he had been hit by a revolver-bullet and he fell to the earth, and was there rolling at Ransom's feet, slavering and chattering and tearing up the moss by handfuls" (p. 96). Like Chillingworth, like Rayber, like Simon Clerk in Charles Williams' *All Hallows Eve*, this possessed Un-man becomes a grotesque monster and meets a monster's end. As Ransom engages him in physical duel, he resembles a mandrill, the living death, the "eternal Surd in the universal mathematic," a Thing with tripartite body, an It which Ransom smashes with a stone and hurls into a sea of fire.

Also meeting a violent end is the demon-possessed Rechele in *Satan in Goray*. "For a long time now someone inside her had been thinking twistedly, someone had been asking questions, and replying as though a dialogue went on in her mind. . . " (p. 139), a disputation between the sacred and profane spirits. Samael, a prince of Hell, came to her at night and violated her, and "a destroyer demon grew in her womb" (p. 145). She "fell prisoner in the net of the Outer Ones and a *dybbuk* possessed her. . . . Her shape was completely changed and her face was as chalk and her lips were twisted as with a seizure . . . and the pupils of her eyes were turned back after an unnatural fashion: And the voice that cried from her was not her voice: For her voice was a woman's voice and the *dybbuk* cried with the voice of a man with such weeping and wailing that terror seized all that were there and their hearts dissolved with fear and their knees trembled" (p. 148).

The notion of possession by a *dybbuk*, according to Jewish folklore the spirit of a departed human, is, like the notion of Regan's possession by the spirit of the departed Captain Howdy in *The Exorcist*, in violation of Scripture, which seems to teach that demons are fallen angels. Nor does the act of exorcism in the two novels conform to Scripture. In Singer's novel, Reb Mordecai Joseph first relies upon the Torah scroll and the smoke of incense to drive out the *dybbuk*, but the result is only more violent oppression of Rechele. Eventually, blasts of the ram's horn and sacred adjurations supposedly cause the spirit to depart, leaving the victim to die shortly thereafter. In Blatty's novel, the repeated rite of exorcism is futile until the evil spirit leaves the child at Karras' challenge and enters the exorcist, driving him to a violent death.

In the Scriptures, Christ "cast out spirits with a word" (Matt. 8:16), and Christ's disciples simply cast out demons in the name of Jesus (Mark 16:17; Luke 10:17), not resorting to ritualistic conjurations and not invoking the name of Jesus as a magic talisman or power in itself, but trusting in the power of the omnipotent person behind that name. On at least one occasion, when the disciples failed in their attempt to exorcise an evil spirit, Christ told them, "This kind goeth not out except by prayer and fasting" (Matt. 17:21; Mark 9:29).

At the end of Blish's *Black Easter*, the demons loosed upon the earth, and possessing it, refuse to return to hell, even when Father Domenico adjures them in the name of Christ. To the ecclesiastical practitioners of white magic, the name of Christ is only a talisman with no power of the person behind it. And a world which declares God dead, and lives as if He were, learns to its own peril that Satan and his cosmocrats are not dead. The center broken, "circles of desolation spread away from the ritual circles" (Blish, p. 165); the gyre widens, and things fall apart.

The "core of faith is lost," and so the demonic cosmocrats overwhelm mankind. Herein lies at once both an indication of the *cause* of the widening circle of diabolism, as reflected in modern literature, and its *cure*. The center, the core of faith, can be broken by self-serving materialism. "When materialism is rotten-ripe, magic takes root," Huysmans wrote in *La Bàs* (p. 261). Poet Richard Wilbur has remarked: "Since the 'pursuit of happiness' too often entails stupid goals and a strenuous selfishness, it's not surprising that the 'diabolic' should often be found in American life. Is that what Lawrence means?" (letter to the present author, October 20, 1974). In his poem entitled "Matthew VIII, 28ff." Wilbur expresses it as follows:

> Rabbi, we Gadarenes
> Are not ascetics; we are fond of wealth and possessions.
> Love, as you call it, we obviate by means
> Of the planned release of aggressions.
>
> We have deep faith in prosperity.
> Soon, it is hoped, we will reach our full potential.
> In the light of our gross product, the practice of charity
> Is palpably inessential.
>
> It is true that we go insane;
> That for no good reason we are possessed by devils;
> That we suffer, despite the amenities which obtain
> At all but the lowest levels.
>
> We shall not, however, resign
> Our trust in the high-heaped table and the full trough;
> If you cannot cure us without destroying our swine,
> We had rather you shoved off.

There can be no exorcism when the True Exorcist is rejected in favor of a "gross" product, when swine are preferred to the Savior. Perhaps demon influence and possession are increasing because men choose to possess their demons. In his novel *Mr. Sammler's Planet* (Greenwich, Conn.: Fawcett-Crest, 1970, p. 71), Saul Bellow put it this way: "Consciousness and pains? The flight from the consciousness into the primitive? Liberty? Privilege? Demons? The expulsion of those demons and spirits from the air, where they had always been, by enlightenment and rationalism? And mankind had never lived without its possessing demons and had to have them back!"

Perhaps Huysmans' *La Bàs* provides the most pertinent expression of the cause, and, by inversion, the cure of demonism: "The unsatisfied need for the supernatural [is] driving people, in default of something loftier, to spiritism and the occult" (p. 6). Man's "unsatisfied need for the supernatural" which only Christ can satisfy, his broken center which only Christ can mend, turns him to Satan and his cosmocrats. And whose default is it? His, to be sure, but also that of every believer who does not offer that "loftier" supernaturalism to be found only in Christ. "In Christendom," Emerson asked, "where is the Christian?" Where indeed? Surely this is the time of which Yeats wrote, a time when "the best lack all conviction, while the worst/ Are full of passionate intensity." In such an apocalyptic time, the believer is perhaps best represented by the Christian knight in Randall Jarrell's poem "The Knight, Death, and the Devil," based on Durer's 1513 engraving illustrating, as the artist's diary says, "the knight of Christ riding by the side of the Lord Jesus, and guarding the truth":

> . . . In fluted mail; upon his lance the bush
> Of that old fox; a sheep-dog bounding at his stirrup,
> In its eyes the cast of faithfulness (our help,
> Our foolish help); his dun war-horse pacing
> Beneath in strength, in ceremonious magnificence;
> His castle—some man's castle—set on every crag;
> So, companioned so, the knight moves through this world.
> The fiend moos in amity; Death mouths, reminding:
> He listens in assurance, has no glance
> To spare for them, but looks past steadily
> At—at—
>   a man's look completes itself.
> The death of his own flesh, set up outside him;
> The flesh of his own soul, set up outside him—
> Death and the devil, what are these to him?

His being accuses him—and yet his face is firm
In resolution, in absolute persistence;
The folds of smiling do for steadiness;
The face is its own face—a man does what he must—
And the body underneath it says: *I am.*

Or it says, "Greater is he that is in me than he that is
in the world." Though things in the macrocosm fall apart
and the blood-dimmed tide is loosed, with *Him* at the center
of the microcosm, *it will hold.*

Notes

1. J. Dwight Pentecost, *Your Adversary, the Devil*, p. 37.
2. *The Undying Fire* (New York: M. A. Donohue and Co., 1919).
3. *The Devil in Legend and Literature*, pp. 272-73.
4. *Speak of the Devil* (Garden City, New York: Doubleday, 1945), p. 1.
5. *The Devil in 16th Century German Literature: The Teufelsbucher* (Frankfort: Peter Lang, 1972), p. 7.
6. Preface to *The Screwtape Letters* (New York: Macmillan, 1959).
7. Joris-Karl Huysmans, *La Bàs (Down There): A Study in Satanism*, p. 316.
8. *Mystery and Manners*, ed. Sally and Robert Fitzgerald (New York: Farrar, Straus, and Giraux, 1961), p. 32.
9. *Three by Flannery O'Connor* (New York: Signet, 1962), p. 326.
10. *Radical Innocence* (Princeton: Princeton University Press, 1971), p. 27.
11. "Baudelaire," *Selected Essays, 1917-1932* (New York: Harcourt, 1932), p. 337.
12. "Flannery O'Connor's Devil," *Sewanee Review* (Summer 1962). pp. 395-407.
13. One of the most perceptive reviews of *The Exorcist* and its flaws is D. Keith Mano's "The Gimlet Eye: Exorcise the Body," *National Review* (April 12, 1974), pp. 432-33.
14. "Baudelaire in Our Time," *Essays Ancient and Modern* (New York: Harcourt, 1932), p. 72.
15. "The Writer in a Changing Society," *Thoughts in the Wilderness* (New York: Harper, 1957), p. 219.
16. Randall Jarrell, "The Knight, Death, and the Devil," *Complete Poems* (New York: Farrar, Straus, 1969).
17. James Blish, *Black Easter, or Faust Aleph-Null* (London: Faber and Faber, 1968), p. 28.
18. Isaac Bashevis Singer, *Satan in Goray* (New York: Avon Books, 1955).
19. *Modern Poetry and the Tradition* (Chapel Hill: University of North Carolina Press, 1939), pp. 136-72.

20. *Perelandra* (New York: Collier, 1962; originally published in 1944).

21. *Cotton Mather: The Puritan Priest* (New York: Harcourt, 1963; originally published in 1891), p. 71.

A Selected Bibliography

I. Primary Sources

Andreyev, Leonid. *Satan's Diary*. New York: Boni and Liveright, 1920.

Arthur, Robert. "Satan and Sam Shay," in *Speak of the Devil*, ed. Sterling North and C. B. Boutell, Garden City, N.Y.: Doubleday, 1945.

Auden, W. H. "Danse Macabre," *Collected Poems*, 1927-57. New York: Random House, 1967.

Baldwin, James. *Go Tell It on the Mountain*. New York: Knopf, 1953.

Barbey, d'Aurevilly. *Les Diaboliques*. Translated by Ernest Boyd. New York: Knopf, 1925.

Barry, Philip. *War in Heaven*. New York: Coward-McCann, 1938.

Baudelaire, Charles. *Fleurs Du Mal (The Flowers of Evil)*. Edited by George Dillon and Edna St. Vincent Millay. New York: Harper, 1936 (originally published in 1857). (See especially "The Litanies of Satan.)

Beerbohm, Max. "Enoch Soames," *Seven Men*. London: W. Heinemann, 1919.

Benet, Stephen Vincent. *The Devil and Daniel Webster*. New York: Farrar and Rinehart, 1937 (originally published in *Saturday Evening Post*, 1926).

Bernanos, Georges. *Sous le Soleil de Satan (Under the Sun of Satan)*. Translated by H. L. Bensse. New York: Pantheon, 1949.

Blatty, William Peter. *The Exorcist*. New York: Bantam, 1971.

Blish, James. *Black Easter, or Faust Aleph-Null*. London: Faber and Faber, 1968. (Cf. the other two novels in the trilogy: *Doctor Mirabilis* and *A Case of Conscience*.)

Bowen, Elizabeth. "The Demon Lover," *The Demon Lover & Other Stories*. London: Jonathan Cape, 1945.

Boyle, Virginia Frazer. *Devil Tales*. New York: Harper, 1900.

Cabell, James Branch. *The Devil's Own Dear Son*. New York: Farrar, 1949.

Caldwell, Taylor. *Dialogues with the Devil*. Greenwich, Conn.: Fawcett-Crest, 1967.

Collier, John. "Thus I Refute Beelzy," "Bottle Party," "The Devil, George, and Rosie," from *Presenting Moonshine*. New York: Viking, 1941.

———. *Defy the Foul Fiend*. New York: Knopf, 1934.

"Devil Take the Skillet," "The Devil's Pretty Daughter," "Casting out the Devil," from *The Devil's Pretty Daughter, and Other Ozark Folk Tales*. Coll. by Vance Randolph. New York: Columbia University Press, 1955.

Doderer, Heimito von. *The Demons*. Translated by Richard & Clara Winston, New York: Knopf, 1961.

Eliot, T. S. *Murder in the Cathedral*. New York: Harcourt, 1935.

Flaubert, Gustave. *The Temptation of St. Anthony*. Translated by Lofcadio Hern. New York: Alice Harriman Co., 1910 (originally published in 1874).

France, Anatole. *La Revolte des Anges (The Revolt of the Angels)*. Translated by Mrs. Wilfrid Jackson. Paris: Calmann-Levy, 1914.

Garnett, Richard. "The Demon Pope," from *The Twilight of the Gods*. New York: Dodd, Mead, 1924.

Gide, Andre. *The Counterfeiters*, with Journal. Translated by Dorothy Bussy and Justin O'Brien. New York: Random House, 1973 (originally published in 1925).

Graves, Robert. "The Devil's Advice to Story-Tellers," in *Collected Poems*. New York: Doubleday, 1961.

Greene, Graham. "The Hint of an Explanation," in *Twenty-One Stories*. New York: Viking, 1947.

———. *Brighton Rock*. New York: Viking, 1938.

———. *The End of the Affair*. New York: Viking, 1951.

Huysmans, Joris-Karl. *La Bàs (Down There): A Study in Satanism*. Translated by Keene Wallis. New York: University Books, 1958 (originally published in 1891).

Jarrell, Randall. "The Knight, Death and the Devil," in *Complete Poems*. New York: Farrar, Straus, Giroux, 1969.

Lagerkvist, Par. "The Lift That Went Down to Hell," in *The Marriage Feast*. New York: Hill and Wang, 1954.

Levin, Ira. *Rosemary's Baby*. New York: Dell, 1967.

Lewis, C. S. *The Screwtape Letters*. New York: Macmillan, 1961.

———. *Perelandra*. New York: Macmillan, 1944. (Cf. the other novels in the trilogy: *Out of the Silent Planet* and *That Hideous Strength*.)

———. "Wormwood," in *Poems*. Edited by Walter Hooper. New York: Harcourt, 1964.

MacLeish, Archibald. *J.B.* New York: Houghton Mifflin, 1958.

Mano, D. Keith. *Bishop's Progress*. Boston: Houghton Mifflin, 1968.

Masefield, John. "The Devil and the Old Man," in *A Mainsail Haul*. New York: Macmillan, n.d.

Mencken, H. L. "From the Memoirs of the Devil," in *A Book of Burlesques*. New York: John Lane, 1916.

Merejkowski, Dmitri. *Romance of Leonardo da Vinci*. Translated by Bernard Guilbert Guerney. New York: Modern Library, 1928.

North Sterling, and C. B. Boutell, eds. *Speak of the Devil*. Garden City, New York: Doubleday, 1945.

Oates, Joyce Carol. "Demons," from *The Wheel of Love.* Greenwich, Conn.: Fawcett-Crest, 1972.

O'Connor, Flannery, *The Violent Bear It Away.* New York: Farrar, Straus, 1960.

Paget, Violet. *Satan the Waster.* New York: John Lane, 1920.

Pirandello, Luigi. "The Evil Spirit," in *The Naked Truth, and Eleven Other Stories.* New York: E. P. Dutton, 1934.

Powys, John Cowper. *Lucifer: A Poem.* London: Macdonald & Co., 1956.

Powys, T. F. "Only the Devil," "The Devil," in *God's Eyes A-Twinkle.* London: Chatto and Windus, 1947.

———. "The Devil and the Good Deed," in *Rosie Plum, and Other Stories.* London: Chatto and Windus, 1966.

Rudwin, Maximilian. *Devil Stories.* New York: Knopf, 1921.

Sand, George. *The Devil's Pool.* New York: George Richmond, 1894.

Sartre, Jean-Paul. *The Devil and the Good Lord.* New York: Knopf, 1960.

Sayers, Dorothy. *Devil to Pay,* in *Four Sacred Plays.* London: Victor Gollanz, 1948.

Shapiro, Karl. "The Progress of Faust," in *Trial of a Poet, and Other Poems.* New York: Reynal and Hitchcock, 1947.

Shaw, George Bernard. *Man and Superman.* Westminster: Constable, 1903.

Singer, Isaac Bashevis. *Satan in Goray.* New York: Avon Books, 1963 (originally published in 1955).

———. *The Seance.* New York: Avon Books, 1969.

Stevens, Wallace. "Esthetique du Mal," in *Transport to Summer.* New York: Knopf, 1947.

Stewart, Fred M. *The Mephisto Waltz.* New York: Coward-McCann, 1969.

Tryon, Thomas. *The Other.* Greenwich, Conn.: Fawcett-Crest, 1971.

Twain, Mark. *The Mysterious Stranger.* New York: Harper, 1916.

Wagner, Sharon. *Shades of Evil.* New York: Beagle Books, 1974.

Wallerstein, James S. *The Demon's Mirror.* New York: Bellamy Press, 1951.

Wilbur, Richard. "Matthew VIII, 28ff." *Hudson Review* XXI (Winter 1968-69), p. 645.

Wilder, Thornton. *The Cabala.* New York: Albert and Charles Boni, Inc., 1926.

Williams, Charles. *All Hallows Eve.* New York: Farrar, Straus, 1948.

———. *The Greater Trumps.* New York: Avon-Bard, 1950. (Cf. other works by Williams, such as *War in Heaven*, 1930; *Descent into Hell*, 1937; et al.)

II. Secondary Sources

Bamberger, Bernard J. *Fallen Angels.* Philadelphia: Jewish Publ. Society of America, 1952.

Barnhouse, Donald Grey. *The Invisible War.* Grand Rapids: Zondervan, 1965.

Bounds, E. M. *Satan: His Personality, Power, & Overthrow.* Grand Rapids: Baker, 1963.

Carus, Paul. *The History of the Devil and the Idea of Evil.* Chicago, 1900.

Chafer, Lewis Sperry. *Satan: His Motive and Methods.* Grand Rapids: Zondervan, 1919.

Coulange, Louis. *The Life of the Devil.* London: Alfred Knopf, 1929.

Cushman, L. W. *The Devil and Vice in English Dramatic Literature Before Shakespeare.* London: Frank Cass & Co., 1970.

Defoe, Daniel. *History of the Devil.* Philadelphia: Leary & Getz, 1726.

Devils and Demons: A Dictionary of Demonology. New York: Pyramid, n.d.

Elwood, Roger. *Strange Things Are Happening: Satanism, Witchcraft, & God.* Elgin, Ill.: David C. Cook, 1973.

Emmanuel, Pierre. *Baudelaire: The Paradox of Redemptive Satanism.* University, Alabama: University of Alabama Press, 1970.

Fishwick, Marshall W. *Faust Revisited: Some Thoughts on Satan.* New York: Seabury, 1963.

Hansen, Chadwick. *Witchcraft at Salem.* New York: Braziller, 1969.

Hawkes, John. "Flannery O'Connor's Devil," *Sewanee Review* (Summer 1962), pp. 395-407.

Houston, John Porter. *The Demonic Imagination: Style and Theme in French Romantic Poetry.* Baton Rouge: Louisiana State Univ. Press, 1969.

Hughes, Pennethorne. *Witchcraft.* Baltimore: Penguin, 1952.

Huxley, Aldous. *The Devils of Loudun.* New York: Harper, 1952.

Kelly, Henry Ansgar. *The Devil, Demonology, & Witchcraft: The Development of Christian Beliefs in Evil Spirits.* Garden City, New York: Doubleday, 1968.

Langton, Edward. *Satan, A Portrait: A Study of the Character of Satan Through All the Ages.* London: Skeffington & Son, 1945.

―――. *Essentials of Demonology: A Study of Jewish and Christian Doctrine, Its Origin and Development.* London: Epworth, 1949.

Lyons, Arthur. *The Second Coming: Satanism in America.* New York: Dodd, Mead: Award Books, 1970.

McCasland, Shelby Vernon. *By the Finger of God: Demon Possession and Exorcism in Early Christianity in the Light of Modern Views of Mental Illness.* New York: Macmillan, 1951.

May, John R. *Toward a New Earth: Apocalypse in the American Novel.* South Bend, Ind.: University of Notre Dame Press, 1972.

Michelet, Julian. *Satanism and Witchcraft.* New York: Citadel, 1939.

Nevius, John L. *Demon Possession* (originally titled: *Demon Possession and Allied Themes*). Grand Rapids: Kregel, 1968.

Oesterreich, T. K. *Possession, Demoniacal and Other.* New York: University Books, 1966 (originally published in 1930).

Penn-Lewis, Mrs., and Evan Roberts. *War on the Saints.* London: Marshall Brothers, 1912.

Pentecost, J. Dwight. *Your Adversary, the Devil.* Grand Rapids: Zondervan, 1969.

Praz, Mario. "Metamorphoses of Satan," in *The Romantic Agony.* New York: Oxford, 1933.

Roos, Keith L. *The Devil in 16th Century German Literature: The Teufelsbucher.* Frankfort: Peter Lang, 1972.

Rougemont, Denis de. *The Devil's Share.* New York: Pantheon, 1944.

Rudwin, Maximilian. *The Devil in Legend and Literature.* New York: AMS Press, 1970 (originally published in 1931).

Sargant, William Walters. *The Mind Possessed: A Physiology of Possession, Mysticism, and Faith Healing.* Philadelphia: Lippincott, 1974.

Satan, A Collection of Essays. Introduction by Charles Moeller. New York: Sheed and War, 1952. (The "green-bound volume" alluded to in Blatty's *The Exorcist.*)

Sayers, Dorothy. "The Faust Legend and the Idea of the Devil," in *The Poetry of Search and the Poetry of Statement.* London: Victor Gollancz, 1963.

Scott, Sir. Walter. *Letters on Demonology and Witchcraft.* New York: Ace Books, 1970 (originally published in 1830).

Starkey, Marion L. *The Devil in Massachusetts.* Garden City, New York: Doubleday-Dolphin, 1961 (originally published in 1949).

Stein, William Bysshe. *Hawthorne's Faust: A Study of the Devil Archetype.* Gainesville: University of Florida Press, 1953.

Summers, Montague. *The History of Witchcraft and Demonology.* New York: Dell, 1956 (originally published in 1925).

Thompson, R. Lowe. *The History of the Devil: The Horned God of the West.* New York: Harcourt, 1929.

Unger, Merrill F. *Demons in the World Today.* Wheaton, Ill.: Tyndale, 1971. (Cf. his earlier book *Biblical Demonology*, 1952.)

Wall, J. Charles. *Devils.* London: Methuen, 1904 (reissued, Detroit: Singing Tree Press, 1968).

Wedeck, Harry E. *The Triumph of Satan.* Secaucus, N.J.: Citadel Press, 1970. (See especially Chapter XII, "Satan in Literature.")

Williams, Charles. *Witchcraft.* New York: World, Meridian, 1959 (originally published in 1941).

Wilson, Colin. *The Occult: A History.* New York: Vintage, 1971.

Woods, Barbara Allen. *The Devil in Dog Form: A Partial Type-Index of Devil Legends.* Berkeley and Los Angeles: University of California Press, 1959.

PART FOUR

Demonology in
Anthropological Perspective

8

Spirit Possession as It Relates to Culture and Religion

A Survey of Anthropological Literature

A. R. TIPPETT

This paper has been prepared by a social anthropologist. His assignment has been to bring together (1) a body of data about possession manifestations over the globe, and (2) some information on the relationship of possession to culture. For purposes of this paper "possession" is taken to include both individual and collective manifestations, individuals attacked by evil spirits and the possession of mediums for communal purposes.

For purposes of space a large portion of the paper presented at the Symposium has been omitted. This covered the distribution of possession through history, through the geographical regions of the world and through the great religions. However, the sources for this eliminated section have been retained in the bibliography.[1]

Theoretical Preamble

Any study of spirit possession necessarily takes us back to Tylor's *theory of embodiment*. One reason why Western theologians, medical men and psychologists have trouble with the cross-cultural study of demon possession is that they refuse to do their thinking outside their own scientific world view. If there is anything that an anthropologist may contribute to this colloquium it would probably be at that point—a request (at least for the experimental purpose of this present discussion) for us to consider spirit possession in cross-cultural situations by our "sitting where they sit" and trying to consider things in the logico-philosophical frame of reference of the communal societies themselves.

Tylor did not argue the scientific rightness of his theory of embodiment for his own day and civilization, but rather that religion had evolved through this stage on its way to monotheism. But having given birth to the theory, he was never thereafter really able to dispose of it, as we shall see when we come shortly to discuss the research of John L. Nevius on *Demon Possession* (1894). But even so, it was Tylor who exposed the ethnopsychology of peoples who believed in the possibility of possession.

Briefly stated, the theory says:

> Spirits are supposed able either to exist and act, flitting free about the world, or to become incorporate for more or less time in solid bodies. . . .
>
> The theory of embodiment serves several highly important purposes in savage and barbarian philosophy. On the one hand it provides an explanation of the phenomena of morbid exaltation and derangement, especially as connected with abnormal utterance, and this view is extended as to produce an almost general doctrine of disease. On the other hand, it enables the savage either to "lay" a hurtful spirit in some body and so get rid of it, or to carry about a useful spirit for his service in a material object, to set it up as a deity for worship . . . (Radin's ed., 209).

From this definition Tylor went on to argue that "the savage theory of daemoniacal possession and obsession" still remains the dominant theory of disease and inspiration among the "lower races" (210).* His personal view was that this would gradually be superseded by higher medical knowledge (221), although a century later the problem and indeed the whole subject is very much with us still (enough for the Christian Medical Society to call this conference to discuss it).

"When the evil spirit is expelled," said Tylor in developing the theme further, "it is especially apt to enter some person standing near: hence the common saying 'idle spectators should not be present at an exorcism' " (221). More recently, in discussing the worldwide belief in intrusive evil spirits, the anthropologist Norbeck also resorts to common

---

* All citations to literature in this paper may be found in the appended Bibliography under the name of the author or editor. Numbers in parentheses refer to pages (210) or to date of publication and page (1961:215).

idiom—"the devil in me," "what possessed him?" He also points out that "behavior regarded as psychotic in our society occurs frequently in contexts which make it valued and normal," so the "borderline between pathology and normalcy is very difficult to draw" (Norbeck 1961:215). Neither is he the only anthropologist to point out this basic fact for our study. There is I. M. Lewis for example:

> Such is the incidence of mental stress and illness in our contemporary culture, that we do well to ponder how so many beliefs and experiences, which we relegate to abnormal psychology, find in other cultures a secure and satisfying outlet in ecstatic religion (1971:35).

Ruth Benedict wrote a significant article on the subject (1934).[2] Research emanating from Ohio State University has revealed its universality. A project investigated and coded 488 societies and identified cases of trance possession in 437 of the 488—90%. The societies were grouped regionally—Sub-Saharan Africa, Circum-Mediterranean, East Eurasia, Insular Pacific, North America and South America —and in no region did the percentage drop below 80% (Bourguignon 1974:10).[3]

Anthropological Perspective

Social anthropologists have been forced to interest themselves in spirit possession as a theme because they have been confronted with it personally in their field research— problems of multiple personality, accompanied by trembling, sweating, glossolalia and other forms of unusual behavior. Even if they got no further than objective description, they could not bypass it. Not all social anthropologists are competent to deal with the psychological aspects of dissociation, but most of them have gone considerably further than mere description. They have pressed for the relevance of such things as the social position of the medium, the cultural context of the performance, the expectations of the group and the religious world view within which the possessions are set by the participants themselves (cf. Firth 1969: ix-xiv). For these reasons it seems appropriate for the Christian Medical Society Symposium on Demonology to have an anthropological survey before them.

Perhaps anthropology should also warn a scientific audience like this against hoping for too much statistical data. Many of the situations which result in performances of possession are spontaneous and cannot be set up experimentally. This is why we are so dependent on the literature and notebooks of anthropologists, missionaries and colonial servants. Most of the performers cannot be recalled for interviewing. Even those cases which are stimulated deliberately, and in which communal assemblies have waited in expectation, many of them, especially those associated with esoteric cults, have been religious acts which must be performed in their entirety without interruption by any foreigner. The anthropologist or missionary has been able only to sit and observe, without any camera or tape recorder. Yet such case studies exist in abundance for the researcher who is willing to search them out one by one over many years.

Unexplained Data

If these cross-cultural records indicate any commonality, it is the association of possession with a variety of enthusiastic experience. *I fail to see how the experience can be interpreted, either psychologically or socially, without taking into account the world view and philosophical system of those who practice it.* I have a strong methodological problem with any attempt to dismiss the observed data of these accounts, because they create spiritual and psychological problems. As long as there are unexplained data the case is open. One recalls the work of Herskovits, recently republished (1971), which took possession seriously (apart from cases of manifest simulation), and reacted against any tendency to deal with everything within range of psychopathology, which he said "is to approach it handicapped by a fundamental misconception" (148). He considered the phenomena of possession as still yet "unsatisfactorily explained" (147). Anthropologically speaking, his work cannot be lightly dismissed, especially with respect to Afro-Americans, who share the biblical view of possession.

In the face of the unexplained data I want to suggest that it is possible to deal with such ideas as possession in either a pagan or Christian conceptual schema. It seems to me that a westerner can become subjectively involved with pagan enthusiasm in either one of two ways: he can *give himself over* to it and become possessed by the demonic power, or he can *confront* it on the same phenomenological level. In either case he believes in the reality of demonic presences. This he can do within the biblical world view. But to be a *disbeliever* disqualifies him for either experience.[4]

The old Haitian told the padre in Cave's novel *The Cross on the Drum* that he was not likely to be possessed because—

> You're too questioning. Even if you wanted to be [possessed] and tried to be, you'd be searching your own feelings too much. To be possessed a man has to let himself go . . . (250).

Eliminating the Spurious and Psychopathological

Manifestations of real or supposed spirit possession first need to be differentiated as belonging to one of three basic categories, which for the want of better terms I shall call *spurious, psychopathological,* and *prima facie genuine.* Of the first two I intend to say little in this paper, but even so they have to be noted and placed in the taxonomy (Lechler in Koch 1972:147-86).

Many critics have dismissed the whole business as completely phony and few field researchers will deny that they have met phony cases of simulated possession. Sometimes there is a simple motivation for these spurious cases— social or psychological—but usually there has to be *an acceptable climate for credulity.* (See "Cultural Context" below.) It may even be that the undesired presence of the missionary or anthropological observer is itself the cause of the supposed possession and prophetic utterance, the purpose of which is to get rid of him. And this may be a social rather than an individual felt need. It may be a defense mechanism or it may be exploitative, ventriloquistic or hypnotic. I merely indicate the diversity of possible motives and means, and leave a slot for it in my taxonomy.

In those cases where demon possession is connected with sickness and expressed in religious idiom shared by the whole community in a cross-cultural situation, at least for purposes of description and diagnosis, they will need to be treated as if genuine, within that world view or belief system. It may be that after the event they should be transferred to the psychopathological category. But as long as the patient, his corporate group, and the exorcist think in terms of possession, diagnosis and cure and even description can only be made within the idiom and behavior pattern.

A good example of this is described at length by Obeyesekere (1970), where a woman of Ceylon was possessed by an inferior ancestral spirit. The diagnostician, a Buddhist monk, used hypnosis and conversed with the demon. Demons being the embodiment of evil, clash with the higher Buddhist values, and the demon, not the woman, was held responsible for her behavior. All parties understood the situation. If the supposed demon possession is eventually found to be a cultural coping mechanism, then the case would be transferred to its correct category in the taxonomy, but this cannot be done by presupposition, because the group presupposition is that it is religious. It must be described first within its own idiom and belief system.

S. and R. Freed (1964:152-171) also discussed spirit possession as illness. This seems to be common in North India (see also Opler, 1958). The possession was frequently by a ghost from somewhere within the extended family complex (maybe the ghost of an elder brother or of a close friend from the mother's brother's village, etc.), and often the subject had unpleasant sex experiences and no help at hand. Here again data should be collected at its local face value (as religious) because not all cases of sickness can be explained as due to social conflicts.[5] In the same way in the New World African world of Voodoo and Spiritism Herskovits claims that we investigate a normal world, in which members of society view possession as something which could happen to them in the ordinary course of events (1951: 66-68, 371-372; 1964: 52-53). He also pointed out the remarkable consistency of motor behavior under possession in the "slavery area" where shaking and learning to "speak in tongues" is part of the initiation, and where interpretations tended to be prophecies, new cures, or how to cope with hostile magic (1958:216-217; cf. Métraux 1972:135ff.).

When one has eliminated the spurious and psychopathological cases one is still left with a considerable residue of material which appears to be genuine possession. I must agree with Montague Summers (cited in Nauman 1974:311):

> ... When every allowance has been made for incorrect diagnosis for ill-informed ascriptions of rare and obscure forms of both physical and mental maladies, for credulity, honest mistakes, and exaggerations of every kind, there will yet remain a very considerable quota which it seems impossible to account for and explain, save on the score of possession by some evil and hostile intelligence.

Within *prima facie* possession several anthropologists have devised their own classifications. Each makes a useful distinction of some kind.[6] Let us look at Firth and Lewis.

Spirit Mediumship and Spirit Possession

Firth (1969:x-xi) distinguishes between *spirit medium-*

ship and *spirit possession*. They are phenomenologically similar—an extra-human entity enters the body and takes control, and the individual passes through a personality change. The spirit medium, however, is involved in the function of communication, either one or two way, which invariably involves him in a speech utterance of some kind. In spirit possession the behavior does not necessarily (and certainly not intentionally) convey any message at all.

Both spirit mediumship and spirit possession have conceptual and operational fields (xi-xii). Conceptually they validate the reality of the spiritual world view of the group. Operationally they permit individuals a certain flexibility of behavior (rebellion within limits) and provide mechanisms for restoring control of the social group, which would otherwise be disrupted by the performance. Thus the very irregularity of the performances and the approved mode of treatment or adjustment may even work out for religious and social benefit. It certainly validates the religious world view, which holds the society together.

The conceptual complex of spirit mediumship and spirit possession contains an inbuilt explanation of sickness and its method of treatment. It identifies the normal channels of expectation and enjoys the confidence of the community.

Peripheral and Central Cults

Lewis differentiates between possession in *peripheral* and *central* cults, because a person subject to possession in the former lives a normal life in a normal social system, and the cult does not deal with the whole of life nor deny a man his place in the larger world, or even in its central religion. Central possession cults involve the autonomous deities, cosmological religion or ancestral cults, which maintain the moral integrity of the community. Peripheral possession tends to pay attention to women, downtrodden categories of men and odd depressed persons, or at the other end of the scale, individuals striving for status or prestige. The primary function of peripheral possession tends to emerge as "an oblique aggressive strategy" (1971:32) and is amoral or evil. Central possession cults are essentially moral. Peripheral possession tends to focus on individuals; central possession is individual only as this relates to the community. The two kinds may be found side by side in the same society.

Lewis illustrates this from the case of the Veddas in Ceylon (C. & B. Seligman 1911). The Veddas were a hunting and honey-gathering people. The shaman had the power to summon the spirit of a deceased ancestor or kinsman, who thereupon possessed him and spoke through his mouth. He approved the ceremony, gave advice on hunting and honey-gathering, and enquired of the health of the community. This is a central possession cult, concerned with public morality, communal activities and health. However, among the same people another possession cult was reported, in which an evil and foreign spirit afflicted a woman with illness. Thus the central and peripheral cults can be found side by side (Lewis 1971:133-35).

Illustrating from the case of the Korekore Shona of the Zambesi Valley (Garbett 1969) Lewis (1971:136-39) demonstrates the patterns of a central ancestral guardian cult through the operation of a possessed shaman. In this way natural phenomena—rainfall and fertility—is controlled, and also the moral order. Under possession the medium exhorts the people to avoid incest, adultery, homicide, sorcery and other practices which would upset the harmony of the social relations.

Lewis outlines the procedure whereby the shaman is validated. Upon his original manifestation of possession, the first assumption is that the individual is possessed by a foreign, and therefore, an evil spirit. The regular rituals for exorcism are, therefore, employed to "bring out" the spirit. If this fails, then he is put through a series of tests to see if the possessing spirit is really the ancestor. This process is "strictly controlled by the hierarchy of established mediums" (138). Thus the status is achieved rather than ascribed. Here is an interesting institutional mechanism for differentiating between kinds of possession which exist side by side: the moral guardian spirit and the evil foreign demon. As with the Veddas of Ceylon (see p. 13), the inspirational possession is a male monopoly, but the foreign spirits more often concentrate on women, who may use them to improve their condition.

One has to discover how ecstasy and possession operate with a moral quality in a total situation, to maintain values, morals or social equilibrium; to assure perpetuity, fertility, economic effectiveness, and so forth. Thus possession is "ultimately construed as ancestral inspiration" (147), and this moral significance is virtually an article of faith. (Lewis is not writing of all ancestral cults—only those using possession for inspirational moral purposes [148].)

Not all central possession cults are ancestral, but like the ancestral cults they are found side by side with peripheral possession. Knutsson's research on the Kallu institution among the Macha Galla of Ethiopia (1967), which is also one of Lewis' sources, may be cited here. This is probably the least-acculturated sub-unit of the large Galla tribe, the largest ethnic component of the country. To the Macha, the pan-Galla god, Waka, is the guardian of morality and punishes those who do wrong by withdrawing his support and exposing them to disaster and sickness. Waka is the central deity with cosmological dimensions. His religious practitioners, although hereditary officials, nevertheless compete for power and leadership in the local assemblies of kinsmen. They demonstrate their power through trance and possession, and depend on public recognition of their achievements—the drama of the performance and the skill of the divination, etc. This differs from the ancestral cult, but it is, nevertheless, equally a central possession cult. Among the same people one also meets with peripheral cults which concentrate on demons or evil spirits (*Zar* or *Setana*), which once again specialize in possessing women. (See Knutsson 1967, or Lewis 1971:150-58, for a commentary on this phenomenon.)

During the regular kallu ceremony, after an hour or so of drumming and singing, some participants may be possessed with somewhat violent results. When this happens the drummers surround the possessed and intensify the rhythm. When the possessed falls exhausted on the floor, the kallu intervenes to exorcise the possessing spirit. These spontaneous possessions are regarded by the kallu as negative and destructive, in that they bring sickness and suffering. In confrontation with these *zar* or *setana*, the kallu acts as an exorcist (Knutsson 1967: 91-92). Here is a power encounter between the *ayana* and the *zar* or *setana*.

Varieties of Possession

It was not by accident that the Society for Psychic Research was formed in the eighties. The theories of Darwin and Tylor stimulated much research by people in cross-cultural situations—especially missionaries. A good example of this is the research of John L. Nevius in China on possession and, among its manifestations, glossolalia. The time and the conditions were ripe for such research.

Research in China

1. *E. B. Tylor's Theory of Demonical Possession:* One of the early accounts of the theory of possession which may be considered as belonging to modern anthropology was that of E. B. Tylor, the father of the anthropological study of primitive religion. Tylor's theory of *daemoniacal possession* was based on a great many descriptions of the phenomenon which he had from travellers and missionaries who had observed it. Among the significant physical manifestations, the possessed individual's enthusiasm demonstrated "giant strength" and also "eloquence beyond his sober faculties to command" and afterwards the possession experience left him exhausted. Tylor pointed out that this tied up with "the dominant theory of disease and inspiration among the lower races": that is, Tylor was here reporting *animist theory*, not his own speculation about it. He regarded "the animistic interpretation, most genuine and rational in its proper place in man's intellectual history." This is Tylor, the early evolutionist placing this notion in the period of *savagery* according to the anthropological theory popular at that time. Tylor took from the animist theory of possession the idea of two kinds of spirit possession. He called them *disease-spirits* and *oracle-spirits* (Vol. II, 124). Spirit-possessed persons manifested godlike powers—strength and special skills—and the spirits were frequently vocal so that the possessed person became a medium.

2. *John L. Nevius' Research on Possession:* The Missionary, John L. Nevius, better known among missiologists than anthropologists, made a serious attempt to survey demon possession in China as early as 1879, although his findings were not published until 1894. The resultant work is still a significant compendium of data on the subject. He used a questionnaire sent to Protestant missionaries in all parts of China to be placed with "intelligent and reliable native Christians," who had the option of answering either in English or Chinese. He asked his respondents for identification of cases cited, with locations and dates. Among the questions, he asked one seeking a minute description of the symptoms, and another about the utterances of supposed possessed persons; he asked if these seemed to proceed from a different personality, and if the subject retained recollection of those utterances after the passing of such an abnormal state (41-43).

His respondents were scattered all over China. One informant, reporting from Fukien in the south from the city of Fuchow, and the district of Tu-ch'ing, and Chang-lo, after describing the enthusiasm said, "The voice of the spirit might be of a deceased husband or wife or a demon of 'the fox community' or a 'quiet demon' who talks and laughs. Some have the 'voice of a bird' and others speak in Mandarin (Northern Chinese) or some dialect" (46-47). The personality of the spirit was recognizable as a scholar or warrior, etc. (49).

Wang Wu-Fang's experience (Shantung) was that these possessing spirits could be classified in two types as those who clearly declare themselves and those who do not (53). He found the singing of a Christian hymn led the possessed person to cry out as if disturbed by it (55).

Wang Yung-ngen of Peking pointed out that persons who had no ability for song might become competent singers under possession, and others with no natural capacity for poetry could compose rhyme with ease under possession. He found northerners speaking the languages of the South, which they did not know, and oblivious to it after the conclusion of the experience (58). A Chefoo boy was possessed of a demon who spoke of his friends in Nanking (65). Many of the cases reported contained details of conversation with the demon: bargaining with respect to the price of the demon's departure—a dual personality type of thing.

A case reported by Chang Ah-liang of an incident at Yang-fu-Miao, forty *li* southeast of Taichao, records the question of a Christian exorcist, "Why do you talk in this foolish confused manner?" And this suggests that the language of the possessing spirit was not quite normal. One missionary informant at Foochow spoke of the spirit's speech "as far as I could follow it" (86), but the woman in this incident could have been speaking her home dialect. Here, the interesting thing was not that she used an uncommon dialect, but the theological content of the utterances which were identical with those in Mark 3:11. Only with a foreign spirit would these utterances be in a foreign language, otherwise the conference between the person and the spirit possessing him would be a meaningful conversation (83). However, even when meaningful, the subject might be ignorant of the conversation after the experience ended (85).

One of the findings (No. 9) of Nevius' survey was that

> many persons while demon possessed give evidence of knowledge which cannot be accounted for in ordinary ways. They often appear to know of the Lord Jesus as a divine person and show an aversion to, and a fear of Him. They sometimes converse in foreign languages of which in their normal states they are entirely ignorant (161).

3. *Nevius' Research and Tylor's Theory:* Nevius discusses Tylor's possession theory as argued by him as the natural animistic rationale to account for certain pathological facts "in its time in man's history"; that is, within the limits of savagery. He takes him to task for confining this to the period of savagery "while admitting that many causes have been medically explained in other ways." Nevertheless, he insisted on the continuity of possession unto his day (166ff.). He criticized Tylor for raising questions and dismissing them unanswered—why persons in abnormal states assume a new personality and act it out consistently, how they rise above their natural state with poetical and metaphorical utterances of a professional orator, how they speak accurately languages they have never heard or learned (173-174), and how highly cultivated civilizations have continued to accept the idea of possession—Egypt, Greece, Rome, India—supposedly a phenomenon limited to the savage level (183). Nevius felt that although possession has many forms which are similar to complaints known to pathology, this by no means proves that these are the only possible diagnoses (185).

Nevius differentiated types of possession in the following way. (1) *The automatic presentation and consistent acting out of a new personality.* This is not mere dramatization but has linguistic and other cultural validations developed as sub-points in his analysis. He distinguished it from that form of insanity by which a subject imagines he is, say, Napoleon (186-190). (2) *Knowledge and intellectual power, not possessed by the subject*—oratory, poetic capacity, speaking an unknown tongue (190-194). (3) With the change of personality there is also *a change of moral character* (194).

The Society for Psychical Research was formed in 1882 to organize and investigate various sorts of "phenomena which are *prima facie* inexplicable." It recognized "amidst much illusion and deception, an important body of facts to which this description would apply" (cited in Nevius, 222).

Nevius' survey ended with two appendices which contained a number of reports or testimonies. These permit us to see that he was aware of both cases of *spontaneous* possession and *induced* possession.

Voodoo in Haiti

Probably there is no better extant example of possession phenomena in the whole world than the form known as voodoo, especially that variety known in Haiti,[7] where it threatens to become the national religion, and bears on every aspect of social and political life (Courlander & Bastien 1966). Two good critical descriptions of the performance are provided by Métraux (1972, especially pp. 120-41, 394-97) and Herskovits (1971 [1937], 154-200, 314-17). The roots of this religion are found in Africa. It came to the new world with the slaves and mixed itself with Indian religion and Spanish Catholicism, so that Christian saints are identified with African *loa*. This has been researched by Herskovits, who has identified the specific *loa* equated with the saints in Brazil, Cuba and Haiti as a comparative study, and has traced out their respective African origins (1937: 635-43).

In the idiom of voodoo "the relationship between the *loa* and the man seized is compared to that which joins a rider to his horse"—mounting, saddling, riding, etc. When the possessed person experiences "an invasion of the body by a supernatural spirit," it is said that "the *loa* is seizing his horse" (120).

The intensity of the demonstration depends on the character of the *loa*. The possessed person is the *loa* himself for the duration of the performance. He behaves like him and speaks like him. The *loas'* characters are well known by the audience. The trance may last for two or three hours or even several days, and the "victim" remembers nothing of it afterwards. It may be that the person possessed is an aged woman, very much overweight and infirm, who during the performance will dance nimbly to the drum beat as she could never possibly have done in normal life. Yet she is not playing a part. She is indeed possessed. Métraux described a number of these characters and how they performed under possession (124-29).

A rather dramatic scene is described in the novel *The Cross on the Drum* in which a character is "married" to the deity Erzulie. This man turns in disgust from advances of an "old drunken bag of bones." However, the latter becomes possessed by Erzulie and the deity speaks in *lan-*

gage, a syncretistic speech of African, Indian and Spanish terms,[8] through this normally "obscene rack of bones" whom he despised. Possessed by Erzulie, he can no longer resist her, and he responds to the voice of the possessing deity, and the hag takes him by the hand and leads him off into the darkness (Cave 1958: 153).

The voodoo trance occurs in religious ceremonies either public or private. The spirits *must* take part in the performance. Considerable sacrifices have been offered to them, and their appearance at the correct moment is expected (Métraux 1972:130). The more *loa* who appear the better the omen, because it means they are pleased with the sacrifices (Herskovits 1971:177).

Possession may be induced by the *hungan* (voodoo priest) if he takes a woman by the hand and spins her round and round (170). Many cases are reported of unauthorized possession, a highly educated person, a white woman visitor, a woman under the taboo of mourning, for example (185-200, see also Deren 1953). If a person is really determined not to be possessed, certain precautions may be taken, a way of doing the hair, and wearing a certain charm. This is known as "mooring" the *loa*. The cautious person merely obtains the effect of mild intoxication, which soon passes (Métraux 1972:131).

In his description of the voodoo worship service and dance, Herskovits (1971:154-200) records the full text of a number of the voodoo songs (165-75, 187, 192-94) and describes at length the instruments of the band—three kinds of drums, which have to be baptized (183-85), irons and rattles. The drums are hollow logs of an African type, tuned by means of wooden pegs, and a goatskin stretched over them. The iron is the blade of a hoe, with a metal spike to strike it, and the rattles are calabashes with seeds or pebbles (cf. Jahn 1961:36-39). Herskovits also pointed out that it was no accident that the type of Protestantism most successful in Haiti is the form most hostile to voodoo, because it comes into *encounter* with it on a meaningful level, and he compared it with "the shouting sects" whose ritual behavior has a similar pattern (1971:290). Johnson said the same thing of the encounter between Christianity and Spiritism in Brazil (1968), a view endorsed by Willems in a book on Pentecostalism in that country (1967:123, 257).

Spiritism in Brazil

As Voodooism is to Haiti, so Spiritism is to Brazil. Despite their very great differences the two have a number of interesting similarities, among them the African world view brought to America by the slaves, the identification of African gods and spirits with Catholic saints (both for *Candomblé* [McGregor 1966:56-57] and *Umbanda* [185-91]), and many of the forms and occasions of sacrifice. Also common to them both is the phenomenon of spirit possession (see illustration in *ibid.*, opposite pp. 65, 79, 192), its equestrian terminology (203), the place of drums and rhythm, and glossolalia due to possession (78, 79, etc.). McGregor gives us a detailed description of the ceremony in which possession takes place (80-82), including an evaluation of the syncretism of its identification with Brazilian Catholicism (83).

The best critical analysis of Spiritism which I know is a master's thesis written by Harmon Johnson. He provides a table of the main features of possession in ten different forms of Spiritism, which he has differentiated in his thesis. I set out hereunder his table (65).

He confirms the equestrian terminology: *cavalos* (horses) have to be prepared for the planned ceremonies, although in four of his ten types, spectators are also possessed. As with voodoo, the possessed person's behavior is according to the character of the possessing divinity (1969: 51). These possessing gods or spirits may be alternatively spirits of the dead in six of the forms. In Kardecism they are never anything but spirits of the dead. He distinguishes between conscious and unconscious possession experiences and between spontaneous and induced performances, and enumerates a number of the stimuli used for inducement.

POSSESSION IN SPIRITISM

	Kardecism	Umbanda	Quimbanda	Macumba	Batuque	Para	Xango	Candomble	Caboclo Cults	Pagelance
Spirits of the dead	+	+	+	+			+		+	
Supernatural beings		+	+	+	+	+	+	+	+	+
Who is possessed										
Mediums	+	+	+	+	+		+		+	+
Initiates		+	+	+	+	+	+	+	+	
Anyone		+	+	+					+	

	1	2	3	4	5	6	7	8	9	10
Trance										
Ecstatic		+	+	+	+	+	+	+	+	+
Conscious	+	+	+	+				+		
Unconscious		+	+	+	+	+	+	+	+	+
Spontaneous	+	+	+	+	+			+	+	+
Induced	+	+	+	+	+	+	+	+	+	+
Sacrifices		+	+	+	+	+	+	+		
Drums		+	+	+	+	+	+	+		
Singing		+	+	+	+	+	+	+		
Dancing		+	+	+	+	+	+	+		
Tobacco		+	+	+	+	+	+	+	+	+
Drinking		+	+	+	+	+			+	+
Prayer	+	+	+	+	+	+	+	+	+	+

(Source: Johnson 1968:65)

Possession and Culture

What other data remains for me to give I shall use to illustrate some focal points with which we need to come to grips in our dealing with the dynamics of possession. These are (1) the importance of the social context, (2) the reality of the personality change, (3) the locus of control, and (4) the nature of the stimuli—spontaneous or induced.

The Importance of the Social Context

Some consideration needs to be given to the relationships of the manifestations of possession to their social context.

Plog's research on glossolalia at U.C.L.A. with two thousand questionnaires and two hundred personal interviews showed that glossolalia cut across classes, ages and sexes (Kelsey, 1964:129). Stark linked the rise of West Coast millenarian cults and "an increasing number of encounters with agents of the spirit world" with the sagging stock market of 1962 (Stark 1965:101). Martin (1960:36, 51) has argued its association with minority groups discriminated against by the intellectually privileged, thus regarding glossolalia as anti-rational and anti-intellectual protest.

Now, it should be pointed out that these are researches in scientific western society within the western world view and economic system. Furthermore, they are all *crisis* or *stress situations* and impose a negatively loaded bias on many situations of glossolalia which are not under stress at all. We need to remember that glossolalia is experienced by many ethnic groups as a perfectly normal thing.

Several anthropologists have taken up this theme of *deprivation* as a cause of possession. Harris (1957) discussing a possession complex in Kenya, known as *saka*, saw the subjects as deprived persons within the social structure, and the performance as the ritual mechanism whereby the problem is corrected. Lewis (1966) argued from the usual role of women in possession performances that this was due to their exclusion from authority in male-dominated society—i.e., spirit possession as a sex-war. Unfortunately, there are many societies where males are both dominant and possessed. Wilson (1967), in replying to Lewis, attributes the phenomenon to conflict, tension and jealousy between members of the *same* sex. If any one of these is adequate in the case discussed, obviously none can stand as a generalization.

I think we may move to an adequate solution if we begin by recognizing first that possession experience may be *individual* or *collective*. Most research on glossolalia has been done on western Pentecostals. I do not see that this can be done on a basis of "so many individuals," or "random samples"; because this is a *group experience*. Two thousand questionnaires and two hundred interviews can never record the shared experience between the glossolalist and his hearer within the groupness to which they both belong, or the emotional corporate concern of a gathered social unit that seeks a healing word from a friendly spirit, or the glossolalia of a peyote meeting. This complex multi-individual sharing cannot be recaptured by a random sample of individuals. The collective aspect is hard to measure (Métraux 1972:130).

In his study on possession in Haitian voodoo, Métraux makes a point of the "sympathetic concern" of the whole community gathered for the occasion, which "provides an atmosphere of moral and physical security which is conducive to total abandon in the state of trance" (Métraux 1959:22). Sadler describes a devotional songfest (*qawwali*) in a community of Indian dervishes where

> ...the community showed its concern and involvement and sense of brotherhood with the individual who went into trance and sustained him ... and at the same time shared in his enthusiasm—until the spirit left him and he fell to the ground exhausted, and the community that left the *qawwali*, when it was done, was a radiant, a transformed, a loving community (1964:86).

The finding that glossolalists cut across ages, sexes, and classes suggests that they are not all deprived or under stress. The important fact is whether the possession and glossolalia take place with a single individual or a group; or if an individual, is he by any chance a mediatorial figure in the group. The group must be identified. Herskovits devotes a chapter to this in *Life in a Haitian Valley*, and finds that the group involved is a "family," but not a simple nuclear family. It is "an extended set of relationships" frequently involving plural marriages (1971:xv).

The social context also seems to bear on the language spoken by the glossolalist, although this does not appear to have been researched. Lindblom described a possessed woman in the state of ecstasy. The words were taken to be foreign because they came from foreign spirits and significantly enough the demands made by the spirit were similarly culturally appropriate to that foreign tribe (Harris 1957:1046). This lines up with an experience of my own in southwest Ethiopia, where a group of converted witch doctors informed me that the tribe of the possessing spirit could be identified by the language he spoke; but when I mentioned a nearby language as one they had not included in their list, the spontaneous response was that this could never be, because that was the language of an uncircumcised tribe.

According to May (1956:86), the leader of the Dancing Religion Sect recognizes two kinds of "speaking spirits." One of these is a *foreign spirit*, a wandering ghost seeking salvation. The possessed subject will speak in the foreign language of the troublesome spirit. If it is an animal or nature spirit, the sounds will be meaningless. The second type, also foreign, is a *saved spirit*. A person possessed by such will speak in his native language.

Herskovits argues that possession and glossolalia occur only because the cultural world view permits them—or rather makes them normal and desirable:

> In terms of the patterns of Haitian religion, possession is
> not abnormal, but normal; it is set in its cultural mold
> as are all other phases of conventional living (1971:148).

Bourguignon also points out that the Haitian peasant does not consider possession to be abnormal. It is a sign of the choice of the gods and of their approval, even though the mechanisms encountered may be familiar in psychopathology. There is dissociation, the performance is unacceptable to the self in the normal roles of social life, and unacceptable to the group as a whole in normal life, and the persons involved are not blamed for what they do when the god is possessing them. Even so, the aim of the self may be furthered by the experience. Yet this also is dependent on the social consensus.

> Discontinuity in personal identity, the temporary substitution of other "selves" in the context of a belief in ritual possession by spirits, cannot be considered deviant in the reference system of Haitian culture (1965:56).

What I regard as important about Bourguignon's article is its recognition of cultural conditioning: the acceptance of spirit possession as a feature in Haitian culture, its relation to social structure and social situations, the needs of the self and the group, and its functioning within the frame of reference of the Haitian world view. In this it is vastly superior to much supposed cross-cultural scientific analysis which merely inflicts an agnostic world view upon what is after all a religious experience (cf. Métraux 1972: 129).

Thus it may be said that in those places where possession and glossolalia are most common the people are *expectant*. A society accepts the regularity of the notions of possession and glossolalia as normal, and the forms are highly institutionalized.

A good many of the cases described in this essay have reflected *a slavery ingredient* in the social context. In the cases of Voodooism and Spiritism it was the dominant causal factor, in that there was no other way whereby these religions could have merged or fused African gods and spirits with Catholic saints. But even back in Africa, the slavery complex, which was itself an African institution—the slavers merely capitalized on what was already there—still appears to have been a causal factor in the development of trance and possession cults.

Greenbaum studied trance and possession in Sub-Saharan Africa seeking to discover if it is random, and therefore the cases need unique explanations. She studied institutional correlations in terms of political and social structures, economy, settlement pattern, kinship, population and marriage arrangements (her structural variables). She used a sample of 114 societies relating possession trance with slavery and social stratification, and worked out a societal tree diagram. She found possession rather significantly related to slavery and by no means a random distribution (1972:39-57).

It seems to me, then, that the first essential for the researcher who sets out to explore possession manifestations is to master the world view of the people who practice it. It is only thus that we will discover why it is regarded so often as *normal*, why it is *expected*, and why it is so often *valued* so much.

Among the Eskimo, for example, whose shaman is highly ecstatic, the relation between man and nature, the taboo system, the seasonal rules and general life-style obtain cohesion from the world view. To this end the Eskimos depend on the shaman to deal with the weather, the chase, and the sick. Against this envirnomental background the shaman seeks the aid of his helping spirits through trance and possession. He draws confessions from those who have broken taboos, and searches the conscience of the whole community, demanding repentance. The ceremony is cathartic and lasts for hours (Rasmussen 1929:133ff.).

The Reality of the Personality Change

One cannot escape the reality of the personality change associated with the experience of possession—change in customary behavior, timbre and pitch of voice in glossolalia, capacity to walk on burning coals, self-castigation and extraordinary bodily strength (Herskovits 1951:371-372, etc.). This is said to be due to his possession by the god, who "comes into his head" and takes over the control of his body (1958: 215):

> Fundamentally, to be possessed by a *loa* means that an individual's spirit is dispossessed by that god. Personalities undergo radical change in accordance with the nature of the deity . . . (1971:146-147).

Métraux, speaking of the same people in Haiti, writes:

> The person "mounted"* by a god loses his identity. So complete is the change in his personality that he refers to himself in the third person (1960:86).

Bourguignon narrates an incident at length where the subject called the deity, Ogû, according to the proper ritual, but was also possessed by another, Guédé. The

---

* "Mounted": "the whole occult vocabulary is derived by analogy with horsemanship" (84; see also Métraux 1972:93, 120).

latter appears to have been stimulated by an uncomplimentary reference to him by the former possessing spirit. The attributes of the two gods were different: Ogû, powerful, dominant, rum-drinking and speaking French; Guédé, low-class, parodying upper-class pretentions, eating lowly foods, obscene. The subject's behavior reflected each character, but she was unaware of this after the performance. Bourguignon points out in a footnote that Haitian *loa*, when they speak in foreign tongues, frequently do so in English, French and Spanish as well as *phonations frustes* (1962:52). Apparently, dual possession by Ogû and Guédé and arguments between them were frequent (Métraux 1972: 128).

So completely could the possessing god or spirit take over the personality that fixed social norms of behavior might be reversed under possession. Such implications might include participation in social dancing and glossolalia where these were normally strictly prohibited (Dittes 1971: 376). We have the record of an American woman who was involved in spirit-possession ceremonies and wanted to have a set of drums baptized. The possessing deity happened to be Guédé, with the result that a stream of obscene talk came forth from her mouth, to the amusement of the spectators.

Mbiti (1969:174) records the personality change which took place under possession among the novices of Fon and Yoruba convicts who, when possessed, spoke in a foreign language, and after emerging from the experience had to relearn their own language.

Oesterreich declared that the most important particular of this "invasion" of the person "by a strange individuality" is that "the new voice does not speak according to the spirit of the normal personality, but that of the new one." He went on to describe it as "coarse and filthy" and "opposed to accept ethical and religious ideas." He gave several cases. This personality change is also often accompanied by "contortions which cannot, as a rule, be executed voluntarily, and with remarkable strength" (1966:21-23).

The process for restoring the possessed person to normalcy is exorcism, frequently after an exchange of conversation between the exorcist or audience and the spirit (cf. Métraux 1972:128). The possession state may lead to a manifestation of violence, which the exorcism brings under control. "The chief characteristic of demon possession," says Merrill F. Unger, in *Demons in the World Today*, is the *automatic projection of a new personality in the victim.* During attack the victim's personality is completely obliterated, and the inhabiting demon's personality takes over completely (1971:102-103).

This is typical of many descriptions in missionary literature, and more and more it is appearing also in the Western world of our own day. It all lines up with the New Testament experiences (Luke 8:26-40; Acts 19:13-16).

The Locus of Control

Somewhere in this study we must discuss the significance of the locus of control in ecstatic experiences. Is the medium or shaman in control of the situation, or is it the god who possesses him? Does he understand what is going on, or is he ignorant of it all when he subsequently reflects on it? This has to be discussed because both experiences are well known, though they are often confused.

It is interesting to notice that Plato in *Timaeus* distinguished the prophet from the glossolalist on the grounds that the latter was spirit-possessed and unable to discern what he said while he was speaking, being not in perfect control of himself. People in Plato's day were confusing the oracles and the prophetic utterances, and Plato made the differentiation. It is also interesting to put this fact beside the current distinction between shamanism and spirit possession in the writing of Eliade (1964:6, for example).

In true possession the god, demon or spirit takes over complete control. This is what Bourguignon calls the *discontinuity of the self*, or the *dissociational state*. Maya Deren put it (and she had been unintentionally so possessed):

> To understand that the self must leave if the *loa* is to enter, is to understand that one cannot be man and God at once (1953:249).

Then, eventually,

> when the individual returns to his customary mode of behavior and expression, he claims to know nothing of the intervening events and must be told of the behavior of the *loa*, even to the extent *loa* leave messages for their "horses"; the cultural tradition demands such ignorance, and in many cases this post-dissociational amnesia is undoubtedly genuine. There is a discontinuity in personal identity (Bourguignon 1962:46).

In a study of possession in Japan, Lowell (1894:291) discussed the character of a spirit dispossessing a body of its own personality and manifesting a different personality of its own.

Wallace, in dealing with the goals of religion (the rituals of salvation), saw possession as "socially sanctioned alternation of identity" and spoke of the experience as "like that of a true multiple personality" (1966:141).

Although Oesterreich (1966:374) agreed that glossolalia coming from a state of possession was the mouth speaking without the subject being willing, or even knowing what he says, on the other hand, in the same volume he cited several cases of what he called a "double type of personality" (61). We also saw in the Nevius China data this same kind of dual personality in conversational exchange. More recently (1969) the African scholar, Mbiti, has reported a case of a diviner conversing with a spirit, whose voice was entirely different from his own, in a state of possession. Mbiti taped the conversation for fifteen minutes. Subsequently, when interrogated, the diviner could recall nothing of his conversation under possession.

Both of these should be differentiated from Shamanism, although this term has a wide range of meaning in anthropological literature. Strictly speaking, although the shaman enters a state of ecstasy, he does not fully lose touch with reality, whether he exorcises a spirit which causes his patient's sickness, or sends his own soul off on a journey to capture some wandering soul for its sick owner. Not all ecstasy or trance experiences are possession. (Two different theories of sickness are involved here. They may exist side by side.) By this definition a shaman retains control of the situation:

> ... A shaman differs from a "possessed" person, for example; the shaman controls his "spirits" in the sense that he, being human, is able to communicate with the dead, "demons," and "nature spirits" without thereby becoming their instrument (Eliade 1964:6).

So the question of the locus of control has to be taken into account when any enthusiastic experience of this kind is described or evaluated. The key question is: Does the subject lose contact with reality (as we see reality)?

Some discussion should be devoted to the sociopsychic atmosphere or environment in which possession and its resultant forms of enthusiasm normally take place. Frequently a stimulant of some kind is used. The "mood" might be brought about by means of music or rhythm, drumming or singing, chanting or hand-clapping, dancing or the use of drugs. The instruments vary. Drumming is described in the majority of cases (the drums have to be baptized [Deren 1953:257ff.]), and it is almost always accompanied by hand-clapping on the part of the spectators (Métraux 1972:66; Herskovits 1958:215, etc.). These are constants. Rattles and bamboo wands are common but not constant; but there always is some beat. Boal's description is quite typical. The performance is

> accompanied by incessant rhythmic strumming from a bamboo wand, swinging the body, then dissociation, the arrival of the spirits who speak, argue or direct her (1966:253 [Kond Hills, India]).

In his *Life in a Haitian Valley*, Herskovits devotes a whole chapter to the worship service, especially the singing, and another chapter to the dancing. Sometimes the possession state is induced by drugs, such as the betel nut among the Micronesians of Palau (Force 1960:57) and the cactus fruit of the Peyote Religion, for which the references are legion. Sometimes pungent aromas have been generated and inhaled. It has been pointed out that the Delphic oracle of classical fame operated in a subterranean cavern in which certain fumes were emitted (Martin 1960:21), although this has been challenged by some archaeologists (Parke & Wormell 1956:19-20).

In the mystery religions, *ecstasy* and *enthusiasm*

> might be induced by vigil and fasting, tense religious expectancy, whirling dances, physical stimuli, the contemplation of the sacred objects, the effect of stirring music, inhalation of fumes, revivalistic contagion (such as happened in the church at Corinth), hallucination, suggestion, and all the other means belonging to the apparatus of the mysteries (Angus 1928:101).

Undoubtedly many who partake of these communal ceremonies seek to induce the possession experience, but it is equally true that a few innocent spectators also get spontaneously involved. Maya Deren went to Haiti to study and film Haitian dancing, but fell under the effects of the drumming, and was possessed by Erszulu, the goddess of love. She did not induce it: she gave way to it (1953:257-260, 322-324).

Normally, to return to an earlier distinction I made, central possession is *communal, strongly institutionalized,* and *ritualistically induced*, but peripheral possession is more normally *individual* and *spontaneous*. The tendency may well be for us to think of demon possession as something that involves scattered individuals, who require attention for their mental health. Quite apart from the probability that it is more often their spiritual health which needs repair, I hope that this paper will direct your attention to many highly institutionalized, induced, communal possession cults in our midst. The study of Western Satanism and drug cults is beyond the frame of reference given to me, except that I feel I ought to say that the world of *organized animism* is not far away.

> Mamma and Papa began shaking and writhing. . . . Her jerking became more violent. She flung her arms towards the black north sky, and her head rolled violently on her shoulders as if her neck were broken. A scream ripped from her throat . . . curses and sacred words poured from her lips. She was possessed. The god had accepted her as an oracle. . . . Papa presented Mamma with a bowl of warm blood from the sacrificial kid. She drank. . . .

This is a much abbreviated account of a highly institutionalized, induced, communal performance and manifestation of possession. It could be a description of some tribal community in a tropical forest—but it isn't. It takes place regularly in a great American city with a million inhabitants (Tallant 1962:17-28).

Conclusion

1. You have asked an anthropologist to survey spirit possession in other cultures; I can only hope that this essay will provide some help as you evaluate analogous phenomena in this country. Apart from the fact that America is a multi-ethnic nation, with hundreds of homogeneous units contributing their own folklore and values, I think that everything mentioned in this paper could be found in, say, Los Angeles. If so, my analysis should have more than just theoretical interest.

2. I have another concern; I question whether the Christian churches have provided their members with an adequate faith for this kind of ever-increasing confrontation with spirit forces. My thinking is stimulated on the point by Mary Douglas, who takes up an idea of Keith Thomas, that the world of the Christian West has been in trouble

with demons ever since it lost the religious techniques for dealing with them (confession, absolution, exorcism and protective blessings) in the late Reformation period and during the rise of Enlightenment rationalism (1968:xxxiii). Here is Thomas' statement:

> Before the Reformation the Catholic Church had provided an elaborate repertoire of ritual precautions designed to ward off evil spirits and malevolent magic. . . . A good Christian who used holy water, the sign of the cross, and the aid of the priest ought not to be so afflicted at all. After the Reformation, by contrast, Protestant preachers, strenuously denied that such aids could have any effect. They reaffirmed the power of evil, but left believers disarmed before the old enemy (1970:58).

This is a major question for thousands of tormented church people today: if the Church reaffirms the reality and activity of evil spirits in our midst, how does it arm its adherents against them? The Reformers tried to shift the faith of Christians from artifacts and institutions to the Lord Christ. Granted the fundamental rightness of such an approach, how is each generation of Christians to be brought to this faith-position? Are we not back again in the biblical world of power encounter? Ought we not to return to the scriptural word and to the classic teachings of the historic church consistent with it when faced with modern demonic attack?

　　3. I have also tried to recognize the ethnofunctional dimension of possession manifestations. There can be no possession without a cultural situation that makes it credible and possible and renders the human spirit vulnerable to possession. When the communal medicine man, medium or diviner is possessed by a friendly spirit for purposes of healing or oracle, the most reasonable interpretation of the phenomenon is usually found in the cultural context. At the same time I believe that if we consider the demonic in our midst in the light of the contemporary context which makes it credible, it will immediately become more meaningful. The witch covens of San Diego (more than twenty of them) and the drug cults of Los Angeles (some of which mix the sacrificial blood of cats and dogs with LSD) are communal, institutionalized groups—sodalities of persons who share common disillusionment with society. A great deal more research needs to be done on the relation of these demonic forms with the social situation which makes them credible. My plea is that while we consider possessed but scattered

individuals, we will not overlook the many collective manifestations of possession which are a feature of our times.

Notes

1. The sources used for this distribution study were Mbiti 1969 and
1970, Parrinder 1961, Tidani 1950, Leinhardt 1961, Shorter 1970, Lewis
1969 and 1970, Junod 1962, Middleton 1960, Smith 1923, Gussler 1972, Sundkler 1961, Gray 1969, Codrington 1891, Fox 1924, Rivers 1924, Culshaw 1949,
Kroeber 1948, Elliot 1955, Tambiah 1970, O'Malley 1935, Hoffmann 1961,
Sargant 1957, Presler 1971, Norbeck 1961, Reichard 1950, Kluckhohn 1944,
Lowie 1960, Radin 1953, Fison 1904, Rasmussen 1929 and La Barre 1969.
2. Says Ruth Benedict: " . . . One of the most striking facts that emerge
from a study of widely varying cultures is the ease with which our ab-
normals function in other cultures. . . . It is hard for us, born and brought
up in a culture that makes no use of the experience, to realize how important a role it may play and how many individuals are capable of it;
once it has been given an honorable place in any society" (1956:184).
3. The regional distribution of institutionalized forms of altered states
of consciousness (trance or possession) in percentage of societies coded
broke down in the following manner:

Sub-Saharan Africa in 94 of 114 societies	82%
Circum-Mediterranean in 35 of 44 societies	80%
East Eurasian in 61 of 65 societies	94%
Insular Pacific in 81 of 86 societies	94%
North America in 116 of 120 societies	97%
South America in 50 of 59 societies	85%

4. See the hypothetical case of missionaries A and B, one who met
these problems on the level of experience and the other on the level of
intellect (Tippett 1960:416-17).
5. The matter of accepting the situation at its face value has been
discussed by Welbourne and related to the missionary situation as follows:
"The successful cure by diviners which resist the techniques of western
medicine suggests that within African culture it is necessary to accept,
as a serious therapeutic hypothesis, the existence of ghosts and witchcraft.
This conflicts with the deep-rooted assumptions of Western doctors, who
prefer to talk in terms of psychosis and neurosis. But as Christians we
have no right to prefer one hypothesis to the other. The belief in the
objective character of spirit-possession is an ineradicable part of the
thought-form of the New Testament. It is possible that Western science
has gone too far in eliminating psychic factors in the external world"
(Welbourne 1963:15-16).
Welbourne goes on to cite Jung in saying that "the concept of the
unconscious is simply an assumption for the sake of convenience" and
suggests that his therapeutic approach would have been that "so long
as the patient believed in ghosts and witchcraft, it was necessary for
the doctor also to make the same assumption." He raises another question—
has the "new" (i.e., the scientific) world to rediscover some of the insights
of the old? : "It might be that Christian doctors working side by side
with—instead of in opposition to—their tribal counterparts, could enter

into a dimension, of the aetiology and cure of disease, of which the scientific West has never dreamt" (1963:22-23).

6. There is a dimension of anthropology which reaches out towards psychology in the study of dissociation that is currently receiving more and more attention. One of the valuable recent contributions at this focal point deals with possession, especially as it relates to social change and stress situations. A symposium, *Religion, Altered States of Consciousness, and Social Change*, demonstrates an anthropological focus on marginal religious groups which manifest some form of possession: the Umbanda of Sao Paolo, the Shakers of St. Vincent, the apostolics of Yucatan, and spirit cults of Micronesia and Africa. This research probes the relationship between the belief-behavior complex and the social structure, its complexity and rigidity, and applies the comparative method to the assembled data.

7. Loederer figured that 95% of the Black population of Haiti was involved in some way in voodoo (1935:257).

8. This was an interesting switch, because people possessed by this divine Aphrodite, who swung her hips with seductive glances at the opposite sex, normally spoke in a high-pitched but elegant French. The subtlety, if not the language, is true to her type.

Bibliography

Aberle, David F. *The Peyote Religion among the Navaho*. Chicago: Aldine Publishing Co., 1966.

Angus, Samuel. *The Mystery Religions and Christianity*. New York: Charles Scribner's Sons, 1938.

Beattie, John & John Middleton. *Spirit Mediumship and Society in Africa*. New York: Africana Publishing Co., 1969.

Benedict, Ruth. "Anthropology and the Abnormal," 1934. In: Haring 1956: 183-201.

Boal, Barbara M. "The Church in the Kond Hills—An Encounter with Animism." In: Hayward (ed.) 1966:221-350, *Three Studies of North Indian Churches*. London: Lutterworth Press, 1966.

Bourguignon, Erika. "The Self, the Behavioral Environment, and the Theory of Spirit Possession." In: Spiro 1965:39-60.

———. "A Framework for the Comparative Study of Altered States of Consciousness." In: Bourguignon (ed.) 1973:3-35.

Bourguignon, Erika (ed.). *Religion, Altered States of Consciousness, and Social Change*. Columbus: Ohio State University Press, 1973.

Brown, Peter. "Sorcery, Demons and the Rise of Christianity from Late Antiquity into the Middle Ages." In: Mary Douglas (ed.), 1968:17-45.

Cave, Hugh B. *The Cross on the Drum*. New York: Doubleday, 1958.

Codrington, R. H. *The Melanesians: Studies in their Anthropology and Folk-lore*. Oxford: Clarendon Press, 1891.

Courlander, Harold & Rémy Bastien. *Religion and Politics in Haiti*. Washington D.C.: Institute for Cross-Cultural Research, 1966.

Culshaw, J. W. *Tribal Heritage: A Study of the Santals*. London: Lutterworth Press, 1949.

de Waal Malefijt, Annemarie. *Religion and Culture*. New York: Macmillan, 1968.

Deren, Maya. *Divine Horsemen, The Living Gods of Haiti*. London: Thames & Hudson, 1953.

des Mousseaux, Gougenot. "The Concepts of Possession and Obsession," 1855. In: Nauman, 1974:87-98.

Dittes, J. R. "Religion, Prejudice and Personality." In: Strommen, 1971: 355-90.

Douglas, Mary (ed.). *Witchcraft, Confessions and Accusations.* London: Tavistock Publications, 1968.

Eliade, Mircea. *Shamanism: Archaic Techniques of Ecstasy,* trans. W. R. Trask. New York: Pantheon Books, 1964.

Elliott, A.J.A. *Chinese Spirit Medium Cults in Singapore.* London: The Anthropology Department of the London School of Economics, 1955.

Field, M. J. "Spirit Possession in Ghana." In: Beattie & Middleton, 1969:3-13.

Firth, Raymond. "Foreword" to *Spirit Mediumship and Society in Africa,* ed. Beattie & Middleton. New York: Africana Publishing Corp., 1969.

Fison, Lorimer. *Tales From Old Fiji.* London: Alexander Moring, 1907.

Force, Roland W. *Leadership and Cultural Change in Palau.* Chicago: Chicago Natural History Museum, 1960.

Fox, C. E. *The Threshold of the Pacific.* London: Kegan Paul, Trench, Trubner, 1924.

Freed, S. A. &. R. S. Freed. "Spirit Possession as Illness in a North Indian Village," *Ethnology* 3:2:152-71 (Also in: Middleton 1967:295-320), 1964.

Garbett, G. K. "Spirit Mediums as Mediators in Valley Korekore Society." In: Beattie & Middleton (ed.) 1969:104-127.

Gray, Robert F. "The Shetani Cult Among the Segeju." In: Beattie & Middleton, 1969: 171-187.

Greenbaum, Lenora. "Societal Correlates of Possession Trance." In: Bourguignon, 1972:39-57.

Gussler, J. "Social Change, Ecology, and Spirit Possession among the South African Nguni." In: Bourguignon, 1973:88-126.

Haring, Douglas G. (ed.) *Personal Character and Cultural Milieu.* Syracuse, N.Y.: Syracuse University Press, 1956.

Harris, Grace. "Possession 'Hysteria' in a Kenya Tribe," *American Anthropologist* 59:1046-1066, 1957.

Herskovits, M. J. *Man and His Works.* New York: Alfred A. Knopf, 1951.

———. *The Myth of the Negro Past.* Boston: Beacon Press, 1958.

———. *Cultural Dynamics.* New York: Alfred A. Knopf, 1964.

———. *Life in a Haitian Valley.* New York: Doubleday; first published in 1937; E. Braithwaite contributes an Introduction to the 1971 ed.,

Hoffmann, Helmut. *The Religions of Tibet.* New York: Macmillan, 1961.

Jahn, Janheinz. *Muntu, the New African Culture,* trans. M. Grene. New York: Grove Press, 1961.

Johnson, Harmon A. "Authority Over the Spirits: Brazilian Spiritism." Unpublished M.A. thesis, Fuller Theological Seminary, Pasadena, Calif., 1968.

———. *The Growing Church in Haiti.* Coral Gables: West Indies Mission, 1970.

Junod, Henri. *The Life of a South African Tribe.* New Hyde Park, N.Y.: University Books, 2 vols., 1962 (1912).

Kelsey, Morton T. *Tongue Speaking: An Experiment in Spirit Experience.* New York: Doubleday, 1964.

Kluckhohn, Clyde. *Navaho Witchcraft.* Boston: Beacon Press, 1944.

Knutsson, K. E. *Authority & Change: Study of the Kallu Institution among the Macha Galla of Ethiopia.* Goteborg: Etnografiska Museet, 1967.

172 / *Demon Possession*

Koch, Kurt E. *Christian Counselling and Occultism.* Grand Rapids: Kregel Publishers, 1972.

Kroeber, A. L. *Anthropology.* New York: Harcourt, Brace, 1948.

La Barre, Weston. *The Peyote Cult.* New York: Schocken Books, 1969.

Lessa, Wm. A & Evon Z. Vogt (eds.). *Reader in Comparative Religion: An Anthropological Approach.* Evanston, Ill.: Row, Peterson, 1958.

Lewis, I. M. "Spirit Possession and Deprivation Cults," *Man* [N.S.]. 1:307-329, 1966.

———. "Spirit Possession in Northern Somaliland." In: Beattie & Middleton, 1969:188-219.

———. "A Structural Approach to Witchcraft and Spirit-possession." In: Douglas, 1970:293-309.

———. *Ecstatic Religion: An Anthropological Study of Spirit Possession and Shamanism.* Harmondsworth, England: Penguin Books, 1971.

Lienhardt, Godfrey. *Divinity and Experience: The Religion of the Dinka.* Oxford: Clarendon Press, 1961.

Loederer, R. A. *Voodoo Fire in Haiti.* New York: Doubleday, Doran, 1935.

Lowell, Percival. *Occult Japan, or the Way of the Gods: An Esoteric Study of Japanese Personality and Possession.* Boston: Houghton Mifflin, 1894.

Lowie, R. H. *Primitive Religion.* London: Peter Owen, 1960.

Martin, Ira J., III. *Glossolalia in the Apostolic Church.* Berea: Berea College Press, 1960.

May, L. Carlyle. "A Survey of Glossolalia and Related Phenomena in Non-Christian Religions," *American Anthropologist.* 58:75-96, 1956.

Mbiti, John S. *African Religions and Philosophy.* London: Heinemann, 1969.

———. *Concepts of God in Africa.* London: S.P.C.K., 1970.

McGregor, Pedro. *The Moon and Two Mountains: The Myths, Ritual and Magic of Brazilian Spiritism.* London: Souvenir Press, 1966; the American edition was issued in 1967 under the title, *Jesus & the Spirits.*

Métraux, Alfred. *Voodoo in Haiti,* trans. H. Charteris. New York: Oxford University Press, 1959.

———. *Haiti: Black Peasants and Voodoo,* trans. P. Lengyel. New York: Universe Books, 1960.

Middleton, J. *Lugbara Religion: Ritual and Authority among an East African People.* London: Oxford University Press; International African Institute, 1960.

Middleton, John (ed.). *Magic Witchcraft & Curing.* Garden City, N.Y.: The Natural History Press, 1967.

Nauman, St. Elmo (ed.). *Exorcism Through the Ages.* New York: Philosophical Library, 1974.

Nevius, John L. *Demon Possession and Allied Themes.* Chicago: Fleming H. Revell, 1894.

Norbeck, Edward. *Religion in Primitive Society.* New York: Harper, 1961.

Obeyesekere, Gananth. "The Idiom of Demonic Possession," *Social Science and Medicine,* 4:97-111, 1970.

Oesterreich, T. K. *Possession, Demonical and Other, Among Primitive Races in Antiquity, the Middle Ages and Modern Times,* trans. D. Ibberson. New Hyde Park, N.Y.: University Books, 1966.

O'Malley, L. S. S. *Popular Hinduism: The Religion of the Masses.* Cambridge: University Press, 1935.

Opler, Morris E. "Spirit Possession in a Rural Area of Northern India." In: Lessa & Vogt, 1958:553-66, 1958.

Parke, H. W. & D. E. W. Wormell. *The Delphic Oracle.* Oxford: Basil Blackwood, 1956.
Parrinder, G. *West African Psychology.* London: Lutterworth Press, 1951.
———. *West African Religion.* London: Epworth Press, 1961.
Pauw, B. A. *Religion in a Tswana Chiefdom.* London: Oxford University Press; International African Institute, 1964.
Presler, M. "Hal on Giyarhwin Sherif: A Study of Spirit Possession," *Indian Christian Quarterly*, 27, 3-4:118-126, 1971.
Radin, Paul. *The World of Primitive Man.* London: Abelard-Schuman, 1953.
Rasmussen. *The Intellectual Culture of the Iglulik Eskimos.* Copenhagen: Fifth Thule Expedition [1921-24], Vol. 8, No. 1, 1929.
Reichard, Gladys A. *Navaho Religion: A Study of Symbolism.* New York: Pantheon Books, 2 vols., 1950.
Rivers, W. H. R. *Medicine, Magic & Religion.* New York: Harcourt, Brace, 1924.
Sadler, A. W. "Glossolalia and Possession: An Appeal to the Episcopal Study Commission," *Journal for the Scientific Study of Religion*, 4:84-90, 1964.
Sargant, Wm. J. *Battle for the Mind: A Psychology of Conversion and Brainwashing.* Melbourne, Australia: Heinemann, 1957.
Schurz, W. L. *Brazil: The Infinite Country.* London: Robert Hale, 1962.
Scott, Sir Walter. *Letters Addressed to J. G. Lockhart, Esq.* New York: Bell Publishing Co.; reprint of 1830 ed., 1970.
Shorter, Aylward. "The Migawo: Peripheral Spirit Possession and Christian Prejudice," *Anthropos*, 65:100-26, 1970.
Smith, Edwin W. *The Religion of the Lower Races as Illustrated by the African Bantu.* New York: Macmillan, 1923.
Spiro, Melford E. (ed.). *Context and Meaning in Cultural Anthropology.* New York: Free Press, 1965.
Stark, Rodney. "A Taxonomy of Religious Experience," *Journal for the Scientific Study of Religion*, 97-116, 1965.
Stromen, M. P. (ed.). *Research on Religious Development: A Comprehensive Handbook.* New York: Hawthorn Books, 1971.
Sundkler, B. G. M. *Bantu Prophets in South Africa.* London: Oxford University Press, 1961.
Tambiah, S. J. *Buddhism and the Spirit Cults in Northeast Thailand.* Cambridge: Cambridge University Press, 1970.
Thomas, Keith. "The Relevance of Social Anthropology to the Historical Study of English Witchcraft." In: Mary Douglas, 1970:47-79, 1970.
Tidani, A. Serpos. "Rituels," *Le Monde Noire (Présence Africaine).* 8-9: 297-305, 1950.
Tippett, A. R. "Probing Missionary Inadequacies at the Popular Level," *International Review of Missions.* 49:411-419, 1960.
———. *Solomon Islands Christianity.* London: Lutterworth Press, 1967.
———. *Peoples of Southwest Ethiopia.* South Pasadena, Calif.: Wm. Carey Library, 1970.
———. "Glossolalia as Spirit Possession: A Taxonomy for Cross-Cultural Observation and Description." Unpublished paper, 1972.
Tylor, E. B. *Primitive Culture.* London: John Murray; I have used Radin's 1958 ed. of this work, 1871.
Unger, Merrill F. *Demons in the World Today.* Wheaton, Ill.: Tyndale House, 1971.
Wallace, A. F. C. *Religion: An Anthropological View.* New York: Random House, 1966.

Welbourn, F. B. "The Importance of Ghosts." In: Hayward, *African Independent Church Movements*. London: Edinburgh House Press, 15-26, 1963.
Willems, Emilio. *Followers of the New Faith*. Nashville: Vanderbilt University Press, 1967.
Williams, Thomas & J. Calvert. *Fiji and the Fijians*. London: Charles H. Kelly, 2 vols. (Vol. I is by Williams), 1967.
Wilson, Peter J. "Status Ambiguity and Spirit Possession," *Man*. 2:366-78, 1967.

9
Possession, Trance State, and Exorcism in
Two East African Communities

DONALD R. JACOBS

This paper examines the way in which two African cultures, one Nilotic and one Bantu, have adjusted their possession, trance state, and exorcism rituals to respond to the rapid social change which overtook them. The impinging factors were the Muslim and Christian religions plus the forces of westernization which accompanied the colonial and post colonial eras.

In each of these cultures, in addition to the belief in the Creator God, which was a belief of great antiquity, they also held to a belief in other spirits who had the proclivity of possessing the living under certain circumstances. These spirits were clearly ancestral or kin spirits among the Bantu and usually so among the Nilotics.

The point of interest in this study is the analysis of the way each culture reflected and even provided for social change by the continuation and modification of their possession ritual.

It is assumed that possession phenomena had traditionally served a sociological and psychological need in both cultures. As new needs arose in response to social reorganization and social threat, how, we will ask, did the experience of possession phenomena change or did it simply persist as a dysfunctional ritual act?

We are fortunate to have two significant studies, both recently published, by two recognized analysts of East African cultures. The one dealing with a Bantu culture is *Ritual and Symbol in Transitional Zaramo Society* by Marja-Liisa Swantz (Uppsala, 1970), which details how the possession and exorcism rites are modified both by Islam and modern social change. In *Basic Community in the African Churches* (Orbis Books, 1973), Marie-France Perrin Jassy traces the consequences of the introduction of Christianity and the impact of social change upon the ritual life of the Luo communities in the Lake Victoria area. These studies taken together throw significant light on the persistence of the possession, trance state, and exorcism rites.

We will give our attention first to Bantu culture, the Wazaramo, who inhabit the coastal area north of Dar es Salaam in Tanzania. The Wazaramo lived in close proximity to the Arab Muslim trader for centuries but it was not until the era of the German occupation prior to World War I that they espoused the Muslim religion. Therefore, the Wazaramo faced westernization and its massive innovations at roughly the same time that they began to absorb Islam. The possession rites reflected this change as the culture employed the phenomenon to deal with the expanded options which the socialization process introduced.

Traditionally the Wazaramo world view acknowledged the existence of two types or categories of possessing spirits—the coastal kin spirits with which the peoples are very familiar and the exotic spirits which have come along with the foreign people and influences.[1] The two main coastal spirits are those which are associated with what might be called "limited" possession and those who possess more or less persistently. The former are exorcised through dancing and vigorous movement in which the possessed participates, while the second is usually performed when the spirit has incapacitated an individual. In each case the rites are conducted by practitioners who operate within the context of the traditional world view. They are either those who have themselves been possessed and exorcised or local doctors who receive power and direction from the traditional spirits. These rites have not changed very much at all. According to Swantz, "Basically, these rites affirm the interpretation of them as being constructive from the point of view of traditional family coherence."[2] These possessing spirits are recognized as forces threatening communal unity. Possession dramatizes the discordant tendencies and exorcism reintegrates the possessed back into society. These rites are very common today and evidence is lacking to support the contention that the need for the rites is diminishing.[3] They deal with spirits which are well within the traditional framework.

Traditional possession and exorcism provided a way whereby an individual could project anxiety or even a "mania" onto a spirit which possessed him and then through the process of exorcism disown not only the possessing spirit but its antisocial deeds as well. The trance state provided for this dissociation and reintegration. On the part of society, unacceptable behavior could thus be identified and abolished.

In a general way, possession highlights a problem in a dramatic fashion which requires social reintegration for solution. The society, if it wishes to assist a possessed person, must help that person to come to grips with the demands of the ancestral spirit. This process of possession and subsequent exorcism establishes links with the ancestral spirits, it highlights the nature of antisocial acts which are unacceptable to the group, and it also, in a way, cleanses a person who has problems of antisocial nature.

From the societies' point of view,

> It is a considerable relief from the point of view of immediate social relations when a conflict can be projected to spirits which in a way are part of the society, and yet can be driven out and kept at a distance. If the practices of sorcery and witchcraft should receive the bulk of the load of suspicion, it would make the life of the society unbearable. In this way the hidden causes and suspicions are diverted into socially constructive channels. . . . [4]

Among the Wazaramo, Swantz observes: "The intense practices of spirit exorcism and other methods of curing reflect the prevalent attitudes of social mistrust." [5] As social mistrust increases, asserts Swantz, one can expect an increase in the incidence of healing and exorcism.

The possession and exorcism rituals, inasmuch as they take place in the context of subliminality, provide a way by which deviant individuals in society can enter the realm of death and decay in the trance state. By so doing, the unconscious may be enabled to express itself. And so, according to Jung: "In this way they grant life to the shadow yet prevent it from taking an upper hand in their daily life." [6]

The experience with death as symbolized in the trance state can be part of a renewal ritual in which, through exorcism and cleansing, an individual can be reborn, hopefully no longer dependent upon the undesirable spirit, and can then be reintegrated into society.

Within the Wazaramo society the communal ethic is

strong and is certainly reinforced by experiencing ancestral spirit involvement. The goal of the experience should be the ongoing solidification of the society. The fact that they continue to observe these rites indicates that the basic world view of the peoples remains essentially unchanged. The rites continue to meet individual and social need.

But the two categories of spirit which were experienced traditionally were not sufficient to meet the demands of social change which was at once sociological and religious. The Wazaramo, therefore, added to their repertoire of possessing spirits a third category, the exorcism of which is called "killinge." "This particular form of exorcism," according to Swantz, "has been adopted by the people now living in the area of study, *after their becoming Muslim.* It is, however, an interesting mixture of new and traditional elements, and a form of ritual which is easily adaptable in situations of new culture contacts." [7] The possessing spirits are considered to be local spirits, however, but they are not as localized as the former two. In fact, the spirits in question may have absolutely no connection with the family line at all.[8] They can even include spirits of Europeans, Arabs, or Asians.

As a result of culture contact the traditional rites were greatly elaborated.

> This does not only indicate the ways of adaptation, but points further to the need for a new way of handling problems of an individual who meets life situations in which the traditional ways are not adequate. A changed spirit-possession cult may then be an indication or a process of individualization taking place in the society.[9]

Even though the possessing spirits are not kin spirits, they are controlled by kin spirits. So if one becomes ill because of the possessing spirit, the exorcism must take place in the context of the kin spirits, the social group. The "killinge" rites are kinship rites, therefore, even though the possessing spirits are not their own ancestral spirits.

The fourth category of possessing spirits is a relatively recent introduction. They are called *majini* ("jin spirits") or *mashetani* ("satans"). These spirits have no definite connection with ancestral spirits. They come from up country or from across the water. They act arbitrarily. The "majini" cannot be exorcised according to traditional ritual because the ritual must include a Muslim priest or teacher and the Koran is necessary as an element in the exorcism act. But the rite must be performed in the context of the group.

This form of a trance cult can be classified as being peripheral, an extension of the traditional forms, which facilitates the solving of acute problems and individual frustrations rising in a transitional situation.[10]

The trance rites with subsequent exorcism among the Wazaramo deal with the following problems: (1) Persistent physical illnesses, such as stomach ailments, legs, head, etc. (2) Acute illness resulting in nervous disorders, such as hallucinations or paralysis. (3) Sudden attacks of hysteria. (4) Social problems, such as loss of employment, etc. (5) Sexual and reproductive disorders.

These symptoms can be identified in any of the four possession categories. They are illnesses which attack the individual, but the cure must include a temporary removal from normal communal life after which the society receives the individual back. Swantz remarks: "I consider the question of actual physical cure less significant than the degree of integration resulting from these rites, individually and socially. The therapeutic value of the trance rites is seen in terms of integration effected through them. . . . "[11]

The process is therapeutic as long as healing is experienced. When such does not occur, the situation becomes pathological and social disintegration takes place. Swantz feels that the organic unity of the Wazaramo persists. "This relatedness has changed through migration, the acceptance of Islam and new contacts, but its basic elements are still intact."[12] She concludes: "It has become evident from this study that Islam did not cause any major cultural or social disruption in the Mwambao Zaramo Society."[13] This conclusion is not unique to this particular area but could apply to dozens of Islamized Bantu groups along the East African coast and inland.

The addition of nontraditional "majini" spirits enables the society to undergo significant social change which is radically discontinuous with their traditional practices. It would probably be safe to predict that if the Wazaramo should experience a subtle erosion of their faith in the efficacy of the ancestral spirits as many East African peoples are not experiencing, the possession and exorcism rites will persist but less attention will be paid to ancestral or kin spirit possession and more to "majini" possession because the "majini" can personify almost any sort of disruptive influence.

The trance state ritual acts can be modified to absorb new situations. "In any ritual experience, belief and familiarity are needed before a ritual act can be related within an individual to the store of symbols in his unconscious." [14]

In times of extreme social stress, the trance state phenomenon is likely to increase in incidence. "In the myths as in the symbolism the predominant theme is death from which new forms of life are created. . . . The transitional society is facing a crisis comparable to that in the life of an individual. The trance rites are an expression of this social crisis. . . . A form of death experience is found in the rites based on trance experiences. . . . It is one piece of evidence which shows that society does not tackle the core of its problems." [15]

In summary, when Islam was espoused by the Wazaramo, which incidentally occurred simultaneously with the German colonial rule, the possession phenomenon did not only persist in its traditional patterns but new types of possessing spirits were added to the repertoire. The expanded and extended possession and exorcism rituals served as a means whereby the community could dramatize the internal conflicts they experienced, and change to meet new circumstances.

In contrast to the Muslim accommodation to the possession phenomenon, the carriers of the Christian religion in East Africa refused to incorporate exorcism ritual into their religious services. The reasons for this are not really germane to the present study, but one does wonder why this deliberate avoidance of the possession phenomenon in cultures where it is experienced. Perhaps they felt that confrontation would simply add credence to the belief in the power of these possessing spirits. Seen through the eyes of the local Christians, it must have been quite perplexing, especially in light of the fact that the Gospel is so clear on the confrontation issue. Jassy quotes a very interesting African rationalization which is widespread among Kenya Luo people:

> When Jesus expelled the demons from the Gerasene demoniac and sent him into the pigs, these threw themselves into the Lake but did not drown. In fact, they swam to Africa and came to infest the Africans with demons from which Jesus had delivered the Europeans.[16]

And here is the testimony of a Luo Christian lady:

> The Western missionaries do not understand the sufferings of the Africans. When we complain in confession of

being tormented by an evil spirit, they answer that the spirit torments the body but not the soul and that there is no reason to be upset. However, the Gospel is clear on this point. Jesus did give his disciples the power to expel demons. If the missionaries do not use it, they are either refusing to put it at the service of Africans or they have lost it.[17]

Bishop Girpas Wayoga of the Legion of Mary, a recent (1962) breakaway movement from the Roman Catholic Church in Western Kenya, cites a typical example:

The priests of the Nyarombo Mission refused one day to pray for a woman who was possessed by a bad spirit and running naked in the bush. It was their advice to have her cared for in the traditional way, that is, by bathing her in water in which a magical substance had been mixed, and having her drink a potion prepared from certain plants, sacrificing a goat to the spirit and having her wear the skin of the animal. She was cared for in this way and once cured returned to church. But when at home she served her spirit and when at church she served God. Now nobody can serve two masters. That was not good. If you ask the priests to pray in church to have a spirit expelled, when you get home the spirit returns and torments you twice as much, saying, "You took me to an unpleasant place and now I want a spotless chicken (or cow, or goat) and I wish to eat it, otherwise I am going to kill you." And sometimes spirits do kill people.[18]

The consequences of the avoidance are very hard to define. One thing is clear, however, possession and exorcism rituals persisted in the communities alongside the rites and beliefs of the church. The Christians assumed that as long as a person is walking in faith with Jesus Christ, he need have no fear of witchcraft or possession. If a Christian were to become bewitched or possessed, it would be a clear demonstration of the fact that the person was living in a state of disobedience to Jesus Christ. But if in this state, exorcism could be obtained only in the traditional rites and not in the Christian Church.

The temptation, however, for Christians to acknowledge traditional power structures became very real when persistent misfortune occurred. And local practitioners are always ready to assist in such cases. What should the Christian do? The church's position when faced with this problem has been an enduring point of ambiguity over the years. The churches established by mission societies tend to disregard totally the possession and exorcism phenomenon.

If a baptized member exhibits classical symptoms of possession, he is usually treated medically or disregarded entirely. In twenty years as a missionary in Tanzania and Kenya, I know of only a few cases where the "mission type" churches exorcised demons.

I cannot help believing that this reluctance on the part of mission churches to speak and act meaningfully in face of the possession phenomenon has contributed significantly to the startling rise of Christian independency in many areas of Sub-Sahara Africa today. Generally speaking, these independent churches confront the traditional power constellations in a forthright manner. They experience Jesus Christ as one from whom power is received to resist the spirits who threaten to possess or harass.

The Legion of Mary (referred to earlier) is rather typical of the confrontationists. They exorcise in the following manner.[19] The community gathers around the person who is possessed and who is now the object of the exorcism. They require that the person bring all medicines, amulets and other objects which he used in occult practices. These are then burned in the presence of the one to be exorcised while the community of faith kneel and recite the rosary and the Catena. While in prayer, the priests pass a rosary over various parts of the body of the possessed. The possessed then goes into convulsions and begins to speak in tongues. The officials rebuke the spirit and order it out of the person. Dialogue with the spirit or spirits ensues until as a result of communal prayer the spirit announces its departure. If a spectator also trembles and begins to speak in tongues during the rite, he, too, is exorcised. If the spirit returns to someone already exorcised, the person, in order to maintain a resistance to the threatening spirit, is required to join the healers and the exorcists and help others who are sick and possessed. If possession persists, it could indicate that a person is living in a demon-infested situation. The solution is to move away.

This ritual contains the essential ingredients of pre-Christian exorcism rituals. Jassy observed a number of exorcisms in several independent churches and concludes,

> In all cases, the indispensable element is the presence of the community, which gives those officiating the rhythmic support necessary to force the spirit to manifest himself and then the power of prayer and faith to expel him.[20]

The exorcism reintegrates the person into the group.

The religious leaders, in spite of the predominant role they play in some churches in prayer rituals for the sick and in exorcism, can officiate only in the presence of the assembled faithful. The essential element in the ceremony is not the imposition of hands but the gathering of the community around the patients and the possibility that these will become a part of the community after the cure. Prayer for the sick and exorcism are above all processes of social integration.[21]

The confrontation process is evident both in healings and exorcisms. The practitioners whom I know report that they deal most often with cases of witchcraft. This is common, especially when it is remembered that the vast majority of all sickness among the Bantu is believed caused by witchcraft. They also report that cases of ancestral spirit involvement are not uncommon, but only rarely do they confront possession which requires exorcism. I recall speaking to Prophet John of the Africa Independent Pentecostal Church who said matter of factly, "Curing those who are ill as a result of witchcraft is simple in the name of Jesus, but casting out evil spirits is very difficult. However, they too must eventually yield before the power of Jesus Christ." I would guess that Prophet John performs one hundred healings to one exorcism. But the exorcisms are so dramatic that they eclipse the other healings in profound effectiveness.

The belief in the possibility of possession persists in East Africa. While it is quite impossible to quantify any trend, from the research I have been able to do, I am convinced that healings and exorcisms are just as common today as they were forty or fifty years ago in East Africa.

As far as I know, no one has made a study of Christian exorcism as Swantz did the Wazaramo Muslim's rites. Jassy does not differentiate between the different types of possessing spirits among the Luo, Christian and non-Christian. In my own limited research, I have discovered that in addition to ancestral spirits, other categories have been added. In the late 1960's, for example, the Masai exorcists in the Moshi area of Tanzania were unable to cast out a strange and highly malevolent demon by traditional means. They observed, however, that people who were baptized into the Christian faith were immune to the power of the strange new demon. I understand that many Masai were baptized, therefore, as a sort of immunization against attack.

I believe that healings and exorcisms serve to reinforce

community among the Christians who practice them. Generally speaking mission churches do not experience very significant community. The independent churches do. How much these rites contribute to the solidarity of the groups is not certain but I believe it is a significant factor.

Both exorcisms and healings serve to reincorporate individuals back into society. They also provide a way so that an individual need not carry the full burden of responsibility for his deeds which may be intolerable. He can identify a power outside himself which he feels is ultimately responsible for his unacceptable behavior. In a way, this is a technique for avoiding responsibility, yet it has a therapeutic function for the individual as well as for the community. It enables the community to believe: "We are basically good, the evil which pulls us apart exists outside ourselves." And, too, it affords an opportunity for the community to dramatize unwanted behavior or attitudes. Possessing spirits must, after all, identify themselves. In this way the community updates in a very significant manner its current views on community ethics. It is almost a perpetual object lesson in ethics. This can be said of illness as well because the cause of the illness must too be identified and dealt with in the power of Christ.

In times of extraordinary social change when conflict situations are multiplied in culture, healing and exorcism make it possible to cohere. This is true for Christians as well as non-Christian people. The modern African cities present a situation which has high potential for conflict. It is little wonder that the case load of the 750 or so traditional practitioners in the city of Dar es Salaam is roughly equal to that of all of the hospitals, health centers, and clinics in the city. Witchcraft activity and possessions appear to be on the increase.

East African Christians gain many benefits from the rituals of healing and exorcism in addition to the obvious assistance to community solidarity discussed above. I shall mention only a few others.

In their power conscious societies, the experience of Jesus Christ as the one who has dominion over the spirits of evil is a tremendous boost to faith. If in the name of Jesus all spirits must yield, then He must surely be the Anointed One.

Knowing that Jesus Christ empowers a group of Christians gives them courage to witness because they believe they can truly help people who have fallen prey to the evil spirits.

Some groups actually use the healing and exorcism ministry to advertise, so to speak, the Gospel. I was startled when Prophet John told me that he heals and exorcises Hindu Asians in the name of Jesus even though they are not Christians! He said he does it so that they will believe.

Healings and exorcisms make it possible to live in traditional society while at the same time overcoming the dominion of the bewitching and possessing spirits. The Christians need not separate themselves physically from others if they are truly separated by the extraordinary power of Jesus Christ. This makes it possible to affirm one's own culture without at the same time coming into bondage to the culture's power centers.

There are, on the other hand, several things which concern me. Healings and exorcisms, while making it possible to project unwanted guilt, may also have the tendency of allowing a person or a community to live irresponsibly. Rather than dealing with disobedience and sin (in the Christian sense) in an ongoing repentant way, the healing and exorcism rites present a model of accumulated sin which can be very devastating to the individual and the community.

The East African revival movement does not emphasize healings or exorcisms; instead, a daily repentant walk in light fellowship where Jesus' leading and loving care is emphasized rather than His power.

Judging from information which I have at hand, healings and exorcisms in many of the independent churches approximate in frequency the healings and exorcisms in a similar non-Christian community where traditional practitioners officiate. This, one must remember, is after a century of Christian and Muslim influence and in the midst of a modern educational system. The essential world view of the vast majority of East Africans remains very much unaltered. The change one sees is not the withering of the traditional rites but the addition of new possessing spirits whose presence makes the modern world understandable and bearable.

I do not envision that the situation will be altered very much in the foreseeable future. The possession, trance state, and exorcism rites will be with us for a long time to come.

Having examined the possession phenomenon culturally, I am not inferring that demons and ancestral spirits do not in fact exist. As a matter of fact, I am far more ready to acknowledge their ontological reality today than

I was before association with East African peoples. It is quite impossible to prove the existence of possessing spirits. Yet, if one believes, much of what was incomprehensible begins to make sense.

Conclusion

In these two case studies, the possession, trance state and exorcism rituals do not only survive the pressures of social change processes but also they in fact help to rationalize and enable sociological development. They are sociologically functional. And to assume that urbanization, religious reorientation, western-type education and medicine will render these rituals (or adaptations of them) unnecessary is not supported by the findings.

The Christian community, as it pursues its evangelistic and nurture ministries, must be aware of the persisting nature of these rituals and should pray for a proper understanding of the way Jesus Christ would have the church deal with the issue in each cultural setting.

In summary, some of the sociological functions of possession, trance state and exorcism rituals follow.

1. Identify and dramatize unacceptable behavior by assuming that the affected persons will behave in ways counter to the accepted cultural mores. Following exorcism he is in turn expected to exhibit "normal" behavior.

2. Make the group aware of the belief that there are sinister forces seeking to disrupt social solidarity and that the consequences of not resisting them are great.

3. Enable groups to clarify in a specific way new forms of evil, thus enabling social change to occur. By isolating the unacceptable elements of an innovation the culture is in a sense exorcising the evils so that innovations can be incorporated in modified form.

4. Provide a way for the group to reincorporate certain deviant individuals. If the unacceptable behavior is expunged, the person reenters the group clean.

5. Reestablish community. This is accomplished by ridding the community of undesirable elements and by involving the total community in the exorcism. The thrust of the exorcism is the assurance that the group will make a place for the exorcised individual.

6. Reinforce and update the group's cosmology. Every time an exorcism occurs, the group reconfirms their beliefs.

7. Provide a way of dealing with problems which the community is unable to handle in traditional legal or executive ways. Through exorcism, therefore, the group has an alternate method of conflict resolution.

8. Guarantee the endurance of community "protectors," thus providing the community with guards against disintegration.

9. Provide a way to expunge capricious malevolency.

10. Provide an opportunity to reenact death/resurrection ritual in the context of the spirit world.

11. Demonstrate the belief that the living have ultimate control over malevolent spirits.

Notes

1. Marja-Liisa Swantz. *Ritual and Symbol in Transitional Zaramo Society* (Uppsala: Almqvist and Wiksells, 1970), p. 201.

2. *Ibid.*, p. 200.

3. *Ibid.*, p. 190.

4. *Ibid.*, p. 118.

5. *Ibid.*, p. 119.

6. Carl G. Jung. *The Integration of the Personality* (London: Routledge & Kegan Paul, 1963), p. 92.

7. Swantz, *op. cit.*, p. 193.

8. *Ibid.*, p. 153.

9. *Ibid.*

10. *Ibid.*, p. 202.

11. *Ibid.*, p. 311.

12. *Ibid.*, p. 337.

13. *Ibid.*, p. 340.

14. *Ibid.*, p. 345.

15. *Ibid.*, pp. 354-5.

16. Marie-France Perrin Jassy. *Basic Community in the African Churches* (Maryknoll, N.Y.: Orbis Books, 1973), p. 204.

17. *Ibid.*

18. *Ibid.*, pp. 204-5.

19. *Ibid.*, p. 206.

20. *Ibid.*, p. 209.

21. *Ibid.*, p. 212.

PART FIVE

Demonology on the Mission Fields

10

Demonism on the Mission Fields

G. W. PETERS

Introduction

The world of religious experience, pneumena and phenomena is perhaps the most mysterious, complex, and dynamic of all human encounters, functions, and psycho-socio-religious constellations. This should not seem strange to us. Religion involves the totality of personality and its relationships. It implicates in principle at least three realms—the human, the divine, the demonic; the natural, the supernatural, and the supranatural. It is broader in its embrace and more complex in composition and implications than any other human experience and relationship. The religious phenomena is the most comprehensive and most inclusive reality in human life. Because of this, no satisfactory definition of religion has come forth. It constitutes the content, purpose, motivation, and substructure of the life of much of mankind. It is the cement which holds life together and shapes the way of life of multitudes of people.

The study of the religious increases in complexity as we move beyond the borders of the Western world and the realm of Greaco-Hebrew conditioned traditional Christendom.

Well does Sir S. Radhakrishnen say: "The Western mind is rationalistic and ethical, positivist and practical, while the Eastern mind is more inclined to inward life and intuitive thinking. . . . Speaking in general terms we may say that the dominant feature of Eastern thought is its insistence on creative intuition, while the Western systems are characterized by a greater adherence to critical intelligence."

It is an indisputable fact that the Greaco-Hebrew tradition has established a unique mentality and a unique world and life view. Mankind, therefore, is divided into two great blocks, the Greaco-Hebrew world of thought and the non-Greaco-Hebrew world of thought. Both worlds have their premises and their basic frame of reference.

In order to penetrate the religious milieu of the various peoples, it becomes imperative to know some of the basic premises and their world and life view within which their experiences take place and are being interpreted. These, of course, must be evaluated in the light of the Bible rather than our own culture.

Premises

For our purpose I project four such premises: They live in (1) a world of continuum and nondifferentiation; (2) a world of spiral rise and enlargement of power potency and personalities; (3) a world of nonabsolutes and non-polarities in the realm of good and evil, of truth and falsehood; (4) a world which is dynamic and governed by caprice and fiat of the ancestors and by the spirits rather than by a God of "law and order."

We must make allowances for variations in degree in these matters as well as for numerous individuals and some areas of life which have been conditioned by Western education and Western invasions of thought forms and life patterns. A few comments on each of these points follows.

1. *A world of continuum and nondifferentiation*

The Western mind is conditioned to think in terms of definitions, delineations, classifications, and departments. We section and divide, separate and analyze, diagnose and compartmentalize. Everything has its own rightful label. This seems natural to us. We would, however, quickly admit that this is not the way life is being lived. Life is more existential than it is logical and clearly classified. Yet, in our minds the former pattern seems to dominate at least in our more rational moments.

This is not the way non-Western people live. They live in a "total," in a "whole," in a "unit." Particularization is of a very low level, and subject and object, and again object and object flow together. Their world is one without sharp differentiations. They live in a continuum, in a reality that shades and fades from one sphere of experience into another without much tension.

Therefore, the non-Western mind does not formally distinguish between the sacred and the secular (to him secularism is foreign), the religious and the nonreligious, the spiritual and the material, the temporal and the eternal, the living and the dead. To him all of life is religion related and religion dominated. All constitutes one great even flow and unified stream.

While this sounds good, it has its serious consequences. Continuum penetrates all of life and experiences and wears down all edges of differentiations. The mentality of continuum and nondifferentiation makes analytical and critical approaches most difficult. Its logic seems to follow different processes. It is built more upon intuition and "discernment" than upon emperical facts and evidences. The rational is often replaced by the mystical, imaginative and intuitive. It is a kind of "mystical thinking" (Lévy-Bruhl). The range of experiences becomes comprehensive and complex and appears to shade from the extremely positive to the extremely negative without clearly defined delineations. Thus the spiritual seems to fade into the religious, into the psychological, into the psychosomatic, into the occultic, into the demonic and ultimately into the satanic. It is a religious "mystical symbiosis" (Lévy-Bruhl). It becomes most difficult to delineate and to define what is what since the experiences seem to swing from side to side and move from realm to realm without serious tensions and without registering in the consciousness of the individual. Consciousness seems more a stream and flow than conceptualization; it is a mystical awareness rather than an object comprehension.

2. *A world of spiral rise and enlargement of power potencies and personalities*

The cosmic dynamism appears in this world in different manifestations which ascend in a spiral manner from the impersonal (Malenesian *mana*, West African *nyama*, East African *bwanga*, Chinese *feng-shui*, Sanskrit *shakti*) to the personal; from the impersonal dynamism or animatism to animism, to spiritism, to demonism, to deities.

Thus there is not a wild confusion of forces floating about in the universe, but explanations are given as to why some powers are more potent than others. Plants and animals have spiritual forces akin to those of men, but generally they are of a lower grade than man's. They are, therefore, less potent. Man's potency is of a less grade than that of the spirits', and these in turn of lower grade than that of the gods'. It should be noted, however, that none of these power levels and embodiments are totally good or totally evil. Good and evil is relative and therefore not mutually exclusive.

It is here where the specialist enters the scene and gains in significance. The secret of the specialist's power for good or evil is his knowledge of the source of the power and his skill to relate himself to the higher grade of power to "possess" such power and/or being possessed by it and to manipulate it to do his biddings for good or evil.

3. *A world of nonabsolutes and nonpolarities in the realm of good and evil, truth and falsehood*

Such a premise is, of course, a natural consequence of the previous presuppositions. Insofar there is more "natural" logic than is often allowed to the non-Western mentality, especially the mentality of the "primitive" people. The primitive man is, indeed, a philosopher. He is intuitively causal without proceeding on the same path we do.

The premise of nonabsolutes and nonpolarities comes to its ultimate heights and fruition in Hinduism. In a sophisticated form it is most vigorously advocated and defended by the able apologist, brilliant philosopher, and modern exponent of Neo-Vedanta, the first and late president of India, Sir Sarvepalli Radhakrishnan. Rajah B. Manikam summarizes the position in four statements which I borrow with some changes and additions. The axioms undergirding nonabsolutism and relativism are:

(1) Ultimate Reality is essentially beyond-personal, indefinable, and unknowable. For the best it can be known only in part. Only lower forms of knowledge ascribe to it personality with its concretization and limitations and thus bring Ultimate Reality down to the level of man. This may take the form of henotheism, polytheism, idolatry, or spiritism in its various forms.

It is therefore more pious to remain religiously agnostic and without doctrinal formulations about the nature of Ultimate Reality than to be affirmative and definitive about its nature. It is more reverential and religiously mature to be agnostic-worshipful than to be theological-dogmatic.

This axiom, however, must be modified for much of

Africa and many American Indians. Here an impersonal, cosmic dynamism is intermingled with a cosmic personality or god concept. Dr. John S. Mbiti argues at great length for the theistic god concept in African tradition, and so does Dr. Edwin Smith and several other authorities on African religions.

In general, however, it is agreed that in popular religion even in Africa and American Indians the interaction and interrelationship between cosmic dynamism and cosmic personality is of such a nature that it becomes practically impossible to ascribe ultimate reality and ultimate authority and power to one or the other, at least in the minds of the vast majority of people.

(2) No one religious system (in revelation and tradition as preserved in its sacred writings) and theological formulation about the nature and function of Ultimate Reality can honestly claim absolute validity. No religion is wholly true and good. All religious formulations and practices are a mixture of truth and error even in their ultimate sources. No religion can claim absoluteness and finality.

(3) No one religious system and theological formulation can claim totality of truth and comprehensiveness. Ultimate Reality is too great, too complex, too variable, too rich to be compressed into and expressed by one religion or the religion of any one people, revelation, comprehension, or practices. Only the sum total of all partial truths as manifested in all religions can lead us to the desired and aspired goal of completeness and comprehensiveness of truth and reality.

(4) It is more religious to recognize the right of every man to accept whatever beliefs and way of life he finds most useful and practical to his mode of thinking and his peculiar circumstances. To seek by persuasion and/or enticements to make converts is to violate the inherent rights of man and the nature of ultimate reality.

The four axioms can be summarized by four loaded and dynamic words—agnosticism, relativism, syncretism, pragmatism. They leave man in the plight of uncertainty and groping, the predicament of continuous search without hope of finding, the futility of incompleteness and unguided independence, the dilemma of becoming relevant in the midst of relativity. They confine man to a mist of "beginningless and endless faith" without foundation, direction, and hope. They lift the anchor of the soul and set it adrift in the midst of an ocean of tumultuous storms and waves in a ship without a rudder and captain. In fact, it has no shore in sight and no harbor to aim for.

4. A world of dynamism, governed by caprice and fiat of the ancestors and the spirit world rather than by a God of "law and order"

Various words have been employed to describe the belief that the universe is not static but that it is a dynamic, "living," and powerful cosmos. It has been spoken of as animism (Edward Tylor), animatism (R. R. Marett), vital force (Temple), dynamism (Edwin Smith). The latter describes the situation as "belief in and practices associated with the belief in hidden, mysterious, supersensible, pervading energy, powers, potencies, forces."

Dr. John S. Mbiti of Kampala, writing from the African point of view states: "Every African who has grown up in the traditional environment will, no doubt, know something about this mystical power which is experienced, or manifests itself, in form of magic, divination, witchcraft, and mysterious phenomena that seem to defy even immediate scientific explanations." Somewhat later he remarks: "This mystical power is not fiction: whatever it is, it is a reality, and one with which African peoples have to reckon." [1]

No student of "popular religions" of Asia would deny that cosmic dynamism constitutes the basic source from which oriental shamanism, mysticism, spiritism, occultism, and ancestor worship spring. The universe is alive, charged with dynamism, life force, souls, spirits and gods—good and evil. The pleasure and caprice of these potencies govern the universe and determine the fate of man. To please, appease, capture, persuade, manipulate these impersonal and personal powers is the secret of all success and welfare. "It is chiefly the specialist, and particularly the medicine man, diviners and rainmakers, who use their knowledge and manipulation of this mystical power for the welfare of their community." This is "good magic" or "white magic." "Evil magic" or "black magic" involves the belief in a practice of tapping and using this power to do harm to human beings and their property. It is here where witchcraft, sorcery, and evil magicians come in.

My Personal Premise

In considering the above outlined premises and world

and life views, we are tempted to write off strange and peculiar psycho-socio-religious phenomena and experiences as subjective projections, as the result of imagination, superstition, hallucination, hypnotism, ecstaticism, personality dissociation or disorganization, and psychopathology of one kind or another. This is, of course, a simple way of getting rid of a complex situation, at least academically. I must state, however, that such would be neither historical, existential, nor theological. History has had strange ways of mocking man in his dogmatic optimism and rationalistic certainties. Today demonism is invading our countries more than ever before. Existence has had peculiar ways of making itself felt and known in a mysterious, yet in a persuasive manner. Also, the testimony of multitudes of people and the witness of men of good training and close observation of the experience, pneumena and phenomena compels us to take a closer took at it. And theology assures us that there are reality experiences beyond human comprehension. *Positively*, there is joy unspeakable and full of glory, a peace that passeth understanding, a knowing which passeth knowledge. There are objective realities which become subjectively real by appropriation and not rationalistic comprehension or by logic. There are truths and realities which flesh and blood cannot reveal. They come as a heavenly bestowment. *Negatively*, there are principalities, power (authorities), rulers of darkness (world rulers), spiritual hosts of evil, and there is the craftiness of the devil. Christians are warned to arm themselves against this evil not as fiction and fantasy, but as objective realities.

While I am most ready to admit that much rests in subjectivism and abnormalities, I am equally ready to believe that there is a realm that continues to elude all scientific investigation and that refuses to submit to all human manipulation, correction and direction. There is intelligent *evil* in this world.

Instead of writing off the experiences as spurious, as unreal, as false, as sham, or attributing them to subjectivism, mental abnormalities, and psychopathology, I am inclined to believe that both the divine as well as the evil, God as well as Satan, are accommodating themselves to the psychology and mentality, and the world and life view of the people and are operating within the milieu as it is. This appears to me as scriptural, factual, and existential. With this *premise* in mind, I turn to demonology as I have found it in the Third World.

Demonism and Possession

To define demonism within the above outlined frame of reference is not a simple matter. Whatever else it may mean, it is a reality, a force, a dynamic, *an intelligence.* It operates as an extraneous force and influence and in the form and patterns of intelligent personality. It functions mediately and immediately and makes its dynamic felt in various ways. The interpretation of the force can be disputed, but the presence of the fact is difficult to deny.

Thinking in terms of a spiral staircase, we may think of demonism and possession in the Third World on four levels that may not be sharply divided but that spiral upward and increase in intensity.

1. *The creation of an oppressive, general "atmosphere,"*
   an "air" of fear, suspicion and animosity

Experientially it is realized as a general, negative dynamism, an oppressive influence upon the mind and emotions and creating suspicion and distrust. It generates a counteracting, oppressive, repelling social and mental environment, a tone and an "air" that is nonconducive to position, action, and progress. While its presence is felt, it is most difficult to define and to describe. It rests like a heavy cloud upon the community. There is a feeling of discomfort, uneasiness and restlessness, uncertainty, and insecurity. Such have been repeatedly my personal experiences. Well do I recall the almost overwhelming depression that came upon me as I entered the premises and inner "sanctuary" of the "goddess" (Kali) in Nandi, Fiji with its horrifying blood-smeared image. The pace of walking became abnormal and breathing irregular. Similar was the experience in the Kali temple premises in Calcutta, India. Attendance at a ceremonial dance in eastern Zaire brought an impact of oppression and ill feeling to me in the "electrified" general, negative, and depressive atmosphere of the situation. It was very similar in Dahomy, West Africa, as we observed a priest at the altar sacrificing chickens and chanting incantations to appease the evil spirits at the bottom of an "indwelt" tree. Robert Peterson is describing his experience after a visit to a Festival of the First Full Moon after New Year when the Chinese of Kalimantan (Borneo), Indonesia, devote several days to the worship of evil spirits. The story is worth reading. He reports it in *Are Demons for Real?* [2] His depression, awful spiritual struggles and thoughts of suicide are quite common to such an oppressive atmosphere and influences. They are not attacks and encounters but mental and emotional pressures of the darkest nature. They are not the arrows of the Wicked One but the strangling atmosphere of Satan.

However, oppression is not the only experience. Often there is irrational fear to the degree that it generates terror and phobia. Suspicion and animosity are a very common phenomena and make life wretched for the whole community.

The judgment of many anthropologists is not necessarily absolute and final to attribute *all* fear, suspicion and animosity to cultural differences and to mistakes missionaries have made in their initial contact with people. Many missionaries are well aware of the operations of an extraneous, intelligent force opposing them and sustaining over prolonged periods an atmosphere of hostility and fierce opposition which made gospel ministries most difficult. Why such hostility should express itself through special personages will become evident later.

2. *The focalization of demonic powers in objects and practices*

The risk of not differentiating sufficiently between occultism, spiritism, and demonism, and perhaps falling prey to a mentality of continuum is always serious. Yet, I cannot help but believe that there is such a thing as demonic focalization in certain objects and operating uniquely through certain formulas. These objects (including words) become special embodiments and vehicles of demonic powers and convey supra-human and supra-natural potency. Strange phenomena proceed from them. Sounds and voices are heard, flames are seen shooting forth from rocks and trees as lightning or bright flashes, and strange and destructive influences are emanating from them. Dr. John S. Mbiti reports several rather peculiar experiences in *African Religions and Philosophy* (pp. 194-97). Trustworthy eyewitnesses have informed me that they have seen flames shooting up from rocks repeatedly in Timor, Indonesia, and trees have been seen burning without being destroyed. Experiences as described by Dr. Mbiti and the reports from Timor are quite common in Southeast Asia and the South Pacific. Of course, we may dismiss such stories as imagination, fables, the product of a mythological nonreality mentality, as hypnotism, as phobia objectified. But such "explanations" do not necessarily make these experiences such. It could also be that our "explanation" is the projection of our mentality and the objectification of our prejudices. One possibility is as real as the other.

It has been experienced that the transportation of an idol has actually brought serious physical disturbances, destruction, and death to the new locality and community. In some instances, nothing but the return to the former place could restore peace and tranquility to the new locality. At other instances a former priest and specific sacrifices could atone for and placate the outraged spirit. The books *Demon Experiences: A Compilation* [3] and *Are Demons for Real?* (mentioned above) report numerous instances to support the view. My personal experiences in Africa, especially in Dahomy and certain villages in Nigeria and in Timor, Indonesia, leave no room for doubt in my mind. Unforgettable are the impressions and mental pressures that I experienced in the peculiar atmosphere that surrounded two very large trees in the interior of Dahomy at which trees numerous twin children had been sacrificed to the spirits of the ancestors who were supposed to *indwell* those trees. Peculiar stories were being told of terrifying phenomena that seemed to proceed from those trees, especially in the evening hours and at times of "sacrifices."

It is my impression that the focalization of demonic powers in objects and practices is the secret of "magical" powers of charms and fetishes. Here also is the secret of the potency of the "curse" in witchcraft, sorcery, the evil eye, etc. Let no one imagine that words do not carry power, that they cannot become embodiments of dynamics. It is so with the Word of God. His Word is power-bearing. It is a living and powerful Word. Can the opposite be true also? Can words become bearers of destructive forces? Can the curse carry paralyzing effects and the power of death? Perhaps no other man has penetrated into the "mystery of iniquity" more deeply than Dr. Pieter Middelkoop in his doctor's dissertation at the University of Utrech in Holland. After spending some twenty-five years in Timor, Indonesia, he wrote his dissertation under the title: "Curse-Retribution-Enmity, a study of the Natural Religion in Timor, Indonesia." This study is most illuminating, and his reports and conclusions are quite convincing. A new world of operations is opened to us as we read such a book.

Much can be explained on psychological levels, and more will become natural as the sciences proceed in their investigations. I also want to make room for incited imaginations, superstition, projection, and mythological nonreality mentality. Yet, when everything has been said and subtracted, many experiences appear to be of such a nature as to lie beyond the psychological and the natural. There are sufficient indications that the power is supra-human *and intelligent*. That on the one hand it responds to acts of obeisance and worship, and on the other hand that it bows to and flees from the Name of Jesus and the power of His blood.

The realization of the reality of the focalization of demonic powers in objects and practices is also the key to the understanding of the uncompromising attitude of the Bible to all forms of idolatry. We cannot enter into a comprehensive study of the biblical attitude to the curse, witchcraft, sorcery, and black arts.

Two things, however, are clear. First, the Bible realizes the reality of evil in these practices. It does so not because they are superstitions and pagan cultural and religious "hang-overs," but because they are *embodiments of evil*. Second, the Bible condemns such practices without compromise and apology.

Even broader and deeper is the biblical approach to idolatry. Idolatry according to the Scriptures is evil in the final degree. *It is a confrontation of God.* It is not a denial of God but a substitution for God. Because of this, it is branded as iniquity, terror, nonentity, horror, figure, cause of grief (different Hebrew words used for an idol). Paul associates it with demonism (1 Cor. 10:20, 21). In clearest words does the New Testament exclude the idolaters from the kingdom of God. Why? Because idolatry is the most serious form of human and demonic confrontation of God and the sharpest and deepest focalization of evil under the cloak of a religious object.

3. *Demon Possession of a Violent Nature*

This is the phenomenon we are most familiar with. Here is something that is so evident, so obvious that no one can doubt the abnormality. The debate, of course, may be whether such experiences are mental, psychological, psychosomatic, occultic, or demonic. While the debate in the academic realm continues and ought to continue to seek to differentiate and delineate if and wherever possible between various kinds and/or gradations, the Bible believer and the down-right realist in the midst of life situations has no choice in the matter of the *fact* and *reality* of possession. The Bible relates sufficient instances to establish the fact of demon possession of the most violent kinds. And eyewitnesses of present-day demon possession are too numerous to bypass the evidences. Perhaps the best arguments are witnesses who have been victims of demon possession and then have been gloriously and victoriously delivered by the power of Christ.

Since this is a phenomenon so general and so similar wherever found in this world, I need not dwell upon it here. It is a fact too broadly experienced to be ignored and too well established to be denied.

4. *Demon Possession and Cultic Possession*

Perhaps the finest summary of this aspect of our study is presented by I. M. Lewis in "Ecstatic Religion." His book is *An Anthropological Study of Spirit Possessions and Shamanism.* It should be noted that Dr. Lewis uses the word shaman in a very broad and general way to designate religious practitioners. He begins his exploration of the shaman phenomenon as found in wide areas of the world with the following paragraph:

> This book explores that most decisive and profound of all religious dramas, *the seizure of man by divinity.* Such ecstatic encounters are by no means uniformly encouraged in all religions. Yet it is difficult to find a religion which has not, at some stage in its history, inspired in the breasts of at least certain of its followers those *transports of mystical exaltation* in which man's whole being seems to fuse in a glorious communion with the divinity. Transcendental experiences of this kind, typically conceived of as *states of "possession,"* have given the mystic a unique claim to *direct experiential knowledge of the divine* and, where this is acknowledged by others, the authority to act as a privileged channel of communication between man and the supernatural. *The accessory phenomena associated with such experiences, particularly the "speaking in tongues," prophesying, clairvoyance, the transmission of messages from the dead, and other mystical gifts, have naturally attracted the attention not only of the devout but also of skeptics.* For many people, in fact, such phenomena seem to provide persuasive evidence for the existence of a world transcending that of ordinary everyday experience.[4]

It must be kept in mind that the number of religious

practitioners or "specialists" (Mbiti) differs considerably in the various religions. Dr. John S. Mbiti mentions the following: medicine men, rainmakers, kings, priests, witches, sorcerers, prophets or seers, diviners, mediums, and magicians. While the first four perform more positive and constructive functions, the latter five are mostly negative and destructive. Therefore, they are feared and hated. It may happen that all or most of these functions are performed by one and the same person or by two or three people. The classification is seldom clear and precise. However, all of the functions are related in the mind of the people to "possessions" of one kind or another. Because of this, these specialists are "made." They are not considered as men and women naturally gifted with abilities to function in their role and "calling." Only possessions can endow them for their office and work.

The "making" of the practitioner varies considerably from area to area and from "calling" to "calling." For many it is a series of strenuous, time-consuming experiences. It is not my intention to burden ourselves with these details in procedures. However, there are certain specific and perhaps universal aspects and principles in the experiences of "making" which we need to note.

First, we observe that few of the specialists are conscious "volunteers" in their calling. A shaman is considered first and foremost a man who has been summoned and seized upon by his "gods." He does not enter upon a self-chosen path. Rather, he responds to a summons, he yields to a pressure, he succumbs to a pursuit, he surrenders involuntarily to a "calling" of an extraneous dictate and power. The initiator is thus an outside agency. We are, of course, inclined to think of the above experiences as psychological and, perhaps even social, predispositions to becoming a religious specialist. The signs of such pursuit are:

> hiding from the light, hysterically exaggerated crying and singing, sitting passively in a withdrawn state on a bed or on the ground, racing off hysterically (inviting pursuit), hiding in rocks, climbing up trees, etc. Unless there are contra-indications, people who exhibit these symptoms of hysterical flight are likely to be regarded as possessed by a spirit, and may or may not, be encouraged to become shamans. If they do receive support and encouragement, they quickly learn to cultivate the power of experiencing demonstrable ecstasy. And when in response to such appropriate stimuli as drumming and singing they can produce

this state at will, they are well on the road to public recognition as "masters of spirits." The controlled production of trance is taken as evidence of controlled possession by spirits.[5]

Second, we note that the initiatory experience is a violent culmination of being possessed by an invading, transcendental power which overwhelms the individual and submits him to the power and authority of the intruder. This results in temporary psychological disorders, trances, and mental dissociation:

> Thus the shaman's initiatory experience is represented as *an introductory surrender to disorder*, as he is thrust protesting into the chaos which the ordered and controlled life in society strives so hard to deny, or at least keep at bay. *No matter how valiantly he struggles, disorder eventually claims him and marks him with the brand of a transcendental encounter.* At its worst, in peripheral cults, this is seen as a baneful intrusion of malign power. At its best, in central possession religions it represents a *danger-laden exposure to the powers of the cosmos.* In both cases the initial experience withdraws the victim from the secure world of society and of ordered existence, and exposes him directly to those forces which, though they may be held to uphold the social order, also ultimately threaten it.[6]

Third, the secret of being an effective specialist, however, does not lie in the fact of being possessed by "transcendental mystery and power" but in mastery of this possessing and indwelling potency to do the will and biddings of the specialist. The possessed person must become the possessor and lord of the spirit within him. His training and practices must continue until he becomes the master of the god within him and makes him subservient to his biddings. The specialist thus becomes a god in his own right. "From being subject at the whim of the gods, to involuntary, uncontrollable experiences of disorder, the shaman has progressed to a point where he has achieved a stable and dominant relationship with the grounds of affliction." Therefore and eventually the shaman is not the slave, but the master of anomaly and chaos. He ultimately triumphs over the chaotic experiences of "raw power" which threatened to drag him under. "Out of the agony of affliction and the dark night of the soul, he breaks through into the daylight of ecstasy and spiritual victory. In rising to the challenge of the powers which rule his life and by valiantly overcoming them in this crucial initiatory rite which reimposes order on chaos and despair, man reasserts his mastery of the universe and affirms his control of destiny and fate."

"The shaman is thus the symbol not of subjection and despondency but of independence and hope." Through him the otherwise unfettered, mysterious power of the world beyond society as well as the spirit world are harnessed purposefully and applied to minister to the needs, demands, and wishes of the community. However, the harnessed potency can also be manipulated into the greatest destructive power and bring misery and calamity upon the enemies. It serves to bless and prosper as well as to avenge and destroy.

Lewis summarizes the making of the professional in the following words:

> *The essential process* in the making of a shaman is thus as follows. Suffering interpreted as possession involves an invasion of the human body which is usurped as a vehicle for the spirit. In trance the host's personality fades away and is replaced by the power of the possessing agent. But while this is a general experience which may befall any socially appropriate member of society, for the shaman it is merely the first indication of his future vocation. By overcoming this spiritual assault a new relationship is forged with the spirit which makes the victim of this experience a shaman with a consequent change in his status.[7]

In his book, *African Traditional Religion*, Parrinder speaks of various "sacred specialists." After describing the priest and his functions, he presents the "mediums" and their making:

> The mediums often have a hard training to undergo. After the initial possession, which may come upon them spontaneously at a dance, they exert great efforts, and endure privations, in the attempt to induce the return of spirit possession. For times of varying length the medium tries to produce coherent messages in a state of trance. These will often be almost unintelligible at first, but gradually they become clearer till they can be produced at will while the medium is in a genuine trance.
>
> In parts of West Africa, especially Dahomey, there are communal training centres for mediums and assistants to priests, called cult-houses or "convents." Here the novices are secluded for months or years. The entry to the cult-house is generally preceded by an acted ritual of death, to symbolize the death of the neophyte to the world. Finally there is a resurrection to a new life. When the

mediums emerge at the end of their training they come out into the world as new personalities, they speak a new ritual language, bear new names, and profess to be returning home from a distant country.

The spirits believed to possess the mediums are very varied. Mediums may impersonate the type of god they represent, strutting like a warrior, waddling like a pregnant woman, or barking like a dog. The mediums dress up to fit the part, and have their special regalia, with bracelets and other ornaments which are put on when the beating of drums has induced the ecstatic state. In their heavy necklaces and adornments of cowrie shells and seeds, and many other accoutrements, they are impressive to look at.

There is a clear difference between mediumistic possession and that of seizure by evil spirits who come to trouble man and make them ill. Many tribes do not think that ancestral spirits possess men, but rather accompany and control them, giving messages through them. The spirit is not an alien invading force living permanently with the medium, but it only comes occasionally. On the other hand people are believed to become sick when some troublesome demon comes to take up its abode in them, and the assistance of a doctor is sought to cast out the evil.[8]

A distinction thus exists in the minds of the people between what I call "violent possession" and "cultic possession." In either case, however, it is *possession*.

Such, in general, is the philosophy which underlies the "making" of the religious practitioner.

It is difficult to deny or doubt reality and mystery back of the religious specialist. The very persistence of the specialist over vast areas of the globe over the millennia and the air which surrounds these personages are a peculiar human and religious phenomena. And the fact that scientism and secularism, philosophy, and education have not been able to eradicate it even in the Western world speaks a language all of its own. It appears to be an argument for a mystery which by its very existence and ineradicability demands attention.

The third aspect in the "making" of the specialist, however, needs a comment. Does the "shaman" *really master* the spirit within him? Three answers are given. Some would insist that this actually happens. It establishes the fact of "man's absolute autonomy" and his mastery of all around him. Hegelian idealism may support such a view. Man's lordship and autonomy must be absolute and triumph.

A second answer points in the direction of absolute

identification of the spirit of man and the invading spirit. In the process of his training, not mastery but accommodation and identification have been achieved to the degree that differentiation becomes difficult. The fusion has been solidified, and functional harmony has been established to the degree of perfection of unity without serious tensions.

A third answer would suggest that not mastery but deception has been achieved. The practitioner may achieve a *conscious feeling of mastery* but that such conscious feeling of mastery is not real mastery. It is subconsciously dominated, motivated, inspired, and empowered. Thus possession by the invading power and intelligence has laid hold of man's deepest resources. Possession has become complete on the deepest level and irrevocable on the purely human level.

Be it accommodation, identification, or deception, in the final end possession has become an awful reality, demonism has triumphed, and man becomes the victim and tool of powers beyond him to accomplish the anti-God purpose within certain individuals and communities.

Conclusion

I conclude my study by the affirmation that demonism is real and demon possession is an awful fact. While much mystery surrounds the whole phenomenon, its reality is difficult to deny. Much in so-called occultism, spiritism, and demonism will be explained by further explorations in psychology and psychiatry. However, there is a realm of reality which functions and operates on the level of intelligent personality. There is intelligent Evil in this world.

Notes

1. John S. Mbiti, ed., *African Religions and Philosophy* (New York: Praeger, 1969), pp. 194, 198.

2. Robert Peterson, *Are Demons for Real?* (Chicago: Moody Press, 1972).

3. *Demon Experiences: A Compilation* (Wheaton, Ill.: Tyndale House).

4. I. M. Lewis, *An Anthropological Study of Spirit Possessions and Shamanism*, p. 18.

5. *Ibid.*, p. 54.

6. *Ibid.*, p. 188.

7. *Ibid.*, p. 189.

8. E. C. Parrinder, *African Traditional Religion* (London: S.P.C.K.), pp. 102-3.

11

Demonism on the Mission Field:
Problems of Communicating
a Difficult Phenomenon

W. STANLEY MOONEYHAM

Let me say right at the start that I feel like something of a charlatan in venturing upon this subject before such a distinguished company. My training is in journalism. I am a mission executive and, for what it's worth, a world traveler. My remarks come therefore from one who assesses rather than makes reports, and who can lay no claim to being either anthropologist or missiologist. The different types and more technical aspects of demonism I confidently leave to other papers and more expert hands.

I fully recognize the widespread interest in the occult which has sprung up here at home over the past few years. Perhaps this is a positive reaction to the widespread materialism and spiritual dryness that is so evident. However, I readily accept the suggestion that this paper should focus outside North America and Europe.

Finally, even if it is relevant to the subject given me (and I doubt it), I do not feel qualified to discuss exorcism, a very specialized ministry which, properly understood, involves unusual qualities of faith, prayer and fasting (Matt. 17:19-21).

As a journalist, then, I feel that our common purpose can best be served if I deal with such questions as these: What is happening on the mission field today? How are we to understand what is being reported? Are the reports credible? Do we understand them correctly? What do they contribute to our Western grasp of demon activity? I also

210 / Demon Possession

want to touch on the problems of Western bias in approaching the subject, and some of the factors necessary in establishing a balanced perspective.

The most widely read reports of demonism come from very different sources: missionaries, national church leaders, national laity, semi-experts, nonexperts. The accounts frequently appear as brief items in mission magazines, as occasional (often superficial) feature articles in Christian or secular periodicals, and as contributions to so-called popular publications oriented to the weird, the bizarre, and the occult.

Let me set the scene by citing ten examples of, or comments on, demonism from three continents. For these I am indebted to sources we have every reason to regard as reliable. The mission field is vast and varied; you will, I know, understand if I seem to jump abruptly from one thing to another. The examples are brief, involving no more than the passing of bones from one graveyard to another in the time-honored manner of Ph.D. candidates, but hopefully these will give enough background to indicate the complex range of our subject.

1. From an editorial survey in *Christian Life* magazine, June, 1958:

> Indians at Arajuno mission base knew in a few hours what had happened when five missionaries deep in Ecuador's Auca territory in 1956 failed to make radio contact with anxiously waiting fellow missionaries. How? They asked a local witch doctor. He obliged by falling into a trance, calling up his favorite demons and asking them to tell him where the missing missionaries were. According to the friendly Indians, they heard the demons leave the scene and, in a short time, return with the message that the missionaries were in the Curaray river with Auca lances in them.

2. From Dr. William D. Reyburn, writing in a 1958 issue of *Practical Anthropology*:

> It is common for the missionary to recoil emotionally when a trusted convert turns up describing in vivid detail how spirits from the spring chased a man into the forest and nearly killed him.

3. From *Demon Experiences in Many Lands*, a symposium published by Moody Press in 1960, in which W. E. Wright, a missionary in Western Nigeria, tells of his encounter with a witch doctor:

He volunteered to read to me from his book, and before I could stop him, for I had seen enough, he began nonsense reading in an ordinary voice. Then suddenly his voice changed. He was possessed, and I heard a demon through his lips telling me that I had a sick little girl in my house. (My daughter had been sick for several days, and as he was a total stranger it was unlikely that he would have heard it.) I silenced him as quickly as I could, reading to him from my Book.

4. From a 1964 issue of *Practical Anthropology* comes this testimony of a Choco believer in Latin America, quoted by Dr. Jacob A. Loewen:

I am so glad for the powerful Spirit of God who keeps those who have given God the hand and walk on God's road. A few nights ago we had a real testing. . . . A Colombian witch doctor came to visit a relative who lives in my house. I used to be afraid of devils, and so when this witch doctor was going to "sing demons" at night, I became worried that I would again become afraid. So before going to sleep I told God about the things that were on my heart. I told him, "You have brought me from the devil's hand; you have taken my fear away. Don't let me or my family become afraid this night." It was after midnight when I suddenly awoke hearing someone talking loudly. When I listened, I heard the witch doctor say, "Who has been praying? My hai won't come tonight." I was happy to know and to see again that God is stronger than all the devils. When the Spirit of God watches my house, the devil's can't even come there.

5. From Hugh White, veteran Southern Presbyterian missionary in China:

Demonism as seen today is the same as in the time of Christ. The terminology is so identical as to make one feel that he is walking the streets of Nazareth or Capernaum. It is a common experience that the demon "vexes" one, the demon talks, comes and goes, throws the patient down, tries to kill him.

6. From Robert Peterson, Overseas Missionary Fellowship worker in Borneo, writing in his book *Storm Over Borneo* about the 1967 Dyak uprising:

The Dyak is completely dominated by his belief in an invisible spirit world. A spirit is his life-long companion and leaves him only after death. If the spirit is malevolent, nothing will go right. If benevolent, good fortune will follow him. There is also a vast host of other spirits living in the jungle, and exerting a tremendous influence on his life. They must therefore be treated with the utmost respect, and periodical blood sacrifices must be made. . . . Evidences of demonic power were witnessed at Andjungan. Dyaks used their fists and feet to break display cases with glass flying all over the place. Some actually danced on it with bare feet but no one was injured. One missionary watched Dyaks step into pans of acid used to coagulate rubber. Undiluted, this acid can normally burn the flesh to the bone, but these men were unharmed. Others struck locked and barred doors with their bare hands, breaking them down as easily as if they had been rammed by a truck. . . . These things are hard to understand, but we realize that Satan is powerful and . . . able to endow men with his power when it suits his purpose.

7. From a paper given by the Reverend Detmar Scheunemann at the 1974 International Congress on World Evangelization at Lausanne:

A very rich family in Java has achieved its riches through making a covenant with Satan on one of the famous mountain peaks (Kawi) on condition that one member of the family dies every year. This is taking place.

8. From *Whitened Harvest*, a 1970 publication of the West Indies Mission:

James G. Leyburn has created a creed which expresses most of the common ideas of the vodun system in Haiti: "I believe in scores of gods and spirits, guardians of earth and sky, and of all things visible and invisible; I believe that all these vodun . . . are potent, although less majestic than le bon Dieu of the Christians; that some of them came with our ancestors from our former home in Africa, while others we have learned about in our Haitian fatherland; that these loa have power to possess us, their worshippers, informing us of their needs and desires, which we must faithfully satisfy; that these loa, like us, are capable of good and evil, gentleness and anger, mercy and revenge. I believe in the efficacy of sacrifices; in the pleasures of living; in respect due to twins; in the careful cult of the dead who may return to our abodes; in the spiritual causation of diseases and misfortune; in the dance through which we may be 'mounted' by our loa; in the possibility of interfering with the normal flow of events by means of magic; in the efficacy of charms and spells; and in the Holy Catholic Church."

9. From Dr. Frank Cooley, longtime missionary in Indonesia, in a private letter written in December, 1972, about the revival in Timor:

> In all parts of Timor and the surrounding islands, belief in spirits, demons, occult powers, black and white magic is prevalent. This is not uncommon even amongst those who call themselves Christians and are baptized church members. The teams therefore concentrated heavily on cleansing and liberating individual Christians and the church from these burdens. . . . The atmosphere in Timor villages is almost wholly traditional, tribal, only half a century out of a completely indigenous ("animistic") religious sphere, and 94.36% of the people live in villages. In the indigenous situation belief in and practice of miracles, the visible, physical acts of the spirits and demons, the vivid manifestation of power in curse and blessing, the unquestioned authority of functionaries related to the world of the spirits and demons was practically universally held and experienced.

10. From the Reverend J. M. Brodie, a Scottish missionary, in a personal letter dated October, 1974:

> There is a real fear of demons among the people with whom we were living in North-East India. Sickness is often attributed to a demon, and the witch doctor called in to expel the demon. . . . In Christian high schools skits are often performed at school functions by the senior "enlightened" students, making the witch doctor a figure of fun, but the fear of demons goes deep and is not easily eradicated. Among certain Indians we have met, very young boys are dressed as girls to deceive the evil spirits who might otherwise harm the child, since a boy is regarded as of so much more worth than a girl. Missionary colleagues have told me of a demon possession in Nepal, and of evil spirits being called back into the monasteries by the lamas of Bhutan, as the trumpets are sounded at twilight.

The quotations I have just read not only testify to the reality of demon activity, but at the same time link it with such powers as the knowledge of distant events, the use or understanding of an unknown language, and abnormal displays of physical strength. The examples show also, among other things, that there are even baptized Christians who somehow learn to coexist with demon activity; that there are others whose "Spirit-consciousness" enables them to recognize and refute evil spirits through the Holy Spirit;

that missionaries have found startling parallels in occurrences of demonism separated by nineteen centuries and thousands of miles; that demons demand slavish obedience and payment of tribute; and that the centuries-old belief that a deal can be made with the king of demons himself is far from being discredited in our modern age.

A further point is made by anthropologist and Bible translations consultant Dr. Jacob Loewen, who has had considerable experience in Latin America and Africa. He says that, while in Latin America the evil spirits were part of the original creation, in Africa they are ancestral spirits who have become malevolent because they are no longer being remembered and have lost their connection with humans. Where they *are* remembered, they are benevolent and helpful. Now I do not profess to understand all of this, but I report it as the view of a responsible observer.

Despite the ten illustrations given above, which I regard as credible, there is considerable difficulty in obtaining accurate information about demon activity unless a reliable person is actually an eyewitness. Details often come at second or third hand. They may be supplied by someone unfamiliar with demonism or without Christian perspective. They may be reported only partially, without giving the cultural context. They may come from someone whose aim is personal gain or notoriety, or who simply likes a good story.

From this it becomes apparent that, in more than one sense, some spirit-discerning is called for. It is not unknown for individuals to simulate the symptoms of those who are "possessed" and, by alleged communication with spirits, make a tidy living as fortune-tellers or healers. Embellishment and deception are part of human life as a whole, and the serious investigator will not be put off by bogus operators, nor will he fall into the trap of assuming that because we cannot take everything literally we cannot take it seriously.

There are other obstacles to getting at the truth of demon activity. In China during the latter part of the nineteenth century, medical missionary Dr. J. L. Nevius found that to have a case of spirit possession in a family was usually regarded not only as a great misfortune, but as a disgrace, just as leprosy is in some areas today. To tell a foreigner about a neighbor's demon possession would incur not only the resentment of the neighbor, but the vengeance of the demon. And, of course, there is the continuing barrier in all generations and among all peoples about speaking of personal and domestic matters with foreigners.

But there is a difficulty more fundamental about demonism, especially for the first-term missionary. For Westerners, demon activity is something alien. For a major part of the world, on the other hand, including the great ethnic faiths of Asia and the animistic religions of Africa and South America, demonism is a natural part of life in which there is no dichotomy between material and spiritual, no division into rational and nonrational.

Westerners have often scoffed at occult matters—and many of them still do. Because of this, we may note in passing, African students who went to study in Britain would seldom speak of their fears—or their knowledge—openly. Such Western denial of part of another's heritage does nothing for the establishment of rapport with those who come from regions where a man gives traditional respect to the religious feelings of his neighbor.

In my own experience traveling overseas, I have never personally come across demon possession that I could recognize. I have, however, many times been conscious of spiritual battles, where the presence of evil was very real, and I was conscious that a spiritual conflict was taking place.

I am sure that had I had a different cultural background and different "eyes" for perceiving the world, I might have seen the visible manifestations of this demonic activity. My technology-oriented, rationalistic, Western culture simply prevented me from seeing what the people of other cultures see and experience in a more tangible way.

Ironically, my only definite encounter with demon possession was here in the United States. I was in a counseling session with a lady and, even with my knowledge of how demon powers operate, I didn't recognize that demons might be involved. She had been to psychiatrists, had been in mental institutions, and I just did not consider the possibility of demonism, although I kept sensing, in some nonverbal way, that something was wrong. It was only some time later, when she came back and told me of her complete deliverance from demons, that I learned what the situation had been. Then things made sense. And in her case, the change of personality was dramatic. No longer was there the wild look of terror in her eyes; she had become poised, relaxed and attractive. Here again, I feel that my cultural orientation prevented me from clearly recognizing demon activity. And I think this is often true for missionaries and observers from the Western world.

The Western missionary inevitably carries with him his own culture and his own prejudices, conscious or unconscious. Coupled with youthful enthusiasm, these attitudes might add up to a new broom sweeping away the garbage of centuries—with no thought that it could perhaps be sifted and recycled. It has taken us a long time to learn that people must be dealt with according to their situation and environment. Missions were often founded on bases reflected in their valedictory hymns: "Far, far away, in heathen darkness dwelling . . . / The heathen in his blindness bows down to wood and stone." And of course it was true. The danger lay rather in the side effects that encouraged a certain arrogance toward indigenous culture, including the belief that the savage mind was utterly devoid of truly religious thoughts.

"I brought with me to China," wrote Dr. Nevius, "a strong conviction that a belief in demons, and communications with spiritual beings, belongs exclusively to a barbarous and superstitious age, and at present can consist only with mental weakness and want of culture." When Nevius and his colleagues first encountered demon possession, they attributed it to fear or hallucination or epilepsy—assumptions still not infrequently made. The fact that they are frequently also true points to a significant principle: a diagnosis of demonism should be preceded by the elimination of every other explanation. Or, if you know your Sherlock Holmes, you will remember his rhetorical question: "How often have I said to you that when you have eliminated the impossible, whatever remains, *however improbable*, must be the truth?"

Where indigenous beliefs about demonism were condemned out of hand by missionaries, as in parts of Africa, there was a predictable reaction. As Dr. Reyburn has pointed out, the African spirit world went underground. African converts to Christianity were understandably bewildered by the missionary's summary rejection of a whole dimension of life. Did he not, after all, teach about a Holy Spirit, and an evil spirit that pulled the other way? So the missionary's testimony is damaged. Dr. Loewen, in an unpublished paper, suggests why this is, in a concise summary of how the African might see the missionary's life:

> He reads the Bible and preaches about evil spirits and the Spirit of God, but when you suggest that a certain person has fever spirits, he resolutely says, "No, that is malaria! That does not come from a spirit, it comes from a mosquito bite!" Missionaries speak long, loud, and emphatically about the need of being led by the Spirit; but again and again, when members of the indigenous church feel the Holy Spirit's leading in one direction, the missionary's decisions go in another direction. So what do you believe? What the missionary says or the way he lives? Furthermore, since the missionary usually controls the purse strings, national believers have found that it pays to listen to the missionary. . . .

There is no need to underline the dangers inherent in that line of thought, with its parallels with the "rice Christians" of another continent. An added danger is that the whole question of evil spirits may remain just beneath the surface, never brought into the light of day for the sort of open discussion that would benefit all parties, except the devil who thrives on secrecy—and perhaps make symposia like this one unnecessary. Some missionaries, unfortunately, do not possess the scientist's or the journalist's faculty of curiosity. Some may feel secretly appalled at the prospect of precipitating a situation with which they may not be able to cope (and if they have doubts, they *won't* cope). Satan and his emissaries must be defeated, not ignored.

At the same time a balance must be maintained. It is possible to develop an unhealthy preoccupation with the demonic and thereby lose sight of the fact that it is only one facet of the diabolic strategy. At one of the group discussions at the Lausanne Congress, someone suggested as a guideline: "Never go looking for demons, but if one appears under your feet, tread on it!"

African attitudes have been strongly influenced in modern times by Western secularization. The latter introduces elements not strictly within the scope of this paper, but we must acknowledge their existence, for they associate Western education with an even more clearcut materialism that divorces matter from spirit.

One more example of the missionary's discrediting of native spirits in Africa is reported in Donald H. Bouma's *Anthropology and Missions*, published in 1957. These spirits were believed to keep a check on whether the village women kept things clean around their houses. If they neglected to do so, the results would be serious, not just for the offender, but for the whole society. When the missionaries dismissed the whole idea, the cleaning no longer seemed important, and so grew the unenviable reputation of "dirty Christian villages." The devil is nothing if not opportunistic, and has that unique capacity for fudging an issue that confirms his reputation as the author of confusion.

What can we learn from such accounts of demonism on the mission field? We find, for example, that less "developed" societies have no difficulty in seeing this world as a perpetual struggle in which evil spirits play a prominent part. Western Christendom once knew it only too well. It is our loss that a creeping materialism even in the church itself serves the devil's cause so well that we seldom sing some of the percipient old hymns such as the one translated from Andrew of Crete by John Mason Neale; it begins:

> Christian, dost thou see them,
> On the holy ground,
> How the powers of darkness
> Compass thee around?
> Christian, up and smite them,
> Counting gain but loss;
> Smite them, Christ is with thee,
> Soldier of the cross.

Unlike our own society, pagan communities are seldom guilty of depreciating evil spirits. Converts from such societies are potentially good expositors of such biblical warnings as 1 Pet. 5:8: "Your enemy the devil, like a roaring lion, prowls about looking for someone to devour"; or, as the Living Bible's striking paraphrase of Eph. 6:12 expresses it: "For we are not fighting against people made of flesh and blood, but against persons without bodies —the evil rulers of the unseen world, those mighty satanic beings and great evil princes of darkness who rule this world; and against huge numbers of wicked spirits in the spirit world." Where can the Holy Spirit find more receptive hearts than those who have gone down to the depths and who have known the stark fear of the evil spirit world? It is reported from southwestern Zambia at the present time that young people are putting their lives in God's hands as a protection against a wave of indiscriminate attacks by evil spirits.

Enough is known to show the advisability of new missionaries being directly trained about demonism so that on the field they will not be taken unawares, but will be ready to recognize it and point the way of deliverance from it. At the Lausanne Congress one missionary told how many Arctic missionaries from his society came under a demonic activity and apprehension with which they could not cope and, as a consequence, left that particular sphere of work. This resulted in the inception of a training and preparation program so that whether the missionaries-to-be accepted the existence of the demonic or not, they were at least prepared when confronted by it.

Both those who must deal firsthand with demon activity and those who read about it from a distance need to continually pray for a scriptural and balanced perspective. Let me summarize three considerations which would apply to persons in either category: (1) We must constantly remind ourselves of the need to appreciate the vast differences between Western and non-Western cultures. We may strive to speak in common terms, but we are looking at the same phenomena from widely divergent perspectives. People of other cultures will perceive these matters far differently than ourselves. (2) We must realize and appreciate that spirit activity is a natural and accepted (though often feared) part of daily life in many cultures. This realization should caution us against casual dismissal of the reports and views of fellow Christians from these cultures. (3) We must challenge, with a sanctified skepticism, reports of demon activity which lack detail, which are second- or third-hand reports, and which are sensationalistic in tone and presentation. Headlines and theater marquees which promise titillation about demons may flatter Satan and feed sensation-seekers, but they do little to warn or edify concerning the desperately serious business carried on by the "prince of darkness."

Brethren, I am very conscious of the inadequacy and scattered nature of these remarks. I hope at least that I have raised questions that will further discussion of the subject about which I have so much to learn. Of two things we can be sure. First (I have said this before but it bears repeating), demonism on the mission field, demonism everywhere, is but one manifestation of the devil's activity on earth. Second, that activity is doomed ultimately to failure because of a Greater One to whom alone belongs not only the kingdom and the glory, but the *power*.

PART SIX

Demonology Viewed Psychiatrically

12

Hysteria and Demons, Depression and Oppression, Good and Evil

WILLIAM P. WILSON

The Christian world has witnessed in the last few years a renewed interest in our enemy Satan. A number of books, including a few reprints of classics such as Nevius' *Demon Possession*, have revived an interest in the occult and in demonology. This phenomenon has occurred in reaction to a rise in occultism and Satan worship that has had great popularity among young persons, especially in high schools and colleges. Satan worship, black magic and voodoo, as well as witchcraft have found practitioners among all social classes but especially among "bikers" and "druggies." Since such practices are dramatic, they are certain to arouse reaction. There is, however, a more subtle form of the practice of evil. This is witnessed in the infiltration of churches and schools, but above all in the harassment of Christian workers as they undertake their work to further the causes of God.

If one accepts the reality of God, the sonship of Christ, and the reality of the Holy Spirit, he must also accept the fact that Satan is very much a reality. Chafer has said that Satan's greatest weapon is to convince the world that he does not exist. But those who are not blinded know that there is a force for evil in the world even though the perpetrator of evil is always man. We, therefore, must accept the fact that this evil is guided by a master intelligence. As there is no proof of his existence, we believe that Satan exists simply because God has said so. But how does he manifest himself? How does he control man?

The most popular mode of control is by demon possession. This phenomenon is, of course, scriptural and has been an area of great attraction for neo-Pentecostals such as Don Basham, Derek Prince, and many others among this group. Some of those interested in demon possession have cataloged over two hundred demons which they cast out of Christians and non-Christians alike. These demons "come out" with vomiting, coughing, spitting, roars, growls, barks, etc. The excessive attention paid to demons in some quarters has brought considerable reaction from such spiritual giants as David Wilkerson. He has cited and discussed some of the basic scriptures that refute the notion that Christians can be demon possessed and clarified the biblical position of the Christian in regard to demons.

The reprinting of Nevius' book, *Demon Possession*, has also made available to us an older work that originated in China where ancestor worship made most Chinese readily subject to demon possession. Nevius, through his observations, was able to catalog and describe certain classical signs of demon possession using data he had accumulated by questioning other missionaries. The signs are:

1. The chief differentiating mark of so-called demon possession is the automatic presentation and the persistent and consistent acting out of a new personality.
   a. The new personality says he is a demon.
   b. He/she uses personal pronouns; first person for the demon, third person for the possessed.
   c. The demon uses titles or names.
   d. The demon has sentiments, facial expressions and physical manifestations that harmonize with the above.
2. Another differentiating mark of demon possession is the evidence it gives of knowledge and intellectual power not possessed by the subject.
3. Another differentiating mark of demonomania intimately connected with the assumption of a new personality is that with the change of personality there is a complete change of moral character (aversion and hatred to God and especially to Christ).

Nevius' description of specific cases is very helpful as is his review of the phenomenon in the early church and in other countries. Finally, Nevius provides us with an excellent apologetic for his work in which he reviews popular attitudes among believers as well as Christian workers.

It is not the purpose of this essay, however, to consider

the theological considerations of demon possession, but to present two possible cases of such possession.

Case Reports

The first occurred as a chance encounter in the hospital environment. The details of the history are not known, but the experience was worthy of description.

A young Black male of approximately 19 years was brought to the Electroencephalography Laboratory for examination. During his EEG examination he had three "spells" that were not associated with the electrographic abnormalities. After the examination was completed, he was suddenly thrown from the chair in which he was sitting with a loud thud! He twitched several times and laid still. As this appeared to be a hysterical seizure, a pillow was put under his head and he was left where he fell. When the author walked by, he suddenly lept to a squatting position and with a loud yell grabbed me by the legs and attempted to lift me up and throw me out a window. As I was bigger, and because I had a head-lock on him, he desisted but tried to fight and hurt me. *His facial expression was one of rage and hatred.* He quieted with sedation.

A second similar case was cared for by the author.

This 32 year old, twice-married female was brought in because of falling spells which had been treated with all kinds of anticonvulsant medication. She was examined on the neurosurgical service and after all examinations including EEG, brain scan, and a pneumoencephalogram were negative, she was transferred to the phychiatric service. Her mental status examination was unremarkable and all of the staff commented that she seemed normal until she had her first "spell."

While standing at the door of the day room she was violently thrown to the floor bruising her arm severely. She was picked up and carried to her room all the while resisting violently. When the author arrived, eight persons were restraining her as she thrashed about on the bed. *Her facial expression was one of anger and hate.* Sedation resulted in sleep. During the ensuing weeks, the patient was treated psychotherapeutically and it was learned that there was considerable turmoil in her childhood home, but because she was "pretty" she was spoiled. She married the type of individual described by Jackson Smith as the first husband of a hysterical female. She was a "high liver" and after her separation and divorce, she was threatened with rejection by her parents. She remarried and her second husband was a "nice" but unexciting man. She continued to associate with her "high living" friends. When her husband demanded that she give up her friends and her parties, she started having the "spells."

The usual psychotherapeutic treatment for hysteria including interviews under sodium amytol only aggravated her spells. Seclusion in the closed section brought her assaultive and combative behavior to an end but she would have spells in which she became mute, especially when religious matters were discussed. More dramatically, when the names Jesus or Christ were mentioned she would immediately go into a trance. On one occasion while in a coma, in desperation, a demon was exorcised and her spells ceased. She subsequently accepted Christ as her savior and has been well since.

These two cases are the only cases that the author has seen that meet the rigid criteria of Nevius for demon possession. In both cases there was no self-identification by the demon, but the profound personality change and the violence of both strongly suggest possession. It has not been the experience of the author that he has encountered other hysterics like these.

Other examples of possible "hysterical" demon possession meeting the criteria of Nevius may be found in the *Three Faces of Eve* by Cleckley, and in *Sybil* by Schreiber.

More recently, considerable attention has been focused on the problem of demonic or satanic oppression. The author has during the last several years encountered three patients who have had symptoms that suggested this phenomenon.

A 16 year old female was brought by her father, a well-known Christian layman, because of rebellious behavior. The home from which she came was a stable one with little dissension. Both parents were devout Christians who had not forced their beliefs on their child. She had, however, received too much freedom and too many material things. In high school she fell under the influence of a self-proclaimed "witch" who had a profound influence on her while she was a member of the "witch's" coven. This "witch" introduced her to drug use.

She became increasingly disturbed so that her behavior became erratic and chaotic.

On admission she was not found to be rebellious or angry as were most young persons of her age. She admitted freely to participating in Satanic worship services. She did comment that these always left her disturbed and anxious. She had a feeling of oppression—of being weighted down. She would not, however, cooperate with therapy and rejected any kind of counseling.

Eventually she came under the influence of a young male Christian worker whose spiritual guidance and prayer led her to a renewal of her faith. She is now doing well in college.

Two other cases in females were characterized by a similar type of oppression.

The first was a 24 year old, single college junior who came from a woman's liberation home where the mother had always chafed at being wife and mother. She brought two children into the world; a girl bright and capable and a son who was minimally brain damaged. Her hostile efforts at control drove her husband first to infidelity then finally to suicide after 24 years of marriage.

The daughter, a college freshman, was disturbed by the family turmoil and especially by her father's suicide. After his death, she first tried sex, then "dope," then after a series of unsuccessful affairs, she too had tried suicide. Interestingly, some of her sexual explorations led to orgies that were associated with drugs and Satan worship. She had purchased a number of books on witchcraft and Satan worship.

In the hospital the patient related her story as outlined but was resistant to any type of spiritual intervention until she was taught how to relate to people in love. With this maneuver, she became open to the gospel and finally accepted Christ. After discharge, she did well but called one day to say she felt an oppression every time that she walked into her apartment. When asked if she had burned her books on witchcraft and Satan, she said she had not, but would. She did and her oppression was relieved. She has been asymptomatic for one year.

A third case was more dramatic.

A 32 year old, white female, separated mother of two boys called to seek an appointment. When told she could not be seen for two months, she began to scream and cry so that the secretary handed the phone to the author who was standing in her office. The patient said that a friend had told her to call because she did not feel that she could survive behaving as she had. As it was possible to see her, the patient was given an appointment during which she related the following story.

Raised in a religious home, her mother had used love withdrawal as a disciplinary technique. This was so drastic, however, that the mother would refuse to speak to the patient and would turn her back on her for periods up to two weeks. After much verbal abuse and denegration by her "Christian" mother, she married to "get away from home" during her second year in college. Her husband who was successful but unexciting was a bore so that after her first child was born, she had an affair. The birth of a second child was followed by a second affair. Within months she left her husband and cohabited with a Black man for three months. This came to an end when she met and began dating a "biker" who introduced her to shoplifting ("for kicks"), to drugs, and to Satan worship. During the examination her anguish and turmoil were so profound that one could hardly listen to her story in its entirety.

On this first visit she accepted Christ, and, after doing so, announced: "I'm free, I feel as though a burden has been lifted." She went home and within a few days again felt oppressed, but when she obediently burned her books on witchcraft and Satan, she was relieved. After further psychotherapy she now plans to return to her husband and reestablish her marriage.

These three cases are remarkable in their similarity. Interestingly, they all follow the same pattern of sexual promiscuity, minimal drug use, and Satan worship. Drug use in all three cases was minimal and limited to marijuana and some LSD. The third patient used cocaine on a few occasions.

Although demonic possession is a more popular subject, I have earlier mentioned a more subtle form of satanic influence. This has been encountered on at least seven occasions, five of which are to be described briefly.

In these cases there seems to be a pervasive personality influence that results in evil. These individuals come disguised as angels of light but are wolves in sheep's clothing. In the author's opinion they are the most destructive because of their influence on workers in the church.

The first individual encountered was a neo-pentecostal invited on a lay witness mission. He had been recommended by a friend. He talked much about his "gifts" and encouraged others to seek the kinds of gifts he had received. He condemned others because they did not have his "gifts." When the mission did not go well, a question was raised about the lack of enthusiasm and low motivation of the church members. At this point he suddenly jumped up and in rage accused the coordinator of being judgmental. He told him he was not fit to be a Christian and berated him for his behavior. He refused to pray for the coordinator. During his tirade, his facial expression and attitude was one of vicious anger.

It was ascertained that this individual often behaved in such a manner under similar circumstances.

Two other cases were encountered under similar circumstances.

Case 2 was the lay leader of a large midwestern conference. He too was invited on a mission as an approved witness. On arrival he announced that he had come "to break up the mission." He subsequently urged all in attendance to go home and not to participate for "these missions are destroying *the church*." He denied the divinity of Christ. When asked to leave, he refused to do so for several hours. There was no evidence of schizophrenic thinking and it was said that his work and family life were known to be quite good.

A third case was encountered in a member of the congregation of a large church.

This Sunday School teacher with 20 years of service had a negative attitude toward the mission he was attending. He aroused the witnesses by denying the divinity of Christ and then rejecting their counter arguments which were based on the scriptures. He pricked, goaded and finally antagonized one witness to the point of fisticuffs. Interestingly, his "strongest" argument was that one did not need Christ. All one needed was a closer walk with *God*!

Finally, two persons in attendance at a large meeting that included Christians of all degrees of faith complete our report.

The first was a man who was a participant in a small group at one of these meetings. Among the participants were three spiritual giants. In their discussion of the essentials of Christianity, the necessity for conversion was emphasized. This man responded with the statement, "You think you have it made, don't you? You are all 'saved.' You know you don't need Jesus to have God." The response of the audience was to sit stunned but each began to pray. After a long silence, he got up and left. His facial expression was one of derision.

The second individual was quite similar. While listening to a lecture on Christian counseling, he became incensed when the lecturer made the statement that salvation was a useful tool in changing a personality and that prayer was helpful in uncovering conflict. He indicated his disapproval of such maneuvers with an angry countenance and then delivered an oration on the foolishness of Christ.

All of these cases seem to us to represent a particular kind of satanic spiritual possession. In summary, these individuals (1) were not known to be periodically possessed: (2) their personalities remain constant; (3) they are "anti-Christ"; (4) they had an angry and hostile demeanor during their discourses; (5) all of these individuals were workers of prominence in the church.

Discussion

How then are we to classify them since they do not meet the criteria of Nevius for demon possession? In a like manner they do not seem to be controlled by their human nature as described in the fifth chapter of Paul's letter to the Galatians. We are left then with only one alternative; i.e., they are controlled (not possessed) by an evil spirit.

One has considerable difficulty with such a concept, however, for most do not think of Satan as a spirit. Still there is a scriptural reference to Satan as a "spirit" in Eph. 2:2. Phillips in his discourse on Satan emphasizes the fact that Satan as a spirit does work "by his spirit" in fallen man. His statement leads us to the conclusion that there is a counterpart of the Holy Spirit—an evil spirit—that can control and guide man. Do we have to look any further than at such figures as Stalin and Hitler to see such guidance? What man could in himself conceive of the tortures and diabolical destruction that these men have loosed on the world? Still we will have those who say that such people are not guided by a higher intelligence, but that they in themselves are just evil or that they are what they are because of the childhood experiences that occurred as a result of their families' economic status. Others would blame racism or society. But when we inspect our data, we cannot say that any of our subjects came from the ghetto or from broken homes. Only one was subjected to racism. None of them were in dire economic straits and, as far as we know, they had not been taught evil. How then did they become evil? How did the spirit of evil come into them? We have no answers to this question.

Demon possession and satanic oppression are subjects that defy scientific explanation. Certainly the ownership of books on the occult, witchcraft, and voodoo do not in themselves bring about possession or oppression. One must normally have a personal desire to participate experientially in the occult to become possessed or oppressed. Only in our second case was there no evidence of any discourse with persons involved in satanic practices or in actual worship of Satan. We have not seen similar problems with those who have been involved with Buddhism or Hinduism.

Conclusion

Two cases of a patient who met some of the criteria for demon possession, three cases of satanic oppression, and five cases of individuals who seem to have an evil spirit are reported.

Those who could be considered demon possessed could have been diagnosed as hysteria, those who were oppressed could have been diagnosed as depressed, and those who had an evil spirit would be considered normal variants.

Bibliography

Basham, D. *Deliver Us From Evil.* Washington Depot, Conn.: Chosen Books, 1972.

Chafer, L. S. *Satan.* Grand Rapids, Mich.: Zondervan, 1964.

Cleckley, H. M. and C. H. Thigpen. *The Three Faces of Eve.* New York: McGraw Hill, 1957.

Cruz, Nicky. *Satan on the Loose.* Old Tappan, N.J.: Fleming H. Revell, 1973.

Lindsey, H. *Satan is Alive and Well on Planet Earth.* Grand Rapids, Mich.: Zondervan, 1972.

Nevius, J. L. *Demon Possession.* Grand Rapids, Mich.: Kregel Publications, 1968.

Pentecost, J. D. *Your Adversary the Devil.* Grand Rapids, Mich.: Zondervan, 1969.

Phillips, McC. *The Bible, the Supernatural and the Jews.* Minneapolis, Minn.: Bethany Fellowship, Inc.

Schreiber, F. R. *Sybil.* New York: Warner Books, Inc., 1973.

Smith, J. A. *Psychiatry: Descriptive and Dynamic.* Baltimore, M.D.: The Williams and Wilkins Co., 1959.

Wilkerson, D. "Demons," *The Cross and the Switchblade* [periodical], X (1972), 3-5, 1972.

13

Commentary on Hysteria and Demons, Depression and Oppression, Good and Evil

JOHN WARWICK MONTGOMERY

It is most refreshing to read a paper on demon possession by a professional psychiatrist who does not regard belief in the existence of personal supernatural evil as a hopeless anachronism. The mere fact that Dr. Wilson affirms what Scripture has to say about the devil and his machinations so outweighs any technical problems the paper may present that this critic wishes his comments to be understood in a context of approbation and appreciation.

Bibliographically, I could wish for the establishment of a list of the classical signs of demon possession on a much broader base than Nevius alone provides; such early treatments as those by Weyer, Le Loyer, Delrio, Sinistrari, Rémy, Guazzo, etc., ought to be consulted, as should modern authorities on the level of Summers and Koch.[1] Epistemologically, I am uncomfortable with fideistic assertions that "as there is no proof of his existence, we believe that Satan exists simply because God has said so"; a wider contact with the classical literature of the subject would almost certainly bring the essayist to the conclusion that there is overwhelming extra-biblical data in empirical confirmation of the scriptural claims (even the great French novelist Huysmans' cat became objectively aware of the direct demonic attacks which his master suffered, and the cat, we understand, was not much of a Bible reader.)[2]

But these bibliographical and epistemological peccadillos do not blunt the edge of an excellent essay which endeavors to provide firsthand clinical illustrations of possible demonic oppression, control, and possession. Instead of offering criticism as such, we shall use the opportunity to comment on certain unfortunate tendencies in contemporary evangelical demonology—tendencies to which the essayist himself may not all be a party, but which are alluded to in his paper and which reflect more fundamental theological problems in evangelical circles.

First, the essayist makes reference to certain "spiritual giants" who "refute the notion that Christians can be demon possessed." I must respectfully disagree with these giants. To be sure, Christian believers cannot be torn from Christ's hands by Satan—their ultimate salvation is absolutely assured when they rely solely upon Christ for it (1 John 4:4; Rom. 8:38-39). Moreover, the pattern and direction of their lives is set in Christ, so that nothing occurs which is not for the universal best (Matt. 10:29-32; 1 Cor. 10:13). But, apart from these magnificant ultimate assurances, Christians are as subject to the evil consequences of a fallen world as any non-Christian. Their physical lives can be snuffed out in a moment in a satanic automobile accident caused by a drunken driver; they can be born blind as a result of satanic venereal disease in a parent; the demonic wars of history can ruin them as readily as unbelievers. The rain of sin, as well as rain from the clouds, falls on the just and the unjust. Kurt Koch and others have shown beyond dispute that involvement in occult and demonic practices can produce dire emotional and spiritual effects "to the third and fourth generation" in the families of those who engage in such practices, and that not infrequently there is a spill-over effect on the community at large when some members of it are practicing black arts. As *The Exorcist* illustrates, on the basis of the classical literature of the subject, Satan can even bring about the physical death of the believer in these ways. Christians are no more exempted from such calamities than they are from infections, epidemics, or from the wider evils that are part and parcel of a sin-sick society.

Dr. Wilson is compelled by his data to conclude that instances do occur of inner "control" by evil spirits. He allows that "there is a counterpart of the Holy Spirit—an evil spirit—that can control and guide man," but he is not entirely comfortable with the idea: "One has considerable difficulty with such a concept, however, for most do not think of Satan as a spirit." Why the hesitancy to affirm this obvious truth—reiterated by orthodox Christian dogmaticians from Patristic times through the Reformation to our own day—that Satan can function as a spirit and regularly tries to ape the Trinitarian work of the living God? Does the hesitancy perhaps tie with evangelical reticence to admit to the demon possession of Christians—based, I suggest, on the erroneous notion that a personal commitment to Christ ought to clear the inner life completely of satanic influence and create a fortress area of holiness whose ramparts evil cannot scale? Here we witness the great evangelical dualism in action: Satan is given total control of *everything external to the Christian heart* (politics, society, entertainment, literature, art, etc.), but he is kept from *one inviolate utopia—the inner life of the believer.* Here perfect "separation from the world" is always available, even when it is unsuccessful in separationist church activity and condemnation of non-Christian cultural life in general.

But this is nothing less than false doctrine! As the Reformers properly maintained on the basis of clear scriptural teaching: *Totus homo est caro* (the whole man is flesh), i.e., satanic influence, power, and control cut down the center even of man's psychic life. There is no inner area of safety; no utopian retreat from sin and Satan; no dualistic division of sinful "world" from inner holiness. Freedom from satanic wiles must be sought *eschatologically*—in the new heaven and new earth—not in our present existence under the Cross.

I suggest that a significant degree of emotional immaturity, distress, and even nervous breakdowns among Evangelicals could be traced to this utopian error. Convinced that his inner life *cannot* be satanically worked upon, that only the Holy Spirit can *possibly* influence him within, the Evangelical tries to keep up an "I'm so happy" facade which contradicts his real experience and drives him to hypocrisy at best, psychic collapse at worst. Theologically, it deflects him from the one proper recourse: constant return in penitence to the cross of Christ. Perhaps to admit (as Dr. Wilson rightly does) that Satan can control inner life spiritually would be not only a great gain for studies in demonology but also the path toward recovery of a realistic Reformation view of sanctification on the part of contemporary Evangelicals.

Dr. Wilson's efforts to categorize satanic activity in psychic life as "possession," "oppression," and "control" are exceedingly helpful, and suggest the need for an in-depth study of "Varieties of Satanic Experience." Indeed, a major work of this kind, paralleling William James' classic in its scholarship (though not in its presuppositions!) could arise from the very kind of clinical material Dr. Wilson includes in his essay. Such a work might well establish a continuum of satanic psychic activity along the following lines:

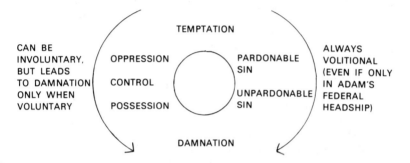

Certainly one needs to distinguish carefully between *sin* (reflecting at least some degree of human volitional self-direction) and *possession*, with its variants (displaying more direct and personal satanic influence, sometimes to the obliteration of human volitional action). Interesting common denominators would arise from such a study, e.g., the experiential fact, attested to in Charles Williams' archetypal novel, *Descent into Hell*, that sin voluntarily persisted in eventually becomes as involuntarily manifest as are the classic signs of demon possession.

A taxonomy of satanic activity would go far to increase our understanding of the tactics of the evil foe, and to be forewarned is always to be forearmed. On the ultimate level, Dr. Wilson is certainly correct that "demon possession and Satanic oppression are subjects that defy scientific explanation," but, as in the biological sciences, a taxonomy can achieve important scientific results even when ultimate explanation of the phenomena studied seems unattainable. Dr. Wilson's own essay points the way toward such a scientific taxonomy of supernatural evil influence.

Notes

1. See the bibliographical notes in my *Principalities and Powers* (Minneapolis: Bethany Fellowship, Inc., 1973), especially n. 7 to chap. 2,

n. 71 to chap. 5, and Appendix D ("Suggested Readings").

2. See Huysmans' *Oeuvres completes* (23 vols.; Paris, 1928-1934), 13:255.

14

Psychological Observations on Demonism

GARY R. COLLINS

Psychologists have always been somewhat embarrassed by the historical background of their discipline. The first people to write about human behavior were philosophers and theologians, a group from which the early psychologists were determined to disassociate. Early publications in psychology concerned formal experiments done in the laboratory of a physiologist and in 1913, when John B. Watson proposed the theory of behaviorism his ideas were readily accepted by the psychological world. Behaviorism sought to study observable behavior only, to the exclusion of concepts like the mind, soul, will, or any other topic which smacked of philosophy and religion.

In order to build their science as an objective approach to overtly observable human behavior, psychologists paid a heavy price. The discipline accepted the assumption that empirical methods provide the only avenues to truth, and that the supernatural, if it exists at all, is irrelevant to the field of psychology. All of this is to say that historically, psychologists have almost defined themselves right out of any discussion of topics which might touch on the supernatural.

Happily, this rigid behavioristic stance in psychology is showing signs of weakening. Increasing numbers of psychologists and psychology students are coming to recognize that there may be more things in earth and (if we can use a theological term) heaven than are dreamed of in the behavioristic or psychoanalytic philosophies. The new "third-force" movement in psychology[1] is not especially sympathetic toward religion, but it does maintain that what they term "peak experiences," "transcendent phenomena," and "transhuman" influences have an important influence on human behavior and should thus be included in the subject matter of modern psychology.[2]

The Christian psychologist must, it seems to me, move even farther away from rigid adherence to empiricism and naturalism. Recognizing the value and importance of empirical methodology, the Christian must also accept the accuracy and authority of God's divine revelation as found in the Bible. In addition, as a follower of Christ, the Christian in psychology has to believe in the supernatural. He may believe that God's world is orderly and that human behavior most often conforms to natural laws which God created and man is discovering. But he must also acknowledge that God, in His wisdom, may at times decide to bypass the natural laws and work in ways which, while consistent with God's nature and creation, are from the human standpoint supernatural.

In a study of so-called occult and demon phenomena, the traditional psychologist's assumptions limit him to the dotted portion of figure 1. He assumes that the world is orderly (without knowing why), and then with his well-developed techniques, he carefully investigates the natural order to find the independent variables which determine behavior. In contrast the Christian, and presumably other believers in the supernatural, starts with belief in the existence of God. The Christian sees God not only as creator of the universe, but also as the source of all truth and as the being who holds the whole world together by His power (Col. 1:16, 17; Heb. 1:1-3).

It would seem to me that the follower of Christ must also believe in the literal existence of the devil and his demonic forces. Only by the most ingenious of hermeneutical gymnastics could one accept the Bible's teaching about the reality and divinity of Christ and then reject the reality of the devil. Whereas God and His Son are described as being *the* Truth (John 7:28; 8:26; 14:6), Satan is called the "father of lies" (John 8:44). He goes about the world like a roaring lion, seeking to devour, hinder and confuse people (Job 1:7; 1 Pet. 5:8; 1 Thess. 2:18). Satan is clearly under the control of God who alone is sovereign in the universe, but the devil is still powerful and even able to do miracles (2 Thess. 2:9). He took upon himself the form of a serpent to tempt Eve, and with Job (1:12-19) he accomplished his purposes by both natural means (using attacking bands of marauders and storms) and means which appear to be supernatural (fire from heaven).

Returning to figure 1, therefore, we see that a given event or behavior could be the result of (1) God, or perhaps Satan, working through comprehendable natural events; (2) God working to accomplish His purposes through means which men would consider supernatural; or (3) Satan using his supernatural powers to reach demonic ends. When Jesus healed the blind and dumb demon-possessed man in Matthew 12, He demonstrated the power of God (No. 2 above), but the critics charged that the healing was from Satan (No. 3 above). Had there been a psychologist in the crowd that day, He would have had to find reason for the healing within the natural laws uncovered by science (No. 1 above). His assumptions about the universe would permit no other explanation.

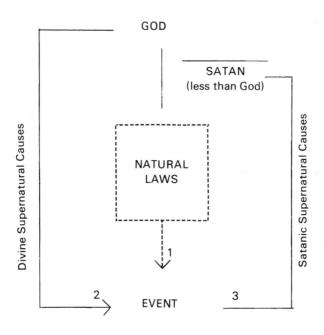

Figure 1

A Personal Clarification

With this introduction it is important, I would suggest, for me to clarify where I, as a psychologist, stand on the issue of the demonic. Not everyone will agree with me, of course, but it is more honest for me to state explicitly what I believe, rather than to leave you guessing.

Like others in this symposium I have been impressed by the oft-quoted statement of C. S. Lewis in the introduction to his *Screwtape Letters.* "There are two equal and opposite errors into which our race can fall about devils," Lewis wrote. "One is to disbelieve in their existence. The other is to believe, and to feel an excessive and unhealthy interest in them. They themselves are equally pleased by both errors. . . . " [3] Perhaps all of us have seen both extremes. Psychologists tend to be disbelievers; some of the Christians I know tend to have an excessive belief and almost morbid interest in the topic of demonology. I try to place myself somewhere in between.

I believe (a) that the devil exists as a real and powerful superhuman creature who, for a temporary period of time, has been allowed by God to wander to and fro throughout the earth seeking whom he may devour; (b) that the devil's work is largely accomplished by demons who are under his control; (c) that the satanic forces are powerful, deceptive, opposed to righteousness, and constantly tempting men to engage in ruinous sin (Eph. 6:12; 2 Thess. 2:9; Heb. 2:14; John 8:44; 1 Pet. 5:8; Matt. 4:1).

I have never had personal experience with an exorcism, but I have talked with several people whom I consider to be mature, serious-minded, educated Christians who have had such experiences. I believe that the devil and his forces are interested in and actively involved in resisting the work of the Holy Spirit and attempting to undermine the effectiveness, especially of Christians (1 Pet. 5:8). I also believe, however, that the Christian need not go around with a paranoid fear of the devil. Christ has already established His control over the world and its forces, and we have the assurance that He who is within us is greater than he that is in the world (John 16:33; 1 John 4:4). I like Luther's attitude toward the devil. "The best way to drive out the devil if he will not yield to texts of Scripture, is to jeer and flout him, for he cannot bear scorn." [4]

This is not to imply that we should ignore the devil. The Scriptures tell us to be alert to his schemes and to resist actively his power through our closeness to Christ and reliance on the Holy Spirit (1 Pet. 5:8, 9; James 4:7, 8; Eph. 6:10-18). It is also important, I believe, to avoid all dabbling in occult and satanic phenomena. Horoscopes, ouija boards, seances, witchcraft, palm-reading, card-laying and similar activities have, in the past, been shown to be harmful and could very well be royal roads to satanic influence in one's life.

General Psychology and Demonology

Turning to the psychological approach to demons, I was not surprised to discover that the literature is relatively silent on this topic. Increasing numbers of books and psychological articles have appeared, especially during the past few years, on such topics as altered states of consciousness, glossolalia, mysticism, magic and similar phenomena, but very little has been written about the psychological influence on demonology. When they do discuss the satanic, psychological writers usually attempt to explain away the supernatural influence of demons and to come up with a more viable scientific explanation for occult phenomena.

Freud, for example, suggested that both God and Satan were mental substitutes for human fathers. He concluded that what men once called evil spirits are really "base and evil wishes" deriving from "impulses which have been rejected and repressed." What people in past centuries called demon possession in the present day are called neuroses.[5] Victor White states the issue somewhat differently:

> . . . Finally, it must be made clear that we do not of course contend that "devils" and "complexes" are altogether synonymous and interchangeable terms. When the theologian says that somebody is afflicted by the devil, he is describing his situation in relation to God. When the psychologist says he is suffering from an unassimilated autonomous complex, he is describing an inherent, functional disorder. He speaks a different language; each describes an observed occurrence from a different point of view, or as the scholastics would say, in a different *ratio formalis qua.* Our contention is that the meanings of the two sets of terms (the theological and the psychopathological) are, however, not mutually exclusive; and we would offer for expert consideration the suggestion that, while the meanings are different, each term may be, and commonly is, referable to the selfsame phenomenon or occurrence.[6]

A much more contemporary discussion of this issue appeared in *Human Behavior* magazine. Discussing those events which culminated in filming *The Exorcist*, the authors present their "conviction, after several years of investigating this topic, that demons have never existed, clear-cut cases of possession have never taken place and that exorcisms . . . should be abolished because they are useless and potentially harmful." [7]

Christians in the psychological sciences are more open to the reality of demons, but there is considerable reluctance to in any way equate possession with so-called "mental illness." In an informal survey of some "Christian friends in Social Science," Vincent found responses ranging from outright rejection of the demonic to a guarded willingness to believe that demons exist and, in some undefined ways, influence the psychological functioning of people today.[8] Vincent himself gave a cautious but challenging psychiatric reflection on the issue of demonology and the psychological. "Demon possession today is either fact or fiction," he wrote. "Its existence can only be resolved by those who are well-informed on human behavior; well-informed about Scripture; and open to the possibility that demon possession exists." [9]

Regretfully, there are not very many people who meet these high but, I believe, necessary prerequisites, but Christians in the behavioral sciences should be among this select group. The psychologist, it would seem to me, especially can apply his training and expertise to at least three general areas: the social psychology of the current interest in occultism; the influence of the demonic on learning perception, emotion and other psychological functioning; and the role of the demonic in counseling. I would like to comment on each of these and conclude with some observations about psychological research and the study of demon activity.

The Social Psychology of Demonology

Interest in the demonic is, at the same time, both an ancient and a recent phenomenon.

The Old and New Testaments are both filled with references to Satan's demonic hosts, and one need not be an historian to realize that at certain times in history (such as the 16th and 17th centuries[10]), there was great interest in and fear of the devil and his legions. As recently as fifteen or twenty-five years ago, most educated westerners probably would have agreed that belief in demons had finally been laid to rest—at least in highly civilized parts of the world. It generally was assumed that the symptoms and evidences of demon possession could either be dismissed or explained away scientifically. Never did we suspect that in the 1970's an interest in demons, Satan, witchcraft and similar phenomena would sweep over the country, catching not only the attention of mystics or religious people, but invading the very sanctums of academia. Even in psychology classrooms, people who once dismissed the supernatural with a sneer, are beginning to have some second thoughts. Some are even concluding that "psychology, like natural science, may need alternative and even contradictory hypotheses to deal with the complexity of the human psyche." [11]

This widespread contemporary shift of interest towards the supernatural undoubtedly has many complex causes but with characteristic perceptivity Paul Tournier gets to the crux of the issue:

> ... Modern man, despite appearances, is less aware of his own nature and motives, and is lonelier as he faces them. We pity the savage amid his mysterious, menacing spirits, but at least he shares his fears with all his tribe, and does not have to bear the awful spiritual solitude which is so striking among civilized people. And the primitive tribe does at least lay down a certain magical interpretation, which, however mistaken, is satisfying because it is unquestioned. In the same way, the modern fanatic, who unhesitatingly accepts all the dialectic and the slogans of his party, is happier than the sceptic. And this explains the strange resurgence of the primitive mentality which we are witnessing today.
>
> Uncertainty is harder to bear than error. Now, science, by claiming to do away with the problems to which it has no answer, has left men alone in their grip. It leaves man in complete uncertainty as to the meaning of things, and the question still haunts him. [12]

During this century we have lived in the shadow of science. Two world wars, economic depression, erupting crimes in the streets—nothing, it seemed, could shake our faith that everything could eventually be solved scientifically in the end. But this is changing. We finally are discovering that science does not have all the answers. It says little about the meaning of life and death or the reasons for suffering. It gives us no real hope for the future; no

244 / Demon Possession

reason to believe in our own significance or eternal destiny. Some have even suggested that science, while solving one set of problems has created a whole new set. Men, therefore, are looking for a substitute which goes beyond science. Christianity has attracted many, but others are moving to Eastern philosophy, mysticism, meditation and belief in the demonic. Disillusioned with the rational, men are seeking answers in the nonrational and experientially based areas of life.

This decline of science and distrust of the rational are not the only reasons for a shift to the supernatural. Many, I believe, are losing faith in the long held humanistic view that man can solve all of his problems alone. Apparently, man cannot solve all of his problems so we are looking to horoscopes, ouija boards, and other devices which give some reassurance and guidance. In addition, it may be that many people are bored with life. Surrounded by incredible luxury, labor saving devices and leisure time, we are like the men of ancient Athens who spent their time trying to find something new to occupy their minds and time (Acts 17:21). Demonic and related occult phenomena are mysterious, exciting, and containing enough truth to make them credible and popular. It is unusual but no longer surprising to read in a psychology journal that "psychology is once again flirting with theology. Minimal adjustment to the savage glory of the human condition is drab. From a different world view, some seek transcendent citizenship in divine order." [13]

There is at least one other reason for a popular shift to the demonic: it absolves us of responsibility for our actions and problems. Christ demanded that His followers repent of their sins, turn from their evil ways, take up a cross and follow Him. The rewards for such dedication are high, but so are the costs. Many people prefer the ecstasy and ease of experiential religion. Closely related to this is a willingness to avoid personal responsibility by blaming one's problems on demons. One can hardly be held accountable if "the devil made me do it!"

In summary, therefore, it would appear that a decline of science, a move towards the nonrational, a disillusionment with human potential, and a desire to escape from boredom and personal responsibility all contribute to the current interest in occult phenomena including demonology. Man is searching. His needs are not being met, but he is flirting with forces which could be far more destructive and immobilizing than any of the problems from which he is trying to escape.

Human Behavior and Demonology

Apparently demons influence human behavior in a variety of ways. According to the accounts described in the Bible, they may create deafness, an inability to speak, blindness, convulsions, self-injury, screaming, fierce aggression, intense strength, withdrawal, and other socially inappropriate behavior.

Let us assume that the people who showed these characteristics were, as the biblical accounts state, actually possessed by demons. If we can assume further that the New Testament writers were accurate in their various (remarkably consistent) descriptions of the demonic behavior, then we know at least some of the ways in which demons influence psychological functioning.

From the psychologist's perspective, however, there are two difficulties with the list. First we are by no means certain that the Scriptures were intended to give a complete listing of demonically produced behaviors. Perhaps there are other demonic behaviors which are not mentioned in the Bible. A perusal of the literature in this area would suggest, for example, that demons might produce trances, visual or auditory hallucinations, obsessive thoughts, bad language, extreme discomfort in the presence of discussions about Christ, etc. One writer cites an inability to say the name of Jesus, special powers of telepathy or clairvoyance, instant lying, and mocking at the mention of Christ—all as evidence of demonic involvement.[14] To this might be added a lack of interest in spiritual matters, an inability to perceive spiritual truth and the very significant statements in 1 John 4:1-3 that the evil spirits will not confess that Christ is from God. The list could go on but already we are faced with our second difficulty.

The symptoms mentioned in the Bible, or added by later observers, can almost all be explained in some naturalistic way. Of course this does not rule out possession as the cause of these behaviors, but it shows that what people call demonic today, may not be demonic at all. Drugs, loss of sleep, psychosis, epileptic seizures, transcendental meditation, physical disease, intense fear—these are among the factors which can lead to symptoms that apparently are identical to the cited signs of demon possession.

One other psychological observation must be mentioned at this point. There is abundant evidence from studies in perceptual psychology that people see and act in accordance with the expectation of those around them. If someone convinces me I am demon possessed, unconsciously I might begin to experience the symptoms and show the behavior which fit the diagnosis. In like manner, if I assume someone else is possessed, I may begin looking for symptoms to prove my hypothesis. It is easy to develop a demonology mind-set in which almost everything we see or do is attributed to the devil. This tendency is apparent in some of the more spectacular books about demons. The authors appear to be giving the devil a lot more credit than he deserves. One can also see how much damage can be done by well-meaning exorcists who, by the very act of exorcism, suggest to the counselee that demons are present. If the "exorcism" fails, the counselee is left not only with his original symptoms but with hopelessness and despair because he thinks his body is possessed by stubborn demons who refuse to leave.

The Bible makes a distinction between those who are demon possessed and people who are physically diseased (Matt. 4:24; 10:1; 8:16; Mark 16:17, 18). It also differentiates between demon possession and what we now call mental illness (Matt. 4:24; Mark 1:32; Acts 5:16). In spite of this, and the previously mentioned passage in 1 John 4:1-3, we still have few clear-cut distinctives that enable the modern counselor to recognize demonic involvement. In a discussion of "the distinction between disease and the demonic," Lechler has even suggested that "one frequently finds psychopathy and demonic subjection occurring simultaneously, so much so that the two conditions are often almost indistinguishable." [15] It is hardly surprising, therefore, that most counselors, even those who accept the reality of demons, work on the assumption that the possibility of demonic involvement can be ignored in any consideration of the causes or treatment of psychological problems.

Counseling and Demonology

The name *Satan* means "adversary," and the evil one is pictured in the Bible as being an enemy opposed both to God and man. In accomplishing his purposes, Satan sometimes exercises control over natural events like storms or disease (Job 1, 2), but more often he does his work by tempting men. Being finite and open to temptation, we often fall as did Adam and Eve. This gets us into all kinds of difficulties some of which lead to behavior disorders and physical disease. In one sense, therefore, even without possessing a person, the devil and his angels are behind most of the problems that the counselor and his counselee face.

To deal with these problems, a variety of techniques is used. Among the more familiar are listening while the counselee talks, helping him gain insight, giving advice and encouragement, or applying reinforcement to modify his behavior. All of these, and dozens of other techniques, have been found to have success with at least some counselees. More recently, within the helping professions there has been an emphasis on the importance of values, individual responsibility, and even the confession of sin.[16]

In His counseling, Jesus used a variety of methods. In like manner the truly competent Christian counselor is skilled in the understanding and application of a number of psychological techniques, but he is also aware of the influence of sin in the counselee's life. This spiritual dimension is an important part of counseling and, in my opinion, should not be overlooked as treatment proceeds.

All of this implies that the devil's influence in lives is being attacked whenever counseling takes place. This, in fact, is what counseling involves—an attempt to undo the harm caused by the devil and his hosts. The counselor or counselee may not recognize this, but in essence, this is what is happening. The Bible clearly teaches, however, that Satan is deceptive, harmful, and extremely powerful. If he works to bring problems or chaos into a life, through either the natural or supernatural routes shown in figure 1, then it is unthinkable that man alone will be able to resist and reverse this satanic influence. To most effectively resist the devil we must acknowledge his existence, be alert to his schemes, and be shielded with the power of God as we go into battle (Eph. 6:10-20). In his work the Christian counselor will also make use of established psychological techniques but we must view these as tools which the Holy Spirit uses in our hands to defy the destructive work of Satan.

This is not to imply that the Christian counselor is always effective or that he alone is competent to counsel. Sometimes the Christian counselor fails because of his poor counseling techniques, inadequate training, or inclination to resist the Spirit's influence in his life and work. At other times God, in His divine will, may not want the healing to occur so the counseling is ineffective. There are also many occasions when the nonbeliever is used to bring healing into a life, just as God used nonbelievers in the Old Testament to accomplish His purposes.

I am arguing, therefore, that most, if not all, counseling involves resisting the devil whether or not the counselor realizes this. The same is true of all medical healing. Notice that I have not mentioned exorcism. Exorcism implies that the counselee is possessed by demons. Most of our counselees are demon influenced but probably are not demon possessed. In counseling we can resist the devil without resorting to exorcism. Indeed, I agree with those who believe that exorcism should be used as a last resort and only when demon possession seems apparent. Because of the potentially harmful effects of suggesting demonic involvement, the counselor should attempt exorcism only after every conceivable medical, psychological and spiritual counseling technique has failed.

As indicated earlier, I have neither experience nor expertise in the topic of exorcism. Because of this I will limit my comments to a few general conclusions which have been gleaned from lengthy conversations both with pastors who have engaged in exorcism and with one or two of their counselees.[17]

Some writers have noted that Jesus never engaged in exorcism as we know it today. He simply spoke to the demons who recognized His authority and obeyed His commands, usually without even putting up any resistance. Unlike people today, the Son of God had the ability to "diagnose" demon possession without ever making a mistake. His authority was unquestioned by the demonic world and unlike the disciples who sometimes failed in their exorcism attempts (Matt. 17; Mark 9), Jesus had faith in His power and a spiritual alertness (prayer and fasting) which His followers apparently lacked. It would appear that a prerequisite for successful exorcism is that the exorcist be a believer in Christ, walking close to God aware that our power over demons only comes because of a strength from Christ, and probably possessing the gift of being able to distinguish or discern the spirits (1 Cor. 12:10).

One of my missionary acquaintances who has engaged in several exorcisms always begins with personal prayer and confession. Then he reads such passages as Col. 2; Heb. 2:14-18; or 1 John 1, 2 or 3 to the counselee and observes the reaction. Often the listener goes into a trance, finds that he has no understanding of the passage or tries to overwhelm the reader with a theological discourse which is invariably confused and/or unbiblical. Sudden headaches, belching, hearing of voices, extreme anxiety, or rapid breathing are all seen as further indications of demonic involvement. At such time the demons are called to attention in the name of Christ, asked for their names, commanded to describe their jobs within the possessed person and then cast out "to the pit" in the name of the Lord Jesus Christ. God is then thanked and praised because of His power and His having removed the demons. The process is, of course, more lengthy than is described here, often extending over several sessions and involving the casting out of numerous demons—a few at a time. The counselee is then given encouragement, instructed to avoid all contact with the occult, presented with the importance of committing one's life and works to the lordship of Christ, reminded of the cleansing power of the blood of Christ, and discipled to walk in the newness of life as described in Heb. 2:14-18; Phil. 4:4-9; and 1 Tim. 4:1-2.

Psychological Research and Demonology

The Christian psychologist should be an expert in human behavior, a trained researcher, and an individual who takes both science and the Bible seriously. The Christian behavioral scientist has ideal and somewhat unique qualifications for doing empirical research in the area of the demonic. Regretfully, however, very little of this research has been done. Work in this area does not lead to much professional prestige and the subject matter of demonology is difficult to define and study empirically.

Perhaps we should begin with some careful observations of the exorcism procedure as practiced today. Eventually we might get some precise descriptions or measurements of counselee behavior both before and after an exorcism. More careful study could be made of the characteristics of the apparently possessed as opposed to the nonpossessed. Because of the complexity and multidisciplinary nature of the demonic phenomena, it would doubtless be best if a team of researchers (consisting of a psychologist, sociologist and psychiatrist, for example, aided by a biblical scholar) could tackle these issues together.

Biblical scholarship is making good progress in its study of the demonic. Historians and anthropologists have added their conclusions. But there continues to be an increase in popular books and papers dealing with the pet theories and colorful observations of a variety of writers. These people are no doubt sincere and often deeply committed to Christ, but they are not trained in the careful observation and precise study of human behavior. In contrast, the behavioral scientist has this training. He has begun to apply his skills to topics like conversion, glossolalia and faith healing. The time is now ripe for psychological and social science techniques to be applied to an understanding of the occult. Such an application is necessary if we psychologists are to take our place alongside scholars in nonpsychological disciplines so that together we can bring greater understanding to a field which is still filled with contradictions, mystery and continuing confusion.

Notes

1. This is the name of a loosely defined but influential and growing movement within psychology. Known also as "humanistic psychology" the movement is presented as a third alternative to the more traditional two movements of behaviorism and psychoanalysis.

2. These terms were all used by A. H. Maslow who is accepted as the founder of the third force movement. See A. H. Maslow, *Motivation and Personality* (2d ed.; New York: Harper & Row, 1970), p. xxvii.

3. C. S. Lewis, *The Screwtape Letters* (London: Collins Fontana Books, 1942), p. 9.

4. *Ibid.*, preface.

5. S. Freud, "A Neurosis of Demoniacal Possession in the Seventeenth Century," *Collected Papers*, trans. Joanne Riviere, IV (London: Hogarth Press, 1949), 436f.

6. V. White, *God and the Unconscious* (London: Harvill Press, 1952), p. 189.

7. J. B. Cortes and F. M. Gatti, "Exorcising 'The Exorcist'," *Human Behavior*, III (May, 1974), 16-23.

8. M. D. Vincent, "What in Hell is the Devil doing on Earth?" *Christian Medical Society Journal*, I (Winter, 1971), 1-9.

9. *Ibid.*, p. 9.

10. See, for example, H. R. Trevor-Roper, *The European Witch-Craze of the 16th and 17th Centuries* (Baltimore: Penguin Books, 1967).

11. S. Keen, "Transpersonal Psychology: The Cosmic versus the Rational," *Psychology Today*, VIII (July, 1974), 56-59.

12. Paul Tournier, *A Doctor's Casebook in the Light of the Bible* (New York: Harper & Row, 1954), p. 104.

13. Keen, *loc. cit.*

14. A Lechler, in K. Koch, *Occult Bondage and Deliverance* (Grand Rapids: Kregel, 1970), Part Two, pp. 133-98.

15. *Ibid.*, p. 184.

16. K. Menninger, *Whatever Became of Sin?* (New York: Hawthorne, 1973).

17. A much more complete discussion of counseling and the occult can be found in Kurt Koch's classic volume, *Christian Counseling and Occultism* (Grand Rapids: Kregel, 1965).

15

Commentary on Psychological
Observations on Demonism

JOHN WHITE

Dr. Collins has raised many points in his broad coverage
of the topic. With some points I heartily concur, and all
points he raises are stimulating.

I will confine my remarks to the intriguing suggestion
he makes at the end of his paper, namely, that the time
is ripe for psychological and social sciences "to apply their
skills to an examination of occult phenomena." Dr. Collins
does not specify what aspects would be of most pressing
importance—which is hardly surprising in view of his limited time.

Good research, whether empirical or not, begins when
you delineate what you want to find out. It begins with
the formulation of clear, plain questions. What exactly do
you want to know?

In the case of the occult we could ask many types of
questions at different levels, all of which would pose formidable difficulties for the researcher and many of which
could never be answered by scientific methodology alone.
If research were to attempt to test hypotheses, we would
encounter many blind alleys.

Three areas suggest themselves. First, one could attempt to establish criteria for the diagnosis of demon
states. Secondly, an attempt could be made at some sort
of classification of demon states, according to their severity, along the lines of possession/oppression, or according
to some other principle. Thirdly (and in my mind most

importantly), one could attempt to evaluate "treatment" methods.

Diagnosis presents us with a thorny problem. John's reference to "trying the spirits" (1 John 4:1-3) can hardly be taken as a rule of thumb for detecting demons. It seems rather to be directed at the "spirit" underlying anti-Christian teaching. In any case, in the Gospels, demons seemed ready enough to confess that Christ was come in the flesh (e.g., Luke 4:33-37). In the absence of scriptural diagnostic principles we are forced to fall back either on the direct illumination of the Holy Spirit to guide us in a given case, or else to devise rules based upon experimental evidence.

My own conviction is that science is helpless in the face of the diagnostic problem. I can conceive of no demonic state which cannot be "explained" by a non-demonic hypothesis. I can likewise conceive of no experiment to give conclusive support to demonic rather than parapsychological hypotheses. It also seems to me that Christians should not be found floundering in the steps of J. B. Rhine.

We could ask the question: What is the most effective method of changing episodic blasphemous outbursts of rage? We would have to assign blasphemers randomly to different treatment methods—exorcism, counseling, psychotherapy (and ideally to a control group also), a procedure which raises both technical and moral difficulties.

If we did not assign subjects *randomly* to different groups the subjects would choose the treatment method they believed in most. In that case we could not possibly rule out a "placebo" effect. (A placebo, in medicine, is a pill that works only because you believe it's going to.) On the other hand, random assignment would only go part way in ruling out placebo effects. There is no way in which a single-blind, let alone a double-blind, study could be carried out. All the blasphemers would know what method was being used. And their faith in a given method would introduce a placebo factor.

I should make it clear, doubly clear, since I am addressing Christians, that the fact that faith works proves nothing. I can believe (mistakenly) that I have picked up fleas from a flea-infected patient—and I will itch. But the itch does not prove I have a flea. Similarly, faith in any healing method goes a long way toward producing healing. My faith produces psychological effects on physiological mechanisms in my body. We called these effects psychosomatic.

Faith in God can, however, produce effects of an entirely different order, effects that cannot be explained solely on the basis of psychological mechanisms. They are not "placebo" effects, but represent the operation of supernatural power. The problem in exorcism is to distinguish between the supernatural and the purely psychological.

The only way I can see around the difficulty would be to scrap a more limited approach and to take the bull (or the goat!) by the horns. But to do so we would require three conditions: (1) A panel of judges, preferably from different disciplines and theological backgrounds who would have a high rate of concordance in their assessments as to whether a distressed person were demon-afflicted or not. (2) A group of subjects diagnosed independently by all panel members as being demon-afflicted, but including in the group some who did not see themselves in this light, but who were anxious to receive some kind of psychological help, rather than exorcism. (3) A group of therapists with deep convictions about the superior effectiveness of their treatment methods—whether of exorcism or of psychological counseling, who would devote themselves to helping whoever sought their help.

If all three conditions could be met (and I am by no means sure they could), placebo effects would be minimized, i.e., would partly cancel one another out.

The findings of such a study, whatever they might prove to be, would not prove the presence or absence of demons. Such would not be its purpose. Supposing, for example, the results in the exorcised group were significantly better than in the psychologically treated group. All we would have demonstrated was that exorcism, for some reason, works better than other methods in changing behavior rightly or wrongly attributed to demons.

Again, if results in the two groups were comparable, or if "psychological" treatment proved superior, we would not have demonstrated that demons didn't exist, nor even that the panel members were wrong in their diagnosis. We might simply have demonstrated that there are more ways than one of counteracting demonic influence.

But a more serious difficulty raises its head at this point. I have been talking as though the right method is all-important in treating behavior regarded as demonic. And as I do so our attention is automatically focussed on human activity, human techniques, formulae, methods or procedure, etc.

I have hardly mentioned faith in God. And if I do talk about faith in God, how can I compare my faith with yours? Or how can I know whether my faith is a misplaced faith (i.e., a faith that expects God to do something He has no intention of doing)? Most difficult of all, if faith is as Luther asserted, in no way a virtue, but a mere channel by means of which the saving grace of God reaches our hearts, by what research instruments may we detect or measure such a sovereign operation of God's power? And would not the attempt to calibrate divine power border on gross presumption, if not blasphemy?

And all this is not to discourage careful investigation but to warn against a light-hearted approach to it, and to caution would-be researchers that while trained observation is always of value, scientific research can give only very limited answers. In the final analysis we will have to rely on faith in the Holy Spirit's ability to give us divine insight.

16

Reflections on the Demonic:
A Psychiatric Perspective

BASIL JACKSON

In coming together in conference, as we do on this occasion, it should be useful to attempt to delineate both our motives and our goals for the particular enterprise which now occupies our attention. I cannot, with authority, speak for anyone but myself in this regard, but my ideas regarding our various reasons for being found here are as follows. Like any other motivation, our reason for coming to this conference was not only determined, but v. as overdetermined. That is to say, we had many motivations coexisting on different levels of the psyche at the same time. In general, however, it is safe to say that most of the important motivational factors which lead to any significant decision are related to an internal sense of dysphoria.

There are many reasons for the existence of such discomfort and, in this case, I would suggest the following for our consideration: (1) Because of the increasing interest in occult activities in the world and, in particular, in the United States. (2) Because of the sense that we might be missing something psychologically, spiritually, and perhaps exegetically. (3) Because of a sense of desperation as clinically we cope with so many problems, which show so little response to all our professional ingenuity. (4) Because we are somewhat guilty for having so long ignored this area in spite of specific statements and illustrations in the Sacred Scriptures. (5) Because of a keen sense of embarrassment at what so many of our fellow Christians are saying, writing, and practicing. (6) Because, like the rest of mankind, we have a fascination with the unknown and the mysterious.

In view of such a wide variety of possible motivational factors, potential goals for this conference are relatively easy to visualize. However, I do not believe that anyone in this conference really believes that we will come up with the last word on the subject of demonology, and most of us will be satisfied with more realistic goals.

First, out of this period of dialog, I would like to see an increased awareness that a prerequisite to any form of treatment is the necessity of not just diagnosis, but precision in differential diagnosis. Such is essential before the initiation of any treatment program unless one would be satisfied with a rather "medical shot-gun, multi-vitamin" type of approach which is, at most, directed toward the removal of target symptoms rather than underlying causes. Demonic states (whatever these may prove to be) are presumably to be recognized in their phenomenology by symptoms and signs which, together with the course of the condition, make up the clinical picture as a "disease entity," or "demonic entity." Let us consider just what is meant by the term *symptom*.

(1) A symptom is an indication of some type of disorder in which there are both subjective and objective aspects.

(2) Such a symptom is a subjective or objective indicator of some type of somatic or psychic disorder.

(3) Subjective symptoms are states of dysphoria. Objective indicators, whether verbal, psychological, etc., cannot be denominated as either psychopathological (or demonic) unless the social context is taken into consideration. Thus, screaming, sweating, tachycardia, aggressive behavior, mutism, convulsions, etc., may or may not be psychopathologic symptoms, depending on their social and physical appropriateness. In particular, consideration must be given to the expectation level of the immediate environment. It would seem reasonable to make similar assumptions for demonically induced symptoms.

One of the most frequently reported observations we read today concerns the increase of occult activities in the United States and around the world. If indeed this current increase in the occult is a reflection of an actual, rather than an apparent, increase in demonic activity, we should not be unduly surprised. The Bible tells us that a marked increase in such activity occurred in the antediluvian days and also during the period of Christ's ministry on earth. We are also warned to expect an unprecedented increase of such activity in the "last days," which is to be similar to the days of Noah and which, in the opinion of many students of the Word, seems to be fast approaching.

In this connection, it is most noteworthy that the "last days" are described by Paul as "perilous times." "This know also, that in the last days perilous times shall come" (2 Tim. 3:1). This word *perilous* is very closely associated with the idea of demonic activity in its only other occurrence in the New Testament in Matt. 8:28, where two demonized individuals are described as exceedingly "fierce" or "perilous": "And, when he was come to the other side into the country of the Gadarenes, there met him two possessed with demons coming out of the tombs, exceedingly fierce so that no man might pass by that way." This would appear to be a foretaste of what the world has to face in the "last days."

It is, however, comforting to remember that even the greatest possible avalanche of demonic hordes which may eventually erupt on the earth will still be only a puny effort against the power and strength of Almighty God. It is reassuring to remember that, no matter how great their strength, they are still no match for God.

Paul, in describing the "last days," in 2 Timothy, chapter 3, indicates that those days will be characterized by a recrudescence of Egyptian darkness similar to that which occurred when Jannes and Jambres withstood Moses. After these magicians of Egypt had successfully simulated the initial miracles of Moses, they reached a point where they failed to bring forth lice as Moses had done. "Then the magicians said unto Pharaoh, this is the *finger of God*" (Ex. 8:18). In Luke 11, the same phrase occurs again. Christ is in confrontation with the Pharisees who have accused Him of casting out demons by the power of the devil. Christ replied, "But, if I, with the *finger of God* cast out demons, no doubt the kingdom of God is come unto you." God's finger is involved in the struggle with demonic agencies, and His power and strength are more than sufficient.

As a Christian who, without any reservation whatsoever, accepts the Sacred Scriptures as inerrant and inspired by the Holy Spirit in every jot and tittle, I accept the existence of Satan and his demonic agencies, and the reality of demon possession or demonization. I also recognize that this is no more scientific than a belief in either creationism or, on the other hand, evolution, since my belief is not related to personnally observable and reproducible phenomena.

This is not, however, so very different from some of the bases on which one conducts the clinical practice of psychiatry. There is little that is final and definite as regards etiology in the conditions seen in clinical psychiatry and yet one has to proceed, often by trial and error, to mediate some degree of comfort to one's patients. In my practice, for example, I rely to a large degree upon the idea of unconscious mentation, which I have never actually proved to exist. However, it remains a useful hypothesis and, although I don't "believe in it," I will use it until I find something else more useful and potent.

Often, when I am asked about the validity and reality of the demonic, the question arises as to whether Jesus really meant what He said about demons, or whether it is not more accurate to consider Him as adapting himself to the prescientific age in which He lived. Another possibility which is raised is that, as part of the kenosis of the incarnation, there was a limitation of the knowledge of Jesus as regards demons as well as other subjects, principally those of a scientific nature. I do not personally accept either view, and I accept the words of Jesus at face value.

In connection with the current interest shown in occult activity in this country, I have noted that there is an increased tendency for attraction to the occult in those Christians who have a basic paranoid personality structure. It is also very interesting that this same type of person tends to be attracted towards a type of hyper-Calvinistic theology which also is very much concerned with hidden things and the selective revelation of "occult" information to the initiated. It is this type of personality which appears to be particularly attracted to interest in the occult and it is this kind of evangelical Christian who often falls prey to it. Thus, I have noted that Christians who claim to be soundly evangelical and who demonstrate this particular personality position often become fascinated with the occult, with the burning of candles, pinning of dolls, etc., in order to express their feelings for or against some other person. In addition, this type of Christian is often particularly attracted to involvement in the deliverance ministry.

Another question we must ask concerns the relationship between participation in occult activities and the possibility of subsequent demonization or, perhaps, subsequent psychiatric decompensation. A frequently stated objection to dabbling in the occult is that such an activity tends to make the individual more susceptible to invasion by outside agencies. I have read and re-read this in works on the subject, particularly from evangelical writers within the last few years, but even though it seems a reasonable hypothesis, and I tend to accept it, I have seen no attempt at objective confirmation. I hasten to add that, because the possibility seems reasonable, I always encourage Christians to stay away from this kind of activity. In view of what has just been noted regarding certain types of personality being attracted to the occult, the question arises as to which is the cart and which is the horse.

Another area in which a high degree of naiveté in both current writers and workers in this field is seen is the frequent recurrence of the phrase, "a typical case of demon possession." In my practice, I have had referred to me such "typical" cases from all over the United States. After prolonged examination and observation, often the only typical feature discovered has been the ignorance of the referring source of the basic phenomenology of psychopathology. In psychiatry, we have learned that the more ignorant we are of precise etiologic factors, the more esoteric are our interpretations and explanations likely to be.

One of the most important areas of fallacious reasoning with which we have had to deal in psychiatry and which is now almost universal among Evangelicals who choose to write about or work in the area of the demonic is the venerable "post hoc, propter hoc" fallacy—the trap of "pill before change is proof that change is due to pill." Similarly, the fact that "cure" follows upon a psychoanalytic interpretation does not mean that the "cure" was due to, nor in fact, was in any way related to the interpretation. Again, the fact that a client is "cured" of demon possession and feels better or behaves differently after the most sincere rite of exorcism does not prove that demons were involved or that the devil had anything whatsoever to do with the particular client or his condition.

A question which is very often posed to me as I speak in various parts of the world is, Do you believe in demon possession and have you encountered demonization in your clinical work? In all honesty, I have to say that I certainly

do believe in demon possession or demonization because
the Bible teaches it. However, I remain unconvinced that
I have ever seen or, at least recognized, demonization in
a patient with whom I was working. The nearest thing that
would approach demonization in my work has been my experience with drug users. These pharmacophiliacs often
tend to become completely dependent upon a drug, which
does not produce physiologic dependence, in a manner which
is not representative of their general psychiatric state. Often
I have wondered, when I have seen youngsters deliberately
do that which they know will be harmful to them, if there
is not an outside agency at work pushing them towards
misery and/or self-destruction.

Today, I believe we are seeing a most unhealthy interest in the area of demonology so that many of our evangelical friends have, in effect, become "demonophiliacs"
as a result of their fascination with the occult. They tend
to see a demon under every tree and, thus, quite commonly
today, we hear of demons of tobacco, alcohol, asthma, and
every other condition imaginable. In this connection, it is
noteworthy that, by far, the majority of cases of demon
possession which are diagnosed in the deliverance ministry
today are mental in phenomenology. This is in marked contrast with the only safe records we have of accurately diagnosed cases of demon possession—namely, the Gospels, in
which at least half the people possessed had physical problems rather than any psychiatric difficulties.

Another frequent query concerns the question as to
whether a regenerated person can be demonized. First of
all, let us note that it is still a little premature to attempt
to give a definitive and final answer to this question until
such time as we can decide just what demonization is. Before one can answer the question as to whether a born-again
Christian can be demonized, it is first of all necessary to
be precise in the definition of terms. By born-again Christian, I mean an individual in whom the Holy Spirit has
come to reside within the personality, and who makes available His source of energy in an ego-syntonic manner. This
is particularly true of those ego functions pertaining to volition. I have great difficulty in believing that such an individual could ever volitionally give over all control of conative function to an outside demonic agency. Therefore, I
have difficulty believing that such an individual, in whom
the Holy Spirit is resident, can be demonized in the New Testament sense of the term. Of course, every Christian is sub-

ject to attacks and oppression by demonic forces of which we are clearly warned in Ephesians, chapter 6.

At this point, it might be useful to emphasize the fact that, irrespective of the degree of oppression, or even demonization, to which a Christian may be subjected, we have been assured in the Bible that God will not permit us to be tempted above that which we are able to bear. Thus, even if a Christian theoretically could be demonized, he would still be fully responsible for his actions in view of the above-mentioned promise. If this were to be fully realized, it would completely take away the value of the mechanism of projection in these situations and the value of the devil and demonic agencies as scapegoats. Then there would be no validity in the idea that "the devil made me do it." Rather, "I myself am fully responsible, with God's help, for what I do" would be the observation.

In the last few years, while working on the integration of psychology and theology, I have attempted to examine the psychologic components of the regeneration experience. Using a psychoanalytic model of ego, super-ego, etc., I have found it useful to think of the Holy Spirit as, after volitional invitation, coming to take up residence in the ego of the individual. If such a spatial model is offensive as perhaps being too mechanistic, we may think of the strength and power of the Holy Spirit being given to bolster certain ego functions and, thus, coming to play a specific ego-syntonic role within the personality. Similarly, I have considered the ego ideal as being modified, the same process, by the introjection of the person of Christ and what He represents.

Using the same model, I have found it useful to consider a similar sequence of events in the process of demonization. Psychological processes require energy and this energy may be supplied, not only by the psyche and the Holy Spirit, but conceivably also by demonic forces. Such an agency could enter the ego especially, and perhaps only, if the conative functions were volitionally given over and begin to act in a completely ego-dystonic manner. It is also reasonable to assume a similar reconstruction of the superego and ego ideal with the incorporation of the father the devil, who is also the father of lies.

It is clear that the Bible teaches the reality of demonization, but little in the way of facts useful in making a precise diagnosis are found in the Bible. Nor should we assume, as most have, that demonic influence on the human body and mind today would have to have effects similar to the clinical pictures described in the New Testament, scanty as they are. It is a well-known fact that clinical pictures can change according to the socio-cultural matrix in which they occur. As previously mentioned, they also tend to change very significantly according to the expectation levels in the immediate environment.

In tackling the problem of differential diagnosis between the psychiatric and the demonic, we will encounter a special series of difficulties. As we have seen, we have to deal with and understand specific symptoms before we can reach this point and accurately diagnose. We also have to examine symptom complexes before we can begin to formulate any degree of taxonomic understanding. For our purposes, we may consider a symptom complex as follows: (1) It is composed of a group of two or more symptoms, (2) which tend to be found together in a sizable number of cases, but (3) this does not necessarily point to a single underlying pathologic (or demonic) process, nor does the symptom complex imply a similar etiology.

Some of the special difficulties are now immediately evident—for example, even if we were to meet a case which demonstrated exactly the same phenomenology as a case recorded in the New Testament record, we could not assume that the process or etiologic agent was the same in each case. It is clear, from even a cursory examination of the cases of demonization recorded in the New Testament, that psychopathologic and demonic states share many of the same symptoms and symptom complexes.

The difficulties in the differential diagnosis are then further enhanced by the fact that both psychopathologic states and demonic conditions may coexist. As a matter of fact, as the low resistance associated with certain physical conditions increases the susceptibility to physical diseases, so the presence of certain psychological conditions may increase potential for surrender of the will to outside demonic forces. It is, therefore, not surprising that most cases referred to me as "typical" cases of demon possession are clinically seen to be schizophrenic in nature and which present with one outstanding symptom—namely, ambivalence, which represents a basic defect in the will aspect of ego function.

The possibility must still be considered that the fact that a person is suffering from a schizophrenic process makes him or her more susceptible to invasion by outside agencies. However, this possibility, in itself, raises a problem. If we accept this possibility, then we must also consider the possibility that preexisting conditions of a psychopathologic nature might be conducive to voluntary commitment to the Holy Spirit as another type of outside agency.

The area of differential diagnosis is certainly a most difficult one, but this should not come as a special surprise to us because, as has been well demonstrated, the devil is a master of both simulation and imitation. The difficulty is further aggravated by the fact that Scripture teaches that Satan can use recognized etiologic agents to produce illness—for example, the boils from which Job suffered presumably were secondary to an invasion by staphylococci. Similarly, Satan may be behind dumbness and epilepsy, not as the proximate or immediate etiologic agent, but he obviously has the ability to use scientifically demonstrated etiologic agents for his own ends.

One of the most useful clues the New Testament gives in making a differential diagnosis is the fact that, in the record, Jesus touches those who have physical infirmity, but there is no record of His having physical contact with a demonized individual. This may well have to do with His very sinlessness, but it should be noted that this is just the opposite of what usually occurs in the present-day deliverance ministries in which there is often much physical contact with the client. When Christ was involved with a demonized person, His method was to speak the word of command, and His authority was recognized by the demonic agencies involved.

Another useful clue in making the diagnosis would seem to be the client's response to a confrontation with Jesus Christ as Lord, according to John's recommendation. Of course, to one conditioned to the idea of commitment, etc., and who may be struggling with a problem of guilt, a confrontation with the idea of the lordship of Jesus Christ might be sufficient to produce a massive, hysterical, motoric response, which could very easily be interpreted as evidence of demonic influence.

In the extra-New Testament literature, both ancient and modern, certain features are said to be suggestive of demonization. Some of these features could represent a rather classic description of many psychopathologic states; some could also be spiritual, and some could be learned phenomena. Many of the features which one finds in the literature as being useful from a diagnostic point of view, could well be a combination of severe obsessive-compulsive

states with the processes that one sees typically in schizophrenic patients. For example, religious doubts could be
a reflection of the ambivalence which is part and parcel
of schizophrenia. Distractability and inability to concentrate
during Bible and prayer activities could be a classical example of obsessive-compulsive states and other conditions
associated with high levels of anxiety or, indeed, of brain
damage. A persistent lack of peace and inner unrest sounds
very much like the particular kind of anxiety often seen
in schizophrenia and which I call schizophrenic perplexity.
Outbursts of temper associated with blasphemous words
are seen classically in the Gelles de laTourette syndrome.
Aggression and suicidal preoccupation is an everyday occurrence in the field of clinical psychiatry. In this connection, it is most difficult to understand why a demon would
go to so much trouble to become incarnate in the body
of an individual only then to proceed to kill him off as
fast as possible. Compulsions toward drunkenness, sexual
immorality, smoking and drugs, etc., are very, very frequent
manifestations of a wide variety of psychopathologic states.

Mendacity was one of the evidences of demonic activity
considered to be significant by the primitive church. However, it is of little value today in the formulation of a precise
diagnosis because it is so widespread. Not only do so-called
normal people frequently lie, but it is a veritable way of
life for the narcissistically oriented psychopath. Similarly,
glorification of the self is possibly due, in some instances,
to demonic activity, but is much more frequently found
as an expression of a high degree of primary narcissism,
or in some of the hysterical states. The trance state has
also been mentioned as useful in the differential diagnosis,
but it is also a salient feature of the dissociative conditions
and of the hypnotic states.

One of the chief characteristics of demonization is the
possession of the will of the individual with resulting control
over his body. If we are to believe many of the records,
it appears that, in those instances where the possessing
spirit was prepared to speak, it not only often spoke with
a different voice, but it spoke of itself as an entity separate
from the possessed individual. This would perhaps be a
more useful tool for diagnostic purposes if it were to occur
more frequently but, again, it must be remembered that
the same phenomena may occur in certain dissociative
states, even to the change in voice, etc. Other writers have
emphasized the quality of the voice in cases they consider

to be secondary to demonic activity. The voice has been described as a weird minor chant which clearly distinguishes it from insanity. Unfortunately, things are not so clear as they sound because often the diagnosis of certain pathologic states is made merely after listening to a patient's weird monotone.

Supernatural knowledge has also been mentioned as a possible useful clue in making the diagnosis and, if we were to see this more frequently, then perhaps we would be nearer our goal of precision in diagnosis. We would still, however, not be justified in immediately assuming that we had arrived at our goal because we would still have to evaluate our findings in terms of the recent work being done on precognition, ESP, etc.

Tentative Suggestions for Differential Diagnosis

What, if any, positive features of demonic states can be considered which might be useful in terms of making a diagnosis?

1. One of the principal rules in making any diagnosis in medicine is not to look for two etiologic agents until it is clear that one such agent cannot be productive of all the features manifested. Similarly, I feel it is an excellent rule to follow never to look for a supernatural cause without ruling out all possible natural causes.

2. The diagnostic value of confrontation with the name Lord versus the name Jesus has been stressed.

3. Perhaps the most useful clue is the presence of symptoms which are not in keeping with the known personality structure of the individual and with recognized psychopathologic states.

4. It is also well to remember that the demonic factor in etiology tends to increase pro-rata with our lack of knowledge and ignorance.

5. 1 John 4:1 indicates that we should test the spirits as part of the diagnostic procedure. Unfortunately, it does not exactly explain what this means, nor how one can develop this ability.

6. It is a safe rule to expect sin not to be due to demonic agencies, but rather to be secondary to the expression of narcissism. I cannot think of one sin, in life or mentioned in the Scriptures, which in the final analysis is not due to an expression of narcissism and selfishness. It is not a question of "the devil made me do it," but "self made

me do it." Of course, as has already been pointed out, the devil may use for his purposes one's own reservoir of narcissism.

17

Taste and See

R. KENNETH McALL

It is a great privilege for me to be among such a learned gathering of people and to be able to share with you some of my experiences. We all here have learned through our training the value of experiment, working through trial and error until a theory is proved and faith becomes assurance.

I do not intend today to discuss divine healing of phsyical conditions nor the release of those caught up in the ramifications of psychosomatic illness, although in many of these the casual influences may be recognized by us as satanic. My subject for this talk concerns those who are in the grip of often identifiable and always evil control or by forces external to themselves. In this sphere of disturbance, the need is for deliverance often coupled with the process of exorcism. There is no doubt that the need to recognize such cases and deal with them in the appropriate manner is greatly on the increase throughout the modern world. The examples I shall give come from over one hundred and fifty documented cases in which exorcism has been used.

In the 1930's when I was a missionary surgeon in the interior of China, devil possession was not uncommon, though the diagnosis could sometimes have been in question. The only treatment offered to those possessed was death by stoning, unless the case occurred within reach of a Christian community in which case the villagers would send for the highly trained and extraordinarily fearless Bible women who would lay hands on the victim, pray and release him. The effect was always immediate. At the time,

I was afraid of the whole subject, dismissing it as "primitive." However, over the next few years during which I spent varying periods of time in Communist and later Japanese hands, I found myself quite shaken by the transformation of some of these people who were obviously in the grip of evil and by the fact that it was our prayers which had initiated the cure.

The first case in England which I suspected to be one of control occurred after the war. An elderly woman came to consult me about her "heart condition." Her incessant talking about her son roused my suspicions, but my insistence that this sphere of her life might need dealing with made her so angry that she refused further help. However later, when she was sitting resting in a nearby church, she heard a voice, which at first she thought was mine, saying, "You have never cut the umbilical cord of your youngest child." This was repeated until she finally knelt down and prayed that God would cut this bond. From that moment her own symptoms disappeared. The next day she told me the full story of her son. After her husband died, she had taken her eight-year-old son out of boarding school to be with her and from that time had emotionally depended on him. He had developed a schizophrenic illness and was in a hospital four hundred and fifty miles away at this time and was thirty-five years old. Exactly at the moment when his mother was praying in the church, he had begun to feel normal. His wife was in the hospital with tuberculosis. From that time she too was healed. They have remained well for over twenty years of follow up.

Differential diagnosis in these cases is often difficult, but the multiple diagnoses given to them is often an indication of the real trouble.

I had become a consultant psychiatrist, and one called Mavis was sent in 1965 to see me, her seventeenth psychiatrist. She complained of "blackouts," sometimes lasting three to fourteen days at a time during which she would behave in a bizarre manner with a clouded consciousness and little memory afterward. She was a school teacher, and at these times would go to bed. Her job was threatened. She was a physically fit twenty-six-year-old of pyknic build wearing fantastically gaudy clothing. At the beginning of her second interview she said, "I cannot tell you a lie, but the truth and I have been strangers for years." She told how she retreated to bed because her "voices" had been mocking her again. She thought that in this new job she had escaped them. One day she had been asked to take some school money to the bank, but instead she found herself loaded with useless presents which she had bought without knowing what she was doing.

She could recall four admissions to the hospital. On the first occasion she was given eight months of deep insulin treatment and ECT, and then she left without being discharged. In the second she was diagnosed as a schizophrenic because of her hallucinations, withdrawal from reality, and inappropriate affect. After a few weeks "suddenly" everything cleared and again she left on her own. She says that she never took any of the tablets given to her in that hospital and thought "the hospital didn't know." In another hospital she was thought to have a pre-frontal tumor and underwent air studies and angiograms. At the fourth hospital she was labelled a hysterical psychopath. Now in this last interview with me she told me about a lesbian relationship she had had with a girl called "Jean" over a number of years. This girl had died sometime previously, but in her dreamy states she still carried on this relationship with Jean's spirit. I sought the help of an experienced priest who in a service of exorcism ordered the possessing girl to leave Mavis alone. Suddenly from Mavis' mouth during the prayer came the words in another voice: "Go away and leave us alone." Afterwards when we asked why she had shouted, she said, "Oh that was Jean, but now I feel as though there is a huge hole in my head." She felt empty and clean. Shortly after, she found another job and also went back to teaching Sunday school, which she had not done for many years. Ten years later I heard from her, telling me that she was married and had children and that her experiences had been of help to other people.

Another case illustrating this syndrome was that of a married woman in her twenties. She had been diagnosed a schizophrenic and had been passed from one hospital to another. Her last two years had been spent in a padded cell where only her husband had been able to approach her. She had not spoken for two years and was violent. Neither electro-convulsive therapy nor drugs had helped her. In fact, she demonstrated the interesting paradox often seen in these cases, that of responding in the opposite way to drugs, sleeping when given amphetamines, and being wide awake on large does of barbiturates. When I spoke to her husband, mentioning devil possession, about which he knew nothing, the woman, huddled in her dark corner and dishevelled, stood up and spoke for the first time the name of the possessing spirit and asked to see a priest. She was released and for the past seven years has lived as a normal housewife again and helping her husband in his business.

In analyzing this first group of stories, we may say that in the Chinese cases, certainly witnessed at a time when I had little experience or appreciation of these conditions, there were transmarginal stress situations where there was no belief or strength of character to promote self-control or claim protection, so other forces took over. In the second case, the mother, a possessive type, had compensated for the death of her husband by taking over the life of her youngest son. She had controlled every aspect of his life. Thus we have a living person being used to control and destroy another living person. In the third case, in which two women had been in a close lesbian relationship, the control of one over the other had continued after death. The fourth case, misdiagnosed for years but with the correct diagnosis confirmed by the results of exorcism, demonstrated the specific control by an unknown entity, apparently bent on destruction of the personality of the patient.

These cases all showed no response to known treatment but were cured instantly through prayer, not necessarily with the approval or consent or even awareness by the victim. These people can be classified as being controlled or possessed by external entities: multiple or single, dead or alive, willingly or without the patient's volition.

Naturally there has been built up, according to the various disciplines, a language descriptive of attitudes to, and beliefs in, these phenomena. In ordinary language one may talk of the person who dabbles and is intrigued by or plays, perhaps inquisitively, with occult material, becoming infested or dirtied by contact with it. They could be "under attack" but not "got down." They might come under the control of occult forces and later, unable to release themselves, would become "possessed" or "demonized." Children are especially susceptible; whole families may be the target where accidents, illness or even financial disaster occur. Perhaps all these descriptions are gross over-simplifications of the true position, but they are adequate for an introduction of the subject. In psychiatric terminology we would refer to the neurotic, hysteric or suggestible type often with middle grade intelligence. These are particularly susceptible and show a dissociation and in severe cases, ultra paradoxical reactions. The obsessive, critical, highly intelligent person who can retain insight is less prone to this type of possession, but may well come under other forms of attack more insidious and less readily recognized. This leaves a large group of humanity, usually physically tough and superficial in their attitudes and reactions, with little insight, who may appear immune to the attractions of either good or evil. Theologians may well consider them as already "lost." Others may call them hedonistic.

In this talk I do not intend to analyze or attempt to deal with the mass group hypnotic or hysterical "possession" seen so frequently in devil dances or voodoo, and similarly in the fervor of mass revivalist meetings. The various conversion techniques for good or evil are not in the scope of this lecture. In these mass exercises nervous illness can be cured or induced. Faith may be created or destroyed. I am concerned with individuals presented for psychiatric assessment and help. In these cases we must always and increasingly be on the alert for any evidence of occult involvement. In the stage of infestation by would-be controlling entities, the Christian can resist and through his faith achieve not just a defeat of the negative, but positive growth to higher goals and a quicker recognition of attacks by the occult. Certainly you want a deliverance from the power of Satan, but even more, a deliverance into the new life of forgiveness and cleanliness in the Lord; some would understand it to mean through the veil. A Christian who has dabbled in the occult "for fun" or out of curiosity is more quickly aware of the strange power of these things and the need to avoid them absolutely. There is much in Leviticus, Deuteronomy and Samuel to warn us and give us laws to follow: "These things are an abomination in the sight of the Lord."

Those without Christian awareness may be helped but come to rely on tranquilizers, analysts or psychosomatists. When the state of actual control or possession is reached, many illnesses can be imitated, mostly in the psychiatric field.

Classifications

P. M. Yap calls this "the possession syndrome"—a

term close to the "smother love" type of control—and clas-
sifies the whole according to the depth of consciousness:
complete, partial, histrionic. This is a useful guide to the
use of ECT in Eastern cases but not to an eradication of
cause, nor of the depth of psychotherapy needed for a cure.

Dr. Jean Lhermitte, the French neurologist, has had
a large number of cases of possession pass through his
hands. Can one therefore presume that in a predominately
Roman Catholic country doctors and priests are more
alert to this problem? Lhermitte insists on the cooperation
of doctors with priests, or to use his words, qualified theologians. He uses the term "demonopathy," which is closer
to the Greek translation, and suggests an infestation by
occult forces. He considers that the one who is demonized
is not necessarily sinful in himself, but that the infestation
enters via an area which lies between mind and soul,
especially when a person has been weakened through illness. In his classification he describes the genuine cases,
where there is a full replacement of the personality by the
possessor. The cases in the New Testament are of this
type and need highly qualified exorcists to release them.
He discusses at length the paroxysmal hysterical or mytho-
maniacal types. Some of these have a clouding of consciousness. These persons, seemingly possessed, regress to
an earlier stage with a dissociation of their personality
and of the elements which should have held it together;
thus the personality escapes rational self-criticism. They
can make believe through untrue romances and lying statements. Their episodes "miraculously" end when life is
threatened. They need sympathy and patience, for this
state has built up slowly from an early age. To the analyst
Lhermitte says that though today we accept telekinesis,
telepathy, and the like, the possession syndrome can appear
as a projection or personification of our own tendencies.
In the form he calls lucid possession, he considers that there
is a battle going on within the person as to which force
is going to take control.

Those who respond to ECT and physical means are
therefore probably not part of the possession syndrome.
It is true some manifest many facets of other diagnoses,
and where this becomes confusing and a multiple diagnosis
is given, then this syndrome should be suspected.

In the light of the above readings, and in retrospect
over the cases experienced, the following is suggested as
the possession syndrome or demonosis. Two or more person-

alities are involved; they may be dead or alive.

Differential Diagnosis

Possession syndromes may be associated with psychoses or neuroses; some with clouding of consciousness, some with epileptic form convulsions. Others with a more insidious onset may remain lucid and with full insight be able to discuss the possession, the passivity, and feelings. Or there may be abnormal somatic sensations, weakness, anxiety and depression.

The problem of psychosomatics in this connection may be one of degree only. Where hatred and resentment produce manifestations (e.g., Luke 13:11, "A spirit of infirmity binds her"): Fear—asthma; pride—stiffneck; temper and indulgence; resentment—rheumatism.

The first question has to do with the soil for easy flourishing of infestation, or infestation which breaks down the personality. A strong, integrated person who is spiritually mature, not only is immune, but by this very fact saves others from their danger. Depression is a common concomitant and can manifest as exogenous or endogenous in symptom pattern. Such people are emotionally labile. Possessed people, at times, speak with a high-pitched scream, low-pitched croak or stutter. They differ from hysterics in that there is no motive of gain, no attention-seeking, and most of the attacks are isolated. "There is a suspension of criticism and a posture of retreat," says P. M. Yap. Many such cases are labelled as atypical schizophrenics. None of them show the complete symptom-complex of schizophrenia, but they may present one or two unusual features such as catatonia or delusions.

Dr. Skottowe, in his textbook, *Psychiatry for Students*, states that "in differential diagnosis for schizophrenia, a differentiation must be made from those who have 'been involved' in occult practices."

There is a need to ascertain if there has been any involvement in drug addiction, as it is common for addicts, especially those addicted to heroin and alcohol, to become involved in black magic, and vice versa. "Folie-à-deux" is usually found in closely related people who echo each other's thoughts and reactions of a commonly bizarre paranoid nature. These persons have been known (in some cases) to have been very religious people who have defaulted and thus left themselves open to some power other than God to control their lives.

Passivity feelings, as described by Mayer, Gross and Slater, are considered by some to be pathognomonic of schizophrenia, but when they are the only presenting symptom and all other criteria necessary for the diagnosis of schizophrenia are absent, then the possession syndrome must be suspected. Heightened suggestibility is of course very common in the sensitive, artistic group of the religiose. Some would say, "If you sup with the devil, you need a long spoon." In the majority of cases quoted there is no question of suggestion. Possession is obvious immediately. In two cases where suggestion was used, other factors were revealed in later interviews, and exorcism had only partially helped. These are not quoted as success stories. In many cases the patient was cured without knowing that any exorcism was taking place—nor had it been mentioned to him.

The analyst would postulate that the ego hypercathects the pre-loss-self and reinforces denial in an ego arrest, especially in the sphere of self-image and self-object relationships, with resistance to new integrations and change and a retreat into a known or imaginary relationship. Analysts would agree that growth can be resumed under appropriate conditions, after unconscious conflicts have been talked out and resolved. The differential diagnoses are in themselves a fascinating study, but more important for us is the illumination which may be found by listening in quiet to our Lord with an open mind. It is even more fascinating to see how accurately He will point the way both to the correct diagnosis and to the answer. The following cases will illustrate this better than any theorizing of mine.

For seven years a young nun's acute bouts of disruptive behavior had shattered the peace of the closed community to which she belonged. I asked her to draw a family tree and this she was able to do. It showed clearly a repeated pattern of behavior. I was asked to speak to the nunnery on the subject of Satan's use of this family pattern to destroy and disrupt. Forty nuns produced similar problems, including family suicides, mental breakdowns, disrupted relationships and sudden deaths. With the two chaplains we designed a service which began with praise, then exorcism, confession and absolution. This was followed by their bringing to the altar steps paper on which was written all the problems raised, including the names of the departed; the papers were laid on the altar. Finally there was a shortened service of the Eucharist and, for those who wished, the laying on of hands and holy unction at the altar. The effect on many of the participants' lives was dramatic, both in the order and beyond the nunnery.

In conditions of this type, where exorcism seems indicated, study of the family tree often reveals repeated patterns related to the position of those afflicted: For example, the eldest daughter of seven succeeding generations; the eldest male of each family; the youngest, weakest person at the time of onset.

An elderly Canon of the Anglican church became quite terrified when he found himself appointed as official exorcist for the diocese. He asked for help. I asked why and he replied: "My daughter is locked in a padded cell in a mental hospital, and there is nothing they can do to help her." Her main trouble was that she had an overwhelming urge to gouge out the eyes of her children. I remarked that this seemed a very primitive form of behavior and inquired who her ancestors were. He informed me that her mother, his wife, was a titled lady from an ancient castle. I knew from having visited this castle that at one time this form of torture had been practiced there. The present family apparently never went near the place and knew nothing of it. I suggested to the Canon that he should see his bishop and ask his advice. The bishop said that we should have a eucharist of remembrance and that he would be free in five days' time to celebrate this with the two of us. From the moment he made this promise, the Canon's daughter became perfectly normal. A few days later we heard that her aunt who was—unknown to me—in another mental hospital had been cured at the same time. Neither of these two knew anything of the conversation with the bishop. The Canon, too, was released from his anxieties and has helped many others since then.

Quite commonly one finds in what are known as the "back" wards of mental hospitals patients who have been labelled atypical schizophrenics or depressives. Some such cases have been completely cured by the prayer of exorcism—sometimes with, and even at times without, the patients' permission and sometimes in their absence. Even in a true schizophrenic the hallucinations and delusions may sometimes be removed as a result of exorcism. They then regain an increasing degree of insight and with the help of a spiritual discipline can learn to control their own medication. It seems that those with borderline or established mental disturbances are easy prey to occult or demonic control.

Nancy was the daughter of a medium. She had become a heroin addict. During a prayer of exorcism she stood, objecting loudly and stamping her feet, but in spite of her objection, her addiction ceased overnight and she had no withdrawal symptoms. Since that time she has completed two years of training at a Bible college.

A Nigerian student attending a school of Military Survey in England showed a schizoid pattern of behavior until he was exorcised from the curse of a witch doctor, put on him at the request of a jealous uncle. Or we could tell of the exorcism of a pseudo-epileptic, of the Spiritualist medium who then became a Quaker, or of haunted places. Enough to say that as far as types and occurrences go their name is "Legion."

No two instances are exactly alike. They may be drug addicts or alcoholics, ignorant or educated, materialists or spiritists—but at some time they have been attacked and later possessed by external forces. This has sometimes come about through their own dabbling in occult things or by their own voluntary acceptance of control. It may result from cursing by others or may occur during a state of ill health at a time when the victim is vulnerable and unprotected.

We have been considering the effects of occult possession and control on the lives of individuals. Equally important is the effect on society as a whole. Through the media—radio, television, newspapers, magazines—the whole subject of the occult is made to seem fascinating. We *must* be aware that much of this, along with the traffic in drugs, pornography and smear campaigns, may be part of a vast spiritual program intended to undermine our Christian heritage and character.

Effective exorcism does not depend on permission from a church hierarchy or the authority of any senior churchman. Nor is any specific formula of service or prayer required. It is not even necessary in exorcism to have the victim's approval. The possessed is often not in a position to understand what is going on. But success in exorcism *does* depend on the intent and faith of two or three who pray in the name of Jesus Christ. We can only have glimpses of God's purposes and we can only dimly comprehend the mysteries underlying these events. We step out in faith with a profound, nonrationalistic conviction of the truth of the proposition. Christ commanded us to preach, heal, and cast out evil, and this apparently we can do with effectiveness far beyond our human understanding. We have proved the truth that the grace of our Lord is adequate for every situation. Taste and See!

PART SEVEN

Demonology and Pastoral Care

18

Problems and Procedures in Exorcism

JOHN WHITE

I am both a psychiatrist and a minister. In the local congregation I spot neuroses and psychoses. I am aware of sociological and psychological laws just as I am aware of the powers of the world to come. On the other hand, in my office, functioning as a psychiatrist, I am unable to close my eyes to moral and theological issues. The skills and the insights of each profession affect my perceptions and practice in the other. In both professions I say with Charles Wesley:

Forth in Thy name, O Lord, I go
My daily labor to pursue,
Thee only would I seek to know
In all I think, or say or do.

Common to both professions is an encounter with the occult. I am sometimes forced in the office to ask myself whether I am dealing with patients whose emotional problems are secondary to, or concomitant with, the operation of demonic forces; while in church and in conversation with other ministers, I grow concerned about what seems an overzealous use of techniques of "deliverance." I wonder whether some of the advocates of spiritual warfare do more harm than good. I also wonder whether their effectiveness may sometimes be explained in psychological terms alone.

Clashing Epistemologies

There are difficulties with the cross-over of insights from one professional sphere to the other. As a psychiatrist I am as much a scientist as an artist. I am trained skeptically to examine hypotheses and to subject them to experiment. But the scientific method, limited enough in dealing even with material realities, collapses altogether in the face of the nonmaterial. To "deal with" demons I must *know* that they exist and I must also *know* that they are a factor in Joe Smith's distress. No scientific experiment could be devised to demonstrate conclusively the presence of Joe Smith's demon. Evidence, yes; proof, never.

Now, no good scientist believes in the hypothesis he is examining. Yet you cannot exorcise demons you do not believe in. I am therefore obliged in the office to make a long stride where the occult is involved. The objective skeptical scientist must step across a chasm and *believe*.

Herein lies a difficulty. No one in the New Testament ever disagreed about the presence of demons in a specific case of possession. There seemed always to be a common understanding among those concerned as to the true state of affairs. One did not need to be a follower of Christ, even of Jehovah, to spot the occult. Everyone, believer and unbeliever alike, seemed just to *know*. The question of *how* they knew is never discussed in the New Testament.

Yet in extra-biblical literature the "how-to-diagnose" theme is central. Unfortunately the criteria for diagnosis are often the criteria the psychiatrist uses to diagnose mental illness. There can thus arise a clash of opinion as to whether someone is demon possessed or psychiatrically sick, a clash which is at heart a clash of epistemologies. And before we leap to take sides it would be well to scrutinize the epistemological bases on which both systems rest. For the exorcist has as much right to challenge the doctor as has the doctor to challenge the exorcist with the question: How do you *know* that such-and-such is the true cause of the patient's difficulties?

Let me review for physicians and non-physicians alike, the basis on which medical diagnosis rests. To do this, you must keep three concepts in mind: the *"clinical picture,"* the *diagnosis* and the *etiology*. The *clinical* picture has three components. There is Joe Smith's story: how his trouble started, what happened next, and what made him come to see you. This component is called Joe's *history*. Then there are *symptoms*, the things Joe feels and complains about, but that you yourself cannot observe (e.g., a headache). Finally there are signs, things you can see and sometimes measure about Joe (like a red rash on his left arm). To these three, extra "signs" may be added because of the advances of technology—Xrays, blood examinations, etc. For the sake of simplicity I will include everything—the history, the symptoms, the signs and the special tests—into what I am calling the clinical picture.

From the clinical picture the physician makes a *diagnosis*. The term originally implied a profound understanding of the patient's condition, a knowing through or by means of. But as often as not diagnosis amounts merely to naming or labelling the condition. If you were to ask the doctor why he chose a particular "diagnostic label," you would find that he had done the same thing you used to do yourself when as a child you gathered flowers or collected butterflies. You divided them into different kinds because of their different appearances. Though all butterflies had wings and antennae, their shapes, colors, and sizes differed. You also gave them names, because you found out that other people before you who had also spotted the differences (plus some you never thought of) had given them these names and published books about them.

In the same way, the doctor groups and names illnesses in his mind by the distinctive patterns of different clinical pictures, and on the basis of previous labelling fashions.

To name something, whether a sickness or a moth, is to profess to know something about it. The longer and more obscure the name you give it the greater your knowledge appears to be.

It would have bothered me when I was a medical student to be told that I understood very little about the diseases even though I could diagnose them. After all, I could give an account of their *etiologies*. Not only could I name Joe's sickness, but I could explain its cause. I knew why he got to be sick. I could describe what was happening to and in the cells of his body, giving rise to the symptoms he complained of. We knew such a lot thirty years ago.

Two things have happened since I was a medical student: one of them to the diagnostic process and the other to me. I now see (as a skeptical scientist) that what I referred to as the *etiology* of a sickness was at best a partial explanation. Indeed it would be better to refer to it as *description* rather than explanation. My "etiology" of an illness was a crude and inaccurate description of body mechanisms associated with it.

More recent research has revealed how inaccurate the descriptions were. What *seemed* to be happening inside Joe was rather different from what it *now* appears was happening.

In the meantime the labelling process itself has changed. Diagnosis has shifted, at least in physical medicine, to greater concern with supposed etiology and therefore to more dependence upon complex testing. Some old diagnostic labels have disappeared and new ones have taken their places—all in response, not to the appearance of new diseases, but to greater knowledge about old ones. The new names reflect new insights. Reality has not changed; only the way we doctors perceive it.

But presumably the process of changing perceptions of reality will continue as knowledge advances. If it does, our present descriptions and labels will in the future be seen also as crude and partial, and our classifications as subject to revision. The quantity of our knowledge has increased and may increase yet more, but its *essential quality* remains the same—a matter of observation and shrewd guesswork, forming a basis for making classifications.

My statements are not disparaging. However incomplete and illusory our understanding of the disease processes is, it has led to the alleviation of suffering. We have learned to tamper clumsily with laws of the universe and our tampering seems to do more good than harm. We do not altogether know what we are doing to Joe but we are fairly sure it helps.

Evangelical Christians tend to be impressed by the scientific discoveries of modern medicine. Only when those discoveries, and the etiological theories that go along with them, attempt to explain disturbed emotions and behavior do they begin to feel threatened. Yet there is no difference between the weakness of the etiological theories of physical medicine and those of psychiatry. Two things immediately become apparent, however, as we make the transition from medicine to psychiatry.

First of all, the psychiatrist is embarrassed by the necessity of coping with the concept of *mind*. His colleagues in physical medicine can be totally at ease as materialists. But the psychiatrist is forced either to accept *mind*—a nonmaterial entity—or ingeniously to reconstruct his hypotheses so that he largely avoids the concept. And this is difficult.

The second thing is in some way connected with the first. Few psychiatrists admit that they were created in the image of God, yet in every psychiatrist as in every man there exists a profound awareness of his essential nobility, and the wonder of his being. The innate determinism of physical medicine presents no problem to the surgeon or the internist. But the determinism of psychiatric theories demeans and belittles man. It matters little whether the determinism is psychoanalytic, biochemical, anthropological, behaviorist or whatever. The thinking psychiatrist therefore often finds himself rebelling against the idea that he himself, like his patients, is merely a link in complex interacting chains of cause and effect.

When we turn to psychiatry we become acutely and uncomfortably aware that there are gaps in our understanding of human disease, and that the very paradigm within which science operates seems ill equipped to give us satisfactory answers. We cannot discuss what is wrong with man until we have answered the prior question: What is man?

That is not to say (and I must make the point again) that psychiatric knowledge is useless. It has practiced value. It offers partial solutions, but useful ones.

Up to now we have been taking a cursory look at what grounds the doctor has for claiming to know what is wrong with Joe. When we turn to make the same challenge to the experts on exorcism, we find that their claims are based on knowledge from two totally distinct sources. On the one hand they appeal to revelation. On the other, they follow the same process as the physician, though in a much less sophisticated fashion. They elaborate hypotheses from observations and tradition.

They appeal to the Scriptures as an infallible guide to truth. And in the Scriptures they (and we along with them) discover statements about evil spirit beings, their relationship with God, with Jesus Christ, and with the age we live in, with the earth, etc. The teaching is straightforward, but limited. There is much we do not need to know. We also find descriptions of Christ's encounters with Satan and with demons, and of how the apostles dealt with demons. From these descriptions it is possible to make inferences.

However, the difficulty lies in the fact that in none of the Bible's teaching is there a discussion as to *how* one determines when a demon is present. Are the few descriptions in the Gospels and Acts typical of all cases? Even if they are, the details are meager and case histories almost nonexistent.

In addition to the Scriptures, then, a body of knowledge

about "diagnosis" has arisen in a manner identical to the rise of psychiatric and medical knowledge. The etiology (of occult activity) is assumed or inferred from the observed data. A "clinical picture" is described. It must be clearly understood that this body of knowledge is *extra-biblical.* Neither its advocates nor its detractors seem aware of this. It has the same innate strengths and the same underlying weaknesses as the extra-biblical theories of sciences, or of history. At best it depends upon the accuracy of the observer and the limitations of his reason. Yet as such it should be taken at least as seriously as other bodies of knowledge.

There are, of course, men and women who claim to *know* when demons are present—to know with intuitive immediacy. They believe that their knowledge is from a divinely imparted gift. But such a knowing cannot be imparted to someone else. If I ask, *"How* do you know?" the answer will be, "I just know," or "I can feel it." But their gift, if it is a gift, is only of limited help to the rest of us.

When we turn to the extra-biblical literature, there are four principal classes of data that make up the "clinical picture." These are (1) the history; (2) the signs and symptoms pathognomic of demonism; (3) the signs and symptoms common to both psychiatric illness and demonism; and finally, (4) epiphenomena in the vicinity of the victim.

The History

The history is sometimes one of contact with magic or the occult either innocently (i.e., with no deliberate defiance of God in mind) or in chosen rebellion. Anything from Satanism to teacup reading may be implicated. There is strong evidence that real demonic manifestations can follow such contacts. Many of the more popular authors go further and suggest that any "giving place to the devil" opens the way to demonic states requiring exorcism. But it would seem unwise to assume that even direct contact with the occult necessarily means that a subsequent disturbance must be demonic. It may be, but on the other hand, it may not. All cats are animals, but not all animals are cats.

Signs and Symptoms Specific to Demonic Influence

These consist of a virulently hostile or fearful reaction

to the things of God, so that the mention of His name, the name of Jesus, or specific references to the redeeming blood provoke agitation and blasphemous outbursts of fear in the affected subject. Sometimes the victim is described as speaking in another voice, or even another language. These signs are manifest. They should be distinguished from obsessive thoughts which, though they may be blasphemous or obscene, are symptoms common to psychiatric conditions and demonic manifestations. Of course the fact that the manifest signs are not features of recognized psychiatric illness does not mean that they could not be "explained" in psychological terms. It only means that something other than what we call psychiatric illness is implicated.

Signs and Symptoms Common to Mental Illness and Demonic Influence

The number of such signs and symptoms is legion. They may concern the subject's volition—a lack of control so that Joe performs actions which seem alien to him. He may experience violent swings of *mood*, inexplicable depressions, fears, hallucinatory voices or visions, suicidal or homocidal urges. There may be changes in his *consciousness*. He may appear to pass into fugue states or trances or to perform actions of which he seems to have no subsequent memory.

Epiphenomena

By epiphenomena I mean things happening *around* Joe— things that can be observed by other people, like tappings, knockings, or unexplained movements of physical objects like the shaking of a bed or the transfer of china across a room. Such phenomena have been reported by many observers. Some of the phenomena have been subject to scientific investigation in an attempt to explore parapsychological hypotheses explaining them. Others have been recorded by newspaper reporters featuring poltergeist activities. They are uncommon, and more usually reported (at least if we read Christian literature) where there is a clear-cut history of previous occult practices.

Other explanations have been suggested to account for the manifestations I have described, explanations which do not have recourse to the supernatural. It would be inappropriate for me to discuss them in this paper and I will make only one comment. Psychological and sociological theories may have light to throw upon the facts. But their light at best is partial. Most psychological and sociological hypotheses reject a Christian view of man. They constitute, like the doctor's etiological theories, an incomplete description of psychological and sociological processes concomitant with the phenomena. We do not necessarily accept them or reject them on an *either/or* so much as on a *both/and* basis. If you ask me why the kettle is boiling, I can "explain" the matter *both* in terms of electrical resistance, heat conductance, and the latent heat of evaporation *and* by telling you my wife wants a cup of tea. Both explanations are true. Both are partial. Each explanation would correspond to a different meaning of the word "why?"

I have taken much space to discuss, even in a perfunctory manner, concerns which are essentially epistemological. My only excuse for doing so is that I am forced in my profession to grapple with the questions I have discussed, in order to find a basis for my attitudes and practices. I find it hard to discuss more practical concerns without sharing with you my own struggle to understand.

I was asked to discuss several things. What is an appropriate level of concern in the church around the question of demonic activity? How ought this concern to be expressed? What resources are there for counselling? What has been the general effect on the church of an interest in demonology? What resources are available to the believer in handling this issue?

How concerned should we be? Certainly our concern should be increasing. The evil that once walked our streets clothed and meekly, now strides naked and contemptuous, openly asserting his rights. In Western countries overt collusion with the Lord of Darkness and his cohorts is more widespread than it has been for centuries.

It affects some congregations not at all, others greatly, but many only minimally. Much depends on where the congregation is and how spiritually vital is its evangelism.

How should the concern be expressed? It may seem surprising, but I would not suggest immediate courses on "How to Cope with the Occult." At least I would not advocate them for church members in general. If we would strengthen the church, we must first discover where her weakness lies. The weakness of the church in the West (a weakness Satan has contrived by his quiet insistent use of insidious temptation) is its materialism. Western evangelical congregations live for *things*.

Our commission is to bear witness. We cannot bear witness effectively unless we place God's kingdom above everything else we hold dear—our security, our family's well-being, our very lives. Of what value is a verbal witness when Christianity in practice is a nice *addition* to life as we know it, icing on the cake, so to speak? I see no reason to instruct churches in dealing with demons. They need first to know how to deal with dollars, with mortgages, investments, material luxuries—by burning and burying them if need be.

There are exceptions to my damning generalization. Yet where the warfare is fiercest and overt assaults from demons are fiercest, there the needed knowledge already exists.

My conservative stance is reinforced by observing the impact of instruction on demonism in a number of congregations. The occult is a new delicacy which titillates the jaded appetites of pulpit-weary evangelicals. It is hot copy. Overnight a lethargic congregation can buzz with a fever of activity. Prolonged prayer meetings, glowing testimonies of deliverance become the order of the day. But when all the excitement dies down, what is the result?

Often one or two people *have* found release from bondage of some kind—perhaps more from besetting sins, resentments and bitternesses than from real demons. (Many "demons" exorcised by charismatic groups differ from those found in the New Testament in that they are "spirits" of psychological bondage, e.g., of anger, resentment, fear, pride, rejections, etc. I would not question their satanic origin, or that charismatic groups sometimes deal very effectively with them—only that what is cast out is not a *being* so much as a sinful attitude. It is probably to such enslaving attitudes that Daniels, the Indian evangelist, refers as "strange spirits." [1] Loving concern has been shown, and this is always good. Marital and group therapy of a cathartic nature has, on the whole, had a sweetening effect. But impact on the darkness around? Usually I have seen none.

In other instances I have seen the initial interest coalesce into a rigid pattern of demon hunting. The church by its behavior displays more respect for demons than for God (this would indignantly be denied). It becomes demon-oriented; and that is bad. If it spent time singing the praises of Jesus, it would be more profitably occupied. We need to learn not respect for demons, but *disrespect* for them.

I believe it is possible to declare a general principle: *teaching to the church as a whole* should not focus excessively on the occult. Teaching about Satan, about demons, about spiritual warfare should be introduced along with regular positive teaching. This is how the apostles distributed it in the Epistles.

You may ask how I can treat so serious a matter in so cavalier a fashion. It is true that we are engaged in a warfare with principalities and powers. But in warfare your principal aim, surprising as it may seem, is not to beat the enemy. Beating the enemy is secondary to some other object, e.g., you defeat his army because he tried to stop you from controlling his oil fields. While it is important to know your enemy and to be alert against his attacks, your main focus is on something else. In spiritual warfare our goal is to set men free. If the enemy can lure us into being too preoccupied with him, he has won a major tactical victory.

A second general principle in teaching the church as a whole is: teaching should not focus on the phenomena of possession, or on fine distinctions between oppression, possession or other esoteric specifics, but on how a Christian should overcome Satan in his everyday living. Paul's famous passage in Eph. 6:10-18 is usually expounded well, but it is losing popularity in the face of more salacious material. The brief mention by John in the Apocalypse (12:11) about the overcomers needs also to be brought home to Christians. These overcame Satan by: (1) the blood of the Lamb, (2) the word of their testimony, (3) preferring death to unfaithfulness. Let us put aside our difference in eschatology and examine the phrases. I shall expound them succinctly in a hortatory manner.

The Blood of the Lamb

This phrase is not an incantation or spell. Though its use as such ("Satan, we bid you depart because we claim the blood of Jesus over this man . . .") may indeed be attended by dramatic results, in Revelation 12 it has nothing to do with exorcism. The context reveals the devil as the Accuser—accusing the brethren day and night before God. One of his prime activities, then, is to induce a burdensome sense of guilt by which confident, spontaneous service for God is strangled. I cannot serve God freely when I *feel* estranged from Him or unaccepted by Him. What the Accuser is telling God in my hearing is that I haven't tried hard enough. I must repent more sincerely, have deeper consecration, etc. Yet God's acceptance of me is not based on the depth of my sincerity but on the death of His Son. The blood of Christ here symbolizes the death of Christ, and it was shed not to cleanse my heart (as in hymnology) but my *conscience.* "How much more shall the blood of Christ cleanse your conscience from dead works, to serve the living God?" Only the man who continually appreciates the relevance and the glory of the death of Christ is continuously free in conscience to serve God for love.

> Well may the Accuser roar
> Of ills that I have done
> I know them all . . .
> And thousands more . . .
> Jehovah knoweth none.

The Word of Their Testimony

This phrase is unquestionably related to the devil in his role (also mentioned in the immediate context) as "that old serpent" that deceives the whole world. To set men free the church has to overcome the deceiver who clouds his captives' understanding in darkness. This is accomplished when the Word of God proceeds from the lips of a witness who can truthfully tell forth what God has shown him from the Word in his own life. He testifies to truth he has discovered.

Death Before Compromise

In the last resort the serpent becomes the devouring dragon. Whom he cannot depress or deceive he devours—or threatens to. And here lies the key for today's church. You may not be able to cast out demons, but is faithfulness to Christ more important to you than life? I do not dramatize the issue; it is very down-to-earth. If your life is not currently threatened, there are many smaller sacrifices you have to make by choosing Christ above all else. Faithfulness in small things may indicate potential faithfulness to the death. And faithfulness in the "crunch" always defeats the adversary.

Such are general teachings I would see hammered home to the church at large.

Special Resources

But there are times when individual Christians, especially those in Christian leadership and physicians in practice, need more specific help. If you ask me to whom they should turn, I am at a loss to answer. It depends on where they live and who is available there. I can only offer general principles for those of you in leadership who yourselves encounter the occult or who may think you do.

Talk to the distressed person. Allow him to describe the nature of his distress. At first do not interrupt his flow of speech except to ask clarification of points you fail to understand. Take time to watch and listen carefully. If the person finds it difficult to talk, do not be overanxious. Be gentle in your questioning and be slow to probe deeply. The genuineness of your interest and your own inner tranquility will be the greatest incentives for him to open up.

As the urgent rush of words slows down you will probably wish to fill in gaps in his story. In your mind will be the questions: Is this an emotional problem? Is it simply a matter of his relationship with others? What spiritual issues are involved? Is it possible that the man is mentally ill? Is there something in the story that suggests the occult? Once he has told you as much as he can, then ask specific questions about the occult.

Where there is difficulty in deciding between demonism and psychiatric illness (incidentally there is no reason why the two could not occur simultaneously), psychiatric consultation may be called for. If there are reasons which cause you to hesitate to refer to a psychiatrist, and if at the same time you lack psychiatric sophistication, you might be helped by the book, *Occult Bondage and Deliverance*.[2] Dr. Lechler's discussion of the distinctions between psychiatric and demonic symptoms are helpful up to a point. He makes the statement, "A mentally ill person is in fact still ill, even when he exhibits certain symptoms characteristic of possession. On the other hand, a possessed person is in fact mentally healthy in spite of the fact that at intervals he may exhibit certain symptoms of mental abnormality." Some might cavil at the second part of Lechler's statement but a psychiatrist would know what he means. One of my own cases may illustrate this:

> A 26-year-old single woman consulted me with symptoms of anxiety, episodic brief depressions and strong suicidal urges. She made occasional use of marijuana and amphetamines, and was living in a loose common-law relationship with a man her own age. She had recently taken an overdose of amphetamines in a suicide attempt.

Her father was religious, rigid, strict, and punitive; her mother, deeply religious but gentle. The patient stated that at times she was subject to visual and auditory hallucinations which had frightened her initially, but were no longer distressing. They occurred only when she entered certain houses, never when she was alone, never when she was under stress, and not necessarily in association with drug use. In certain houses the "appearances" occurred whenever she entered. She "saw" men and women dressed in fashions dating back fifty years or more. She was somewhat reluctant to discuss the apparitions, being more concerned with her depressions.

Several years previously she had at her parents insistence broken off an engagement. She went through a normal grief reaction following her fiance's suicide a week after the broken engagement. For a year she attempted unsuccessfully to "contact" him as she lay in bed at night by "projecting her spirit" in search of him. On the anniversary of his death she stated that he appeared to her in a dream. The dream was deeply comforting, and was followed by more dreams of a similar nature. She saw them as real contact with her deceased fiance, and was aware that she "was dabbling with spiritism."

When I suggested that her symptoms might be connected with her reaching out into the occult she agreed, but was reluctant to break off her occult experiences. A careful psychiatric examination excluded the possibility of any of the schizophrenias. There was no evidence of any other functional psychosis. The patient's manner did not suggest a hysterical personality. At the conclusion of the interview she stated that she would prefer not to see me again. Though she telephoned me once or twice, she would break off the connection whenever I suggested she come to see me.

I viewed her symptoms as rising from the occult rather than from mental illness.

On the other hand, Lechler also mentions mental illness which looks like demonism but *is* mental illness, whatever else it may be. Here the problem is more difficult. Certainly obsessive-compulsive patients may be troubled by blasphemous or obscene thoughts or by fears of harming their children. Similar obsessions arise in some depressive illnesses and can be alleviated and even cured by the use of antidepressant medication. In the more acute schizophreni-form illnesses hallucinatory voices urging suicide or making blasphemous suggestions can similarly be banished by brief courses of electroconvulsive therapy or by the use of psychotropic drugs. It would seem unlikely that demons can be exorcised with phenothiazines or ECT. Lechler describes points of differentiation between illness symptoms and those rising from demonism. But the distinction is not always easy.

> A young married woman, an evangelical Christian, was referred to me in an extremely psychotic condition which I judged at the time to be manic. She responded to lithium carbonate, and later, when depressed to antidepressants.
>
> Over the next two years she was troubled episodically by obsessive, blasphemous thoughts and outbursts of rage. Several exorcisms by visiting experts afforded her relief, but the effects would last only a day or two, and sometimes there would be no relief. At times she would benefit from Christian instruction. She was intelligent but extremely demanding upon a wide circle of friends.
>
> Following the birth of her third child I contacted the Children's Aid Society to protect the baby from her beatings. The child suffered a fractured skull and long-bone fractures.
>
> Two months later, at a time when I was away from home, she underwent one more exorcism during which many demons were cast out of her one by one. The agnostic social worker (an expert in the battered child syndrome) was so impressed with the patient's subsequent condition that she called me on my return, asking me to reassess her. I did so, and found her to be more relaxed and realistic than I had ever known her, and no longer demanding. The child was returned (at first under supervision). The patient has now remained symptom-free for many months.
>
> I listened to a tape of teaching on exorcism by her exorcist. In it I learned that the meaning of the word "double-minded" in James was "schizophrenic," that 25% of the population in North America was schizophrenic —and needed to be released from demons. His talk was a fascinating blend of psychological insightfulness and wild inaccuracy. Yet he seemed, in spite of his misapprehensions, to have helped my patient.

The case history I have outlined raises other issues. It suggests that a reasonably competent psychiatrist who is widely read and has an open mind on the occult can be fooled into thinking a condition is purely psychiatric when it may be totally or in part demonic. Or it may suggest that certain emotional problems are better and more effectively dealt with by believing prayer than by therapy.

Certainly knowledge may contribute comparatively little to one's ability to help. It suggests also that many self-professed Christian exorcists are in the same position as the disciples who could not cast out a certain demon. In dealing, then, with what might be demonic, we shall need both to be realistic and humble. Fortunately most cases are much easier to assess and treat than the one I have described.

The Decision to Help

At some point as you listen to the story of a distressed person, you will be forced to face options: What help is needed? Is there anyone to whom I can send this person? Ought I to try to help him myself? Is the occult involved?

One does not need to "have a ministry of deliverance" to cast out demons. Yet both the Scriptures and extra-biblical literature warn us that not all cases are equally easy to cope with. The same disciples who rejoiced at their power over demons were humiliated before the demonic simulation of epilepsy.[3] I know no way of anticipating how difficult a given exorcism may prove to be. One can only look to God for guidance whether to proceed or not.

How can I know whether I am qualified to proceed? All power in heaven and earth is given to Jesus.[4] In His name (i.e., when executing His commands under His authority) there is no limit to the demonic power His servants may overthrow. Yet I am not acting "in His name" when I neglect the provisions He has made—when His righteousness is not a plate of armor about me or His truth my trusty weapon.[5] Perhaps it is at this point that fasting and prayer are called for—not as a mechanical device for "psyching myself up" to cope with demons, nor yet a mystical pathway to supernatural power, but rather as an opening of my mind and will to God's Spirit that He may reveal to me my ambivalences, my double-mindedness, my unbelief.

The Spirit of God may give special gifts to some (God is still sovereign). But in general terms a Christian's effectiveness in dealing with evil powers arises from his relationship to Christ. My authority over demons will operate effectively in the degree that I rejoice in a clear, unambivalent relationship with Christ—a relationship of trust in His redeeming and justifying grace and of total commitment to His person and will.

Procedure

What do I *do* to cast out a demon? Are there certain words or phrases to be used?

Answers from the literature are contradictory and confusing. This fact in itself would tend to suggest that there is no set procedure. Kurt Koch is very careful before outlining sixteen principles involved in exorcism to state that " . . . a person may draw the false conclusion that there is some kind of pattern or stereotyped method involved. But this is not true. The Holy Spirit needs no pattern." [6] Even the use of the name of Jesus is not a magic spell, so much as a reminder to all concerned as to Who has the final word.

Let me then proceed in simple faith. "It is better," says Koch,[7] "to exercise faith from the very start and be prepared to let God disappoint you . . . than to fail to exercise faith and thereby disappoint God." Faith, it should be noted in the context above, means confidence in the character of the one trusted rather than confidence in the outcome of the procedure initiated. It is the faith of Shadrach, Meshach, and Abednego.[8]

No one who has read widely in the literature of the occult can fail to be impressed by the emphasis on *ritual*. Satanists who seek to control demonic powers and Christians who seek to exorcise them are alike obsessed with it. Mike Warnke, former Satanist High Priest, in his best-selling autobiography confesses, "The study of ritual fascinated me." Anxieties over mistakes in details of ritual also hounded him with fear.[9]

It would be fascinating to pursue the subject of ritual, symbol, witchcraft and demonism, but I will satisfy myself with one comment. A ritualistic approach to overcoming demons seems to have inherent weakness of playing the devil's game by the devil's rules. It may be true that demons are subject to complex symbolic and ritualistic laws, but the Christian's authority does not spring from a manipulation of them (ritual being at best a "figure of the true" [10]) but from the very fountain of all authority. To depend on ritual for the exercise of power is to depend on magic. It undermines dependence on God.

As I have myself proceeded in simple and sometimes very feeble faith, I have encountered surprising results. What I have found has humbled and instructed me. Let me conclude with a brief case history, which offers some interesting suggestions.

A twenty-six-year-old single woman was referred to me following a suicide attempt. Her behavior was agitated and hyperactive, but she gave verbal expressions of despair. She was intelligent and insightful and became more settled on psychotropic medication. She was Lutheran with a comprehensive grasp of Christian doctrine, and regarded herself as a Christian. However, she was the organizing secretary of one of the three "gay" leagues in Winnipeg, and a practicing homosexual, living with a woman who had alcohol and other personality problems.

Soon after her admission to the hospital she had improved to the point where day care seemed appropriate. Shortly therafter I invited her to a "cell group" meeting (for Bible study, fellowship and prayer) in my home. After the meeting she asked me: "What is wrong with you if when other people sing 'Oh, how I love Jesus' you find yourself singing 'Oh, how I *hate* Jesus'?"

Further questioning revealed that her attempts to sing hymns or pray were attended by verbal expressions of blasphemy which took her by surprise. It was not that she struggled against them so much as that she expressed them before being fully aware of what she was saying. The incidents dated back to her living in a haunted house, where a "friendly ghost" could be heard walking across the room, giving rise to creaking of boards and the appearance of depressions in the rug. "We really used to enjoy him," was her flippant comment. More recently she had been plagued at night by rattlings, shakings, knockings and tappings which interfered increasingly with her sleep.

I made an appointment, with the object of attempting exorcism. After praying, and as I commanded the demon or demons to depart, I was careful not to enforce my own wishes or will so much as to insist on the will and the authority of Christ. The patient appeared to pass into a species of trance in which she alternately laughed recklessly or was shaken with terrible sobbing. She made no verbal responses to questions. I had the subjective impression that I was locked in a struggle with an obstinate adversary who threatened injury or death to my wife and children. (Bizarre demonic attacks have been made on my family.) As the time for the termination of the interview approached I was at a loss as to how the conflict would be resolved. Eventually I was obliged to say, "The time is up now." At this the patient again laughed, but this time I had the subjective impression (which afforded me immense relief) that the laugh was one of despair and defeat. I felt (and I can only report my subjective impressions) that the main struggle was over, though the demon or demons had not left my patient.

Emerging from the trance she was somewhat dishevelled. I noticed that the skin on the palmar surface of both hands had been pierced by her fingernails. Her tweed skirt showed a circular patch of wetness of about 9 or 10 inches in diameter, where her tears had fallen. She said: "My God! What have you been doing to me?"

She returned immediately to the Day Care program. Later in the afternoon I was approached by three members of the staff who asked me what had happened in our interview, commenting on the profound improvement in the patient.

Later that week, at a charismatic cell group meeting, a young girl made the command, "Demon, whose name is Legion, I command you to come out of her in the name of Jesus." The patient is reported to have screamed and fallen on the floor convulsively. The members of the group, at first frightened, state that they experienced "a baptism of love" and surrounded her with expressions of love and praise. She regained consciousness to find herself saying, "He could not possibly love me," while those surrounding her gave her assurances of the love of Christ.

At our next interview she seemed open, straightforward and "in her right mind." She stated: "Know what? I'm not a lesbian."

"Oh?" I replied, "when did you decide to give it up?"

"Decide *nothing!*" was the reply, "I'm just *not*—not since the demons left."

She had abandoned her homosexual life-style, resigned from the gay organization, professed to have no homosexual conflict. She stated that the turning point had come in our session in the office. In the two years since then her life has been one of uninterrupted spiritual and emotional growth.

Perhaps the only prerequisite to our overcoming the powers of darkness is that we fear God and God alone. Christ commanded His disciples to be fearless in the face of those powers that were able only to kill the body. For my own part I reecho Martin Luther's words (Carlyle's translation):

And were this world all devil's o'er
And watching to devour us.
We lay it not to heart to sore;
Not they can overpower us.
And let the prince of ill
Look grim as e'er he will,
He harms us not a whit;
For why, his doom is writ;
A word shall quickly slay him.

God's word, for all their craft and force,
One moment will not linger;
But, spite of hell, shall have its course;
'Tis written by His finger.
And though they take our life,
Goods, honour, children, wife,
Yet is their profit small;
These things shall perish all;
The city of God remaineth.

Notes

1. "A Survey of the Situation: India." In: *Demon Experiences in Many Lands* (Chicago: Moody Press, 1960), p. 28.
2. Kurt Koch & Alfred Lechler, *Occult Bondage and Deliverance* (Grand Rapids, Mich.: Kregel, 1970).
3. Matt. 17:14-21.
4. Matt. 28:18.
5. Eph. 6:11-18.
6. Koch & Lechler, *op. cit.*, p. 88.
7. *Ibid.*, p. 122.
8. Dan. 3:17, 18.
9. Mike Warnke, *The Satan Seller* (Plainfield, N.J.: Logos International, 1972), pp. 66-67.
10. Heb. 9:24.

Additional Reading Suggestion

Jessie Penn-Lewis and Evan Roberts. *War on the Saints*. London: Marshall Brothers, 1912. This older and much quoted work has become a sort of Bible on demonology, highly regarded by older evangelicals.

19

Victims Become Victors

W. ELWYN DAVIES

"And without controversy great is the mystery of godliness; he who was manifested in the flesh, justified in the spirit, seen of angels, preached among the nations, believed on in the world, received up in glory. But the Spirit saith expressly, that in later times some shall fall away from the faith, giving heed to seducing spirits and doctrines of demons, through the hypocrisy of men that speak lies, branded in their own conscience as with a hot iron" (1 Tim. 3:16-4:2).

Paul wrote these words to Timothy nineteen hundred years ago. Just as the Bible does not set out to prove the existence of God and the angels, so it assumes the existence of Satan and demonic beings. The apostle warns of increased demonic activities as the present age runs its course, and it is evident that we are now living in the time foretold by him. It is not my intention to argue for the fact of demonism, but rather to examine the situation that exists in the church and the world at present and to seek some answers to the many questions that arise from modern demonization.

It is important to note the conditions which exist in the church of the last quarter of the twentieth century, because these have created a climate within the professing church that is conducive to demonic activities both in the church and in the world:

1. *The humanization of the gospel.* At first it was a denial of the deity of Jesus Christ. In recent decades the battle has largely centered on *the denial of the divine in Christian living.* God has largely been explained away and excluded from the dogma of the church, and now the life

of the church—and of the individual Christian—has become merely human. Such statements as that of Paul in Col. 1:27, "Christ in you, the hope of glory," are disregarded, because it is claimed they are irrelevant to our modern world of technical know-how. Man is now on the Throne!

2. *The materialization of life.* The test tube has taken over from the Spirit of God. The supernatural has been exorcised. In the conduct of the life of the church committees, specialists, programs, and even computers take precedence over the workings of the Holy Spirit. Public relations are considered more effective in filling pews than prayer meetings.

The God-Man has become just the Good Man; the mystical movings of God have become the mechanics of men, and now all at once we are aware of a strange vacuum in the church. Somehow we have been made aware of an area of life that is unfulfilled. The cravings of the spirit of man have been unheeded for too long. Man, according to the Bible, is a spiritual being. His spiritual life must be attended to sooner or later. Now it is "later," and to a large degree, the church is pitifully inadequate to meet his need. Our programs, our material wealth, our high-sounding liturgies, leave man empty. The climate of the church has conditioned millions to regard the Christian faith as good, but not good enough. It satisfied the agrarian community of the past century in part, but it leaves contemporary, urbanized, restless modern man cold.

It is at this point that men in the church have begun to show interest in alternative sources of fulfillment. If this is true of professing Christians, how much more so of the masses of unbelieving yet unsatisfied of our day? Deep down they *want* to be helped. They *want* to stretch their minds beyond the petty limits of all the pat answers of bygone days. They crave the adventure of stepping off limits, away from the cozy security-blanket of affluence and of predictable schedules for living. We should have seen more clearly the warning signs as our young people responded to the Beatles and to drugs. Beyond these lay the occult world, arms opened wide, beckoning and enticing, and promising knowledge, experience, fulfillment—and all that makes for Satisfied Man.

The Contemporary Scene

Within the church today—and I include many evan-

302 / Demon Possession

gelical churches—there are many who have experienced direct or indirect involvement with the occult. For us to turn a blind eye to their plight is to disregard a particularly needy segment of our society. Outside the organized churches the number of occult-oriented people is astronomical. It has always been more comfortable to think of the occult as indigenous to Africa, or India, or China, but now we must face up to its existence in Europe and in North America.

Neither can we continue to relegate it to the lunatic fringe of Western society, and smile tolerantly at the activities of the gypsy in her tent reading palms, or the teacup readings of polite parties. A close friend told recently of finding one of her relatives kneeling before a small image of Satan, praying for help before his day began. In an African village? No, in a great industrial city in Canada—and the praying man is a scientist, holding a doctor's degree, and able to look back on a boyhood spent in Sunday school and church.

The Canadian Broadcasting Corporation recently carried an hour-long TV program depicting the life of a Protestant clergyman in Northern Canada. A native Indian himself, he was shown combining the two offices of Shaman of his Indian tribe with "Christian" minister of the Gospel. The CBC apparently saw no incongruity in such syncretism!

Over 1,200 newspapers bring horoscopes to their American readers daily, while bookstores filled with occult literature make a roaring trade. Colleges and universities throughout North America have their Satan-oriented groups, and the profile of the occult is at an all-time high.

In Britain, following the repeal of the old Witchcraft Act in 1951, there has been a great surge of occult activity. Demonism is very much on the scene.

Reports indicate that in France there are more professional healers, sorcerers, than there are medical practitioners, while in Normandy alone over three hundred chapels are maintained for occult purposes.

Germany may be considered highly industrialized and very sophisticated, but that does not seem to limit very widespread occult practices all over the country. Its society is permeated by all kinds of occultism.

When the government of Italy published social security and retirement plans for various professions, ten thousand witches and warlocks paraded in the streets to protest the omission of their own group!

All these North Americans and Europeans need help. If our Christian faith means anything at all, surely it demands of us that we understand their need and do something about it. We cannot lump them all together and dismiss them as sick, or outsiders, and try to carry on as if they do not exist. They are *here.* They are *our* people, and we must reach out to them. But first we must understand certain important things about them.

1. *Many are escapists.* It has become a cliché to say: "Satan (or the demons) made me do it." The world of the occult becomes attractive to people who find it difficult to face up to their moral responsibilities. Many dabble with "other powers," and are drawn into involvement. They often claim that they have tried "other remedies" in vain, and the alternative empowerment through the occult allures them.

2. *Many more are superstitious.* Going beyond the bounds of revelation and common sense, they profess to see demonic activity in many areas: sickness, depression, anger, any unusual or unexplained behavior. While such may be evidence of demonic action, it should by no means be an automatic assumption. Where natural causes offer a reasonable explanation it is wise to accept them as the origin of the problem. People who jump to the conclusion that demonic influences are responsible for a wide variety of phenomena invariably become obsessed with the thought of demons-at-work, and suffer many of the disabilities commonly found in victims of demonization.

3. *All are victims.* I use the word advisedly. There is no point in being judgmental toward these people, even though as Christians we oppose and condemn all occult practices. From a biblical perspective there is no room for negotiation or compromise here. God judges and condemns all traffic with demons, and we can do no less. In the sight of God they are guilty of transgressing His law. Each one is a victim too—the victim of powers immeasurably more powerful and knowing than he. What kind of person is he?

(1) The curious, who experiments and plays with demonic forces, only to find eventually that they are playing with him.

(2) The conformist, who looks around at his peer group and says, "Everyone does it," and decides to be another who "does it."

(3) The dissatisfied, whose religious experience has left him unfulfilled and skeptical.

(4) The sad, whose bereavement inclines him toward anything that offers knowledge of the dead.

(5) The rebellious, who recoils from the status quo in the church and in society, and seeks a viable alternative elsewhere.

(6) The psychically inclined, who wants to develop suspected latent powers.

(7) The offspring of practicing occultists, who are conditioned from childhood.

(8) The credulous, and every generation seems to produce its quota of them!

Pastoral Response

In view of the growing prevelance of occult interest and participation, it is highly regrettable that so many pastors display great ignorance in regard to the incidence of demonism and ways of assisting its victims. Three groups in particular are commonly found in most evangelical circles—nonevangelicals rarely admit the existence of demons, so that their problems are of a different nature!

1. The first group pretend that the problem does not exist. By theological or psychological rationalization they say that there are no demonized people today. Cases of apparent "possession" or "obsession" are really individuals with mental abnormality or overheated imagination. Unfortunately, pretending the problem does not exist does not solve it.

2. Over-reacting to demons: Some pastoral counselors profess to detect demons in every unusual circumstance. A case was brought to my attention recently where a clergyman rejected the medical profession's diagnosis of terminal sickness in a young lady and claimed that it was "demon possession in the mother." Nothing but harm can come from such a false diagnosis; unfortunately it is frequently encountered.

3. Demon-centric conduct: This kind of response to demonic phenomena is also widespread, and highly suspect. Counselors apparently hold lengthy conversations with demons, carefully recording everything on tapes. Books appear, containing details of such conversations. Since when have we been commissioned to accord demons center stage treatment? Seances reminiscent of a circus, with screaming demons and equally loud exorcists, are surely far removed from the biblical approach to demonology.

The Biblical Approach

I suggest that to handle demonic situations effectively we must first get back to the basic treatment of demons in the Scriptures. First, demons are always depicted as the tools of Satan. They are always allied with Satan in the never-ending conflict of the ages. The adversary opposes every move of God. Demonic forces loyally serve their master in his quest for world dominion, and the overthrow of the kingdom and purposes of God.

Second, failure to be rightly related to Jesus Christ causes man to play into the hands of demonic forces. The only safe refuge for the Christian is the center of the will of God.

These two factors are important. We need to understand the nature of the enmity placed between the Serpent and the Seed of the woman (Gen. 3:15). We also need to appropriate the true defense which is only possible as we dwell under the shadow of the Almighty. Then only are we ready to engage in combat with these dark forces.

How did Jesus Christ meet them? For example, demons spoke of Him. They also spoke of Paul and his companions. Amazingly, every recorded witness by demons to Jesus Christ or Paul in the Gospels or Acts is 100 percent accurate (see Luke 8:28; Acts 16:17). The responses of Jesus and Paul were similar. Although the testimony of the demons was accurate, they refused to accept it. They robbed the demons of a voice! In the New Testament one thing is certain: in pursuance of the objective stated by Paul in Col. 1:18 "That in all things he [Jesus] might have the pre-eminence," demons were never made the center of attention.

One significant reason for not accepting the witness of demons is that with demons there is nothing free. "The wages of sin is death" (Rom. 6:23). It has always been thus. Sin pays wages. Only God gives freely. A Faust may receive much from Satan, but sooner or later he must pay. Missionaries of Bible Christian Union have frequently experienced great difficulty in counseling Europeans who have had previous dealings with the occult. They may have received health benefits through sorcery, and the benefits were real. But once the same Europeans begin to show interest in Jesus Christ, a great force within them asserts itself, adding to their already considerable spiritual blindness. Paul said, "The God of this world hath blinded the minds of them which believe not, lest the light of the glorious gospel of Christ . . . should shine unto them" (2 Cor. 4:4).

Pursuing this biblical approach still further, we note that "deliverance" is not the goal in itself. The modern cult of "deliverance" is gaining ground in many quarters. Generally it flourishes where much is made of demonism, where demons are identified in terms of sickness, the abnormal, or the unusual. Fortunes are made—and lives destroyed—by this approach. In His parable in Luke 11:24-25, the Lord Jesus shows what happens when "deliverance" is seen as merely getting rid of an unwelcome spirit. Surely there must be a better way of dealing with demonization! We do not have to look far for the divine answer.

Luke 11:21-22 is one of the most important scriptures, and a right understanding of the teaching of the Lord Jesus Christ here is vital to all concerned. "When a strong man armed keepeth his palace, his goods are in peace: But when a stronger than he shall come upon him, and overcome him, he taketh from him all his armour wherein he trusted, and divideth his spoils." The strong man armed is of course Satan, who controls his possessions through his demonic forces. The Lord deals with the situation in a direct fashion: "When a stronger than he shall come upon him, *and overcome him*," things change! Here is no talk of lengthy communication with demons. There is a complete absence of the kind of circus atmosphere so common in our day, with a great display of emotional excitement as victims are "delivered." Instead, the Greater than he comes upon him, overcomes him, and robs him of his spoil. This is more than deliverance—this is victory over an enemy and victory planted in the life of the victim.

Deliverance, then, is not merely exorcising the demon. Deliverance is a lifelong relationship to the Deliverer, Jesus Christ. There can be no short cuts here. "Instant" deliverance is meaningless magic. God wants men and women who know the liberating power of His Son at work in them day by day. Being delivered from is only the prerequisite for being committed to—committed to a life of fellowship with the Son who sets men free.

Practical Suggestions

In the light of the foregoing here are a number of practical suggestions which merit consideration:

1. In all counseling sessions, project the person of Jesus

Christ. If demons are real, their enmity must be presumed. If their enmity is accepted as a fact, the object of their opposition—Jesus Christ—must be recognized. *He* is the one they are after. Mere man is incidental. The great goal is always the Son of Man. And He alone is adequate to deal with such a situation.

Jude 9: "Yet Michael the archangel, when contending with the devil he disputed about the body of Moses, durst not bring against him a railing accusation, but said, The Lord rebuke thee."

2. Never settle for "mere" deliverance, exorcism. Much more is entailed. Experience corroborates the teachings of Scriptures here. Demonic beings always rebel at the assertion of Jesus Christ as Lord. Yet this is precisely what Paul teaches. Phil. 2:9-11: "Wherefore God also hath highly exalted him, and given him a name which is above every name: that at the name of Jesus every knee should bow, of things in heaven, and things in earth, and things under the earth; and that every tongue should confess that Jesus Christ is Lord, to the glory of God the Father." It is this insistence on the lordship of Jesus Christ that breaks down the powers of darkness. It is confession of His sovereignty— not merely as a point of doctrine, but as a *way of life*—that releases men from enslavement, and *provides for them continuing freedom from demonization.*

3. Never disregard the victim's own will. If he does not show real desire for help, you are not likely to be effective in your dealings with him. Does God free man from guilt, or sinful habits, against his will?

4. Maintain your own spiritual and emotional balance. Why do so many neurotic people fancy themselves called by God to "deal with demons"? They should flee the devil, not court his attention!

For pastors on one hand, and doctors and psychiatrists on the other hand, it is always wise to seek each other's help. Demonization is a complex, difficult challenge to anyone, and trained help in a number of areas is needful. It is also demanded by one's sense of humility and integrity.

The need for spiritual balance is a very serious one. In the last several years I have observed tragic consequences in the lives of men who have become obsessed with the so-called deliverance ministry. By neglecting major truths, and the "balance of truth," many of these men have shown serious theological, spiritual and moral imbalance.

Paul professed to preach "all the counsel of God." We should aim at no less. Demonology is a subject to be carefully investigated and tested by scriptural standards. It will not go away just by our ignoring it. On the other hand, who wants to give his life to dwelling on it? The answer to the conditions which created the climate for demonic activities in the first place is the continuous assertion of the lordship of Jesus Christ. Recognition of His sovereignty in every area of our lives, so that He will dominate all of life, is God's remedy for this modern scourge.

PART EIGHT

Demonology and Theology

20

Demonology Today

ROGER C. PALMS

My task is to look at what is happening now. That is a big order. It's as large as the world. Do we illustrate by describing individuals who are involved in witchcraft? Do we tell stories of Satan worship or elaborate upon sick tales of unsolved murders? Do we talk of covens meeting on deserted beaches, and spells cast, people injured and blood spilt? Do we talk of horoscopes? Some ten million Americans are guided by astrology, another forty million dabble in it. Shall we talk of the more than two hundred thousand people committed to the cult of witchcraft in our country, or voodoo in Haiti, or spirit worship in Brazil? At what point do we stop and say, "This is an example of the demonic"?

Obviously the subject is much larger than any of these specifics, and because it is and affects every one of us in some way, we have to look at it as more than unusual religious experimentation and more than the subject of entertainment for movie goers and television viewers. The occult with its demonic oppression has become a part of our culture, invading our thoughts at every level. It is being given a degree of sophistication that brings in science, business and education. In short, like any theological event, it influences every aspect of our lives. And, since the Christian gospel does the same, we have to look at everything that is happening from the perspective of where we stand with Jesus Christ.

We cannot understand the contemporary occult scene by looking for patterns, or logical developments or reasons.

Both medical people and theologians would like to do that, but although we will try to get some kind of handle on the demonic in these meetings, there will be frustration because Satan's activity appears as varied as every observer's bias and as different as each occult practitioner's involvement. People come to the demonic from where they are, and every person is different.

When I first began my studies in the occult, I had difficulty putting together—into some kind of package that I could grasp—the various aspects of occult behavior and worship. Then, one day in California, a lady involved in various forms of psychic activity said to me: "Of course you cannot understand it! We take a little bit from this religion and a little bit from that religion and put them together."

In short, the occult is a custom-made religion. And, since there appear to be at least one hundred and fifty subdivisions offered in this cafeteria of selection, the combinations are practically endless. That's why you will find witches who believe in reincarnation and witches who do not. There are astrologers who also study numerology and astrologers who do not. In a recent article in our Bloomington, Minnesota, newspaper, Carl Weschcke, a St. Paul native who has been involved in the occult for many years and has the largest occult publishing firm in the world, told a reporter: "People find they may accept certain parts of the movement which fit into their lives, but they need not commit themselves to the entire scope. They may accept and use astrology and graphology, but deny witchcraft and herbal healing, whatever may seem proper or understandable to them. The practical application of most occult sciences attracts those who wish to know more about themselves, to understand options available to them and apply these sciences to their lives."

Three years ago when my book, *The Christian and the Occult*, was first in the works, it was necessary to convince many Christians that this occult activity was real. That's not so anymore. Today we are not even questioning it as a reality, but we want to know what kind of reality it is, where its limits are, how far it is going in its influence, the satanic elements in it, and what we can do to help in the deliverance of people who are possessed or at least oppressed by it. And we want to know about the legitimizing of the many psychic studies that are opening wide new doors to satanic influence.

It should be made very clear at this point that I am not suggesting that every energy or force being discovered by people is satanic. God is still the Creator of all things. But Satan does use every opportunity to oppress people and we must be alert to that. For example: I would never teach that a person's sexual drives are satanic; they are a gift from God. Yet we all know what can happen when Satan gets control of those drives. When we speak of telekinesis, telepathy, clairvoyance, etc., these are apparently very real, and obviously not unknown or unplanned by God, but definitely doorways for satanic entrance. Neither stones nor bread are satanic, but Satan would have used them both to get to Jesus. Christians need to realize that.

We could follow any one of the many tantalizing directions available to us in occult or demonic study, but it would show only a small part of the whole. I'd rather not take that route, but, accepting the given that the occult is influencing people in very large numbers, go on to examine some of the dimensions of that influence.

In Crockett, California, John Swett High School is the first secondary school to teach occult studies formally. According to the teacher, Robert Beck, the occult deals honestly with what might lie beyond the grave, the limitations of human perception, and attempts to understand intuitive phenomena. It can, says Beck, "become an engrossing and rewarding journey into realms of mankind's deepest, most abiding concerns and fears." [1] We might wonder what would happen if Christians proposed a similar course in the biblical teachings on eternal life, to explore "the engrossing and rewarding journeys into realms of mankind's deepest, most abiding concerns and fears."

From an article appearing in *Business Week* we learn that the Institute of Electrical and Electronic Engineers has presented a panel on parapsychology; the National Science Foundation is considering a conference on parapsychology; the National Institute of Mental Health has granted Maimonides Medical Center in Brooklyn funds for ESP tests; the National Aeronautics and Space Administration has financed a Stanford Research Institute program to teach ESP skills to NASA personnel.

The Pentagon's Advanced Research Projects Agency is monitoring psychic research with the purpose of finding out what the Soviet Union knows because the Russians have been studying ESP far longer than has the U.S. The Central

Intelligence Agency is interested in what they have found. Robert Van de Castle who heads the dream research laboratory at the University of Virginia Medical School says, "The CIA wants to know whether psychics could jam computers and radar screens, and even whether people could be trained to leave their bodies." [2]

Bell Telephone Laboratory scientists are working on telepathy and clairvoyance. Hoffman-La Roche, Inc., as well as other drug companies, are exploring ways to train the mind to control stress. Business executives are being examined for ESP qualities. A professor of industrial engineering at the Newark College of Engineering thinks that ESP makes the difference between the successful and the unsuccessful businessman. [3]

Arthur Koestler in a *Harper's* magazine article tells us: "In some laboratories, an active search is going on for hypothetical 'tachyons'—particles of cosmic origin which are supposed to fly faster than light and consequently, according to orthodox relativity theory, in a reversed time direction. They would thus carry information from the future into our present as light and X-rays from distant galaxies carry information from the remote past of the universe into our now and here. In the light of these developments we can no longer exclude on a priori grounds the theoretical possibility of pre-cognitive phenomena. The logical paradox that predicting a future event may prevent or distort it is circumvented by the probabalistic nature of all forecasts." [4]

Both the Russians and the Americans are asking some serious parapsychological questions. For example, is a schizophrenic really schizophrenic or does he somehow pick up the thoughts of somebody else? In other words, is he being influenced by some other forces than the ones that most of us are hearing, touching or seeing? Is a person mentally ill if he has this kind of unusual sensitivity?

Scientists are alert to vibrations, auras, energies and forces that cannot be measured or explained in the usual scientific ways. The Russians are working on what they call "skin vision." American scientists are wondering about "hypothetical psytrons" with properties similar to the "nutrinos" (particles of cosmic origin devoid of physical attributes—that is, they don't have mass, weight, charge or magnetic field—which are capable of impinging directly on neurons in the recipient's brain, thus serving as carriers of ESP). Axel Firsoff suggests "extrasensory communication by 'mindons,' nutrino like particles of an all-pervasive 'mind stuff.' " [5]

All of this brings to mind the familiar statement of Sir James Jeans: "The universe begins to look more like a great thought than a great machine." [6] Jeans is not a mystic; he works with quantum theory principles. It seems that the principle of complementarity, which Christians have taught and believed on the basis of biblical revelation is at last being discovered by others. There is more to our universe than strict mechanical causality or determinism. Everything has an effect on everything else, and there are forces that heretofore we had not realized were influencing us. Noting this, Arthur Koestler points to Sir Joseph J. Thompson, who was the discoverer of the electron and was also one of the early members of the British Society of Psychical Research, and comments, "Why should physicists in particular be disposed to infection by the ESP virus? The answer is hinted at in the autobiographical writings and metaphysical speculations of some of the greatest among them. The dominant chord that echoes through them is a pervasive feeling of frustration, caused by realizing that science can elucidate only certain aspects, or levels, of reality, while the ultimate questions remain elusive.... We are now asking for something more definite—for data and theories that would point the way to the ultimate fusion of science and parascience." [7]

How much of this activity is an opening for the demonic? How do we distinguish between scientific investigation of God's world and "mind blowing" manipulation by the demonic? Is there danger of demonic possession when psychic experiments are conducted in a psychic's basement but not when they are conducted in government laboratories? If a businessman uses ESP to gain some advantage over his competitors, is he less likely to suffer oppression than the witch who also uses ESP to score a profit? In short, does Satan respect the practitioners of pure science?

The occult, including the full range of psychic activity, has captured the interest of the business world, the scientific mind, the world of spies and counter spies, inmates of our prisons, and our high school and college students (the third annual Psychic Conference was recently held at the University of Wisconsin-Milwaukee with forty special events and workshops). Recently I received the following letter from a man in a Colorado prison: "I have been received by the spirit world (known to some as the Astro

Plane) through much study and concentration with my own spirit within me. On August 23, 1974, my spirit left its earthly bonds and through my third eye witnessed its flight into the ethereal worlds. I will continue to develop myself spiritually step by step until I have reached the 7th plane which is the spirit mind or that of atunement with the universal consciousness of God the Almighty. Upon my release from prison, I will travel and teach the religious philosophies of the East, Yoga, and devote my remaining years to my own development and that of my students."

Most people know that there is far more to them than what can be examined physically. And, they know that there are dimensions to the universe that could, like gravity, have an influence over them and the things around them. There is a desire among many to come into a harmony with these forces, to seek the "universal spirit" or the ultimate source of reality and power. Maybe it was inevitable after the neatly packaged psychology of the thirties and forties gave way to the spiritual quests of succeeding generations. Maybe it was speeded on by the mind-expanding use of drugs.

This quest by man for higher truths or greater powers, this yearning to know how he fits into the larger picture of life, and this longing for some controls or harnessing of the energies he senses should not surprise the Christian. We are wonderfully made, and there is a God-breathed part to all of us. We were created to be related to Him. There is an emptiness and longing when we are separated from the oneness with Himself that He offers. Satan would fill that longing for God with his offerings. Mankind has a built-in need for relationship with the "God out there" who is beyond and greater than anything else. He also longs for an intimacy with this totally other God that gives him strength to cope with life's confusions. Jesus Christ is both Mighty God, before all things and in whom all things hold together, and personal Savior, the one who will be "with you always." Satan will capitalize on man's need, steering him not to Jesus Christ but to his own counterfeits.

Satan is a deceiver. Using the same basic gnostic heresies that he promoted in the first century, he is urging people (through many different occult practices) to find the god beyond the God of the Scriptures. By occult activity a seeker can move through the various spirit planes to the universal mind. And, to satisfy the longing for strength, there are spells, incantations and harnessed energies that can move objects and change situations without the necessity of coming to the One who promised: "You shall receive power when the Holy Spirit has come upon you."

Even professing Christians are being lured by Satan's counterfeit offers. I have yet to speak in a church about the occult, when there has been opportunity for discussion, where there has not been at least one person present who admitted to some form of occult activity. And too often it is with a defensive, "I see no harm in this. . . . "

Christians are involved with ouija boards (not a parlor game when it is prompted by a genuine belief in a fixed fate), seances (I was criticized by a Christian lady who thought it was cute that her daughter was going to take part in a seance with friends), and horoscopes. One pastor is still convinced that God used astrology to mend a broken marriage. When the troubled couple came to understand each other's horoscopes, they understood why they acted certain ways. This was an "answer to prayer," they insist. Their minister agrees. He accuses me of denying a legitimate form of "therapy," no different than professional counseling.

There are Christians who don't want to believe that Satan might be influencing them. There are some who don't want to believe in Satan at all. I remember speaking at a seminary on the West Coast and being treated in a very patronizing way because I expressed belief in a real Satan. And a young friend of mine, presently attending a seminary in the Midwest, says his school teaches a course in psychic phenomena but had real trouble with ideas about satanic influences. One day the professor said to my friend, "Now suppose you believed in Satan," to which this young man quietly replied, "I do!"

A friend told me about a conversation he heard on a radio talk show between a Jewish psychiatrist and a Roman Catholic priest who was trained as an exorcist. When the program host asked the priest if he had ever exorcised anyone, he said "No, it's true I have been trained in exorcism, but we now realize that most of the problems that we once attributed to demon possession are really psychological. We do not need exorcism today; we need proper psychiatric care." The host then turned to the Jewish psychiatrist who said, "We are beginning to realize that some conditions, once explained as psychological disorders, may be demon possession. There seems to be evidence of some kind of demonic influence."

I'm glad for this conference because there needs to be

a clear responsible Christian voice explaining the occult and demonic activity, and what we have available in the lordship and presence of Jesus Christ. I'm grateful to God for a renewed emphasis in the church on the power and ministry of the Holy Spirit. Right at the time when the demonic seems to be most rampant, there is also a rediscovery of what the first century church knew—that in the name of Jesus and the ministry of the Holy Spirit people are delivered, healed and made whole.

We need this balanced emphasis because there are zealous Christians who are pronouncing healing, making prophetic statements and determining who is satanic on the basis of their own emotional adrenaline. They are countered at the other end of the spectrum by Christians who either write off the demonic as silly imagination or who recognize a demonic force but relegate the power of God to ancient dispensations. Thus we need responsible, biblically based voices wholesomely balancing zeal with theological and psychological wisdom.

Central to our thinking, then, in these meetings together should be the power of the demonic at all levels in people's lives and the healing available in the name and power of the Lord Jesus Christ. There is a definite need to grasp as best we humanly can the divine mystery surrounding confession, renunciation and absolution. We also need to clarify our thinking on how, when and where and by whom this is to be done. How does God act through individuals, how does He act through the church? (See my *The Christian and the Occult*, pp. 118-121.) We should explore this knowing that the spiritual warfare with principalities and powers is real (Eph. 6:12ff.) and that the victory over these principalities and powers is assured through the One who has already led them captive (Col. 2:15). We should neither avoid this, fearing the label "unsophisticated," strip from it the mystery of exorcism, nor add to it our own cultural programing.

To conclude, the Bible calls Satan a deceiver (Rev. 20:10), the prince of this world (John 12:31), prince of darkness (Eph. 6:12), accuser (Rev. 12:10), prince of the power of the air (Eph. 2:2), god of this world (2 Cor. 4:4), murderer and liar (John 8:44), and his followers as fallen angels (2 Pet. 2:4 and Jude 6). He will fight against the Light, using any and all means to gain entrance into the minds and souls of people.

But we also know, on the authority of Scripture, that

in Jesus Christ the fullness of God was pleased to dwell (Col. 1:15-19); that we have not the spirit of bondage or slavery but the spirit of adoption (Rom. 8:15); and that we have the Paraclete, the one who stands alongside of us and resides within us (John 14:15-17; 15:26; 16:7-8). We proclaim the one who is the Good News of peace. This is far more than physical or emotional peace; it is total peace for the whole person. It is my prayer that in the studies of this conference, we will find effective ways to communicate this wholeness and peace to a very confused world.

Notes

1. Rose Marie Levey, "Happenings in Education," *The PTA Magazine* (February, 1974), p. 2.
2. Research Article, "Why Scientists Take Psychic Research Seriously," *Business Week* (January 26, 1974), p. 76.
3. *Ibid.*, pp. 76-78.
4. Arthur Koestler, "Order From Disorder," *Harper's Magazine* (July, 1974), p. 60.
5. *Ibid.*, p. 56.
6. *Ibid.*
7. *Ibid.*, p. 55.

21

Response

JAMES D. MALLORY, JR.

Mr. Palms begins his paper with observations on the multifaceted nature of the occult. Actually, the problem is even greater because what he identifies as occult is probably only a small area of potential demonic activity. Specifically, he mentions "psychic activity, witches with and without the doctrine of reincarnation, astrologers with and without numerology, telekinesis, telepathy, clairvoyance, parapsychology, ESP, ouija boards, horoscopes, and scientists studying vibrations, auras, energies, forces" not measurable in the usual ways.

He also reveals the astounding interest in psychic phenomena from such varied sources as secondary schools, National Institute of Mental Health, NASA, the Pentagon, the CIA, Bell Telephone and business executives. Added to this list are those of the general public showing an increasing interest in the occult as evidenced by movie, TV, literature, games on such themes.

All these interested parties in the occult reveal many different motivations. Basically all are seeking experiences or answers that have not come forth for them through their routinely held suppositions, beliefs, practices. Thus some are seeking religious answers or experiences; others are trying to satisfy scientific curiosity; others are looking for materialistic or militaristic gain. Probably one of the primary reasons for the general population's interest in the occult is the spiritual vacuum that exists because of their secularistic mind set.

Palms raises some very crucial issues concerning occultist and psychic phenomena: (1) Are they all from Satan? He apparently thinks not. (2) Are they simply our discovery of energies God has made which may be used for good or bad? An example of this is the unfolding mystery of the atom which may be used to kill one million people or one million cancer cells. (3) Do they all open the door to Satan? Palms says, "Yes." He recognizes a dilemma exists of how to distinguish between scientific investigation of God's world and "mind-blowing manipulation by the demonic."

He doesn't tell us how to make this crucial differential. He does give some clues. As a person tries to find the god beyond the God of Scripture through different occultist practices, becoming enamored with various spiritual planes to the universal mind and to satisfy the longing for strength with spells, incantations and harnessed energies without coming to Jesus Christ of Scripture, he must be opening the door wide to Satan's counterfeit offers. I believe a person who follows this course is moving more and more to a subjective, ego-centric basis for his beliefs and less and less to objective truth of Scripture. He begins to make his own experience the basis for truth. He has made an idol of his own feelings, experiences and interpretations of experiences.

I agree with Palms that professing Christians are lured by Satan's counterfeit offers. In fact, I would add that some Christians who are not involved with what is usually identified as the occult make the same error of canonizing their subjective experiences. I suspect the many "The Lord has told me" statements come from some source other than the Lord.

Scripture gives further clues to help differentiate the works of Satan. It specifically forbids witchcraft, enchantment, divination, magic omens, horoscopes and signs (Amplified Bible) soothsaying, wizards, mediumistic activity, charmers and consulters with spirits. Three basic prohibitions emerge: (1) using any mechanism to predict the future; (2) casting spells; (3) consulting spirits.

It may well be that many psychic phenomena do not fall in these categories and do represent scientific discoveries which could be used for good or evil. However, I agree with Palms that these phenomena particularly potentially open the door to Satan. They are in a special category because by their very nature they can lead a person into a highly subjective, mystical experience that may be very exciting, seemingly meeting the need to find the something

322 / *Demon Possession*

more to life than just the naturalistic, secularistic explanations which do not satisfy.

However, the burning issues for me as a psychiatrist are not the categories Mr. Palms has mentioned. The issues of the current scene which concern me are to what degree of emotional and physical suffering can we attribute to satanic or demonic activity?

Some enthusiastic, if not knowledgeable, Christians about mental illness have concluded virtually all mental suffering is demonic. There are demons of depression, alcohol, guilt, lust, fear, etc.

A recent book popular in some circles based on a supposed revelation from God concludes schizophrenia is a demonic condition. The Bible reveals very few symptoms of demonic activity. They include inability to speak, deafness, blindness, falling to the ground in a rigid or stuporous state with grinding of teeth and foaming at the mouth, acting like a wild animal with superhuman strength, and having the ability to predict the future. Also wasting away and vexation or being tormented is mentioned. The casting out of demons when successful is done by a simple command. However, there is a vast literature regarding demonic activity and their removal that has minimal biblical authority. Rather it comes out of the deliverer's own experience and most particularly his interpretation of his experience. There seems to be a tendency in this literature to attribute to demons what is not understood by the author's limited knowledge of mental illness.

I would like to give some examples of the current scene which I face that pose serious problems for me.

Here is a girl in her twenties who was told if she was filled with the Holy Spirit she should expect to hear God's voice. She began to pray in her closet and to listen very intently. She began to hear voices which she attributed to God. Initially they were quite affirming with such statements as, "I love you, you are my child," etc. Later the voices became accusatory and profane. She became extremely depressed. Now her group concluded she was under demonic influence and began a series of deliverances. After many unsuccessful attempts to alleviate her symptoms, she was more depressed, guilty, and afraid of Christian groups or advice. At this point she was referred to me. With proper medication her hallucinations and depression were relieved.

Another patient was told she should stop her medications and "rely" on the Lord. She became increasingly depressed.

A person in her prayer group speaking in tongues told her the Lord said her depression was now healed. Two years later she was still depressed and doubly discouraged. Christianity apparently wasn't working. Here is a very suggestable, hysterical girl who allegedly had many demons cast out. Now she thinks that every pain, worry, trouble, and alien thought is due to a demon. She takes no personal responsibility for such problems.

Palms' statement that "there are Christians who are pronouncing healing, making prophetic statements, and determining who is satanic on the basis of their own emotional adrenalin" strikes me as very pertinent.

However, there is the other side of the coin. Here is a young woman in her thirties. She has been diagnosed as schizophrenic since her teen years. She has had multiple psychiatric hospitalizations and treatments all without benefit. I failed to help her utilizing standard treatment. After much prayer and after two years of no progress, she revealed that one of her "hallucinations" was a presence that wanted to take over her being. She was tormented by this presence almost constantly. A couple who seem to have a ministry of deliverance prayed for her with very dramatic results. The presence was gone and has not returned for two years now. According to the couple three demons were cast out. However, she still has highs and lows which are probably at least partially genetically and chemically induced and she still has many interpersonal problems. But now she responds to chemical and psychological treatment, whereas prior to her deliverance nothing helped.

My own conclusion is that Satan is the author of all that is destructive. The Christian's heritage is to be in the process of becoming whole, being conformed into the image of Christ. At what point in sin or suffering one crosses some line where he is now under demonic influence that can be relieved only by a special ministry of deliverance is very unclear to me. The Hippocratic injunction for physicians to do no harm should be considered very carefully by those who are engaged in deliverance. There is no doubt in my mind that Christians in the mental health field need to become more aware of the fact that we do fight a spiritual warfare and specific prayers for deliverance are in order in certain cases. However, it may well be that a person who confesses and repents of sin, who places himself under the lordship of Jesus Christ, praying for healing with prayer support from a Christian group, blocks demonic activity without even being aware of it. One thing is certain: We have an enemy who is a liar, deceiver, destroyer; but we have the victory in Jesus Christ, the God of Scripture.

22

Satan and Demons: A Theological Perspective

JOHN P. NEWPORT

This study is an attempt to understand Satanism and demonology from a theological perspective. After participating in discussions on this subject with numerous college and university groups, the author has come to see that the grounds of belief or disbelief in Satan and demons are subtle and profound. The question cannot be dealt with in isolation. What a person believes will depend on many factors. Is there meaning in assertions which cannot be reduced to a summary of physical observations? How valid are experiences which cannot be subjected to typical laboratory testing? A person's viewpoint is also influenced by his or her attitude toward the Bible.[1]

This study accepts the biblical revelation as a normative guide in the difficult and critical areas of Satanism and demonology. It will be an exercise in biblical theology before we turn to systematic or philosophical theology. In other words, we will look at the biblical sources before and not after discussing the credibility of the demonic for the twentieth century.

There is obviously a dearth of knowledge concerning the demonic in the Christian community. It is regrettable that we have waited to study the demonic until such a study has been forced upon us by a culture which could not find its answers in materialistic scientism.[2]

It must be granted that the biblical teaching concerning Satan has been distorted both during the Middle Ages and in recent years. For example, in the Middle Ages, the devil was said to have appeared as a huge, black cat. Later it was said that he changed to a goat. In any case, a horned, tailed, hoofed and hairy Satan with bat wings was a popular image.

The present-day Christian who accepts the biblical teaching concerning Satan is not committed to all of the crude imagery that has sprung up around belief in Satan. In the light of medieval and modern distortions, a careful consideration of the biblical teaching concerning Satan is especially needed.

A detailed doctrine of Satan is not found in the Bible until New Testament times. A number of reasons have been suggested for the relatively limited material on Satan in the Old Testament.

God began his self-revelation in the ancient world of polytheism. God wanted to lead His people to a dynamic practical monotheism. Thus, in the Old Testament, a primary emphasis is placed on the supremacy and power of the God of Abraham, Isaac and Jacob who delivered the Hebrews from the slavery of Egypt.

Despite the controversy over such Old Testament passages as Gen. 3:1-19, Isa. 14:12-15, and Ezek. 28:12 the Bible suggests that from the early moments of the creation of this world Satan was on the scene, a rebel against God. Pride seems to have been the cause of his fall. Following the suggestion in Rev. 12:9, it is said that Satan came disguised as a serpent. He is seen as the agent of temptation for the first man and woman (Gen. 3:10; 20:2). Although there is not much in the Old Testament about Satan, when he does appear he is always the adversary of God's people. He seeks to lead God's people into presumption (1 Chron. 21:1) or slanders them to God's face (Zech. 3:1).

The most extensive Old Testament discussion of Satan is in Job. Here he is seen as God's agent and minister, who tested human fidelity. He makes a wager with God, with Job as the stake. He acts, however, with the express permission of God and keeps within the limits which God has fixed for him (Job 1:12; 2:6).

During the last part of the Old Testament period and the time between Malachi and the Gospel of Matthew, the Jews were thrown into relationships with the Persians. The great religious leader of the Persians, Zoroaster, taught that there were two great powers in the world—good (Ahura Mazda) and evil (Ahriman or Shaitan). Some later Persians taught that these two powers were almost co-equal. Contact with the Persians undoubtedly heightened the concern of the Hebrews about Satan.[3]

For many contemporary conservative scholars, the basic message of both Jesus and Paul is seen as closely related to demonology and eschatology.[4] The work of Christ is seen as primary in the battle with Satan. Evil is radical and rooted in the personal—not the abstract. Evil is greater than man. This is not mere mythology. Other conservative Bible scholars see Christ's work as primarily a transaction within the Godhead. The object of Christ's work is God.

There is abundant biblical evidence for both views. For example, Luke 13:16 sees suffering as an attack of Satan. Heb. 12:3-11 sees suffering as a chastisement of a loving Father God. Both views must be held in tension.

The use of proper principles of biblical interpretation, however, demand that if one view is primary in the Bible, it should be determinative and the other secondary. It is the contention of C. K. Barrett, James Kallas, George Ladd, and other evangelical scholars that the demonology-eschatology motif is dominant—constituting some three-fourths of the material in the first three Gospels and Paul. If a limited cosmic-dualism is taken seriously, it means that the New Testament teaches that satanic forces have a measure of real control in the world.

In the first three Gospels, Satan is pictured as a supernatural evil spirit who is at the head of a host of inferior evil spirits called demons. As such, he is the "prince of the demons" (Mark 3:22).[5]

In the Synoptic Gospels, the most characteristic evidence of the power of Satan is the ability of demons to take possession of the center of man's personality. At the very outset of His ministry in Capernaum, Jesus came face to face with demonic powers. Immediately, the demon recognized Jesus by direct intuitive or clairvoyant insight and said, "What have you to do with us, Jesus of Nazareth? Have you come to destroy us? I know who you are, the Holy One of God" (Mark 1:24). The demon recognizes a supernatural power in Jesus which is capable of crushing satanic power here and now.

Demon possession manifested itself in various ways. Sometimes it was associated with other afflictions of a physical nature: with dumbness (Matt. 9:32), with blindness and dumbness (Matt. 12:22), and with epilepsy (Matt. 17:15, 18). There is only one place where demon possession is identified with mental illness. Obviously, the Gadarene demoniac who dwelt in the tombs and was possessed of superhuman strength was insane. Mark 5:15 states that after his healing, the man was found clothed and in his right mind. Perhaps his derangement was due to the center of his personality falling under the influence of demonic powers.[6]

In Matt. 4:24, demon possession is distinguished from epilepsy and paralysis. In exorcising these people, Jesus did not use the crude magic and incantations of His time. He exorcised with the power of His mere word (Mark 1:27).

In Matt. 12:29 Jesus talks about binding Satan. Binding designates in some real sense a victory over Satan so that his power is curbed. This does not mean, of course, that Satan is rendered completely powerless. He continues to be active. He was able to speak through Peter (Mark 8:33) and he entered into Judas (Luke 22:3). Oscar Cullmann describes the binding of Satan as a binding, but with a "long rope." [7] Satan is not powerless, but his power has been broken or qualified (Mark 3:27).

In the early days of His ministry, Jesus sent forth His disciples with power to drive out demons (Luke 10:17). Upon returning, they reported with joy that even the demons were subject to them in Jesus' name. Then it was that Jesus said, "I saw Satan fall like lightning from heaven" (Luke 10:18). The context suggests that Jesus saw in the successful mission of the seventy an evidence of the defeat of Satan.[8]

In Matt. 12:28, we have a record of a very important point made by Jesus about exorcism. It is only preliminary to God's taking possession of the vacant dwelling. Otherwise, a man is like a house that stands in good order, clean, but empty (Matt. 12:44). Unless the power of God enters the empty life, the demon can return bringing seven other demons with him, and the person will be worse off than he was at first. It must be remembered that demon exorcism is the negative side of salvation. The positive side is the incoming of the power and life of God.[9]

Although John's Gospel does not approach demonology in the same way as the first three Gospels, it is clear that the author sees Jesus' mission as involving a basic conflict with Satan (John 16:11). John sees the world as being in the grip of an evil supernatural power called the devil (8:44). Jesus overcomes the power of Satan in the cross.

In Acts 10:38, Peter suggests that a prominent characteristic of primitive preaching was the declaration that Christ freed men from the power of the devil. Paul, when exorcising Elymas the sorcerer, called him a son of the devil (Acts 13:10). In Acts 19:13, we find that Jewish exorcists were already active when Paul came to Ephesus. They were said to have taken up the use of the name of Jesus "whom Paul preached." Philip was used to drive out unclean spirits (Acts 8:7). In Acts 16:16-19, a girl with a supernormal knowledge or perception followed Paul. Paul evidently regarded this case as one of real spirit possession and expelled the demon.

The apostle Paul taught that the world was under the heel of celestial world rulers (1 Cor. 2:8; 2 Cor. 4:4; Eph. 6:12). Man is under bondage to evil powers. Salvation is seen in terms of rescue and God's power. In the Pauline epistles there are several passages which clearly indicate Paul's views. Behind idols are demons (1 Cor. 8:4ff.). In the latter days men shall fall away, giving heed to seducing spirits and doctrines taught by demons (1 Tim. 4:1).

The archenemy of God is an evil spirit who is sometimes called the devil (Eph. 4:27), but usually Satan. Satan is the god of this age (2 Cor. 4:4), whose objective is to blind the minds of men so that they cannot apprehend the saving power of the gospel. Satan's main objective is to frustrate the redemptive purposes of God. At the end of the age the satanic power will become incarnate in a man of lawlessness. He will endeavor by one last final effort to overthrow the work of God and to turn men to the worship of evil (2 Thess. 2:4-10). However, Satan's doom is sure; God will crush him under the feet of the saints (Rom. 16:20).[10]

In Eph. 6:11f., Paul states that the believer's struggle is against the devil and against principalities, authorities, world rulers of this present darkness, and spiritual hosts of wickedness. These spirits are created beings. Evidently some of them have been allowed to exercise a large area of power over the course of this age. Paul deliberately seems to employ a vague and varied terminology in regard to these powers. He alternates between the singular and plural forms of several of the words. Perhaps he is asserting that all evil powers, whether personal or impersonal, have been brought under subordination by the death and exaltation of Christ and will eventually be destroyed through His messianic reign.[11]

It should be noted that only one of the eighteen gifts which Paul lists in 1 Cor. 12; Rom. 12; and Eph. 4 relates to the demonic. This gift is sometimes called the discernment of spirits. It is discussed in 1 Cor. 12:8-10. Scholars disagree on whether or not all of the gifts listed by Paul should be normative for the life of the entire church. Some of the distinct supernatural gifts seem to be primarily related to the apostolic period. For example, gifts of apostleship and prophecy seem to be given for the founding of the church (Eph. 2:20). However, the gift of distinguishing between the spirits seems to be potentially available to all Christians. In practice, however, its exercise will probably be limited to a rather small* number of Christians who will use the gift reluctantly when occasion demands. [12]

The book of James evidently sees a double source of temptation. One source is the inner nature of man. At the same time the author recognizes the existence of the devil and implies that he too is the source of temptation, for he warns his readers to resist the devil and he will flee from them (4:7). This resistance probably has reference not only to temptation to sin, but to every wile by which Satan tries to turn men from the truth. James obviously shares the Jewish Christian view of the existence of demons, although he refers to them only in passing (2:19). James does not develop the method by which temptation can come both from the inner man and from the devil.[13]

A vivid statement in 1 Peter portrays the devil prowling around like a roaring lion seeking whom he may devour (5:8). The passage in 3:19-20 says that Christ went and preached to the spirits in prison. A widely accepted interpretation suggests that Christ proclaimed the victory of the gospel to the fallen angels imprisoned in Hades. The preaching described in this passage may not mean an offer of salvation but rather the triumphant announcement that through his death and resurrection Christ had broken the power of the spirit world.[14]

In 2 Pet. 2:4 there is a statement that is a New Testament source for the idea that evil spirits are fallen angels. There is considerable material concerning this idea in the apocryphal books such as 1 Enoch. According to Peter, there is a class of angels who sinned and who were therefore cast down into Sheol where they are prisoners until the day of judgment (2:4).[15]

Jude 6 tells of angels who left their proper dwelling and who are kept in eternal chains in the nether gloom until the judgment of the great day. This is seemingly a verbal quote from the interbiblical book called 1 Enoch. Jude does not call 1 Enoch Scripture, although it obviously had some value for him.[16]

1 John 4:1 is oftentimes seen as a reference to demon discernment. In this verse, John urges his readers to test

the spirits. It must be remembered, however, that the primary reference is to the so-called prophets. They are to be tested by the norm of orthodox Christian tradition, at the center of which is the real incarnation of Christ (4:2-3). John would imply that Satan was behind any heresy involved.[17]

An important passage in the book of Revelation, chapter 12, portrays a vision of the powers that operate in the spiritual world behind the scenes of human history. The red dragon, or Satan, is seen as seeking to destroy the woman (a representation of the ideal and historic church) in an age-long battle. In 12:4-5, Satan's effort to destroy the Messiah is frustrated. Instead, Satan himself is cast down from his place of power as a result of a spiritual conflict (12:7f.). Because of his defeat, Satan is even more infuriated and seeks to destroy the woman, which is the church. This conflict between the dragon and the woman would help to explain the evil which the church experiences throughout its entire history (12:11). This evil can be seen as beginning at the hands of the Roman Empire and being culminated in the final Antichrist.[18]

In Rev. 12:4, John states that the tail of the dragon draws a third of the stars of heaven and casts them to the earth. This is usually seen as referring to a primeval war in heaven since stars are familiar symbols of fallen angels. In Rev. 19:20, a dramatic portrayal finds the dragon, or Satan, being bound and shut up in the bottomless pit for a thousand years. At the end of the thousand years, he is released and entices men to rebel against Christ and the saints. Finally, he is cast into the lake of fire along with the Beast and the False Prophet (20:10).[19]

From this survey of representative biblical statements, it is evident that the satanic and demonic is a dominant theme of the New Testament. This satanic-demonic teaching, however, presents difficulties for systematic theologians. For example, it demands at least a limited dualism. It should be remembered that biblical thought is not primarily concerned with philosophical difficulties. Rather, the Bible is concerned with a realistic description of human existence and its bondage. It does not give us a fully developed theodicy or a theoretical justification of God and the place of evil in his world. Instead, it tells us of God's action in history to bind and ultimately completely defeat Satan.[20]

The biblical materials, however, avoid an ultimate dualism which would make Satan equal with God. Neither in Judaism nor in the New Testament does this antithetical kingdom of evil opposing the Kingdom of God become an absolute dualism. The fallen angels are helpless before the power of God and His angels. Furthermore, in the New Testament, all such spiritual powers are creatures of God and therefore subject to His power.

There were groups in the first century, as today, who attributed evil to misfortune or capricious fate. For the Bible, however, evil has its roots in personality. Demon possession is almost always related to personal sin. Even though Satan can tempt, he can be resisted by the will. Of course, the human will can yield to him.

In primitive religion, each demon is a law unto himself and acts irrationally rather than according to a predetermined pattern and purpose. In the Bible, evil is not a disorganized chaotic conflict of powers as in animism. Rather, it is seen to be under the direction of a single will whose purpose it is to frustrate the will of God.[21]

At this point, it might be well to point out that to take Satan and the demonic powers seriously is to expect them to work just where we do not expect them. We read in 2 Cor. 11:14 that Satan "disguises himself as an angel of light," and that his servants "disguise themselves as servants of righteousness." It was not to the political subversives, prostitutes, social outcasts and dishonest businessmen, but to the moral, law-abiding Pharisees that Jesus spoke of "your father the devil" (John 8:44). Perhaps, today, Satan and the demonic forces are also at work where people allow their own morality, respectability and law-abiding piety to become more important than the needs of their fellowmen.[22]

To hold a doctrine of Satan does not mean that God is less than all powerful or that He is not love. God evidently limited himself in order to give men and angels freedom. Obviously, there cannot be freedom unless there is the possibility of decision and rebellion.

Belief in Satan and the demonic raises serious theological problems related to man's freedom and responsibility. As has already been indicated, Satan normally cannot possess or control us except by our own consent. Man's original decision, made in the depths of his personality, voluntarily opens his personality to a demonic invasion. It makes it possible for a person to come under bondage to the powers of evil. As men and groups of men give way to the insidious temptation to be as God and usurp their delegated powers for their own ends, this demonic bondage becomes more real.[23]

Only in rare cases could there be anything like complete demonic possession. Even then, man cannot escape the sovereign claims of God.[24]

Another theological problem raised by belief in Satan relates to the sovereignty of God. The Bible teaches that the power of the demonic is limited. Man can never be so totally corrupt that the forces of darkness have complete control over human history. The devil acts only within the limits set by the divine sovereignty. The devil is one whose power was originally granted to him by his Creator. We must beware of ascribing to Satan an authority which verges on the absolute. Actually, evil is always parasitic. Satan feeds on the good and in destroying the good he will ultimately destroy himself.[25]

Satan, because he is a created being, may yet serve God's purpose. The divine justice at times makes use of the rebellious powers of darkness. They may oppose all order, but they cannot escape the judgment of Him who ordained order. Oftentimes, the rebellion is overruled by God to accomplish His will.[26]

The biblical emphasis upon Satan as personal will safeguard any metaphysical dualism which might come if we speak of evil in abstract terms. The realm of Satan is a realm of will, intention and meaning. If evil is organized and dynamic, it must belong to the level of personal and purposeful activity. In fact, the devil and demons seen as personal can better meet philosophical problems than can abstract metaphysical systems.

Eric Rust and other philosophical theologians criticize Paul Tillich at the point of his neglect of the personal. Tillich's approach is ontological and he couches his description of the demonic in impersonal and metaphysical rather than in personal terms. His monistic approach to reality leads him to conceive God as carrying the demonic within his own being. He has obviously been influenced by the monism of Schelling and the mystical theology of Jacob and Meister Eckhart. In God himself there is a kind of duality. God, who is essentially form-creating, has also a form-destroying aspect in the inexhaustible depths of being. This aspect asserts itself when God creates the finite and the creaturely. Out of the depths of being, creative powers surge up into the finite beings as the vital impulses in human personality. Men are tempted to break through the limited form in which they are imprisoned and to realize the infinite in the finite. So sin approaches man from a level beyond his freedom and yet appeals to his freedom. Historical man is thereby tempted to use his creative powers for his own destruction.[27]

This viewpoint, held by Tillich, is basically monistic and abstractly speculative. From one perspective, it would appear to identify the Fall with creation. From another perspective, man has some responsibility. The actual responsibility for sin and evil seems, however, to be placed more upon God than upon man. Tillich's conception of God is grounded more in speculative mystical theology than in revelation.[28]

The biblical portrayal of evil in a personal form, as in the fallen angel story, avoids both monism and dualism. It does not place too much emphasis on the power of the demonic but preserves man's responsibility for his sin. Even though man permits the demonization of his creative works and passes under bondage to them, his life and his world remain in the hands of God. They can never be ascribed to the absolute sphere of influence of the devil. The category of Satan and the demonic is thus seen as providing the necessary theological tool for understanding the sin of man in historical existence.

Donald R. Jacobs, on the basis of extensive mission experience, suggests that great harm has been done to the cause of Christ because demonology and the victory view of the atonement have not been considered respectable during the modern mission era. He makes this statement because he believes that most people in the non-Western world convert to another faith because of seeking more power. In Africa, Latin America and Polynesia the world view of the people resembles that of the New Testament world, a world populated with spirits. Jesus proved His lordship by becoming Lord of the spirits, exorcising demons, healing the sick and forgiving sins. Modern missions has dealt almost exclusively with the sin-forgiving aspect of the faith. But the demons remained and they were exorcised, as they had been for centuries past, by traditional shamanistic practices. Christian faith, therefore, had its limits. What Christ was not expected to do, the local practitioners could! According to Jacobs, by failing to introduce Jesus to all levels of spiritual beliefs in a culture, an undergirding is given to a sort of spiritual dualism in which Jesus answers some questions, and other spiritual powers, others.[29]

Fortunately, as we noted in the discussion of biblical passages, the victory, or triumphant view of the atonement, is coming back into its own. The sacrificial, substitutionary, propitiatory and redemptive views of the atonement all have validity. However, the triumphant view must take its proper place. Much of the New Testament, as has been indicated, has to do with the power of Satan and demons, and this victory view should be seen as quite important. In some unexplainable way the death of Christ has constituted an initial defeat of these powers. This is clearly set forth in Col. 2:15. George Ladd, for example, feels that a more satisfactory translation of Col. 2:15 is that of the RSV, which understands the verse to mean that Christ has disarmed the spiritual powers, stripping them of their insignia of rank or of their arms. Thus the verse states that by His death Christ triumphed over His spiritual enemies, winning a divine triumph over the cosmic powers.[30]

One other advantage of the biblical teaching on the demonic is that it does not show speculative interest in Satan or demons as do many of the Jewish apocalypses and other non-biblical sources. The New Testament interest is primarily practical and redemptive. It recognizes the supernatural power of evil, and its concern is the redemptive work of God in Christ delivering men from these evil forces.[31]

About A.D. 250 Eusebius states that the office of exorcism was the third of four minor orders in the church. One function of the exorcist related to the development of infant baptism and the developing dogma of original sin. Exorcism removed the impediment to grace resulting from the effects of original sin. Furthermore, the whole world was seen as being under the power of the devil. Givry suggests that in those early centuries it was taught that a child entered the world under the auspices of a demon. A voluntary renunciation of the devil was required of a candidate for baptism. When infants were baptized, the renunciation was undertaken by sponsors on their behalf. The pre-baptismal exorcism ceremony included a command "Come out of him, thou unclean spirit!" Books are available giving the exorcism sentences used by such notables as Ambrose and Cyprian.[32]

Since the Reformation, it has been widely debated as to what extent baptism and exorcism are sacramental and to what extent symbolic. In New Testament terms it is difficult to say "baptism" without also thinking "faith" (Col. 2:12). Teaching about exorcism, as has been seen, is not developed by Paul and the other apostles.

The movie, *The Exorcist*, has raised many problems about the relationship of the sacramental system to exorcism. The exorcism in the movie appeared to be semimechanical without any relationship to personal faith.

The Protestant Reformation saw a reaction to the elaborate exorcism rites which are portrayed in the movie, *The Exorcist*. Luther recommended that demonic possession be cured by prayer alone. John Wesley, like Luther, evidently used prayer instead of elaborate exorcist rites. Donald Bloesch contends that we are freed from possession, not by any incantations and magic, but by the proclamation of the gospel and the prayers of the church. Although Bloesch admits that there may be a place for a liturgy of exorcism, the church must be aware of psuedo-exorcism which is magic. Our reliance must not be on psychic dynamics and drama but on the word of the cross which alone is able to expel the demons. We should also recognize a charism of exorcism, which means that certain people are especially gifted at dealing with the curse of demon possession.[33]

The doctrine of fallen angels or demons also presents a problem for the theory of knowledge. In their normal being fallen angels are not perceptible by our senses. Of course, we cannot see our own minds or souls, but we do have a kind of direct awareness of ourselves. Since I am not a fallen angel, I cannot know experientially what it is like to be one. Nor can I learn about these demons from their bodies since in their own being they are bodiless. It is true that in certain instances in Scripture, angels (fallen and unfallen) appeared in human form for a special purpose on a special occasion but these are very rare instances. Even though they do not have bodies, fallen angels are like humans in the sense that they are conscious, intelligent beings.[34]

The essence of our knowledge about fallen angels rests on the authority of revelation. The Bible shows us that the demons are continually at war with God and man. They haunt and exploit the material world and those who inhabit it. They are strong and cunning yet devoid of true wisdom and powerless against the Cross. Theology can seek to draw out the implications of what is said in the Bible.[35]

H. A. Hodges suggests that there are two experiential

sources of knowledge about fallen angels. One source is a kind of direct nonsensory spiritual awareness. The other source of knowledge is based on the effects of their deliberate actions. Men can perceive in themselves the effects of their action and so draw conclusions about them. The scope of their action is limited. Fallen angels cannot act directly upon the will, but they can and do act upon the imaginations, thoughts, emotions and desires. Where they find a passion alive and active in us, they can play upon these passions and fantasies and so intensify the passion. Evidently they can also inject fantasies and feelings which have no ground in our own character and experience. Bodily sensations, too, evidently can be awakened by the same agency.[36]

There are, however, difficulties in relation to these experiential sources. One is that it is too easy to accept an event uncritically as a product of demonic agency, without adequately considering what other causes may also be at work. This is especially true where there is a strong imaginative and emotional interest in the idea of fallen angels and a comparatively slight knowledge of the ways of the world and of the human soul. Discrimination is certainly needed in this area.[37]

J. Stafford Wright contends that the place of possession by an evil spirit is the spirit of man, which is the gateway to the spiritual world. If a person's spirit is empty, he will either be unorganized, or organized around some inadequate center. Unpleasant complexes may develop as a natural consequence, producing mental and physical symptoms. Possession by a demon may intensify these symptoms, and may also produce a flood of supernormal effects. The demon may seize on unpleasant personality groupings that are already forming, and emerge as a new personality in the person. If the case is genuine demon possession, the casting out of the demon in the Name of Jesus Christ will enable the normal personality to function again and the physical symptoms to disappear.[38]

Bloesch suggests that the names of the demons should be understood as representing desires implanted in the heart by Satan, such as death, lust, and hatred. The voices of the demons should generally be interpreted as the voices of the other self, the alter-ego, although the content of what is said may very well be directed by the devil.[39]

A key issue in relationship to Satan and demonology is the problem of demythologizing. The most radical yet straightforward attempt to deal with New Testament demonology is that of Rudolph Bultmann, the well-known German biblical scholar. He frankly admits that demonology (and eschatology) are central in the thought of Jesus and Paul. For modern man, however, Bultmann contends that demonology is irrelevant and invalid. He suggests that modern man does not see sickness, including demon possession, as a theological but as a medical problem. Christians should give up being hypocrites and/or idiots. The answer is to demythologize. Demons are to be seen as our own evil impulses and not as external concrete forces outside of us and acting upon us. Terms like the id, oedipus complex, and compulsive delinquency are more appropriate.

Bultmann claims that he only wants to alter the *form* of the gospel—not its *content*. Kallas and other biblical scholars contend that Bultmann alters the *form and* essential *content* of the gospel. If one says that man is not open to *evil* personal and external powers, then, to be consistent, one must go on to say that man is not open to *good* personal and external powers such as Jesus Christ and the Holy Spirit. The Bible contends that for redemptive purposes God does go beyond the normal laws set forth by science. According to Kallas, many Christians have demythologized, gained an audience, and lost a message.

At least Bultmann is more forthright than other Protestant scholars. James Denny ignored the New Testament teachings on Satan and the demonic as does Vincent Taylor. Edward Langton does not believe Jesus would have deliberately taught a false theory of demons. Langton's own view, however, is that as a part of His incarnation, Jesus was as limited in knowledge of demons as He was in science. Demons, for Langton, are a part of a time-bound world picture. Others, such as C. H. Dodd, suggest that there must be a recognition of the fact that Christ had to adapt His language to communicate to the prescientific mind.

Bernard Ramm suggests tests to distinguish between what is cultural or a part of a first-century world picture and that which is transcultural or part of a perennially valid and divinely inspired biblical world view. There are no simple rules but some general guidelines can be given.

Whatever in the Bible is in direct reference to natural things is usually stated in terms of prevailing cultural concepts. This material about natural things is not antiscientific but prescientific. That which is theological or in teaching form is usually transcultural. An example would be in the area of biblical psychology. The statements about internal organs such as the heart, liver, and kidney possessing psychical properties would be assigned to the prevailing culture. These are physiological ways of representing our deep emotional and volitional life. The statements about man's soul or spirit being in the image of God are trans-cultural. The transcultural truth partakes of the binding character of inspiration, not the cultural vehicle. This same procedure is used in laying bare the essential teachings of the classics such as Plato and other ancient writings.[40] In the writer's book, *Demons, Demons, Demons*, the thesis that the idea of a personal Satan and his demonic cohorts is a part of a perennially valid and inspired biblical world view is accepted.

The approach which differentiates between the world picture and the world view is especially urgent in regard to the doctrine of man. Here the Bible moves beyond secular anthropology. The Christian thinker will be concerned to interpret the scientific evidence in the light of the biblical teachings. He will deny those presuppositions from which different and alien metaphysics may be developed. In rela-tion to God-man categories, the biblical teachings and con-cepts should control our thinking. Satan and demonology are concerned with God-man categories and relationships. This thinking is always to be under the guidance of the Spirit who testifies within our living experience.

The resurgence in the West within the past ten years of many different kinds of occult practices has cast renewed doubt on the confident conclusions of so-called scientific beings. Increasing numbers of Christians have found them-selves confronted with men and women possessed of Satan and have found that they have needed the ability to distin-guish between spirits and to cast them out in the name of Christ. This was especially true in California in the late 1960's.

The Anglican Bishop of Exeter has pointed out that in Western countries today, the widespread apostasy from the Christian faith, accompanied by an increasing recourse to black magic and occult practices, is revealing the presence and the power of evil forces and the contaminating influence of an evil atmosphere in particular places and environments. The need, therefore, for the restoration of the practice of exorcism to its proper place is becoming steadily more ur-gent and more evident.[41]

It is encouraging to note that a number of prominent theologians are emphasizing the biblical perspective on demonology. These include Karl Heim, Gustaf Aulén, Gustaf Wingren, G. C. Berkouwer, Helmut Thielicke, and Eduard Thurneysen. Some psychiatrists and medical men, including A. Lechler, Thomas V. Moore, Bernard Martin, as well as psychologists like Charles Corcoran, also affirm the existence of supernatural demonic powers. A prominent theologian, Thurneysen, states that the demonic view of illness and sin in the Bible is not to be regarded as surpassed by modern psychology and psychotherapy. Whatever psychopathic phenomena may come to light through psychological probing, they are not the primary cause of man's trouble according to biblical thought. Rather, they are the reflection and refraction of that metaphysical bondage to the powers of darkness.[42]

This does not mean that developments in the understanding of mental illness are not to be taken into account. Bloesch contends, however, that mental illness studies and insights are not fully adequate to deal with many cases which represent the bondage of the will rather than disorders of the mind.[43]

Having suggested that the ability to distinguish between spirits is a valid spiritual gift in our time, there is caution that should be expressed. This gift of discernment, like many other spiritual gifts, has been misunderstood and abused by many Christians from time to time.

Oftentimes there is a confusion between demon influence, demon subjection and demon possession. The marks of demon possession are very extreme and quite rare. Demon subjection is perhaps more common. The marks of demon subjection are much less extreme than demon possession. Alfred Lechler suggests some of the characteristics of demon subjection: nonreceptivity to divine things, religious doubt, inaptness for true knowledge of sin, inability to concentrate in Bible reading and prayer, persistent lack of peace, inner unrest, temper bursts, blasphemy, depression, and suicidal thoughts. With these marks is joined various compulsions toward drunkenness, sexual immorality, falsehood, theft, smoking, and drugs.[44]

Bloesch suggests that we should distinguish between being a prisoner of Satan, which is like possession, and being the servant of Satan, which is like subjection. All servants of sin are in one sense servants of Satan in that sin is the will of the devil and not the will of God. Yet to be a prisoner of Satan in the full sense means that one must choose just as the devil chooses. Sinners as such still have the freedom to choose between greater and lesser evils. Some say this should be seen as a distinction between oppression by the devil and possession by the devil. All people, including Christians, are oppressed by the devil, but only a few become wholly possessed.[45]

Another problem concerned with exorcism is the importance of the distinction that must be made between mental illness and demon possession. While the two may occur simultaneously, and while possession may cause or worsen mental illness, there is no necessary connection between them. Just as Christians are prone to physical illness, so they may fall victim to mental illness. Nothing can be more harmful to those who are so distressed than to be told that they are possessed of the devil and for an instantaneous cure to be attempted by exorcism. Mental illness signifies a disorder of the mind whereas demon possession represents the bondage of the will to radical evil. Of course, as has been indicated, one does not discount the fact that psychic illness may in some cases be a symptom and manifestation of spiritual slavery to evil powers.[46]

Donald Jacobs suggests that much of psychiatric work is little more than an exercise of description. Ultimately the question remains, why do people have a tendency to pathological disintegration? At least a partial answer to this question is to be found in the area of the will, where a person makes either positive or negative decisions about the business of living. If the questions about why a person should love or live are not answered, then the demons can move in and produce a variety of symptoms from schizophrenia to suicidal compulsion.[47]

When people reach this low stage, society moves in and tries to help reintegrate them. In most cases, the person is placed in the hands of the modern shaman, the psychiatrist. The psychiatrist is supposed to lead them to self-understanding and convince them that there is purpose in life. If this does not become clear, shock therapy may follow. In some cases, conditioning techniques are used.[48]

Sidney Jourard, a practicing psychologist, feels confident that something goes on at the center of the will which he calls inspiration, or spirit mobilization. Jourard calls for positive hope. Perhaps the doctor helps the patient to catch a positive spirit. Love can also do this as well as prayer.[49]

Jacobs does not suggest that all mental demoralization is caused by demons, but he does think that much of it

342 / Demon Possession

is. Therapy in theological terms calls for the demon present to be exorcised and the person filled with the Spirit of God who consistently affirms life. The Spirit of God has no suicidal tendencies.[50]

Remember, however, the warnings. Demon possession is quite rare. It is most likely after considerable and persistent moral decay has taken place. Recurrent temptations are common to all Christians and these should be dealt with through repentance and cleansing by the atonement of Christ. Insanity is in no way synonymous with demon possession.

The New Testament would seem to suggest that the ability to distinguish between spirits should be sought only when confrontation is made with those who may be possessed. It is significant that in the ministry of Paul we read only once of his casting out an evil spirit, and this he did apparently reluctantly after being bothered for many days by the girl who was possessed (Acts 16:16-18). Some Christian leaders, such as the cases in California, have similarly been forced by circumstances into exorcism. They have told of the mental, physical and emotional exhaustion which they have suffered as a result. While they have rejoiced in the victory which has been accomplished in the name of Christ, they nonetheless speak of shrinking from any further direct confrontation with Satan unless it is absolutely necessary. This is quite different from some Christians who are seeking spirits everywhere to cast out.[51]

Exorcism became so widely prevalent in the medieval period that the Roman Catholic Church had to take decisive steps to control exorcism. The *Roman Ritual*, issued in 1614 under Paul V, offered strict rules for exorcism. Later, exorcism was restricted to priests who had gained episcopal permission. The eminent theologian, Karl Rahner, holds out for genuine possession in rare cases. He agrees that it is very difficult to distinguish between mental illness, parapsychological faculties and demon possession. In some cases both psychological help and exorcism should be utilized.

Rahner is opposed, however, to exorcism as a theatrical ritual in which demons as well as God are addressed. This sort of demonstration emphasized can of itself induce a state of possession (in the pathological sense). Rahner apparently accepts the idea that ceremonial exorcism can act effectively on a sick man's subconsciousness. The adjurations addressed to the demon, the sprinklings with holy water, the stole passed around the patient's neck, the repeated signs of the cross and so forth, can easily call up a diabolical mythomania in word and deed in a psyche already weak.

The debate continues on the dangers of premature exorcism. Sudbrack suggests that the practice of exorcism has in the past caused many medical precautions and treatments to be neglected. Many main-line Catholics urge continuation of exorcism if the demands of the *Roman Ritual* in making certain of the demoniac nature of the affliction are met.

Exorcism and the gift of discernment need wisdom, special care and discernment in their exercise. This can only come from the Spirit of God himself. Bloesch suggests that one should be careful in seeking a special gift such as exorcism without at the same time seeking the divine Healer, Jesus Christ. Our attention should be focused not so much upon the gifts as upon the Giver.[52]

Despite the dangers, the gift of the discerning of spirits is very necessary in our day when pagan cults and alien ideologies are making a bid for the souls of men. But we do not want to end on a note of pessimism. We would state once again that the New Testament teaches that Satan is not co-equal with God. He is a created being who has rebelled and can tempt—but not force. Furthermore, the main concern of the Bible is not with the devil but with God and the gospel of His grace. Satan and the demonic have been overcome by the life, death and resurrection of Jesus Christ. The New Testament never allows complete pessimism. In the end Satan and his angels will be completely overcome. In fact, Jesus came into the world to "destroy the works of the devil" (1 John 3:8). The cross was decisive victory over Satan and Satan's hosts (Col. 2:15). This victory insured that countless numbers would be delivered from the dominion of darkness and transferred to the Kingdom of Christ (Col. 1:13).

In Eph. 6:11-18, Paul describes the armor of God—the biblical gospel, integrity, peace through Christ, faith in Christ, prayer, etc.—which furnishes to the believer spiritual security.

The recent fascination with Satan and demons is partially a reaction to an earlier disbelief. Christians should beware of an excessive credulity as well as extreme reductionism. Satan and the demonic are active but the main thrust of Christianity is on the availability of God's power and love in Jesus Christ and the Spirit.

Notes

1. Eric Lionel Mascall (ed.), *The Angels of Light and the Powers of Darkness* (London: Faith Press, 1955), p. 1.

2. Donald R. Jacobs, *Demons* (Scottdale, Pa.: Herald Press, 1972), p. 7.

3. Edward Langton, *Essentials of Demonology* (London: Epworth Press, 1949), pp. 63-67.

4. James Kallas, *Jesus and the Power of Satan* (Philadelphia, Pa.: Westminster Press, 1968), pp. 202-215.

5. George Eldon Ladd, *A Theology of the New Testament* (Grand Rapids, Mich.: Eerdmans, 1974), p. 49.

6. *Ibid.*, p. 52.

7. Oscar Cullmann, *Christ and Time* (Philadelphia, Pa.: Westminster Press, 1964), p. 198.

8. George Eldon Ladd, *Jesus and the Kingdom* (New York: Harper and Row, 1964), pp. 145ff.

9. Ladd, *Theology*, p. 77.

10. *Ibid.*, p. 401.

11. *Ibid.*, p. 402.

12. Donald Bridge and David Phypers, *Spiritual Gifts and the Church* (Downers Grove, Ill.: InterVarsity Press, 1973), p. 66.

13. Ladd, *Theology*, p. 591.

14. *Ibid.*, p. 601.

15. *Ibid.*, p. 606.

16. *Ibid.*, p. 608.

17. *Ibid.*, p. 610.

18. *Ibid.*, p. 625.

19. *Ibid.*, p. 628.

20. Eric C. Rust, *Towards a Theological Understanding of History* (New York: Oxford University Press, 1963), p. 123.

21. Donald G. Bloesch, *The Reform of the Church* (Grand Rapids, Mich.: Eerdmans, 1970), p. 132.

22. Shirley C. Guthrie, Jr., *Christian Doctrine* (Richmond, Va.: Covenant Life Curriculum Press, 1968), pp. 181f.

23. Rust, p. 124.

24. *Ibid.*

25. *Ibid.*

26. *Ibid.*, p. 125.

27. Paul Tillich, *Systematic Theology, II* (Chicago, Ill.: University of Chicago Press, 1957), 29-44.

28. *Ibid.*, p. 44.

29. Jacobs, pp. 34f.

30. Ladd, *Theology*, pp. 434f.

31. *Ibid.*, p. 51.

32. R. H. Robbins, *The Encyclopedia of Witchcraft and Demonology* (New York: Crown Publishers, 1959), pp. 180-89.

33. Bloesch, p. 134.

34. Mascall, pp. 12f.

35. *Ibid.*, pp. 13f.

36. *Ibid.*, pp. 14-16.

37. *Ibid.*, pp. 16f.

38. J. Stafford Wright, *Mind, Man and the Spirits* (Grand Rapids, Mich.: Zondervan Publishing House, 1971), p. 132.

39. Bloesch, p. 133.

40. Bernard Ramm, *The Christian View of Science and Scripture* (Grand Rapids, Mich.: Eerdmans, 1954), pp. 65-117.

41. Dom Robert Petipierre (ed.), *Exorcism* (London: S.P.C.K., 1972), p. 10.

42. Bloesch, p. 131.

43. *Ibid.*, p. 132.

44. Kurt Koch, *Christian Counseling and Occultism* (Grand Rapids, Mich.: Kregel, 1965), pp. 217f.

45. Bloesch, p. 133.

46. Bridge, pp. 68f.

47. Jacobs, pp. 39f.

48. *Ibid.*, pp. 40f.

49. *Ibid.*, p. 41.

50. *Ibid.*, p. 43.

51. Bridge, p. 69.

52. Bloesch, p. 138.

23

Criteria for the Discerning of Spirits

GORDON R. LEWIS

Suddenly a rather "typical" person, who has done little more unusual than play with a ouija board, has dramatic personality changes, speaks with a different voice, manifests extraordinary strength, uses the most obscene language and expresses hatred of God and Christ. On some of these occasions, objects near him move about by an unseen power.

Probably the first reaction of many to this is sheer unbelief. Is the report accurate? If the alleged phenomena occurred beyond a reasonable doubt, were they stage-managed tricks? Could they be accounted for by physical or mental disorders? Are psychic factors such as ESP at work? Could the spirits of dead people be active in this case? Or might this be traced to demons (fallen angels, agents of Satan)? These and other explanations call for careful consideration.

After a lengthy discussion of possibilities like these, one participant exclaimed, "This field is full of subjectivity!" Another said, "We need help in spirit-discerning." Another noted the prevalence of belief in ancestral spirit influences in the third world and wondered if the criteria for discernment could be different in the East and the West. Another said, "It is impossible to *prove* the existence of a possessing spirit."

This chapter seeks to outline an approach to these basic epistemological questions. Fewer and fewer people can escape the responsibility of making some responsible judgments concerning alleged activities of spirits. That difficult task is not left to a few who may claim a special gift from the Holy Spirit for discerning spirits (1 Cor. 12:10). Clearly, all Christians are to witness, but all do not have the gift of evangelism. Similarly, all Christians are to test the spirits (1 John 4:1-3), though all do not have the gift of discerning them. When that gift is exercised by the power of the Holy Spirit, the judgment will not be out of harmony with reality or other truth about the actual state of affairs. The problem is, how can we know the truth about the cause of these unusual phenomena?

The Meaning of Proof

It is impossible to prove the existence of possessing spirits, if by "prove" is meant a kind of mathematical or logical certainty. But that is possible only in relating symbols with stipulated meanings. In matters of fact, history, law, medicine and life in general we must be satisfied with a preponderance of evidence or conclusive evidence beyond reasonable doubt. On the basis of high probability we often act with moral responsibility and psychological certitude. In matters related to the influence of spirits, we can hope for no higher probability than in other matters of fact and experience.

Observed Phenomena

The diagnostic indications of acute demonic attack collated from eight different authorities by John Richards[1] indicate more precisely the type of phenomena to be accounted for.

A. Change of personality
   Including intelligence, moral character, demeanor, appearance
B. Physical changes
   1. Preternatural strength
   2. Epileptic convulsions; foaming
   3. Catatonic symptoms, falling
   4. Clouding of consciousness, anaesthesia to pain
   5. Changed voice
C. Mental changes
   1. Glossolalia; understanding unknown languages
   2. Preternatural knowledge
   3. Psychic and occult powers, e.g., clairvoyance, telepathy and prediction
D. Spiritual changes
   1. Reaction to and fear of Christ; blasphemy with regret as in depression
   2. Affected by prayer

E. Deliverance possible in the name of Jesus
    As this is a diagnosis in retrospect it falls outside the
    range of pre-exorcism symptoms

Granting that phenomena like these are observed in many different areas of the world by competent witnesses (such as physicians and psychiatrists), numerous explanations may be offered.

Hypotheses, Hypotheses

Faced with phenomena like these, one may yield to the temptation to avoid all causal explanations and simply describe the phenomena as they appear to responsible observers. Phenomenologists challenge the claim that philosophers must start with unexamined presuppositions. Statements are true, not because certain other statements are true, but because they describe the phenomena correctly. The phenomenologist does not frame theories, but simply examines them. He endeavors to avoid all unexamined presuppositions and to examine all phenomena carefully. He desires to take none of them as familiar or understood until they have been carefully explicated.[2] This descriptive approach has a temporary value for those coming to the subject with presuppositions against the activity of spirits in the world and those who attribute too much to spirits. Sooner or later, however, we are face to face with the persistent question, "Why?" Aetiological explanations cannot be ignored. We cannot permanently sidestep the demand to "put it all together."

So bring on the hypotheses! Superstition, suggestion, projection, delusion, manipulation, physical or mental illness, spirits of dead people, spirits of fallen angels (demons), Satan himself, angels or God. No holds are barred in hypothesis making. However, if the proposed explanations are to be considered seriously, they must meet two standards. First, they must be defined with sufficient clarity that others may know what is being proposed. Second, some evidence must be relevant to the verification procedure so that there is a genuine investigation. The case cannot be settled on a priori assumptions. Some evidence must count for verifying or falsifying the proposal.

Christians can no more foreclose a careful testing of explanations in a given case than others. Since God has freely chosen to create the various kinds of beings there are and to permit the fall of some into sin, the world has not emanated from God with an automatic necessity. So none can infer what God must have done, in spite of evidence to the contrary. Christians only can discover what God has in fact chosen to do or permit. Unexamined Christian a prioris are no more likely to square with reality than unexamined, non-Christian assumptions.

In looking at the world of occult happenings, John Warwick Montgomery stresses: "We must 'suspend disbelief,' check out the evidence with the care demanded for events in general, attempt to formulate explanatory constructs that best 'fit the facts,' and at the same time be willing always to accept facts even if our best attempts to explain them prove inadequate." [3]

General Criteria of Truth

Can minds open and closed to the possibility of demonic factors in human events ever meet? Discussion on such emotionally charged subjects needs a meaningful basis upon which to proceed. Some criteria of truth need to be agreed upon in order that interpretation and argument may have some ground rules or points of reference. Christians understand these norms as significant for all men as creatures of God. Because God made man in His image to know and rule the world, man can attain truth about God and the world. God reveals His existence, power and righteous demands to all men (Rom. 1:18-20; 2:14-15). All human beings regardless of their suppression of these matters are responsible to acknowledge the truth before God. [4]

Standards of testing truth-claims regarding spirits, as all other subjects, grow out of who we are and the world in which we live. Criteria of truth are not invented arbitrarily in a vacuum. Truth is the key to reality. A true hypothesis leads us to what actually is the case, not away from it. The following criteria have been held in widely different areas of the world and in different times, by people of very different philosophical perspectives. Those criteria together are often called the coherence criterion. It incorporates the elements of many other criteria and provides the most checks and balances in our quest for truth about reality.

1. *Empirical fit.* In spite of radically different world views, the observable data must be reckoned with sooner or later. We cannot escape reality and live in a dream castle. Differences of perspective on the ultimate meaning of events must not blur the public data given in the phenomena associated with spirit influence. What a naturalist observes as a descriptive scientist is the same as what a

Christian observes as a careful diagnostician.[5] Both see water as H_2O, but one regards its ultimate explanation a product of nonintelligent forces, the other a product of God's creative wisdom and power. Similarly, the phenomena associated with demonic influence (listed above) are given for people of all metaphysical beliefs. And any view that is true must fit these facts.

The truth about a given matter, in Christianity, corresponds to the mind of God on that matter.[6] God created and sustains all aspects of reality. He takes all factors into account in His judgments. Insofar as humanly possible our hypotheses must be consistent with all the facts relevant to a given matter. A proposed explanation of allegedly demonic phenomena should, ideally, account for everything given in relation to the case. Since researchers are limited, it is more realistic to regard that hypothesis as true which accounts for the greatest amount of the evidence with the fewest difficulties (ad hoc explanations). Our question, then, becomes one of deciding which possible hypothesis or combination of hypotheses can explain the many types of phenomena related to allegedly demonic factors in human life. The truth, as God sees it, will account for all the data.

2. *Logical noncontradiction.* A true view of phenomena alleged to be demonic does not contradict itself or other known truth. The universe is a *uni*-verse—one world. In spite of the diversity within it, it coheres. A true view of the reality we experience, while accounting for the diversity of phenomena, cannot meaningfully affirm and deny the same thing at the same time and in the same respect. The law of noncontradiction provides a sure sign of error, but by itself, consistency does not guarantee the truth of a hypothesis. Many proposed explanations may be logically possible (consistent), but not empirically possible (they do not fit the facts).

From the standpoint of Christianity, furthermore, the truth about a matter at issue corresponds with the mind of God on it. How can we know God's mind? As God looks at a case of alleged demon possession, God's view of it is noncontradictory. God cannot deny himself (2 Tim. 2:13). It is impossible for God to lie (Heb. 6:18; Tit. 1:2). A true view of the situation is a noncontradictory view. This was the case even for the Old Testament prophets. Their teaching could not be regarded true, or of God, if it contradicted previous revelation (Deut. 13:1-5); nor their "signs" significant if they did not fit the facts (Deut. 18:21-22).

3. *Existential viability.* A true hypothesis consistently accounts, not only for the external, empirical data, but also the internal data of human experience, such as intellectual honesty, justice and love. As Francis Schaeffer puts it, you are able to live consistently with a true hypothesis.[7] If the diagnosis of a given person's condition calls it epilepsy and that disease is treated but the patient does not improve, the diagnosis is not true. It is not one with which the patient can live satisfactorily. And it is not one that participants in a ministry of healing can live with authentically.

From a Christian stance, acceptance of the God revealed in Christ and Scripture enables a person to be ruthlessly honest with himself before principles of morality. He need not gloss over his unworthy motivations, lack of love, pride, anger, covetousness, lust, faithlessness, prejudice, injustice, greed, etc. With complete candor, he can confess what he really is to God, and receive forgiveness on the basis of the cross of Christ. A Christian has identity as a child of God, purpose in life, love for God and others, and power to say "No" to temptation. In short, he has life abundant (John 10:10). Christianity is a world view and way of life with which you can live life to the fullest.[8]

Are the criteria of truth different in Eastern countries? As I taught in India during a sabbatical and interviewed leaders in several Eastern countries on communicating the gospel to the Eastern mind, I found an initial emphasis upon Eastern people's lack of appreciation for coherence. One former Hindu illustrated them for me. He said, "I am Bhaskar; I am not Bhaskar." From the standpoint of appearance he is a person named Bhaskar, but from the standpoint of the alleged ultimate unity of Brahman, he is not Bhaskar but Brahman. These statements do not affirm and deny the same thing at the same time and in the same respect, however. Two different respects (phenomenal appearance and ultimate reality) are in view. The same is true when he said, "I live only one life, and I live many lives" (in transmigration of the soul). The first statement refers to the single present existence; the second to the supposed transmigrations of the soul. Since the same respect is not in view, the statements are not logically contradictory.

I found that Hindus who were supposed to "buy" contradictions, would not do so with some of their most fundamental beliefs. "All is Brahman," they maintained. They would not listen to the suggestion that something was not Brahman. Again, they maintained that all we can observe is maya or illusion. They were no more inclined to receive contradictions than Westerners when I suggested that some verifiable events are not maya. When one day I purposely contradicted an earlier assignment, I found Eastern students no slower than Western students to challenge the professor's right to contradict himself where their work was concerned.

Just as the law of noncontradiction was operative in the East (underneath its denial), so was the criterion of fitting the facts. Although the material world was said to be illusory, illnesses had to be treated by doctors and nurses, food was essential and on the roads one had to dodge animals, pedestrians, bicycles, bullock carts and automobiles. Labelling sensory phenomena illusory did not reduce the importance of reckoning with them. And one could not live consistently with the denial of the reality of empirical data. Accidents, sickness and death were stark and dreaded realities. Visible money was indispensable to bargaining in the markets, however unreal it was said to be.

Although on the surface it appears that criteria of truth may be different in the East and West, underneath I did not find them totally other. Anywhere in the world the truth about any given matter must without contradiction account for all the empirical data and one must be able to live consistently with it. Integrating all three general tests of truth, Francis Schaeffer shows that Christianity, which, after all, originated in the Near East, not the West, is true for all men everywhere. "Christianity . . . constitutes a non-self-contradictory answer that does explain the phenomena and which can be lived with, both in life and in scholarly pursuits." [9]

On the above criteria there is a conclusive amount of evidence supporting the hypothesis that a personal Creator and Lord of all exists and has revealed himself to men in the person of Jesus Christ and the teaching of the Bible. Belief in the God disclosed in Christ and Scripture gives the most consistent, factual and viable view of all human experience.

In contrast, the spiritualist's hypothesis of communication with spirits of the dead in an evolutionary universe with an impersonal, immanent god fails to meet the criteria of truth. Spirit-messages contradict each other on the nature of Jesus Christ and other things. The spirits allegedly giving the messages and their content are extremely difficult to confirm as leading researchers in the Society of Psychical

Research have acknowledged. Also documented elsewhere[10] is the admission of spiritualists that often the most sincere attempts of people to communicate with the dead over many years may be in vain. When a message does come it may come from a "naughty spirit" intending to deceive, or be a practical joke, unwise counsel on matters with which the spirit has no knowledge or merely a reflex of the message the sitter at a seance wished to hear. The spiritualist's hypothesis of communication with the spirits of dead people is far less consistent, and factual than Christianity, and a person cannot live as consistently with it. In terms of general criteria of any truth, this hypothesis of communication with the dead must be regarded untrue.

A Christian Structure of Reality

In a Christian view of reality, the ultimate being is a personal God. He is infinite, eternal and unchanging in His wisdom, power and holy love. Every other person and thing derives its existence from Him. He sustains and rules the world as Lord of all. In His omnipotence, He can and will overcome all the forces of evil, visible and invisible.

God created angels, spirits intended to implement His general and redemptive purposes in the world (Heb. 1:14). One of the highest of these created, angelic spirits rebelled against God and by his own will (and no more ultimate cause) became the devil. Others who were filled with pride and wanted to become as God joined Satan in his rebellion. These fallen angels are called spirits or demons. Since their fall, there has been a great battle among the unseen powers of good and evil. Teaching on the reality of the kingdom of darkness, as well as the kingdom of God, permeates the Scriptures from beginning to end. To demythologize one or both of these kingdoms is to violate the intention of the biblical writers and do injustice to the ordinary usage of words in their historical, grammatical contexts.

Reality includes not only the divine and the angelic-demonic orders, but also the human level of existence. By nature human beings are children of the devil, prone to deceive, and to destroy the work of God. Unrepentant for their sin and refusing to accept Christ's provision of forgiveness, their spirits after death suffer torment. They do not return to warn others of what lies ahead (Luke 16:19-31). Other human beings, repenting of their sin, and trusting Jesus Christ's provision, are delivered from the kingdom of darkness into the kingdom of God's dear Son (Col. 1:13). Freed from bondage to sin, they share God's fellowship and purposes as long as they live. At death their spirits go to be with Christ who has ascended from the earth (2 Cor. 5:6-8; Phil. 1:22; Heb. 12:23; Rev. 6:9). Miraculously Moses and Elijah appeared in glorified bodies at Christ's transfiguration as did others at Christ's resurrection (Matt. 17:1-3; 27:52-53). But these exceptional events cannot constitute evidence for a regular possibility of communication with disembodied spirits of the deceased. What is thought to be communication with the dead in Bible times is attributed to the deceptions of demons (e.g., Acts 16:16-18). On the human level of reality, then, are the people of God and the people of the world and the spirits of the ungodly dead and the spirits of the dead who died in the faith.

Knowing that biblical Christianity is true on the general criteria of truth, we know that reality includes four levels of existence: (1) God, (2) angels, and demons whose leader is called Satan, (3) the spirits of the believing and unbelieving dead human beings, and (4) the living human beings, both believing and unbelieving.

Morally, reality has two basic divisions. On the side of the good are God, angels, the spirits of the dead in Christ and living disciples of Christ. On the side of evil, are Satan and his demonic hosts, the spirits of the unbelieving dead and the living persons who persist in rebelling against God's revelation in nature, Christ and the Bible. The ultimate source of all evil is Satan (Rev. 12:9). Clearly, on a Christian view of reality, there is no a priori reason why angels, demons or human spirits of the dead could not contact and influence life on earth. Influences from good and bad human spirits and angels and demons are neither logically impossible nor empirically impossible. The question remains whether there is adequate empirical evidence for asserting any or all of them to have actually occurred. Similarly, if demonic possessions should be confirmed, there is no logical or a priori reason why there could not be exorcism by the power of Christ (or even other powers, if the evidence should point in other directions).

Criteria for Distinguishing the Holy Spirit from Satan and Angels from Demons

Granting different orders of intelligent existence in reality, the all-important distinction is moral—between the good and the evil spirits. One of the most blasphemous misjudgments a person can make is to attribute the power of the Holy Spirit in Jesus Christ to evil spirits (Mark 3:22-30). Three distinctively Christian criteria need to be incorporated with the general criteria above to discern the moral nature of spirits at any level accurately.

1. *The Spirit's chief end—God's pleasure.* The highest value on a Christian world view is ascribed only to the living God, Creator of heaven and earth. Worship and service of any created thing, however exalted, more than the Creator is sinful idolatry (Rom. 1:25). When Jesus was incarnate on earth, He was about His Father's business. He called upon people to worship the Father in spirit and truth (John 4:23-24). He said, "My meat is to do the will of him that sent me" (John 4:34). He did not act of His own accord (John 5:19) nor on His own authority (John 5:30). He said He came in His Father's name (John 5:43). He emphasized, "I have come down from heaven, not to do my own will, but the will of him who sent me" (John 6:38). Shortly before His crucifixion Jesus prayed to the Father, "I glorified thee on earth, having accomplished the work which thou gavest me to do" (John 17:4). Christ, as filled and led by the Holy Spirit, exemplifies the chief end not only of men, but angels—it is to glorify God and enjoy Him forever.

Evil men and evil spirits, in contrast, seek to utilize the hidden wisdom and great power of God to their own selfish ends. Their lust for secret knowledge and occult powers leads them from genuine religion to magic. Like the Canaanite nations of old, people today rebelliously attempt to usurp divine prerogatives. Professor Douglas Miller stressed this in responding to my paper, when he said, "These attempts to coerce the divine would have far reaching implications in a religion that affirms a God who is absolutely sovereign and will not tolerate any human effort to intrude upon that sovereignty. God will not be controlled. Any attempt to direct or manipulate God implies rebellious idolatry."

Paul, like Isaiah, knew that idols were nothing in themselves, but he warned that sacrifices to them were to demons and not to God (1 Cor. 10:19-20). He continues, "I do not want you to be partners with demons. You cannot drink the cup of the Lord and the cup of demons. You cannot partake of the table of the Lord and the table of demons. Shall we provoke the Lord to jealousy? Are we stronger than he?" No man can serve two masters! Our ultimate concern cannot be directed to God if it is directed to ourselves or other created spirits.

So one of the clearest indications that deceptive demonic powers may be at work is preoccupation with self-worship, self-glorification. One who refuses to turn from magic to attribute ultimate worth to God in spirit and in truth (John 4:24) may be in the grip of demonic deception. At least he is open to it. Demonic activities cannot be limited to the few instances of possession.

2. *The Spirit's supreme authority—God's Word.* We need to be alert to the counterfeit claims of evil spirits. Do you want to know the future? The final authority is not the stars, not the tea leaves, not the ouija board, not the words of a medium or the words of spirits directly. The final prophetic authority must be God's Word written. Do you want an abundant life of wisdom and power? What is reliable and best for you to know has been revealed in Scripture. "The secret things belong unto the Lord our God; but the things that are revealed belong to us and to our children for ever, that we may do all the words of this law" (Deut. 29:29). All Scripture, Paul says, "is inspired of God and profitable ... that the man of God may be complete, equipped for every good work" (2 Tim. 3:16-17).

On the authority of Jesus Christ, the Scriptures own claims, and an abundance of historical and ecclesiastical evidence, we know that the Bible was written under the direction of the Holy Spirit. Any influence upon our lives tending to discord with the teaching of Scripture is not of God. The Christian's supreme source of information about life after death and fullness of life at present is the Bible.

Do you genuinely seek to ascribe ultimate worth to God? How do we know what pleases and glorifies Him? We know through the revelation of His pleasure in Scripture. To show greater esteem for occult "revelations" than for biblical revelation is an insult to the Almighty God who lovingly created us to worship and serve Him.

3. *The Spirit's preeminent message—God's gospel.* Do the messages from the spirit-world give priority to God's plan of redemption through the person and work of Christ? God's Holy Spirit prepared the way for the coming of the Messiah throughout Old Testament history. Christ incarnated God's loving purposes for fallen men. The New Testament proclaimed the good news of Jesus' completed

atonement and triumphant resurrection. In all the creeds and confessions of the church throughout the centuries, the gospel of Christ has been found to be the central message of Christ and the Scriptures in revealing the Father's grand design.

Where in all the alleged communiques from the spirits of dead people is there any call for repentance from sin and faith in Christ? Why, if either the believing or unbelieving dead communicated with the living, would either fail to warn of the consequences attendant upon rejecting the Savior? Why should the teaching of supposed ancestral dead consistently contradict the scriptural gospel? Why do the spiritualist's messages say that God is impersonal? that men are not lost sinners in need of divine mercy and grace? that men are capable in themselves of endless self-improvement? that Jesus was divine only in the sense in which all people are alleged to be divine? that the cross was not an atonement for man's sin? that Christ's resurrection was a mere materialization? that disciples of Christ are to anticipate no personal fellowship with God? that the basis of man's hope is in human works not divine grace? [11]

As you hear accounts of words from dead relatives which seemingly no one else could know, and when you learn of the distinction between ancestral spirits and evil spirits in African tribes (Donald Jacobs' chapter), the most consistent hypothesis to explain the phenomena seems to be communication from dead people. But when you stop to realize that these alleged messages from the dead give no warning about the torments of the life beyond separated from the Father—the source of all good, you wonder if there is not some deception by Descartes' evil genius. Then you fail to find any references to the gospel of Christ, let alone any priority for that message central to the entire Christian faith. Finally, you conclude that the only consistent account of the content of spirit-messages, so antithetical to the gospel of Christ, is agents of the father of lies.

However good and beneficial the spirit-messages may be thought to be, the gospel of Christ does not have priority in them. Secondary matters, if not outright blasphemy and obscenity, have usurped the place that rightfully belongs to the gospel. As Bernard Ramm has explained, "The chief enemies of man are sin and death (1 Cor. 15), and the divine remedy is Jesus Christ crucified and risen from the dead. This is the first witness of the Bible (2 Tim. 3:15). If the cultists heard the Holy Spirit they would hear this message. The fact that they do not so speak indicates that they do not hear the voice of the Spirit, which in turn means that they have an improper principle of religious authority." [12]

Guidelines for Applying the Criteria

Setting forth criteria in an orderly fashion is one thing; applying them to a difficult case is another. No suggestion is intended that there are easy answers to complex and difficult problems. Little can be done regarding application to a specific case, without a specific case with which to deal. But some tentative suggestions may be made.

The first step is gathering the relevant data in order to know exactly what the phenomena are. Psychiatrist John White in his chapter helpfully outlines a skilled procedure. He inquires about "Joe's" history in relation to the occult. Then he determines if there are any phenomena distinctively characteristic of demonic influence. He is also concerned to detect any signs and symptoms common to both mental illness and demonic influence. Finally, he asks if there have been any surrounding phenomena such as rappings, knockings, and unexplained movement of objects. As full a case study as possible, even in nonmedical language is indispensable.

Second, seek the simplest hypothesis with sufficient explanatory power. If there are indications of physical illness, by all means have these examined by a physician. If his diagnosis and treatment result in a removal of the problem phenomena, seek no further causes. If the phenomena continue, they may be attributed to a mental illness. Any possibilities along this line should be checked out with a psychiatrist. If his diagnosis and treatment result in removal of the troublesome symptoms, you have the truth and need seek no further. Similarly, the simplest consistent explanation of the phenomena may be demonic activity, for occult powers are manipulated for ends other than the pleasure of God, contrary to Scripture and by-pass the gospel. Then the way to deliverance may involve confession of sin and the casting out of the demon(s) in the name of Christ and by the power of His shed blood. When the person is set free, the hypothesis has been confirmed and so is regarded as a consistent account of a matter of fact with which we are able to live satisfactorily.

Although the simplest explanation is sought, many cases may require a complex explanation. These cases may not be limited to just the physical, just the mental or just the spiritual realm. Two areas, or all three, may be affected. In these cases, it is well for Christian physicians, psychiatrists and ministers to cooperate in their healing ministries. Whenever a spirit's influence displeases God, contradicts Scripture and demeans the gospel, it is probable that a demonic factor is part of the problem. If so, no amount of physical and mental therapy will suffice.

To say that a demonic factor may be involved is not to say that a person is necessarily "possessed." Just as it is important to distinguish between God's ordinary prov-idential activities and His extraordinary miraculous ac-tivities, so we may distinguish Satan's ordinary activities from the extraordinary ones.

No one on earth can escape the ordinary influences of Satan and his demonic hosts through the worldly environ-ment and the flesh within. Who can say he perfectly meets the criteria listed? Many may profess allegiance to them, but does anyone perfectly fulfill them? Does anyone *always* lovingly please God, obey the Bible's teaching, give priority in his communication to the gospel and its impli-cations? To the extent that people (believers and unbe-lievers) fail to measure up to these criteria, they "follow the course of this world, the prince of the power of the air, the spirit that is now at work in the sons of disobedi-ence." The apostle Paul adds, "Among these we all once lived in the passions of the flesh, following the desires of the body and the mind, and so we were by nature children of wrath" (Eph. 2:2-3). Christians at Ephesus needed the whole armor of God to stand against the wiles of the devil. "For we are not contending against flesh and blood, but aginst the principalities, against the powers, against the world rulers of this present darkness, against the spiritual hosts of wickedness in the heavenly places" (Eph. 6:11-12).

Clearly both Christians and non-Christians are subject to the ordinary influences of the satanic world order. Through the intermediate means of the fleshly nature with-in and the corrupted world around suggestions occur to us contrary to God's pleasure and revealed will. Tempta-tions strike at the heart of our relation to God and His purposes. A mere temporal advantage may seduce the tempted away from an eternal good. When we should be loving God, we love the fallen world system, yielding to the lust of the flesh, the lust of the eyes and the pride of life (1 John 2:15). Each person who is tempted, James explained, "is lured and enticed by his own desire. Then desire when it has conceived gives birth to sin; and sin when it is full-grown brings forth death" (James 1:14-15). In the usual pattern, then, temptation is an incitement of human desire through the world and the flesh to worship and serve the creature more than the Creator.[13]

The recent publicity concerning possessions and exorcisms must not blind us to the ordinary demonic factors in life. The demonic character of much that is excused and rationalized must be underlined. In contrast to the fruit of the Holy Spirit is fruit ultimately of the devil in the "works of the flesh . . . immorality, impurity, licentiousness, idolatry, sorcery, enmity, strife, jealousy, anger, selfishness, dissension, party spirit, envy, drunkenness, carousing, and the like" (Gal. 5:19-21). Injustice, prejudice, and materialism have no part in God's kingdom.

Aware of the pervasiveness of evil produced by ordinary demonic activity through the present world order and the flesh, we sense the urgency of "deliverance ministries" of evangelism for non-Christians and growth in grace for Christians in their homes, churches, businesses, nations and cultures. We need the whole armor of God and the faithful exercise of the gift of every member in Christ's body to deliver people from the effects of personal and social evils.

As if the ordinary devastations of the demonic were not enough, Satan sometimes resorts to extraordinary attacks upon people in the world. These extraordinary attacks may be of two kinds, one without the person's consent, the other with it. Illustrating the first is Job. This man of God did not seek hidden sources of knowledge and power, but God permitted Satan to attack. Satan used two bands of raiders and a fire from heaven to kill Job's livestock and a great wind to destroy the oldest son's house and all Job's children who were in it. Finally Job's body was covered with loathsome sores and his suffering was very great (Job 1-2). Job's integrity was attacked by Satan's temptations of extraordinary force. These were not invited by any occult curiosity or experimentation. Job was not responsible for this. Some authorities find evidence indicating a hereditary factor in certain cases of demonic oppression.[14] A victim cannot be held responsible if he has not subjected himself to demonic influence.

The second type of extraordinary demonic activity is encouraged by the openness or consent of a person to it. Like any temptation, it may begin in apparently harmless types of curiosity and experimentation. A former spiritualist, Raphael Gasson, explains that in one's first seances "the student is learning to relax his body and to keep his mind on one thing until he has reached a state of what could be regarded as self-hypnosis and passivity, which results in his not thinking for himself. He becomes an automaton through which evil spirits work by taking advantage of his passivity." [15] Those who would experiment with Eastern religions may note the dangers in complete passivity. That leaves an open invitation to evil spirits. The fruit of the Holy Spirit, in contrast, is self-control and biblically guided meditation and activity.

Extraordinary demonic activities with initial consent or not are documented in many other chapters of this book and so their horrors are not rehearsed here.

Summation

By what tests can we discern the activity of spirits? First, can we know that there are spirits? The hypothesis that there are is more consistent, factual and viable than a contradictory hypothesis and so it is true. Another approach may be taken. The hypothesis that the Bible is God's revelation to men (true in all that it teaches) is more consistent, factual and viable than the contradictory hypothesis, and the Bible teaches the reality and activity of spirits.

How can we determine whether a spirit is good or evil? It is good if it loves and glorifies God above all other beings, speaks and acts in harmony with the teaching of Scripture and gives priority to the good news of Christ's atoning provisions for needy men. Ideas and actions from the spirit world exalting a creature above God, contradicting the Bible and ignoring the central message of Christ and the Scriptures (the gospel) is ultimately of Satan.

In applying these criteria to particular cases we may ask whether the hypothesis of ordinary or extraordinary demonic activity consistently accounts for all the related phenomena and whether the hypothesis of human responsibility or the alternative hypothesis consistently accounts for the history and phenomena.

In arriving at these very crucial judgments and acting

upon them appropriately, the Christian is most aware of his need for the Holy Spirit's illumination. The third Person of the Trinity abides with the believer to teach, guide and lead. God has not promised that the decisions in life will be easy, but He has given believers His Spirit to be their counselor. Faced with the agonies resulting from Satan's ordinary and extraordinary antagonism to all God's purposes in the world and the church, the Christian cries out, "Who is sufficient for these things?" Then he remembers that God's grace is sufficient in him through the Spirit of grace. And he knows that God did not give him the spirit of fear, but of power, and of love and of a sound mind (2 Tim. 1:7).

Notes

1. *But Deliver Us From Evil: An Introduction to the Demonic Dimension in Pastoral Care* (London: Darton, Longman & Todd, 1974), p. 156.

2. Richard Schmidt, "Phenomenology," *The Encyclopedia of Philosophy*, ed. Paul Edwards, VI (New York: Macmillan and the Free Press, 1967), 138-39.

3. *Principalities and Powers* (Minneapolis, Minn.: Bethany Fellowship, Inc., 1973), p. 46.

4. Gordon R. Lewis, *Decide for Yourself: A Theological Workbook* (Downers Grove, Ill.: InterVarsity Press, 1970), pp. 15-19.

5. See Edward John Carnell's three levels of meaning, as set forth in his *An Introduction to Christian Apologetics* (Grand Rapids, Mich.: Eerdmans, 1948), pp. 213-15.

6. *Ibid.*, pp. 62-63.

7. Francis Schaeffer, *The God Who Is There* (Downers Grove, Ill.: InterVarsity Press, 1968), p. 109.

8. For the development of this thought, see Edward John Carnell, *Christian Commitment: An Apologetic* (New York, N.Y.: Macmillan, 1957), and Gordon R. Lewis, *Judge for Yourself: A Workbook on Contemporary Challenges to Christian Faith* (Downers Grove, Ill.: InverVarsity Press, 1974), pp. 76-125.

9. Francis Schaeffer, *op. cit.*, p. 111.

10. *Confronting the Cults* (Nutley, N. J.: Presbyterian and Reformed, 1966), pp. 165-68; and, separately published in booklet form, *The Bible, the Christian and Spiritualist*, pp. 7-10.

11. Documented with quotations from the most "orthodox" group, the National Spiritualist Association literature, *ibid.*, pp. 171-93 (in booklet, pp. 13-35).

12. *The Pattern of Authority* (Grand Rapids, Mich.: Eerdmans, 1957), pp. 35-36.

13. Gordon R. Lewis, "Temptation," *Zondervan Pictorial Bible En-*

cyclopedia, ed. Merrill Tenney V (Grand Rapids, Mich.: Zondervan, 1975), pp. 669-71.

14. R. K. McAll's chapter in the present volume; Kurt Koch, *Between Christ and Satan* (Grand Rapids, Mich.: Kregel, 1970), p. 62.

15. *The Challenging Counterfeit* (Plainfield, N.J.: Logos Books, 1966), p. 83.

24

Satan and Demonology in Eschatologic Perspective

CLARENCE B. BASS

The doctrine of Satan as articulated within evangelical churches today seems to focus on the conflict between Satan and man. Satan is presented as the "adversary," lurking within the world, seeking whom he may devour. Demons are Satan's henchmen whose primary purpose is to ensnare men in his program, thus defeating the will of God in their lives. The conflict is seen as one in which man, in weakness, is pitted against the wiles of Satan and demons, and can succeed only as he flees toward God for divine succour.

While the Scripture does describe the relation between man and Satan in these ways, this type of emphasis focuses our attention away from the central biblical and theological understanding of the nature of Satan and demons since it all but eclipses the eschatologic note of the dualistic struggle between God and Satan. It minimizes the striking emphasis which the Scriptures make about the defeat of Satan by Christ and the inaugurating of the Kingdom of God as victor over Satan.

In my estimation the most singularly needed emphasis in the study of Satan and demonology is to recapture one of the most dominant themes in Scripture, that is, an understanding of Satan and demons from an eschatologic perspective.

This eschatologic emphasis is nowhere more forcefully presented than in Mark's Gospel, particularly chapter one, and in Luke's account of Jesus' temptation (Luke 4:1-6). I should like to examine both of these with you.

Let us first note the eschatologic features of the Gospel of Mark. Probably our oldest account of the life of Christ, it is an eschatological book from beginning to end. It begins with an eschatological title: "The beginning of the gospel of Jesus Christ, the Son of God" (v. 1). The term "Son of God" is a messianic concept taken directly from Ps. 2. Mark is here deliberately identifying his understanding of Jesus as the Christ with the eschatological hope expressed in Israel in terms of the messianic Deliverer who is to come. In effect he is saying, "I write about Jesus Christ, who is the Son of God for whom you have been waiting."

As if to confirm this, Mark then quotes two Old Testament texts, one from Malachi and one from Isaiah, both of which are accepted by Israel as announcing that the coming of the true Messiah is to be preceded by an eschatological prophet. That prophet is identified as John the Baptist, who says, "He who comes after me is mightier than I. . . . I baptize you with water, but he will baptize you with the Holy Spirit."

These words of John carry great eschatologic weight. The advent of the great messianic age for the Jews was to be marked by an outpouring of God's Spirit. John says, "He will baptize in the Spirit," as if this is a bold announcement that indeed the Christ is the Messiah.

Bear in mind that Mark is selecting his material in such a way as to demonstrate his central motif—that is, that Jesus is the fulfillment of the messianic expectation, that He is indeed the Christ. Great significance must therefore be placed upon Mark's chronology of events. He records the baptism of Jesus in eschatologic context since he records the voice of God saying, "Thou art my beloved Son, with thee I am well pleased." This quotation comes directly from the messianic imagery of Ps. 2:7 and of Isa. 42.

We can easily surmise the first reaction to Mark's introduction of Jesus to the Jews. Quite clearly it presents the person and ministry of Jesus from the eschatologic perspective. This is no mere historical account of the life of Jesus. Mark is not simply putting down on paper the sum of what Jesus said and did. No, Mark presents him as the Messiah Deliverer, fully documented to be so by the major features of Jewish messianic expectations.

But all of this is merely a prelude to the central thrust of Mark's eschatologic theme, which comes boldly into focus with the temptation in the wilderness and in Jesus' announcement of the inauguration of the kingdom through his own person.

Mark's account of the temptation is cryptically summed up in the phrase, "He was tempted by Satan." For a larger understanding of the significance of the temptation we must turn to Luke's account. Luke's more detailed account helps us to understand the eschatologic note. He records that Satan showed Jesus all the kingdoms of the world in a moment of time, and said to Him, "To you I will give all this authority and their glory, for it has been delivered to me, and I give it to whom I will."

Notice the various aspects of Satan's statement. He had the *power* to cause all the kingdoms of time to pass before Jesus as if in but a moment of time. He had the *authority* to promise it to Jesus. He seemingly had the *right* to do this since the world was his. He said, "It [the cosmos, the world, the temporal-spatial sphere of human history] has been delivered to me, *and* I give it to whom I will." Either Satan was lying, or this world is his. Since Jesus seems not to rebuke him, but rather to accept the statement, we may then conclude that Jesus acquiesced to the fact that the whole world lay in the grip of Satan, even though he had usurped it.

What follows the temptation account in both Luke and Mark is vitally significant to the eschatologic theme. Luke says that after the temptation Jesus went into the temple and read from the prophet Isaiah: "The Spirit of the Lord is upon me, because he has anointed me to preach good news to the poor. He has sent me to proclaim release to the captives and recovering of sight to the blind, to set at liberty those who are oppressed, to proclaim the acceptable year of the Lord." Luke dramatically records that after He had read Jesus "closed the book, gave it back to the attendant, sat down, and the eyes of all in the synagogue were fixed on him. And he said, *Today* this scripture is fulfilled in your hearing." What more bold eschatological claim could Jesus have made than this!

While Luke's account is dramatic, Mark's record of the same emphasis is certainly more pointed. Mark depicts Jesus as preaching the gospel in Galilee saying, "The time is fulfilled, and the kingdom of God is at hand; repent, and believe in the gospel." This is no idle statement on the part of Jesus, but rather a bold and strikingly dramatic announcement, "The decisive hour of God's breaking into human history with deliverance *has come*—it has come *in me*—the kingdom is *here*; therefore repent and believe *in me*. I am the Deliverer. The day of salvation has arrived. The age of the Messiah has begun. Your God reigns in your midst."

Perhaps it would be wise for us to depart from our consideration of the Mark-Luke eschatologic presentation of Christ to structure for ourselves a quite simple approach to the roles of both Satan and Christ in human history, as a prelude to what both gospel narrators develop next.

The accompanying diagram shows the time-line of human history bisected by the Second Coming of Christ.

The Age to Come—Christ's reign over the Cosmos.

The entry of Christ into human history is to usher in the "Age to Come," an age of peace and righteousness. We know that that age is yet to come. However, the age before Christ's return is known in biblical terms as this Present Evil Age.

This Present Evil Age—Satan's reign over the Cosmos.

This Present Evil Age is the time in which the cosmos "Has been delivered into Satan's hands" (presumably at the Fall).

If this were the only reality with which we have to deal, we could conclude that Satan rules this age until Christ comes and that in His second coming Christ will defeat Satan and usher in the Age to Come. However, Mark 1:15 records Jesus as saying, "The kingdom is here" (not "to come"). What did Christ mean? How can the kingdom, which is future, be in the present? That the Age to Come will be when Christ comes again is certainly an eschatological statement. However, it is even more of an eschatological statement to say that the Age to Come came when Christ entered human history as the Incarnate One. The diagram below suggests that when Christ came the first time, He reached into the future, into the Age to Come, and proleptically brought it forward (or back) through time and introduced it into the present.

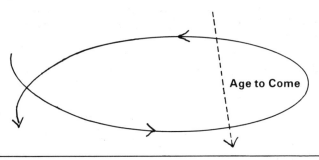

This interpretation follows the motif of Oscar Cullmann's "already but not yet" and suggests that when Jesus announced that the righteous reign of the kingdom was being ushered into the present through His own self, that He also was announcing that He was ready to do battle with Satan for the whole of mankind and the cosmos of human existence.

When this point is understood, Mark's chronology of events in his eschatologic presentation of Jesus becomes highly significant. Immediately after the kingdom announcement, Mark chronicles the call of the disciples and then the first public ministry. Jesus taught in the synagogue where He astounded His hearers, "for he taught as one who had authority, and not as the scribes." There was a man there with a demon spirit. As Jesus taught, the demon spirit cried out: "What have you to do with us, Jesus of Nazareth? Have you come to destroy us? I know who you are, the Holy one of God." Notice that the demon spirit recognized Jesus for who He was, the Holy One of God. Jesus did not point out the demon but rather the demon recognized Him. The demons were terrified by Him because they recognized the divine power within Him which spelled their ultimate doom. Matthew records the cry of two demon spirits as saying: "What do we have to do with you, Jesus Son of God? Have you come to torment us *before the time?*"

The eschatologic note of Mark is sounded throughout the gospel. Jesus' life is presented in terms of a conquest over the powers of evil as personified by Satan and demons. In fact, if we enlarge our consideration to the whole of the New Testament teaching, our central theme of understanding Satan and demons from the eschatologic perspective comes more sharply into focus, i.e., that Satan is the diametric antithesis to God, dominant in this world-order, and that Christ came to break Satan's hold on man by defeating him and setting man free from his enslavement.

Only from this perspective can we finally focus on the two distinctive features of the New Testament: the fall of God's creation (both cosmos and man) under the dominion of Satan; and, the presence of the kingdom of God in human history in the person of Jesus Christ. To put it in less theological terms, the central theme of the New Testament is that of an attack being launched by God against the demonic. Jesus is the Messiah who shatters the forces of evil and restores God's creation to himself.

Let us trace these two themes briefly. The first theme is that Satan and demons are in antithesis to God.

The names ascribed to Satan and demons suggest this antithesis. In addition to the more formal names of Satan, the Devil, Beelzebub, the Wicked One is described as the serpent, the dragon, the lion, the accuser, the tempter, the destroyer, the adversary, the enemy, the prince of devils, the prince of this world, the god of this world. Demon spirits are called principalities, powers, gods, angels, devils, unclean and wicked spirits, spirits of wickedness, elements, rulers of this world of darkness, spirits of wickedness in high places.

These names connote their distinguishing features. Demon spirits are personal beings with demoniacal powers. As personal beings, they have will and intellect, but this will and intellect is invariably directed toward evil ends as they exert their malevolent and demonic powers. Moreover, they are not just evil beings who misuse their power, but are frequently presented in Scripture as evil power itself. They do not merely possess power, but they are power. They exist as power (Col. 1:16). Sometimes they are presented as beings who have power; at other times as powers which have being; but always whether being or power, as evil in intent and action.

These evil powers permeate all existence. They influence men, producing both spiritual and physical maladies. They invade history, affecting both institutions and situations. They pervert the routine affairs of men. The religious sphere is penetrated through lust and greed, even transferring into angels of light to cause error and doctrines of devils.

When the spirits penetrate the world and the circumstances of human life, they conceal themselves in the world and in the affairs of men. Their hidden nature, which seems to be one of their characteristics, makes them impenetrable to human reason. They work through the spirit of this world as princes of the power of "air."

Hence, they penetrate every aspect of human existence—man, the elements, circumstances and institutions of life, even spiritual realities—and subject them to their domination. This domination has as its purpose the distortion, ruin, annihilation and undoing of God's creation. Therefore, their ultimate intent is to bring death to the good creation of God. Satan is the ruler of the "empire of death" holding men "all their lifetime subject to slavery through the fear of death" (Heb. 2:14-15).

Yet, in antagonism to God, the demonic powers present the world of death as good and entice men through seductive design to commit themselves to the evil world-order. They lead men to death by portraying evil as pleasant.

Finally, though ultimately dependent upon God for their source, they become as autonomous in their being, egocentric and self-willed. Precisely because of their quest for autonomy, they place themselves in opposition to God, seeking to destroy not only His creation but their own need to be dependent upon Him. Hence, their opposition to God is not one of mere incompatibility, but malevolently evil in its very intensity.

The second theme in this eschatologic perspective is that the kingdom has come through Christ, and with it the doom of evil powers.

We have already noted the context within which the biblical writers place the exorcisms of Jesus, i.e., they are presented as evidence of Jesus as victor over the demonic. Repeatedly, these accounts show not only the power of Christ over the demonic, but the fear, the abject horror which demons had for Christ. Recognizing Him as the Son of God they cried out, "Have you come to torment us *before the time*?" meaning of course, before the time of their ultimate defeat.

We return now to our basic theme—that when Christ ushered in the kingdom, which is yet to be but now present, He entered into eschatologic battle with demonic powers, the victory which He won not only at Calvary and the open tomb, but through His own incarnate person. The ultimate judgment of God, in the person of Jesus, has broken upon the world and spelled the doom of evil powers.

Though Christ's triumph over evil powers is final in an eschatologic sense, it is somewhat muted by the delay of the final and total entry of the kingdom into time, and in that sense is not yet final as far as the world is concerned. The overthrow of the evil spirits and the breaking of their powers will be revealed at the final appearing of the Victor at the end of time.

Until that ultimate decision, the evil powers are weakened and have no future but to await their final judgment. Until then, they are "princes of this world that have come to naught" (1 Cor. 2:6). Yet, awaiting their certain doom, they thrash about with a frenzy arising out of panic. The recent spate of activity as reflected in the rise of the occult is but an evidence of the desperateness of their acknowledged plight.

Let there be no mistake about the decisiveness of Christ's victory, however. The defeat is not a provisional one, but ultimate, final, and complete. The eschatologic note is sounded by Paul in Col. 2:15. Borrowing the imagery of the ancient world in which a victorious warrior paraded his spoils of war in a triumphant march into his city with all of his captured slaves on display, Paul writes: "And on that cross Christ disarmed the principalities and rulers: he made a public spectacle of them by leading them as captives in his victory procession."

The Contributors

Lynn Robert Buzzard (S.T.D. candidate, San Francisco Theological Seminary). Assistant Professor of Ministry and Director of Field Ministry, Northern Baptist Theological Seminary, Oak Brook, Illinois. Author: *Honor the Doctor: Ancient Wisdom and Modern Medicine*; and articles in several journals.

Dennis F. Kinlaw (Ph.D., Brandeis, 1967). President, Asbury College.

Gordon R. Lewis (M.A., Ph.D., Syracuse University). Professor of Systematic Theology and Christian Philosophy, Conservative Baptist Theological Seminary, Denver, Colorado. Author: *Confronting the Cults; Decide for Yourself: A Theological Workbook;* and *Judge for Yourself: A Workbook on Contemporary Challenges to Christian Faith.*

J. Ramsey Michaels (Th.D., Harvard, 1962). Professor of New Testament, Gordon-Conwell Theological Seminary, South Hamilton, Massachusetts. Co-author: *The New Testament Speaks*; and several scholarly and popular articles.

Richard Lovelace (Th.D., Princeton Theological Seminary). Associate Professor of Church History, Gordon-Conwell Theological Seminary, South Hamilton, Massachusetts.

D. G. Kehl (Ph.D., Southern California, 1967). Associate Professor of English, Arizona State University. Author: *The Literary Style of the Old Bible and the New; The Dual Vision: Poetry and the Visual Arts;* and several articles in Christian and secular journals.

Alan R. Tippett (Ph.D., Oregon, 1964). Professor of Anthropology and Oceanic Studies, Fuller Theological Seminary. Author: *Solomon Islands Christianity; Fijian Material Culture: A Study in Context, Function and Change;* and *People Movements in*

Southern Polynesia. Editor: *Missiology* (Journal of the American Society of Missiology).

Donald R. Jacobs (Ph.D., New York, 1961). Director, Mennonite Christian Leadership Foundation. Author: *The Christian Stance in a Revolutionary Era;* and *Demons.*

George W. Peters (Ph.D., Hartford Theological Foundation, 1947). Professor and Chairman, Department of World Missions, Dallas Theological Seminary. Author: *Saturation Evangelism; Biblical Theology of Missions; Indonesian Revival;* and several scholarly articles.

W. Stanley Mooneyham (Litt.D., Houghton, 1962). President, World Vision International. Author: *What Do You Say to a Hungry World?*; and *China, the Puzzle.*

William P. Wilson (M.D., Duke, 1947). Professor of Psychiatry, Duke, Durham, North Carolina. Author of several scholarly articles.

Gary R. Collins (Ph.D., Purdue, 1963). Professor and Chairman, Division of Pastoral Psychology and Counseling, Trinity Evangelical Divinity School, Deerfield, Illinois. Author: *Search for Reality: Psychology and the Christian; Effective Counseling;* and *The Christian Psychology of Paul Tournier.*

John White (M.B., Ch.B.). Associate Professor of Psychiatry, University of Manitoba; Director of Alcoholism Programmes, Health Sciences Centre, Winnipeg, Manitoba, Canada. Author of several technical and popular articles.

Basil Jackson (M.D., Queen's University, 1957; D.P.M., Dublin, 1963). Director, Jackson Psychiatric Center and Chairman of Department of Psychiatry, Lutheran Hospital of Milwaukee, Wisconsin; Clinical Associate Professor of Psychiatry, Medical College of Wisconsin; Visiting Professor of Pastoral Psychology, Trinity Evangelical Divinity School. Author of several psychiatric and theological papers.

R. Kenneth McAll (M.B., Ch.B., Edinburgh, 1935). Consultant Psychiatrist, Hampshire, England. Author: "Demonosis or the Possession Syndrome," *International Journal of Social Psychiatry,* Spring, 1971.

W. Elwyn Davies. General Director, Bible Christian Union. Author: *As Eagles Fly.*

Clarence B. Bass (Ph.D., Edinburgh, 1952). Professor of Theology, Chairman of Department of History and Theology, Bethel Theological Seminary, St. Paul, Minnesota. Author: *Backgrounds of Dispensationalism; New Testament Writers and Writings*; and several scholarly articles.

John P. Newport (Ph.D., University of Edinburgh, Th.D., Southern Baptist Seminary). Professor of Philosophy of Religion, Southwestern Baptist Theological Seminary, Ft. Worth, Texas. Author: *Theology and Contemporary Art Forms; Demons, Demons, Demons; Why Christians Fight Over the Bible*; and numerous scholarly articles and chapters in published books and encyclopedias.

James D. Mallory, Jr. (M.D., Duke University). Director, Atlanta Counseling Center. Author: *The Kink and I*; and several scholarly articles in medical journals.

Roger C. Palms (M.A., Michigan State University M.Div., Eastern Baptist Theological Seminary). Associate editor, DECISION magazine. Author: *The Jesus Kids*; and *The Christian and the Occult*.

John Warwick Montgomery (Ph.D., University of Chicago, earned doctorate in theology from the University of Strasbourg in France). Professor of Law and Theology at the International School of Law, Washington, D.C. Author: *The Suicide of Christian Theology; The Quest for Noah's Ark; Principalities and Powers: The World of the Occult.*

Symposium Participants

Dr. Donald R. Jacobs
% Mennonite Christian Leadership
   Foundation
P.O. Box 85
Lanidsville, Pennsylvania 17538

Professor D. G. Kehl
Associate Professor of English
Arizona State University
Tempe, Arizona 85281

Dr. Dennis Kinlaw, President
Asbury Theological Seminary
Wilmore, Kentucky 40390

Professor Gordon R. Lewis
Conservative Baptist Theological
   Seminary
Box 10,000 University Park Station
Denver, Colorado 80210

David F. Busby, M.D.
7501 N. Milwaukee Avenue
Niles, Illinois 60648

Dr. Gary Collins
Trinity Evangelical Divinity School
Bannockburn
Deerfield, Illinois 60015

Mr. W. Elwyn Davies
Bible Christian Union (Canada), Inc.
554 Main Street East
Hamilton, Ontario L8M 1J3
Canada

Dr. Paul W. Dekker
1484 Shipley Court
San Diego, California 92114

Basil Jackson, M.D.
9505 North Pheasant Lane
River Hills, Wisconsin 53217

James D. Mallory, Jr., M.D.
Atlanta Counseling Center
3355 Lenox Road, N.E., Suite 1060
Atlanta, Georgia 30326

Professor J. Ramsey Michaels
14 Daniels Road
Wenham, Massachusetts 01982

Dr. Douglas J. Miller
Eastern Baptist Theological
   Seminary
Lancaster Avenue at City Line
Philadelphia, Pennsylvania 19151

Dr. Paul M. Miller
Associated Mennonite Biblical
   Seminaries
3003 Benham Avenue
Elkhart, Indiana 46514

Dr. John W. Montgomery
Professor of Law and Theology
International School of Law
1441 Rhode Island Avenue, N.W.
Washington, D.C. 20005

Mr. W. Stanley Mooneyham
World Vision International
919 West Huntington Drive
Monrovia, California 91016

Professor John P. Newport
Southwestern Baptist Theological
   Seminary
P.O. Box 22000
Fort Worth, Texas 76122

Mr. Roger C. Palms
DECISION
1300 Harmon Place
Minneapolis, Minnesota 55403

Dr. George W. Peters
Professor of World Missions
Dallas Theological Seminary
3909 Swiss Avenue
Dallas, Texas 75204

Dr. Alan R. Tippett
Professor of Anthropology
Fuller Theological Seminary
135 North Oakland Avenue
Pasadena, California 91101

John White, M.D.
Associate Professor, Department of
   Psychiatry
The University of Manitoba,
Faculty of Medicine
Bannstyne and Emily
Winnipeg, Manitoba R3E OW3,
   Canada

William P. Wilson, M.D.
Box 3355 — Duke Medical Center
Durham, North Carolina 27710

Dr. R. K. McAll
Bignell Wood
Lyndhurst, Hants, S04 7JA
England

Dr. Richard Lovelace
Professor of Church History
Gordon-Conwell Theological Seminary
South Hamilton, Massachusetts
   01982

Dr. Clarence B. Bass
Professor of Systematic Theology
Bethel Theological Seminary
3949 Bethel Drive
St. Paul, Minnesota 55112

Haddon W. Robinson, Ph.D.
Dallas Theological Seminary
3909 Swiss Avenue
Dallas, Texas 75204

Scripture Index

Index of Names